*Letters of Carl Van Vechten*

Carl Van Vechten, as photographed by Bruce Kellner, 1956

*Being intimate does not take courage,*
*but it takes experience. . . .*
*I have never been anything else,*
*writing letters or writing books.*
—Carl Van Vechten to Paul Padgette, 3 November 1963

# Letters of
# Carl Van Vechten

*selected and edited by*

## Bruce Kellner

*Yale University Press* · *New Haven and London*

Designed by Sally Harris and set in Meridien type by David E. Seham Associates, Inc.,
Printed in the United States of America by Vail-Ballou Press, Binghamton, New York.

Library of Congress Cataloging-in-Publication Data

Van Vechten, Carl, 1880–1964.
Letters of Carl Van Vechten.

Includes index.
1. Van Vechten, Carl, 1880–1964—Correspondence.
2. Novelists, American—20th century—Correspondence.
3. Music critics—United States—Correspondence.
4. Photographers—United States—Correspondence.
I. Kellner, Bruce. II. Title.
PS3543.A653Z48   1987      813'.52 [B]      86–32400
ISBN 0–300–03907–7 (alk. paper)

The paper in this book meets the guidelines for
permanence and durability of the Committee
on Production Guidelines for Book Longevity
of the Council on Library Resources.

2  4  6  8  10  9  7  5  3  1

All photographs in the book are by Carl Van Vechten, unless otherwise noted.
Photographs from the Carl Van Vechten Collection in the Beinecke Library, Yale
University, those of Langston Hughes and Ethel Waters from The Carl Van Vechten
Memorial Collection of Afro-American Arts and Letters, Millersville University of
Pennsylvania, and those by courtesy of Bruce Kellner are all reproduced with
permission from Joseph Solomon, Trustee for the Estate of Carl Van Vechten.

# Contents

# Illustrations

# *Prolegomenon*

## *1*

There is an intimacy to letters, as Carl Van Vechten knew, if only because of our own thumbs at their margins, a friend's touch, a lover's touch, sometimes a stranger's, and words for us alone. A telephone call is surely more immediate, and eventually we will be facing each other for short as well as long distance communication on televisionphones—extensions in the kitchen to watch each other cook, plug-ins in the bath to eavesdrop on ablutions—as progress has its way. Letters will grow even rarer than they are at present, and letter writers will seem more anomalous than they now must to many people. Already the daily mail amounts largely to batches of catalogs and pleas for worthy causes. An occasional letter camouflaged among them is rare enough. A message travels faster by wire and wind, but hang up the receiver and it's over; hang on to the letter and it's not. Those of us lucky enough to have come in at the end of the written era were luckier still if we were on the receiving end when Carl Van Vechten wrote letters. He worked them into a busy chronology spanning the first half of the century, during which, in the best sense of an old-fashioned word, he was its leading dilettante: a lover of the arts, a connoisseur.

Early on he was in training for the role, first in Cedar Rapids, Iowa, where he was born 17 June 1880, the late and last child in a financially comfortable family. The town was the first stop for traveling theatrical and musical troupes enroute to the west from Chicago, and Chicago itself was only a few hours away by train. By the time Carl Van Vechten had completed his Ph.B. at the University of Chicago in 1903, he was already familiar with most of the leading performers of the period, black as well as white, and with its music, opera as well as ragtime. The preceding Mauve Decade and its *Yellow Book* gave him his colors, and a three-year apprenticeship as cub reporter for the *Chicago American* gave him both experience and discipline. Subsequently, as assistant music critic for the *New York Times*

(1906–13) and then as an independent essayist, Carl Van Vechten was our first serious ballet critic; he championed the music of Igor Stravinsky and Erik Satie and the operas of Richard Strauss; he discovered Spanish music; he advocated musical scores for films; he recognized the value of jazz and ragtime; he extolled the talents of George Gershwin, Ethel Waters, and Paul Robeson—all before anyone else in America.

He popularized the Harlem Renaissance and was largely responsible for white recognition of black arts and letters during the 1920s. He aided several literary careers: those of Gertrude Stein, Ronald Firbank, Wallace Stevens, Langston Hughes, James Purdy; and he resuscitated several others: of Herman Melville, Edgar Saltus, Arthur Machen, Henry Blake Fuller. His *Tiger in the House* is still the best book ever compiled about cats, and he wrote seven volumes of criticism and seven novels, including the controversial *Nigger Heaven*.

At the end of his "Splendid Drunken Twenties" he turned to photography and documented celebrated artists and writers for over thirty years. He established several important archives concurrently, including the George Gershwin Memorial Collection of Music and Musical Literature at Fisk University and the James Weldon Johnson Memorial Collection of Negro Arts and Letters at Yale University, thereby laying the foundation for interracial scholarship long before it became commonplace. Moreover, he continued to keep his collections up to date with constant donations; to write essays, prefaces, introductions, reviews; to stay well aware of the artistic life—in nearly all its forms—around him; and along the route of his productive eighty-four years to write thousands of letters.

Like the best correspondents, Carl Van Vechten wrote *to* his recipients, and his voice was always somehow individualized for them. Formal with one person and silly with another, equally affectionate regardless of gender, baleful with fools and gentle with innocents, he wrote almost always about himself, but with sufficient intimacy to make the letter intensely the recipient's own. Despite his precious salutations—"7 daschunds (housebroken), 4 bowls of India rubies, and a plate of garlic ice cream," "Bright red strawberries to you, a robin, and a proud guitar," "Grace to you, indigence and indolence and porridge," and "Huckleberry Finn and Haddie to you" are not untypical—and frequent penchant for exaggeration and campy jokes, especially as he grew older, the letters are usually more decorous than his reputation as a homosexual dandy would anticipate. He gossiped more than he pontificated, and his occasional wrath was mitigated by his unbuttoned humor, just as in person his ridiculous buck teeth easily vetoed his petrified stare.

The list of his recipients, like the list of his photographic subjects, is staggering, not only in length but in variety, and another volume of equal length and interest can be arranged from those of his letters not included here. This selection makes no attempt to construct a personal biography; I have included none of his childhood letters, and if significant events in his life were only accounted for in otherwise dull letters, I ignored them. Nor is the number of letters to a particular individual here indicative of the size of the full correspondence; other correspondences are not represented at all. Instead, I have chosen letters that seemed to me amusing or informative as signposts along the cultural avenues Carl Van Vechten traveled, including some few business letters of more than routine interest and a greater number of a more personal nature to Fania Marinoff, his wife of fifty years, to whom he wrote sometimes twice a day when they were apart. There are noticeable gaps: only three of perhaps one hundred letters, largely about writing, to Joseph Hergesheimer have survived; three times that number to Emily Clark, also devoted to literary matters, have disappeared; because of their intimate nature, especially those from the ten-year period when Van Vechten and Mark Lutz were lovers, about ten thousand letters, written daily during their thirty-two-year friendship, were deliberately destroyed by the estate executor at Lutz's request; extensive letters to Ann Andrews, Richard Banks, Donald Evans, Richard Hundley, Edward Donahoe, Henry Miller, Grace Zaring Stone, and Edward Wassermann (later Waterman) have disappeared or are unavailable; so, too, Van Vechten's letters to his parents. Finally, some materials are under seal until the twenty-fifth anniversary of his death in 1989.

I have included in this collection only the first and last of my own nearly eight hundred letters from Carl Van Vechten, although passages from several occur as footnotes to amplify information in letters he wrote to others or to supply amusing asides now and then. Some further passages from his letters to me may serve as preface to Carl Van Vechten as a correspondent, a preview of coming attractions, advertisements for a good product.

## 2

We began writing in the summer when as a twenty-one year-old sailor I had ordered a book by Gertrude Stein, whose work I had started reading in college. It arrived accompanied by an unfamiliar envelope and letter, both of elegantly heavy, pale aquamarine laid paper, with an equally unfamiliar name and address engraved in emerald ink, and untidily typed:

Dear Mr. Kellner, [ . . . ] the [ . . . ] Banyan Press has handed me your letter as I am in a better position to answer your questions [ . . . ] as

I am the literary executor of Miss Stein. [ . . . ] Much of her past work is out of print, but if you will tell me what you have I may be able to supply some of your lacks. Miss Stein would be very pleased to hear this voice out of Korea, but she would not be surprised as the army and navy and most young people have been for her for a long time.

I await a letter from you.

sincerely

Carl Van Vechten

August 13, 1951

And from then on there were books and magazines, clippings and programs, phonograph records, an occasional package of exotic foods from Bloomingdale's, dozens of his photographs of celebrated people, and a steady flow of letters. Admittedly, it was disconcerting for my innocent eyes to get postcards of leggy ballet dancers and naked putti statuary and Anna May Wong, and for my midwestern palate to sample marrons glacés and pâté de foie gras. But I learned—and I continued to with pleasure for thirteen years.

He could be contrarily instructive:

I can't answer your questions about literature. [ . . . ] LIKE what you LIKE and pay no attention to the academies. You seem to be getting on pretty well.

He could be informative:

It is curious, but while singers and actors have deteriorated, violinists, pianists, and ballerinas in every department have improved. Indeed, the whole technique of ballet has changed to a terrific extent.

He could be enthusiastic, when he requested (and got) a brief glossary of navy slang:

Shitkickers is now my favorite word. I never heard it before and I know lots of sailors. I shall use it to advantage, but NOT about western movies.

And he could be less than enthusiastic:

I've seen [ . . . Ljuba] Welitch (at long last, and perhaps too late) in Salome, a ghastly embarrassing experience, like seeing a favorite maiden aunt washing her pants at a public dinner.

For the first four months, I wrote to "Dear Mr. Van Vechten"; he was after all seventy-one years old, and I had been reared to respect my elders.

Then: "Dear Bruce, Why don't you address me as Carlo; everybody else in the world does. [ . . . ]" He had been signing himself that way all along, and I had assumed it was just bad penmanship for Carl V. V.

Except for biographical rambles some years later, in answer to my questions when I was writing his public record in *Carl Van Vechten and the Irreverent Decades* (1968), his letters never concentrated at length on any single subject. More often, they were filled with what can be considered only—but in the best sense of an exhausted word—gossip. Usually in the robin's egg blue square envelopes he affected, engraved in green or red or white ink with his name and address, and stamped on the back in sealing wax with the intaglio amethyst ring of Leda and the Swan that Fania Marinoff had discovered in a pawnshop in 1912, Carlo's letters arrived with devoted regularity. Accompanying shipments of his photographs, they came in big gray envelopes covered over with a dozen or so different commemorative stamps for the postage, which he himself judged by means of an erratic small scale on his desk. Certainly, they always gave me the most immediate sense of his presence, which, even with this long passage of time, has not weakened, whether he was writing about himself:

> We were a rough lot in those far-off days, always ready with a quip or a shocker [ . . . ]

or about human behavior:

> Being pure means you are cautious and not very curious, nothing more. It's not very important, but it will complicate your life, unless you continue to remain pure, which is possible. I've seen it done successfully. As a receipt for happiness this is unequalled, because the happiness of impurity is jagged and inconsistent, but occasionally, of course, really tremendous!

About opera, for example when a substitute singer appeared unannounced:

> [ . . . ] the Tristan last night was Ramon Vinay who acted like a sick stick or a frozen marshmallow and sang like a sardine in a frigidaire, but he is a thin boy and when the curtain went up on Act III to expose the fattest boy in captivity, I believed I had lost my mind.

More often about ballet, and at the age of eighty-four he was as enchanted by Mimi Paul, a nineteen-year-old dancer, as he had been by Pavlova or Nijinsky fifty years before:

> I can't wait for the next season when I can loll at her feet. [ . . . ] Please respect my passion and understand it.

Or music:

> I am in my usual state of gaping enthusiasm. (Will it never end? Probably NOT.) I heard André Watts at the Stadium and sans doute he is the greatest living pianist. He has everything, including good taste and he will end in glory, as he has begun.

Or, more economically:

> Oistrakh impaled me at the Philharmonic yesterday.

Sometimes I simply got an account of a busy schedule:

> I am down to solid bedrock work: furnishing an Yvette Guilbert piece for Angel Records (done today), a piece about Olive Fremstad for the Sat Review (done yesterday) and a piece about Marguerite D'Alvarez (to be done next week), any amount of photographs to develop and print, more printed photographs to be put in order, [ . . . ] strange social adventures [ . . . ] new books to read, new pictures and plays to take in, new hands to kiss, new feet to wash, new hours to LIVE.

Some subjects certainly continued from letter to letter, usually various interests in common, surely books, which clearly delineated Carlo's tastes and prejudices and, at the same time, his personality. "I may have a blind spot," he conceded about J. D. Salinger, "but I may be unable to appreciate this great genius." On other occasions he could prove more loquacious:

> I have been reading that goddam bloody fine volume called From Here to Eternity [ . . . ] and love it, love it. I never knew soldiers who used quite such expressive lingo (do Sailors talk like that?) but somehow I wish they did and I did. Somehow I am sure it is true, even the parts of it that are not true and when Lorene the whore almost kicks her lover out when he proposes marriage I could have kissed her and the author and Prew too. What a wonderful scene! In fact, I LOVE this book, as much as if it were Henry James, or Gentlemen Prefer Blondes, or Carl Van Vechten. To think I might have died without reading it!

Sometimes he was more succinct, about a biography of opera diva Olive Fremstad, for example: "as exciting as atom-bombing on skis or self-baking in a fast oven." Sometimes he gave up:

> I find myself utterly unable to read Ivy Compton-Burnett. I have tried several times and never get farther than the twentieth page.

But he was always willing to take a chance on a friend's recommendation:

I have always been terrified by Kinder, cher Bruce, a condition augmented by reading The Innocent Voyage, What Maisie Knew, and The Bad Seed, and watching performances of The Children's Hour. Now I have had the piss scared out of me by reading The Lord of The Flies, and nothing will induce me to remain in the same room with the murderous little brats. A remarkable performance, as you alleged.

And precisely to complain when the recommendation failed:

I've taken a violent dislike to Robert Graves and doubt if I will read any more. It's his inevitability that sets me off. He is ALWAYS right. The fact that this is the truth doesn't influence me.

He liked to deadpan giggle now and then:

I am being regenerated by a new variety of massage which exhausts the operator and excites me.

And to astonish:

Balanchine has had a stroke, had a finger cut off, and is not very well.

And to query:

I've got a new hearing aid. What have you got?

Sometimes he could be impatient, for instance when my wife was expecting our first child:

Margaret is taking too much time. I can't wait. I dare say she is perfectly willing to wait.

Sometimes sympathetic:

I hope your interdisciplinary seminar doesn't destroy your faith in God. Such projects are death dealing.

Sometimes indignant:

Stop calling me grandpa at once. I can do that, but I want no such impertinence from you. [ . . . ]

And sometimes he could add at the foot of a letter a remark to make the heart sing:

I find you the easiest of all my friends to write to. [ . . . ]

Carl Van Vechten wrote his last letter to me when he was eighty-four, just a few hours before his death:

Dear Bruce, Congratulations. I was *sure* it would be a boy and Fania and I are delighted. Hans is a marvelous name with Kellner. Much love to you both and many Kisses.

Carlo
20 December 1964

In editing these letters, I have attempted to preserve their look as well as their spirit by allowing Carl Van Vechten's eccentricities to stand whenever possible. Part of the pleasure in receiving a Van Vechten letter lay in its appearance: the lavish stationery, aquamarine or canary yellow or raspberry, even (during the 1920s) with his own name watermarked into a thick, deckle-edged buff; the body of the letter usually beginning right after the salutation, on the same line; the typing with no spaces after periods and with plenty of capricious capital letters and abbreviations of his own invention; his frequently indecipherable marginal postscripts; his signature, almost always "Carlo," scrawled in green or black or purple ink, sometimes accompanied by exclamation points before and after, and the date typed below; the envelopes decorated with a variety of commemorative stamps and worthy-cause stickers.

I have not indicated the range of Carl Van Vechten's stationery, which embraced a number of variations on his engraved addresses, leftovers from his wife's frequent ocean voyages, and letterheads from foundations he supported. For the reader's ease, dates and addresses appear consistently at the beginnings of letters. I have bracketed conjectural dates and those taken from postmarks; preferring consistency over pedantry, however, I have not bracketed information I have supplied for partial addresses. I have ignored some of Carl Van Vechten's erratic paragraphing; I have made silent corrections for obvious typographical errors, misspellings, and grammatical slips; and I have rectified factual errors in names and titles unless the error bears some significance. Ordinarily, Carl Van Vechten was careful about such matters but deliberately contrary about others. I have not altered his eccentric capitalizations and abbreviations, nor have I altered his long-standing insistence on "incidently" and "coincidently," nor have I changed his punctuation except for sense. Other editorial insertions and deletions are indicated by brackets.

Because I wished to represent the broadest of ranges, both in recipients and in content, during the seventy-five years of Carl Van Vechten's correspondence, I was obliged to edit drastically many of the letters by omitting sometimes substantial sections of them. Except in the rare instance when some observation might embarrass still living people, however, I have not deleted material out of decorum or even good taste. More often, I cut passages to avoid repetition when he had written the same or similar information to several people. Further, it was necessary to cut when he indulged in his "obstinate penchant for cataloguing," as he called it in a dust-jacket note for his 1925 novel *Firecrackers*. Long lists of people he had photographed, guest lists from parties, lists of writers whose works he had collected and subsequently donated to libraries, I frequently deleted to avoid the reader's impatience as well as my own. "Cataloguing is an important part of my personality," he observes in one of his letters to Hugh Walpole, and I believe sufficient evidence of that remains despite my excisions. Still further, I have deleted several passages referring to unidentifiable people or reports to his wife on such domestic matters as who had telephoned or written on a particular day, what bills had come in, and greetings from their maids, although sufficient evidence remains to represent these matters too. In all cases, my ellipses are bracketed, because Carl Van Vechten used ellipses to indicate pauses or changes of subject. I have allowed him his conventional three or four dots, depending on his sentence; but I have ignored his two-dot pauses, since he seemed only to be tapping the key before the next word came to him, and I have truncated an infrequent, long line of dots to four.

Carl Van Vechten added footnotes, x-ing the first, then numbering as he proceeded, scrawling them across the bottom, top, and sides of a letter, not always in chronological order. I have substituted conventional symbols like asterisks and daggers in place of his numbers, and I have numbered my own explanatory footnotes and brief passages from several additional letters that amplify information. However, I have not used ellipses to indicate my deletions of inconsequential notes and postscripts in Van Vechten's margins. Letters that Carl Van Vechten neglected to sign are marked "[unsigned]"; letters I have transcribed from carbon copies or drafts among his own papers are marked "[unsigned carbon copy]" or "[unsigned draft]."

I have identified names and titles for the layman, not the expert, and for the young reader, not the one conversant with Carl Van Vechten's period; and I have considered few sufficiently celebrated or recognizable for exemption. Unidentified names and titles speak more of my failure here than of their success. A list of recipients precedes the letters, setting out dates, occupations, and connections with Carl Van Vechten. If a recipient's name occurs in the text of a letter prior to his own first letter, he is identified briefly in a footnote, as are other people, places, and titles mentioned. Subsequent to footnote identifications, I have bracketed missing names in the text unless they appear with immediate frequency. "Langston" and "Gertrude" are referred to so often that the reader hardly needs reminding that they are Langston Hughes and Gertrude Stein several letters in a row. There is a further exception for Carl Van Vechten's wife: she is referred to interchangeably throughout as Fan, as Fania, as Marinoff, as Miss M, as FM, and as Fania Marinoff in letters to other people, in addition to his own several diminutives and pet names in letters to her. For all of the foregoing editorial decisions, and for the inevitable errors that may afflict this selection, I assume responsibility, defending the former and apologizing for the latter.

I have called upon the resources, memories, and patience of many people, and it is not only my obligation but my pleasure to be able to thank them for their asssistance. Many supplied me with original letters or copies of them; others sleuthed out solutions to puzzles; others kindly responded to questions by mail; still others helped me in deciphering the mysteries of Carl Van Vechten's penmanship.

My first debt is to Donald Angus, who knew Carl Van Vechten intimately from 1919 and whose memory is evergreen. My second debt is to Donald Gallup, whose sound advice has served me well for twenty-five years.

I wish also to thank Dame Judith Anderson, the late Ann Andrews, Desmond Arthur, the late Brooks Atkinson, A'Lelia Bundles, Edward Burns, Sandy Campbell, Marilyn Stone Corey, Charles-Henri Ford, Ruth Ford, Eric Garber, George George, Lillian Gish, George Glauner, Walter Goldwater, Bruce J. Hacker, Larry Hall, James V. Hatch and Camille Billops, Philo Highley, Edward Jablonski, Charles Jahant, the late William Jepson, Kate Kellner, Richard Kirby, Lincoln Kirstein, Lillian Koral, William Koshland, Hugh Laing, Jerome Lawrence, Edward Lueders, Philip Marchant, Paul Motter, Susan Sheaffer Outerbridge, Paul Padgette, Eleanor Perényi, Aileen Pringle, Arnold Rampersad, Jim Ringo, Ned Rorem, Richard Rutledge, Arnold T. Schwab, Anne Seymour, Jack Sharrar, Joseph Solomon, Prentiss Taylor, Henry Van Dyke, Donald Windham, James Yescalis; also the reference librarians in the Ganser Library, at Millersville University where I teach; also, and especially, Hans Kellner.

Indexers get in on the manual labor too late to be acknowledged by name, and they are usually paid in beer and pretzels for time-consuming, boring labor. In the past, as friends and friends of friends have cheerfully gathered around the dining room table for indexing sessions on earlier books, my guilt in not being able to recognize them in print has always been acute. So this time, in advance, many thanks.

Finally, if an editor may be allowed a dedication, this book belongs to One and Three.

Bruce Kellner

# Acknowledgments

For permission to edit and publish these letters, I thank Donald Gallup and Joseph Solomon, Literary Trustee and Lawyer, respectively, for the estate of Carl Van Vechten. Joseph Solomon further kindly granted me permission to reproduce Carl Van Vechten's photographs of his recipients, some from original negatives in the Beinecke Rare Book and Manuscript Library, Yale University, and some from original prints in my own collection.

The letters in this selection, or copies of them, are in the following private collections and in private or public institutions: Donald Angus; A'Lelia Bundles (a letter to A'Lelia Walker); Sandy Campbell; Marilyn Stone Corey (a letter to Leah Maynard); Donald Gallup; Eric Garber (letters to Countee Cullen); Lillian Gish; Edward and Edith Jablonski; Margaret Wilcox Kellner; William Koshland (letters to Alfred A. Knopf); Hugh Laing; Philip Marchant; Paul Motter (a letter to Doris Julian); Paul Padgette; Ned Rorem; Richard Rutledge; Marian Seldes (a letter to Gilbert Seldes, courtesy of George George); Prentiss Taylor; Donald Windham; Atlanta University (the Trevor Arnett Library, Countee Cullen Memorial/Special Collections); Boston University (the Mugar Memorial Library, Alec Waugh Collection); Brown University Library; Columbia University (Rare Book and Manuscript Library, Random House and Edna Kenton Papers); Harvard University (by permission of the Houghton Library, letters to Witter Bynner and Alexander Woollcott); Hatch-Billops Collection, Inc. (letters to Owen Dodson and Ethel Waters); Howard University (the Moorland/Spingarn Research Center, letters to Channing Pollock); the Huntington Library, San Marino, California (a letter to Wallace Stevens); Indiana University (the Lilly Library, a letter to Vincent Starrett); the Library of Congress ( a letter to Irita Van Doren and letters to Arthur Spingarn, Walter White, and Roy Wilkins in the National Association for the Advancement of Colored People Archives); the Museum of the City of New York (Theater Collection, a letter to May Davenport Seymour); the Newberry Library (letters to Henry Blake Fuller); New York Public Library, Astor, Lenox, and Tilden Foundations (the Henry W. and Albert A. Berg Collection, for letters to Ronald Firbank and Hugh Walpole, and the Manuscript and Archives Division, the Carl Van Vechten Papers, letters to Jane Cowl, Muriel Draper, Peter David Marchant, Fania Marinoff, Florine Stettheimer, Charles Duane Van Vechten, Ralph Van Vechten, and the H. L. Mencken Papers); Ohio State University Libraries (letters to Louis Bromfield); Princeton University (a letter to James B. Meriwether); Southern Illinois University (Special Collections, Caresse Crosby/ Black Sun Press Papers); University of California at Berkeley (the Bancroft Library, Gertrude Atherton Papers, C-H 45, and Noel Sullivan Papers, C-B 801); University of Delaware Library (a letter to Louis Untermeyer); University of Michigan Library (Department of Rare Books and Special Collections, letters to R. W. Cowden); University of Pennsylvania (the Van Pelt Library, Theodore Dreiser Collection); University of Texas at Austin (the Harry Ransom Humanities Research Center, letters to Honorable Dorothy Brett, Robert Downing, Joseph Hergesheimer, Fannie Hurst, Blanche Knopf, Philip Moeller, Matthew Phipps Shiel, and Alice B. Toklas); University of Tulsa (the McFarlin Library, Department of Special Collections, letters to Brion Gysin); University of Virginia Library (Manuscripts Department, Papers of Ellen Glasgow, acc. no. 5060, letters to Emma Gray Trigg, acc. no. 5557, Carl Van Vechten Collection, acc. no. 6788a, letters to Scott Cunningham); Virginia Commonwealth University (the James Branch Cabell Library, Special Collections and Archives Department, The Frances Leigh Williams Papers, reproduced by permission of Donald Gallup, Literary Trustee to the Estate of Carl Van Vechten); Yale University (Yale Music School Library, letters to Virgil Thomson, and Beinecke Rare Book and Manuscript Library, Collection of American Literature, for letters to James T. Babb, the Banyan Press, Baroness Karen Blixen, Arna Bontemps, Neith Boyce, John Breon, Charles Byrne, James Branch Cabell, Owen Dodson, Doris Ewing, Max Ewing, Arthur Davison Ficke, Gladys Brown Ficke, Waldo Frank, Donald Gallup, Mary Garden, Hutchins Hapgood, George George, Chester Himes, Avery Hopwood, Langston Hughes, Harold Jackman, Charles S. Johnson, Grace Nail Johnson, James Weldon Johnson, Edna Kenton, Bernhard Knollenberg, Sinclair Lewis, Edward Lueders, Mabel Dodge Luhan, Fania Marinoff, John Martin, Claude McKay, Peter Francis O'Brien, Carlotta Monterey O'Neill, Norman Holmes Pearson, Dorothy Peterson, Edgar Allan Poe, Anna Marble Pollock, Karl Priebe, James Purdy, O. G. Sonneck, Philippe Soupault, Hunter Stagg, Muriel Starr, Gertrude Stein, Carrie, Ettie, and Florine Stettheimer, Alfred Stieglitz, Alice B. Toklas, Henry Van Dyke, Charles Duane Van Vechten, Walter Van Vechten, and Elinor Wylie).

Some of the material in the introduction to this book originally appeared, in different form, in *Carl Van Vechten and the Irreverent Decades* (Norman: University of Oklahoma Press, 1968), pp. viii–xi, 287–88, 294, 297–304, and it is incorporated here with permission of the publisher.

# *Recipients*

Donald Angus (1899–   ), a constant companion during the 1920s, met Van Vechten in 1919 and remained an intimate friend. He was regisseur for the *Revue Nègre* company in Paris and later was employed as a decorator at Jay Thorpe. Van Vechten numbered his friends named Donald: Angus was Donald I and was sometimes referred to as "I" or "One."

Gertrude Atherton (1857–1948) was one of Van Vechten's "literary ladies," as he called women writers of his acquaintance, even professing to admire her garrulously romantic novels.

James T. Babb (1899–1968) was Assistant Librarian at Yale University at the time Van Vechten established the James Weldon Johnson Memorial Library of Negro Arts and Letters in 1941. Babb was Librarian from 1945 until his retirement.

The Banyan Press (1947–50), a private press owned and operated by Milton Saul and Claude Fredericks, issued handsome hand-set and -sewn limited editions including two Gertrude Stein titles through Van Vechten's cooperation.

Baroness Karen Blixen (1885–1962), who wrote under the pseudonym Isak Dinesen, became one of Van Vechten's last literary correspondents when, in 1955, he first read her *Out of Africa* and wrote her a fan letter.

Arna Bontemps (1902–73) was Librarian at Fisk University where Van Vechten established the George Gershwin Memorial Collection of Music and Musical Literature and the Florine Stettheimer Memorial Collection of Books on Art. Earlier, he had been a member of the Harlem Renaissance, that group of young black writers, many of whose careers Van Vechten fostered during the late 1920s.

Neith Boyce (1887–1951), the wife of Hutchins Hapgood, and Van Vechten were compatriots in escaping from Italy when war broke out in 1914. Another of his "literary ladies," she wrote several plays and novels.

John Breon (1923–84) met Van Vechten through his own acquaintance with GERTRUDE STEIN and ALICE B. TOKLAS. Later he wrote a novel and went into publishing.

HONORABLE DOROTHY BRETT (1883–1970) was an eccentric English member of the D. H. Lawrence entourage at MABEL DODGE LUHAN's artists' colony in Taos, New Mexico, and herself a painter.

LOUIS BROMFIELD (1896–1956) wrote a number of popular novels during the second quarter of the century. He is probably best known for *The Rains Came*.

WITTER BYNNER (1881–1968) and Van Vechten shared the same publisher, ALFRED A. KNOPF. Although Van Vechten professed neither interest in nor comprehension of poetry, a warm friendship with Bynner began toward the end of the 1920s.

CHARLES RAYMOND BYRNE (1916–  ) published a paperback version of Van Vechten's *Nigger Heaven* in 1951 for Avon.

JAMES BRANCH CABELL (1879–1958), the Virginia novelist whose literary style had considerable influence on a number of his contemporaries, was one of Van Vechten's best friends and steadiest correspondents.

SANDY CAMPBELL (1922–  ) has been an actor, an editor for *The New Yorker*, and latterly publisher of DONALD WINDHAM's work.

BENNETT CERF (1898–1971) was publisher of Random House and Modern Library books, notably those of GERTRUDE STEIN, 1934–46.

R. W. COWDEN (1893–1961) was Librarian at the University of Michigan and in charge of the AVERY HOPWOOD Awards and the Hopwood Collection there.

JANE COWL (1890–1950) was a popular American actress whose not always successful performances in Shakespeare were of greater interest to Van Vechten than her long and lucrative run in the sentimental romance, *Smilin' Through*, that she wrote with Jane Murfin in 1919.

CARESSE CROSBY (1892–1970), with her husband Harry Crosby, ran the Black Sun Press in Paris.

COUNTEE CULLEN (1904–47) was a young black poet whose early work heralded the advent of the Harlem Renaissance, though he eschewed Van Vechten's help in getting his work published.

SCOTT CUNNINGHAM (circa 1895–1930) prepared Van Vechten's first full bibliography, issued by the Centaur Press in Philadelphia in 1924.

MABEL DODGE. *See* MABEL DODGE LUHAN.

OWEN DODSON (1918–83) was a black writer whom Van Vechten first knew in the late 1930s and later at the Stage Door Canteen.

MURIEL DRAPER (1886–1952) was called "Ma-Draper" by Van Vechten, and she called him "Carlo-Pa" (accents on the second syllables) in later years. They met in London in 1913 but only became friendly after 1925, sharing an interest in the Harlem Renaissance.

THEODORE DREISER (1871–1945), the American novelist, published Van Vechten's first article (about Richard Strauss's *Salome*) in 1906 in *Broadway Magazine,* for which he was editor. They became casual friends and social acquaintances.

MAX EWING (1903–34), one of Van Vechten's "Famous Beauties of the XXth Century," as he called his coterie of young men, was a writer and musician. His "art gallery"—actually his apartment hung floor to ceiling with photographs of celebrities—was well known during the 1920s.

ARTHUR DAVISON FICKE (1883–1945), a now neglected American poet and art historian, was one of Van Vechten's closest friends and constant correspondents.

GLADYS BROWN FICKE (1890–1973), a painter, was the wife of ARTHUR DAVISION FICKE.

RONALD FIRBANK (1886–1926) owed the success of his novels in America to Van Vechten. The mannered wit and precious locutions of this English writer strongly influenced some of Van Vechten's novels, notably *The Blind Bow-Boy.*

WALDO FRANK (1889–1967), the American social critic, was editor of the short-lived magazine *Seven Arts* at the time Van Vechten submitted essays to it for publication.

HENRY BLAKE FULLER (1857–1929) was one of the neglected American writers Van Vechten attempted to resuscitate during the 1920s, favorably comparing him with Henry James because of his subtle humor and irony.

DONALD GALLUP (1913–   ), dean of contemporary bibliography and for many years the Curator of the Collection of American Literature in the Yale University Library, is Literary Trustee to the Estate of Carl Van Vechten. Van Vechten numbered his friends named Donald: Gallup was Donald III and was sometimes referred to as "III" or "Three."

MARY GARDEN (1875–1967), the flamboyant American soprano, was one of Van Vechten's early operatic idols, about whom he wrote incessantly.

GEORGE GEORGE (1922–   ) is an American painter and sculptor who first knew Van Vechten through the Stage Door Canteen.

LILLIAN GISH (1893–   ), the American actress, was an acquaintance through Van Vechten's wife FANIA MARINOFF.

ELLEN GLASGOW (1873–1945), one of Van Vechten's warmest literary acquaintances, documented her native Virginia in a number of successful novels.

BRION GYSIN (1926–1986), a painter and writer who had lived in Morocco, was best known for his hashish fudge recipe in *The Alice B. Toklas Cookbook*.

HUTCHINS HAPGOOD (1869–1944) was an American writer who became an acquaintance through MABEL DODGE [LUHAN] in 1913. His wife NEITH BOYCE was also a friend and correspondent.

JOESPH HERGESHEIMER (1880–1954), whose upholstered novels are now out of fashion, was one of the most popular writers in America from 1917. With the Depression, he lapsed into obscurity. His friendship with Van Vechten began through their mutual publisher ALFRED A. KNOPF and continued until death.

CHESTER HIMES (1909–84), the black American novelist, became one of Van Vechten's closest correspondents and, at Van Vechten's urging, was published by ALFRED A. KNOPF at one time.

AVERY HOPWOOD (1884–1928), the most financially successful playwright of his generation, was one of Van Vechten's closest friends and the model (in part) for his fictional Peter Whiffle. They met in 1906 through Hopwood's early collaborator CHANNING POLLOCK.

LANGSTON HUGHES (1902–67), the best known and arguably the best black writer in American letters, met Van Vechten in 1924, after which their intimate friendship and correspondence continued unabated for forty years. Hughes's career was one of many Van Vechten nourished from its beginnings.

FANNIE HURST (1889–1968), described by Van Vechten on many occasions as one of his ''great friends,'' wrote a number of popular novels during the 1920s and 1930s.

EDITH JABLONSKI (1926–   ) is a magazine editor and the wife of music critic and biographer Edward Jablonski.

HAROLD JACKMAN (1900–60) was a Harlem school teacher who served as the physical model for the protagonist in Van Vechten's novel *Nigger Heaven,* and he founded the COUNTEE CULLEN Memorial Collection at Atlanta University.

CHARLES S. JOHNSON (1893–1956) was President of the Urban League and editor of *Opportunity* during the 1920s; later he became President of Fisk University.

GRACE NAIL JOHNSON (1886–1975) was the wife of JAMES WELDON JOHNSON.

JAMES WELDON JOHNSON (1871–1938), the black humanitarian, author, educator, song writer, diplomat, Van Vechten considered the greatest person he had ever known and for a time his best friend. They were each other's literary executor until Johnson's death.

DORIS JULIAN (?–?) was a theatrical producer and glamorous photographic subject for Van Vechten during the late 1950s.

EDNA KENTON (1876–1954) and Van Vechten were close friends from their meeting in Chicago at the turn of the century until, without any accountable explanation, they ceased all communication in 1934. A member of the Heterodoxy, that group of independent women in Greenwich Village before the First War, Kenton wrote a number of novels and histories.

BERNHARD KNOLLENBERG (1892–1973) was an American historian and Librarian at Yale University, from 1938 until 1945, at the time Van Vechten was building the JAMES WELDON JOHNSON Memorial Collection of Negro Arts and Letters.

ALFRED A. KNOPF (1892–1984) began publishing his Borzoi Books in 1915 and the following year issued Van Vechten's *Music and Bad Manners,* the first of seventeen titles. Knopf and his wife Blanche were warm friends of Van Vechten and his wife FANIA MARINOFF.

BLANCHE KNOPF (1894–1966), ALFRED A. KNOPF's wife, was an active partner of the publishing house, frequently serving as editor for Van Vechten as well as for a number of young black writers whose work he had encouraged the Knopfs to publish.

HUGH LAING (1911–   ), a ballet dancer with several prominent companies, was responsible for roles in most of Antony Tudor's works. His good looks and dancer's body made him an ideal photographic model for Van Vechten who on more than one occasion declared Laing the best model he had ever had.

SINCLAIR LEWIS (1885–1951) was an American novelist who knew Van Vechten from 1906 when they lived in the same rooming house in New York City.

EDWARD LUEDERS (1923–   ) published two critical studies, *Carl Van Vechten and the Twenties* in 1955 and *Carl Van Vechten* in 1965. During the interim, author and subject became warm friends and steady correspondents.

MABEL DODGE LUHAN (1879–1962) and Van Vechten met in 1913. Long periods of estrangement ensued—one of them lasting seventeen years—but they were otherwise intensely close to each other, and Van Vechten considered her the major influence on his taste and aesthetics.

MARK LUTZ (1901–67) met Van Vechten in 1931 and exchanged nearly daily letters with him for three decades. He was Van Vechten's literary trustee at one period, his lover for several years, a frequent traveling companion. After Van Vechten's death, he attended to FANIA MARINOFF's needs. Lutz was a book reviewer in Richmond, Virginia, and later a publicist for Philco in Philadelphia.

WILLARD MAAS (1911–71) was an American educator and writer.

PETER DAVID MARCHANT (1928–57) wrote his Columbia University master's thesis about Van Vechten, and, in the last year before his early death, he enjoyed a genial friendship and correspondence with his subject.

FANIA MARINOFF (1887–1971) and Van Vechten survived fifty years of wedded life—not all of it blissful—in absolute devotion. She made her acting debut at the age of eight and appeared frequently on stage and in films until the 1920s, then intermittently until 1945. Her most notable appearances were in Shakespeare, Shaw, and Wedekind.

JOHN MARTIN (1893–1985) was dance critic for the *New York Times* for many years, and editor of Van Vechten's writings about dancing for a triple number of *Dance Index* in 1942.

LEAH MAYNARD [STONE] (1881–1947) was Van Vechten's earliest childhood friend, the youngest sister of his Uncle Giles Van Vechten's wife Fanny (a bride at thirteen). Later Leah Maynard married Henry Stone.

CLAUDE MCKAY (1889–1948), the West Indian-born poet and novelist, was a member of the Harlem Renaissance who called on Van Vechten for assistance some time after the movement had lost its popularity.

HENRY LOUIS MENCKEN (1880–1956), the social and literary critic, and Van Vechten were friends from the time of their meeting through their mutual publisher ALFRED A. KNOPF, in spite of their widely divergent interests and personalities. One of the richest exchanges, their correspondence covered everything from music to prostate trouble.

JAMES MERIWETHER (1928–   ) is an American educator and writer.

PHILIP MOELLER (1880–1958), the playwright-member and director of the Theatre Guild, knew Van Vechten through actress Helen Westley. Van Vechten wrote a preface to the published version of Moeller's *Sophie* in 1919.

PETER FRANCIS O'BRIEN SJ (1943–   ) is a Jesuit priest interested in black music and singers. He met Van Vechten a few months before the latter's death.

CARLOTTA MONTEREY O'NEILL (1888–1970) knew Van Vechten first through FANIA MARINOFF, circa 1915; then as the wife of Van Vechten's friend, cartoonist Ralph Barton; then as the wife of playwright Eugene O'Neill. In later years he became an unoffical advisor and confidante.

PAUL PADGETTE (1925–   ) is a San Francisco bookseller and bibliophile, Van Vechten's last protégé. He is the editor of *The Dance Writings of Carl Van Vechten*, 1974, and *The Dance Photography of Carl Van Vechten*, 1981.

NORMAN HOLMES PEARSON (1909–75) was a member of the English Department at Yale University from 1941. With DONALD GALLUP he was responsible for the initial cataloging and bibliography of the GERTRUDE STEIN Collection.

DOROTHY PETERSON (1897–1978) was a Harlem schoolteacher and librarian, one of Van Vechten's closest friends from 1925, and the model for the heroine of his novel *Nigger Heaven*. Later she worked to enlarge the JAMES WELDON JOHNSON Memorial Collection of Negro Arts and Letters at Yale by soliciting contributions from friends and associates.

EDGAR ALLAN POE (1871–1961), not to be confused with the American writer, was the recalcitrant lawyer for the Estate of GERTRUDE STEIN.

ANNA MARBLE POLLOCK (1876–1946), wife of playwright CHANNING POLLOCK, was a journalist and author of early vaudeville sketches. Later she was press representative for Oscar Hammerstein when Van Vechten was first reporting musical news for the *New York Times*.

CHANNING POLLOCK (1880–1946), a friend of Van Vechten's from 1906—they may have known each other earlier in Chicago—was well known as a popular playwright prior to the 1920s, at which time his "well-made" melodramas went out of fashion.

KARL PRIEBE (1914–76) was a midwestern artist whose fanciful subject matters often included Negro figures in surrealist settings. After a brief but intense correspondence, Van Vechten suddenly dropped Priebe without explanation.

JAMES PURDY (1923–   ) was one of the last writers Van Vechten championed seriously and continually. Van Vechten arranged for Purdy's manuscripts and letters to be accepted in the Beinecke Rare Book and Manuscript Library at Yale University.

NED ROREM (1923–   ) and Van Vechten met following a recital by black American soprano Mattiwilda Dobbs at Town Hall in 1956, during which she had sung a group of Rorem's songs. He is perhaps as well known for his candid diaries as for his music.

GILBERT SELDES (1893–1970) was an American journalist and critic best known for *The Seven Lively Arts*, published in 1924.

MAY DAVENPORT SEYMOUR (1883–1967) was curator at the Museum of the City of New York, responsible for mounting an exhibition of Van Vechten's photographs of theater celebrities in 1942.

MATTHEW PHIPPS SHIEL (1865–1947), another forgotten writer whose career Van Vechten attempted to revive, was the author of a number of novels published only in England around the turn of the century.

OSCAR GEORGE SONNECK (1873–1928), for many years with the Music Division of the Library of Congress, was editor of *Musical Quarterly* during the period Van Vechten was writing annual essays for it.

PHILIPPE SOUPAULT (1897–?), the French surrealist novelist, translated Van Vechten's *Nigger Heaven* into French but with so many substantial cuts—nearly one-quarter of the novel—that it was published without permission.

ARTHUR SPINGARN 1878–1971), one of the leading white abolitionists of the century, was active in the NAACP as its long-time lawyer.

HUNTER STAGG (1895–1960), a witty and perceptive book reviewer for *Reviewer* as well as one of the editors of that Richmond, Virginia, literary magazine, became an intimate friend and correspondent during the late 1920s; then, again without explanation, Van Vechten simply cut him off, in 1934.

MURIEL STARR (1886–1973) was an actress whose stage success in Australia was never repeated in America. She was an early acquaintance of FANIA MARINOFF and in part responsible for encouraging the Van Vechten-Marinoff marriage.

VINCENT STARRETT (1886–1974) was a journalist and mystery writer. He wrote for the Chicago *Inter-Ocean*, for which Van Vechten also wrote, in 1905. Subsequently he edited the magazine *Wave*, to which Van Vechten contributed.

GERTRUDE STEIN (1874–1946), the American experimental writer, was championed throughout her career by Van Vechten. He was instrumental in keeping her work before the public, and he edited her unpublished work after her death. Always excepting ALICE B. TOKLAS, he was her most reliable friend, as their correspondence attests, and Van Vechten claimed he was the only friend with whom she never quarrelled.

MABEL DODGE STERNE, *See* MABEL DODGE LUHAN.

CARRIE STETTHEIMER (1875–1945), youngest of an extraordinary trio of sisters who kept a salon in New York from about 1915, devoted much of her adult life to furnishing an elaborate doll house, notable for its original works of art by Gaston Lachaise, Marcel Duchamp, and others. It is now in the Museum of the City of New York.

ETTIE STETTHEIMER (1873–1955), second of the trio, published the novel *Love Days* in 1923 under the pseudonym Henrie Waste.

FLORINE STETTHEIMER (1871–1944), best-known member of the trio, was a painter reluctant to show or to sell her work. She designed the costumes and scenery for the GERTRUDE STEIN–VIRGIL THOMSON opera *Four Saints in Three Acts* in 1934. Her work is now in many museums.

WALLACE STEVENS (1879–1955) and Van Vechten met through Walter Conrad Arensberg in 1912. Van Vechten was responsible for publishing Stevens's poems in *Trend* and *Rogue* shortly thereafter and in arranging for

ALFRED A. KNOPF to publish Stevens's first collection, *Harmonium,* in 1923.

ALFRED STIEGLITZ (1864–1946) was America's premier photographer and the husband of painter Georgia O'Keeffe.

NOEL SULLIVAN (1890–1956) was a wealthy west coast patron of the arts, an acquaintance of Van Vechten's through LANGSTON HUGHES.

PRENTISS TAYLOR (1907– ) is a painter and lithographer. He designed Van Vechten's bookplate and the dust-jacket for *Sacred and Profane Memories* in 1932, and he assisted Van Vechten with the lighting in early photographic experiments.

VIRGIL THOMSON (1896– ), music critic and composer, met Van Vechten through his association with GERTRUDE STEIN, several of whose texts he set to music.

ALICE B. TOKLAS (1877–1967), was GERTRUDE STEIN'S secretary and companion for forty years, the author of a celebrated cookbook, and an incisive and witty correspondent for dozens of recipients.

EMMA GRAY TRIGG (1890–1976) was a Richmond, Virginia, matron who wrote poems for *Reviewer* and other little magazines.

LOUIS UNTERMEYER (1885–1977) was an American poet and anthologist.

IRITA VAN DOREN (1891–1966), wife of critic Carl Van Doren, was literary editor for the *Herald Tribune* and for *Nation.*

HENRY VAN DYKE (1928– ) is a black American novelist who met Van Vechten when he won the AVERY HOPWOOD Literary Award at the University of Michigan. After Van Vechten's death, Van Dyke memorialized him with affectionate malice as "Max Rhode" in *Blood of Strawberries* (1968).

CHARLES DUANE VAN VECHTEN (1839–1926), Van Vechten's father, was a prominent Iowa insurance salesman and banker.

RALPH VAN VECHTEN (1862–1927), Van Vechten's brother, was a prominent Chicago banker.

WALTER VAN VECHTEN (?–?) was a distant cousin Van Vechten met during the Second World War at the Stage Door Canteen.

A'LELIA WALKER (1885–1931) was the black heiress to her mother's fortune made through a hair-straightening process. Van Vechten was an intimate acquaintance during the Harlem Renaissance.

HUGH WALPOLE (1884–1941) was a popular English novelist and warm friend and correspondent for nearly twenty years.

ETHEL WATERS (1896–1977), in later years an earthmother figure with evangelist Billy Graham, was a popular black singer and respected actress—in part through Van Vechten's press agentry. They were intimate friends from 1927.

ALEC WAUGH (1898–1983), elder brother of novelist Evelyn Waugh, was an English writer.

WALTER WHITE (1893–1955), powerful gadfly of the NAACP, was Van Vechten's first black literary acquaintance, his entré into Harlem intelligentsia during the 1920s, and a close associate in racial matters afterward.

ROY WILKINS (1901–81) was President of the NAACP from 1958 until his death.

FRANCES LEIGH WILLIAMS (1909–78) was a Richmond, Virginia, historian.

DONALD WINDHAM (1920–  ) is an American novelist and memoirist whose work Van Vechten admired. Windham was Donald IV, having begun as Donald IX and moving up when others were dismissed or dismissed themselves. Unlike DONALD ANGUS and DONALD GALLUP, he was not referred to by number.

ALEXANDER WOOLLCOTT (1887–1943) was a literary and dramatic critic of eccentric tastes and behavior.

ELINOR WYLIE (1885–1928) was an American poet whose novel *Jennifer Lorn* Van Vechten publicized into popularity in 1923, smitten as he was with its artificial style and its author's glamor.

*The Letters*

## TO LEAH MAYNARD

[circa 23 January 1907]

The New York Times
New York City

Leah, my own, you astonish me with your lack of perspicuity. Can you imagine that I intend to put an end to the thousand and one nights as we have started them in Chicago? After intimate excursions—and dinners—which have culminated in the most surprising adventures, it is impossible that I should relinquish the idea of their recurrence. C'est impossible. If we don't meet in New York which is quite what Fate may have in her horrid snaky mind, we shall undoubtedly drift into Chicago at the same time and have a fest compared with which the two preceding summers may be set down as tame. Not that they can be yet. I shall always ascribe to you the most marvelous power of making realistic life pictures romantically interesting. New York, my dear, you would love, with its thousand and one queer places and restaurants. [. . .] Mostly I am going to opera—and *Salome* has got me by the ears and EYES. I wonder if you have read the Oscar Wilde play. If you haven't I must send it to you sometime. It is strangely beautiful literature and the opera makes it even more wonderful. It is overpowering, and strong men are unable to eat or breathe after seeing and hearing it. I have heard four performances now, three rehearsals and the first night,[1] and confess that it has fairly spoiled me for other things along that line. Elsie Janis[2] is doing stunts across the street, even now, and she very definitely reminds me of you. Do write to me more than occasionally and address me care of the New York Times.

Carl Van Vechten

## TO MABEL DODGE

[circa 25 February 1913]

New York City

Dear Mrs. Dodge, Perhaps you didn't see the Monday Times. Perhaps you are ill—(I'm so sorry you were ill Saturday). At any rate here's the clipping.[3] It isn't all that I wanted—my original article was three times as long and four times as amusing but for a daily paper one has to exclude style.

Sincerely, Carlo Van Vechten

---

[1]There was no second performance of *Salome* at the Metropolitan Opera House; the production was cancelled at the insistence of some season box holders, led by J. P. Morgan's daughter Mrs. Herbert Satterlee.

[2]Elsie Janis, American actress, then starring in *The Vanderbilt Cup.*

[3]"Cubist of Letters Writes a New Book," *New York Times,* 24 February 1913, about Gertrude Stein. The article only appeared in the earliest Monday edition, on the financial page. It is not in the microfilm editions of the *New York Times,* but a copy is preserved in CVV's scrapbooks in the New York Public Library.

## TO FANIA MARINOFF
[8 May 1913]

The New York Times
New York City

This, dear Fan-Baby-Baby-Baby, is by way of being a letter you can read, and by the same token it isn't going to be a long one! It's one o'clock in the office and I have just been instructed that hereafter I am supposed to be here until two o'clock. [. . .] My brother[4] is here. He called me up tonight and we arranged to have dinner tomorrow. I am dead sorry you aren't here for with a little assistance from you I think we could get something out of brother—something we need; in fact the only thing we need.—You cunning we-wee-wee kiddie, I've been looking at your pictures—that Steve[5] took—for the longest time today and thinking how sad it is that we are not together. Which reminds me of Eva McDonald in her drunkness, telling me I must never leave you. "We women are crooly treated," she sobbed—real champagne tears—"Men take us and play with us and then they toss us aside. Oh, don't do that to Fan, don't do that to Fan!" Here her sobs made her words inaudible. [. . .] I explained to her if any crool treatment were going on between us that I would be the sufferer.    Good night, darling baby of my heart, I wish you were here with me.   [unsigned]

## TO FANIA MARINOFF
[19 May 1913]

Hotel Longacre
New York City

Darlingest Angelist baby in all words, You are the only one—of that I am sure. Everything else is merely incidental and by the way and preparatory. In one hour I am going to telephone you and tell you this and also that I found a letter here from the managing editor of the [*New York*] Press. I went to see him today and the dramatic position on that paper seems to be mine for the middle of August. Everything does seem to be working out.

I have been busy as anything today. Went to see the Press—and my lawyer—and the Times—and had dinner at Mike's.[6] She is all excited about this pageant and about a benefit that she is getting up for the Paterson

---

[4]Ralph Van Vechten. See List of recipients.
[5]Steve: Stephen Woods Roach, son of shipping magnate John D. Roach, met Fania Marinoff in 1903 when at the age of seventeen she first came to New York. He became her protector, sponsor, and patron, as well as her first lover. He photographed her on many occasions and in several plays, and he was witness to her marriage to CVV in 1914. She remained faithful to his friendship until his death in 1923.
[6]"Mike" was CVV's nickname for Mabel Dodge. He was never certain how it had come about, but within a year or two he had dropped it.

strikers.[7] Bertha Kalisch, Dave Warfield, and Hedwig Deisher are going to be in it and it will probably be given in Yiddish at the Second ave theatre. I suggested [Joseph] Schildkraut, Frank Reuter, Nazimova and Lou Fields— and *you*. That is I told Mike that you could come up for the day, I thought. [. . .] Do as you like, dear girl, about the whole matter, because I told her if she wanted you to write or telephone you.

I can't tell you, darling baby, how proud I am of you. You are the most perfect, the most ideal thing I have ever met. I'm no fool, Fan.—I shouldn't give up any real thing like you for *anything* else. You may be sure of that, and I love you with all my heart, soul, and body.      Yours always, Carlo

TO FANIA MARINOFF                                                    [Paris]
[2 June 1913]

Dearest Fan-Fan, Many amusing things have happened. Almost too many to write about! John Sanborn[8] and I went up to see Polaire[9] at the Folies Bergère at 11.30 one night, and when my card was sent up the response came down to come up immediately. I left John outside and went in to find Polaire doubled up with laughter and *Ann* there.[1] She was very fat and old looking and altogether disgusting, to tell the truth, and very fussed. [. . .]

And I had a marvelous time today at Jacque [Emile] Blanche's.[2] Spent the whole afternoon talking with George Moore[3] and had the most amusing time I've had in ages. Besides I have enough material for an article, which I shall write as soon as I have time. He's an extraordinary person. He called [Gabriel] D'Annunzio a "hair dresser," and said that he knew just what

---

[7]Mabel Dodge conceived of the idea of bringing the plight of the Paterson, New Jersey, silk workers' strike to the attention of sympathetic New Yorkers by staging a "Paterson Strike Pageant." Assisted by Hutchins Hapgood and Max Eastman from her salon, Robert Edmond Jones who designed the sets, her incipient lover John Reed, and ıww leader Bill Haywood, she raised funds, contributing heavily herself, and worked on publicity. On June 7th, an audience—including over a thousand New Jersey workers—stretching nearly thirty blocks lined up to get in to Madison Square Garden. It was a decided success.

[8]John Pitts Sanborn, music editor of several New York newspapers.

[9]Polaire: Emilie Marie Bouchard, Algerian music-hall performer.

[1]Anna Elizabeth Snyder, a Cedar Rapids girl, and CVV were married in London, June 1907. They were divorced in May 1912. By pre-arrangement, a friend, the photographer Paul Thompson, appeared as a witness to verify CVV's "adultery"—the only grounds for divorce in New York at the time—with a prostitute engaged only to render the charge legal. Early letters indicate that the marriage had soured almost immediately. Even earlier, Anna Snyder had been concerned by what she called a "philandering" spirit, and CVV had referred elliptically to his bisexuality as "something fundamental" in himself as the heart of the trouble.

[2]Jacques Emile Blanche, French painter and photographer.

[3]George Moore, Irish writer.

brushes and scents to use!—There was a young widow at the luncheon—
a femme du monde—and turning to her he said, "How are you enjoying
your widowhood?"!! And once he referred to his impotency in the most
careless manner possible—As a result of the Blanche luncheon I am dining
and teaing with other people.

Last night I had dinner at Gertrude Stein's. She is a wonderful personality.
[. . .] She lives in a place hung with Picassos and she showed me some
more sketches of his including men with erect Tom-Tom's much bigger
than mine.

Paris itself is something quite different to me. I don't like it now as well
as London. Last night after Gertrude's as I was well dressed I dropped in
at Maxim's and had a whiskey and soda in the bar. There wasn't a girl
who came in who could touch [. . .] you. In fact if you came to Paris now
I feel you would startle it to the last degree.—You are the dearest sweetest
thing in the world and I adore you.

[. . .] Are you being good? I am good as gold. Tom-Tom sends love and
kisses. I adore you, Fan. Other people simply make me see how nice you
are.     Carlo

TO FANIA MARINOFF                          American Express
4 June [1913]                              Paris

Cherie—Darling—You ask me if I miss you! I can't begin to tell you how
much! [. . .] The other night I saw the Russian ballet and the newest one
"[Le] Sacre du Printemps" is the most extraordinary thing I've ever seen
on the stage. Both the music and the dancing were of an originality appalling. My darling, the French were so startled and offended by this novelty
that they hissed it almost without secession. It was impossible to hear the
last fifteen minutes of the music at all. And how wildly beautiful it was
[. . .]

Yes, darling, I told the [New York] Press I would come back to them if
they wanted me. But I shall probably be back before then.—Will you please
get me an American Express order on Paris for that $75 and send it to me
at once. I shall be very grateful if you will do this. You are the dearest
thing in the world. God never made your like and never will again.

Toujours a toi, Carlo

TO FANIA MARINOFF                                          [Paris]
9 June 1913

Dearest darling Baby, Somehow I felt badly at your account of the "night
out" with the four joli garçons. But if you had a good time, I am glad. You
will be good, tho, won't you darling? And if you feel you need *me* or something why I must come to you. Remember anyway always that I love you
and miss you very much.—Last night again, at the Russian ballet it seemed
impossible to enjoy it without you. You would have loved it so much. It
is the sort of thing we understand so well how to love together. Debussy's
"Jeux"—which was done for the second time, is only less extraordinary
than "Sacre du Printemps." The scene, designed by Bakst, represents the
garden of a modern house. Electric lights play. As the curtain goes up a
tennis ball bounds in—Then Nijinsky in modern tennis costume—very extraordinary—designed by Bakst & made by Mme Paquin—bounds in,
looking for the ball. Karsavina and Schallas follow and then, in the twilight,
the most extraordinary—and indecent—things follow.—Debussy was in
the audience—and the stupid French hissed, but I—and half the house—
broke my gloves applauding.—There were three other ballets including the
extraordinary dances from "Prince Igor."—Baron de Meyer, by the way,
has taken a series of wonderful photographs of Nijinsky in "L'apres-midi
d'un Faune," which I may be able to get.—[. . .]

I have received letters from you on all the posts lately and I hope you
will continue to write to me. I must hear from you often. Remember you
are always in my thoughts. If you hear of a nice cheap studio around
Washington Square I want it for next year. Make enquiries when you have
the opportunity. I have entirely new ideas for an apartment. It's going to
be quite different. It may disgust you in some ways but the bed is for you
alone (avec moi). Est-ce que tu m'aimes? Je t'adore!      Carlo (kiss)
Tom-Tom sends love and. . . .


TO FANIA MARINOFF                                        Pax Hotel
5 July [1913]                                               Paris

Dearest of Fan-Babies, You ought to know how much you are being talked
about nowadays. John Reed is writing a play for which you are to have
the principal part. Mike insists on that.[4] She adores you and we said yesterday that everybody who knows you adores you. [. . .] Mike and I went
to [Henri] Matisse's yesterday. He lives out of town in a villa with a big

---

[4]John Reed, American journalist and poet, Mabel Dodge's lover in 1913.

garden, poisonous begonias and a monkey. He has just returned from Morocco and he has at last painted some things that I really like. Some wonderful Moroccan figures in wonderful colors. His house is filled with picturesque things—and—a touch that you would love—on the side-board in the dining room a tray of orange and yellow gourds.—All my love and I'll write to you en route.     Carlo

TO FANIA MARINOFF                           Villa Curonia
13 July [1913]                                Florence

Dearest darling-Fan-Baby, We arrived in Florence late this afternoon—too late to get mail—and so I must wait until tomorrow to get your dear letters.—I am thinking about you constantly and wondering if you are all right. You *must* be all right because you are all I really have to love, all I really can love—You are the most extraordinary of God's creatures and the only one I have ever found who completely satisfies me. I can't faintly attempt to describe to you how lovely this villa is. But I am writing in my room now, all done in Italian Renaissance, looking out over the mountains. The others have gone to bed. We had dinner out doors in the garden, where there are peacocks and monkeys and Siamese cats. You would love [it] with reason at once, it is so beautiful, and afterward coffee on the loggia—overlooking the Italian garden.—The villa is very old—about 12th century, and belongs to the Medicis. Raphael and Michelangelo used to visit it and the original villa—since added to—was built by the great architect, Brunelleschi. Of course Mike has made it habitable with all sorts of bath-rooms and things[. . .]
     I adore you. *Please* don't forget me.     Carlo
I'm looking wonderful. Quite brown after the long motor trip![5]

TO MABEL DODGE                        New York Press
[circa 6 October 1913]               7-11 Spruce Street, New York

That New Age article, dear Mike, nearly finished me. I didn't know such things existed. It's really the cleverest and funniest thing I have read in some time. . . . Avery,[6] of course, loves you. We had dinner at the Brevoort and I got very drunk and read "Harry" out loud to the assembled dining

---

[5]CVV drove from Paris to Florence with Mabel Dodge, John Reed, and the American stage designer Robert Edmond Jones.
[6]Avery Hopwood, American playwright. See List of recipients.

room, especially salacious passages which you had marked; then I read "The Portrait of Mabel Dodge" [by Gertrude Stein] and Avery was drunk enough by that time to say that he understood it. I went to "Evangeline"[7] in a terrible condition but it didn't do any good; it was too awful. However during the course of the piece Fan and I had a rotten row and she left with authority, nor did I see her again that night. . . . She adjudged my condition to be due to my having seen you and Avery—after all not far wrong. . . . Scenes from "The Younger Generation" were freely enacted. . . . Life and love to you. . .    Carlo

## TO FANIA MARINOFF
[30 November 1913]

Hotel Longacre
New York City

Darling Fan Fan Baby, It was too terrible to think of your being away last night—a night I always spend with you—and just now I have been having my breakfast all alone in my hotel! I suppose you are doing something equally unpleasant. Dearest Fan I don't think you ever cuddled in my arms as wonderfully as you did on our last night. You were like a cunning little animal—some cuddly animal.[. . .]

In the evening I went to Mike's and John Reed and an artist named [Marsden] Hartley—he's Steiglitz's[8] next exhibitor—[were] there. [. . .] I was thoroughly drunk because I had been drinking with J[ohn] P[itts] S[anborn] all the afternoon and I insulted everybody. [. . .] Reinforced by Lincoln Steffens[9] and Hutch Hapgood[1] we went to the nigger show which turned out to be wonderful.[2] Then I came home and went to bed,—missing you like the devil. I hope, dearest baby, that all is going well with you and that you won't have to work too hard.[3] And I send you a thousand kisses and the tightest squeeze I can make!    Always, Carlo

---

[7]*Evangeline* by Thomas W. Broadhurst opened October 5th; CVV pilloried it in his *New York Press* review the following morning.
[8]Alfred Stieglitz, the American photographer, exhibited the work of avant-garde artists at his 291 Gallery.
[9]Lincoln Steffens, American radical journalist of the muckrakers' movement.
[1]Hutchins Hapgood, American social critic. See List of recipients.
[2]"My Friend From Kentucky": *The Darktown Follies* by J. Leubrie Hill, at the Lafayette Theatre in Harlem. CVV wrote about this show at length in the *New York Press*, the first serious criticism ever offered a black entertainment in a white newspaper. It was, in part, instrumental in fostering CVV's subsequent commitment to black arts and letters.
[3]Fania Marinoff had been playing in stock with the Poli Company in New Haven, Connecticut, during the summer; in January 1914 she opened on Broadway in *Thousand Years Ago* by Percy Mackaye. In between, her employment is unaccounted for.

## TO MABEL DODGE
24 December [1913]

New York Press
7–11 Spruce Street, New York

Your cold, but exciting, letter came yesterday and I must say that your experiences, darling Mabel, fill me with envy. What can I do while you are away but resort to cocaine, which, of course, I have done . . . Rumors of the party at your house last Thursday have reached my ears; it was seemingly a dull affair. Somewhere about the middle of it Hutch arises and says, with authority, "This will be the last of these meetings until Mrs. Dodge returns . . . We cannot impose on her good nature in this manner." Whereupon Steffens says, "Isn't it somewhat of a tyrannical attitude, Hutch? . . . Mrs. Dodge said that we might continue these meetings as long as we liked. What right have you to put a stop to them?" Then Lincoln took a long breath and went on as follows: "BUT there are certain people who come here not to listen to the talks but to EAT and DRINK. . . We have a list of these . . . and they are going to be weeded out!" Greenwich Village stands aghast at your performance . . . Somebody who has really done something is too much for the villagers. Admiration mixed with awe describes them. [. . .] Love to Reedio. I fancy him dashing madly over the cacti—how well you know your plurals, Mike!—I hope you are coming home soon . . . Remember that honest hearts and brave beat for you. . . .     with all my soul—tout coeur et tout corps, tou-----jours,
        Carlo

## TO FANIA MARINOFF
[5 June 1914]

Provincetown, Cape Cod
Massachusetts[4]

Darling and forever Baby, [. . .] Today it has rained all day and I have been pasting up Mabel's scrap books. Neith[5] and Hutch have been in. Reed spends the day disporting—and he and Mabel go to a tent, five miles away to sleep.—But right after they had gone I went to Mary Vorse O'Brien's[6] for

---

[4]CVV had gone to Provincetown to write about the little theater group and artists' colony that had begun to develop there, ostensibly for a Sunday feature article in the *New York Press*. As the Broadway season had concluded, however, the newspaper editor dispensed with his services, and the piece was never written. On June 4th, CVV had written to Fania Marinoff that it had been "an awfully fierce journey up here—a good deal like child birth, a thing no one would dare attempt if he realized its horror in advance. From Fall River to Provincetown is a terrible ride—slow, hot, and dirty."

[5]Neith Boyce, novelist and playwright, wife of Hutchins Hapgood. See List of recipients.

[6]Mary Vorse O'Brien, American suffragette.

dinner—with Gertrude Stein's new book,[7] which is extraordinary. The last part refers, I am sure, to things you and I do very well indeed. I love you awfully, darling baby, and I don't mind your showing it. You must be *very, very* good to me.     *Love & kisses* and some to love you. Carlo

## TO FANIA MARINOFF                                               Paris
29 July 1914

Darling Baby, I do love you so. [. . .] Don't worry about the war—if it comes up. It is tremendously exciting here—but not dangerous—at least not for Americans.—and one can always get away.—I shall be much safer with Mabel in case of war than I would be here because there is need of money. Just at present for instance it is impossible to get passage, because of the war scare—everybody is going home. And you can't get a gold piece in Paris at all at all!—Alors, it is best to go stay for a while with Mabel Dodge in Florence—and then from there sail for America. I shall come back *just as soon* as I can—and it won't be long. I am simply *mad* to see you. I can't exist without you. I am as unhappy as I ever have been in my life—because you are away. John Sanborn wants to go to Spain to escape the war and he has offered to take me, but the poor thing has no money. I can't accept his offer altho I'd much rather go to Spain with him than go to Italy with Mabel. [. . .]

I got a Trend today. It seems an extraordinary number. Hutchins Hapgood's story is marvellous.[8] Do send me the August number. No-one else ever will—and that has my Gertrude Stein article in it, I hope.[9] [. . .]

All my love to you, darling baby, and please be well and strong and love me a lot. I simply don't exist without you. I wish we might drift to a desert island and live there alone all the rest of our lives.[1]     Carlo

---

[7] *Tender Buttons*, 1914, published at CVV's instigation by Donald Evans, an American poet who had founded a private press, Claire Marie (named for the actress Claire Burke) to publish his own poems.
[8] "A Modern Episode," *Trend*, June 1914.
[9] "How to Read Gertrude Stein," *Trend*.
[1] Fania Marinoff had returned to the United States, following her European holiday with CVV, to begin rehearsals for *Consequences* by H. F. Rubinstein. CVV to Bruce Kellner, 25 August 1954: "I was never in love until I reached the ripe age of 30 and not very much in love then (tho I thought I was). Love hit me hard when I was 34 and I am probably more in love now than I was then."

TO FANIA MARINOFF                    Albergo il Paradisino
8 August 1914                        Vallombrosa

Darling Angel Baby, Perhaps you will get this letter and perhaps not. There is some talk of sending a boat from Naples on August 13, I believe, but whether it will go or not depends upon whether there is a battle in the Mediterranean or not. My good destiny sent me to Florence. All Americans were sent away from Paris the day after I left, and there were no boats to go down! Nobody has any money—and checks are not good. It is impossible to get money by cable because the banks are closed.—Now there is talk of sending war ships over for us—I hear. But it may be only talk. We have practically *no* money. Mabel [Dodge] has only $500 with her in American Express checks, which are very hard to cash, and there are six of us—and expenses are heavy, and I have *no* money and Neith [Boyce] has *no* money—and there is talk of the Austrians coming down to Italy, and everything is hell! I don't know how we are going to get out. Mabel has cabled [John] Reed to come over and bring *gold* but can he get over, or will he get the cablegram? All cablegrams are going thro France and England. There is censorship and the service is so clogged that private messages are being held up. I haven't cabled you because we are so hard up. [. . .] The trains are being stuffed and used for soldiers. Automobiles are being requisitioned. But Mabel in her cablegram to Reed sent messages to you and Hutchins Hapgood which you will get if he receives the telegram. Under ordinary circumstances I could appreciate the beauty of the place we are in—and I could work here, but now no one thinks or talks of anything but the war. It is very beautiful up here—way up in the mountains—about 2 hours from Florence—but that means nothing now. It has settled me about one thing. I shall *never* put the ocean between us again. Oh, if you knew how much I love you, how much I think about you. I can't get you off my mind. I wonder what you are doing all this time—and I can do nothing. It's maddening and I have not heard one word from you since you arrived,— which is natural. The Post from Paris has stopped. I'll probably never get a cable. *Why* didn't you write me from Cherbourg? or telegraph?

There are funny sides to it all & things which I shall tell you when I see you but on the whole it's too serious!—There are over 500 people waiting in Florence for boats. Imagine how many there must be at Rome, at Naples, at London—Thousands and Thousands of Americans who want to come back and can't.—If you don't hear from me again before you receive this— by wire—I mean I'll wire you if we get any way—try to send me a wire of love—*here*. [. . .] In case anything happens to me I want you to have *everything* I own, my *stocks*, my *insurance*. Show this to my brother. I also told Mabel, and my brother is with the Continental and Commercial Nat'l Bank, Chicago.—Ralph V. V. But, by the time you get this—if you get it at all, I hope to be back on my way to New York, thanks to some American war vessel or what not.—You may be glad that you saw Venice because it probably won't ever exist after this war. We are absolutely *safe* where we are. It's so high in the mountains and not in the line of Florence to Bologna or Roma—but it gets very cold up here and the provisions won't hold out forever—and money won't last,—but the Villa [Curonia] is worse. It's on the main road and near Florence and in case of battle would be seized. We get some news down here but of course all news is censored and if Paris were taken I doubt if we should hear of it.      All all my love—darlingest baby in the world, and don't forget me no matter how long this lasts—Carlo

TO GERTRUDE STEIN                         Hotel Manhattan
6 October [1914]                          210 West 44th Street
                                          New York City

[. . . .]² Perhaps you haven't read *How to read Gertrude Stein* so I am sending it to you. Your postcard came back to me from Paris a day or so ago saying that you are in London. Donald Evans³ thinks you are still there—I am just back from Italy on an immigrant steamer⁴ and, for the present, I am fooling with The *Trend* magazine—sort of editor. I wish you could let me have one of your Spanish dancers for the December number. Where is Marsden Hartley? It's *such* an English name for Berlin. And how are you and Miss Toklas? Do write to me. I may go to jail—for *not* being a suffragette or something—      love, Carlo V. V.

TO FANIA MARINOFF                         Hotel Manhattan
[22 November 1914]                        210 West 44th Street
                                          New York City

Darlingest of Babies, Nobody ever wrote such sweet letters as you do. Nobody ever loved anybody as much as I do you! I could eat you up with love. My! But I'll be glad to see you again.—and I may be in Washington

---

²The first part of the letter is missing.
³Donald Evans, the futurist American poet who founded a publishing house to issue his own work—Claire Marie Press—printed Gertrude Stein's *Tender Buttons* through CVV's intervention.
⁴CVV, Neith Boyce and her two children, and Mabel Dodge's son John Evans escaped from Italy on the lugger *San Guglielmo*, a nightmarish voyage he wrote up at length for the November issue of *Trend*.

the day you arrive.[5] Channing [Pollock] called me up yesterday to tell me that it is very important that I act as a witness. The case has assumed very bad proportions and may run on for several weeks. I may go on the stand the coming Wednesday, or perhaps not until the following Monday. The plan is now to take a private car down on Sunday with *all* the witnesses like Louis Sherwin and myself, and these will go on the stand on Monday.[6] Then I'll come back Monday night. But won't it be *awful* not to be here when my baby arrives. This cuts out the trip west and besides, perhaps you are right, perhaps it wouldn't be best.

I haven't had any salary for four weeks, but I have been managing— but I must get something to do as soon as I can. The Trend has been a great adventure and has been very useful to me. I have learned that I can edit a magazine and I think, also, it has improved my writing! I am more confident. I do want to get a book out now. Perhaps I will. Qui sait?—At any rate you and I don't worry. As long as we have love we should care!— I'll tell you the details of the Trend split up when I see you. I've seen a good deal of Walter Arensberg the last four days, and had dinner with him and Wallace Stevens, the lawyer-poet, last night. I've just come from seeing Donald [Evans], who is sick again, Louise[7] was there and Donald's ex-wife. A most remarkable scene.

O, yes, sweet adorable baby, I can't wait until I see you—and it will be too wonderful your getting back—and we'll go to the Metropolitan Museum—and *everything,* and you are a blessed angel darling kissable adorable baby—and I love you! And there you are! Write much and often. I love your letters.      Carlo

TO EDNA KENTON                Hotel Manhattan
[late March 1915]             210 West 44th Street
                             New York City

Dearest Edna, I've really been postponing writing to you because I expected to be in jail now. Judge Newberger, at the instigation of the redoubtable Ann, has committed me, but it seems to be necessary to yet get an order signed and to send a sheriff after me—in the meantime counting on the

[5]CVV and Fania Marinoff had been married in Connecticut, 21 October 1914; the following month she was appearing in *Consequences* in Chicago following the play's failure in New York.
[6]Pollock was accused of having plagiarized his play *The Beauty Shop* from Washington *Star* columnist Philander Johnson. Pollock was exonerated. Both CVV and American drama critic Louis Sherwin testified on his behalf.
[7]Louise Norton, American writer, wife of American poet Allen Norton; later wife of composer Edgar Varèse.

Fania Marinoff, 1934

Edna Kenton, 1932

intervention of Ralph [Van Vechten].[8] Ralph will *not* intervene and so I am expecting jail daily, from the portals of which I shall send forth manifestos about love, life, and liberty. I have been promised a Matisse, two Persian rugs, and a telephone. Perhaps you will send literature. If I stay there six months I shall have read everything.

Did you get *Rogue?* Harry Thaw[9] has purchased thousands of copies of the last number. You are to appear in the next number and my masterpiece of depravity—to this writing—is to come out in the fourth number.[1] Donald [Evans] by the way after a couple of days in jail due to a controversy with a policeman at 9 A.M. about the vantage corner from which he might view the rising sun, has excommunicated himself from the Times, and is going either to South America or England. I had a wonderful scene with his whilom wife. [. . .] The W[ashington] Sq[uare] Players are doing my new play, I think.[2] Fan has just returned after 2 weeks in Florida with the movies. Give my love to Mabel[3] and write when you can. If I go to jail you are to write oftener than you can.     Carlo

TO EDNA KENTON                              Ludlow Street Jail
[April 1915]                                     New York City

Dear Edna, Your letter and telegram were most cheering, delightful, and delectable. If anything appears in the Chicago papers save me the clippings and I am certainly not averse to anything appearing if you can slip one over. You had not perhaps received Algy [St. John Brennon]'s last story in the Telegraph when you wrote. It *is* clever . . . Fan came back from Florida into this—and we had a week knowing it was going to happen and both became accustomed to the idea by the time it did. I was arrested in the morning and I kept the sheriff by me all day—took him to lunch at

[8]Anna Snyder Van Vechten sued CVV for back alimony ($738), and when he refused to pay, he was remanded to the familiar (even fashionable) Ludlow Street Jail. Correspondence between her and CVV's sister and between CVV and his father, makes it clear she expected the family to pay.
[9]Harry K. Thaw, profligate and eccentric scion of a family whose fortune was made in coal and steel; best known for having murdered architect Stanford White over the affections of his chorus-girl wife Evelyn Nesbitt; less well known for his philanthropy in arts and education.
[1]*Rogue,* a little magazine edited by poet Allen Norton, published work by several people in CVV's circle, notably Gertrude Stein and Wallace Stevens. CVV's "masterpiece of depravity" in the fourth issue was called "How Donald Dedicated His Poem," about Donald Evans.
[2]Aside from some juvenile efforts, CVV's only extant play is an experimental (in the worst sense) one-act piece called "What Do You Think It Is?" and in another draft "After Death What?" Briefly he considered including it in his 1922 novel *Peter Whiffle* but then cut it out of the first draft. First written for inclusion in a 1916 collection to be called "Pastiches et Pistaches," the play has never been produced or published.
[3]Mabel Kenton Reber, Edna Kenton's sister, wife of Neil Reber. The Rebers were cat fanciers and breeders.

15

Pogliani's and introduced him to a *great* many people before he finally brought me here. . . . Ann is crossing her last ditch. Anna Marble[4] came down to see me with the news that Channing [Pollock] was furious with Ann, sorry he ever got her the job with the American dramatists [i.e., the Authors' League], and willing to bounce her as soon as he can. [. . .] However the experience has been far from unpleasant. Ludlow Street Jail, I would have you know, is very comfortable. Hot & cold water, tubs and shower baths on every floor, big airy rooms—no *bugs*. Complete freedom so far as the jail is concerned, except between 10 at night & 6 in the morning when we are locked in cells, but we can have a light and read all night if we wish to—a large court where we race and play hand ball all day—the lilacs are bursting. . . . Pinochle—chess . . . I am reading Turgenev—and the most interesting people with the most interesting stories—and I have the *best* cell . . . I am writing in it now—all kinds of food from without. Louise Norton and Lou Arensberg come down every day with squab, paté de foie gras, etc. Telegrams—letters—visitors—all day, three times a week, and Fan every day—everything but a drink![5]

Fan did a picture with the Kalem Co. in Florida.[6] It is the second of a series called "Broadway Favorites" and will be released in May. I don't know the name but watch out for it. She is now doing *"The Battle"* with the George Kleine Co. a long feature picture—and she is engaged for four weeks *in town,* which is wonderful.

Pitts [Sanborn] wrote me a very sad letter today in which he said he missed you and me and the little French soldier. I may not have the order right.[7]

TO O. G. SONNECK                           151 East 19th Street
12 July 1915                               New York City

Dear Sir, Your long and interesting letter anent my article Shall we realize the ideals of Wagner?[8] has been received and if the pages you sent me and

---

[4]Anna Marble Pollock, wife of Channing Pollock and formerly publicist for Oscar Hammerstein I. See List of recipients.
[5]Later in the month he wrote to Kenton that "Walter Conrad Arensberg has sent me a Matisse etching to decorate Cell Number 11," and in later years he liked to embroider on the trappings. In his old age he even claimed that his cell had had a piano, an exaggeration, although there was a piano in the common room at Ludlow Street Jail, and for the first time in nearly a decade CVV began to play again.
[6]*The Lure of Mammon.*
[7]The letter breaks off at this point.
[8]"Shall We Realize Wagner's Ideals?" was first published in *Musical Quarterly,* July 1916, of which O. G. Sonneck was editor. Either CVV misdated his letter by one year or the article was delayed that length of time.

which I am returning to you include all the revisions you have made, I am perfectly willing to accept them as they do not seem to interfere with the spirit of the article; indeed I want to thank you for one or two of them because I think they at least improve the tone.

Only one question I would beg of you, and I leave this matter to your discretion, after stating my point. It seems to me that the article loses weight by placing "traditional" and "tradition" in quotation marks. To be sure you have only done this in cases you have referred to as being against the wishes of Wagner, but whether Wagner was opposed or not (and I have given plenty of latitude to the theory that a good deal of the tradition has grown up without his sanction, or with a musician's theory of his idea, and always perhaps with no idea on his part that it would be held to so rigidly when better methods presented themselves) there certainly was a tradition abroad that slow tempi and bad singing were somehow connected with Bayreuth ideals. I have never been to Bayreuth, and so have not mentioned that theatre as one I have visited, but I have plenty of authority for this statement. It may be found, I think, in the published writings of Henry Edward Krehbiel, W. J. Henderson, and James Huneker among others, and in personal conversations with singers and conductors I have heard much more. Loomis Taylor, who has had opportunity to study Bayreuth, refers to Bayreuth traditions in his letter (of course not, however, in regard to tempi, and singing). The central idea of the article, which perhaps is a new one, remember, in many particulars, is that Wagner invented a new form of lyric drama before the technical methods of expression which best suited it had been discovered, or singers trained to sing it. That is what I really want to get over. Bayreuth tradition has permitted the adoption of these methods now that they exist, and that the Wagner[9]

As I said in the beginning I shall be very glad to leave the matter of these quotation marks to your judgement. Can you tell me in what issue of the Musical Quarterly, which by the way, it seems to me, has entirely eclipsed all other similar magazines, that I have seen, in importance and interest, my article will appear? Please note that my address has been changed.
very sincerely,   [unsigned draft]

[9]The paragraph breaks off at this point.

## TO EDNA KENTON

[August 1915]

151 East 19th Street
New York City

Dearest Edna, [. . .] You know of course the scandal about the German spies that the World[1] is putting through. George Sylvester Viereck[2] is pretty much on the wrack since it has been proved that he is getting money for *Fatherland*[3] from Germany. And Aleister Crowley[4] and James Keating are both in the *Fatherland* office now so that you can see that Westley[5] may have two of her loves shot at sunrise any morning.

A letter from Sanborn informs me that he is again in the hospital [. . .] (There are of course pages about his ill-luck) [. . .]. This time I judge it is a boil on the back of his neck, although he does not call it even a carbuncle. Some new name. But something more ironic than that has happened to Pitts; he has been arrested as a German spy. I do not know the details or I would write them to you.

Fan broke a contract with Arnold Daly to star in a Mutual picture. She is being heavily advertised. She appears as a Hawaiian girl. The name of the picture is "The Unsuspected Isle," and it is released on Sept. 8 (watch for it). Perhaps I have told you this before and how Fan revenges herself on her seducer by putting him in bed with a leper. I told this to Emily Stevens[6] who said, "My picture is all lust and rum too." "But no leprosy," I demurred. "That," she said, "is in the second generation." [. . .]

Your references to "An Interrupted Conversation" were certainly appreciated.[7] It is a style I cannot will on myself. Sometimes I have it, but of course it is what I am trying to get. I have an idea that in about ten years more I can write a book like that, and of course one can wait, but I shall try to get some of my short things out in a book in the fall. [. . .]     Tum-ti-tum, Carlo

---

[1]*World: A Journal for Men and Women,* 1875–1920 [?].
[2]George Sylvester Viereck, English biographer of English writer G. K. Chesterton.
[3]*Fatherland:* temporary name (1914–17) of *American Monthly,* edited by George Viereck.
[4]Aleister Crowley, English author of occult novels.
[5]James Keating, American journalist, with whom a mutual friend, actress Helen Westley, was then involved.
[6]Emily Stevens, American actress in Philip Moeller's *Sophie* for which CVV supplied a preface.
[7]"An Interrupted Conversation," an essay about George Moore, was published in *Rogue,* 1 August 1915.

TO EDNA KENTON
22 October [1915]

151 West 19th Street
New York City

Dearest Edna, of course it is a great blow to get back from the Bahamas and find New York bereft of you.[8] Even though you are walking the woods in *boots*. Especially as I had a good deal to say to you. We saw a thing which made memories of *Black Mass* descriptions grow faint. T'was called the Holy Jumpers and as it was done by Negroes it became a sort of black mass. Well I'll tell you when I see you, unless you read about it before then. I have written a story. O God, Edna, I have become a popular writer, *Snappy Stories* has snapped up a filthy bit I did about Louise N[9]. [. . .] Do you know, I think I forgot to tell you, I learned in Cedar Rapids that Ann had told many a willing ear that Fan stole me away from her. It's a flattering story and God knows I wish she had and why Ann tells it I don't know (unless drink may explain all) but you and everybody else (including Paul Thompson who introduced us) knows that I never met Fan until after the final decree . . . Anyway the Frank Harris's[1] have separated. She is in Ireland and gives as the reason that he is *pro*-German. And he threatens suicide (he would never do it on time) and people have to sit up with him nights. [. . .] Maurice Sterne[2] is exhibiting 12 more or less nudes of Mabel [Dodge] at the Montross galleries. In one of them she is reading a book with her feet in the chandelier. As you see life is still merry. *Nedra* will be released in December, I think. Watch for it—you will see Fan, 500 niggers and *me* as a naval lieutenant.[3] Give my love to Mabel [Reber] and if you know anything definite about your return please inform me.      Carlo

---

[8]CVV had accompanied Fania Marinoff to Nassau where she was to make a film on location, *Nedra*, based on George Barr McCutcheon's novel.
[9]Louise Norton, then embroiled in the beginnings of a complicated romantic entanglement— see CVV to Edna Kenton, 15 January 1916—unnamed in CVV's "The Fifth Alternative," *Snappy Stories*, 18 December 1915.
[1]Frank Harris, English critic and (unreliable) memoirist.
[2]Maurice Sterne, Russian-born painter, Mabel Dodge's third husband.
[3]Elsewhere CVV refers to his role as a ship's captain. The epithet "nigger" was freely used by white people, in ignorance and without opprobrium.

## TO EDNA KENTON
[6 November 1915]

151 East 19th Street
New York City

Dearest Edna, Doris[4] arrived and departed without my having much opportunity; Louis Sherwin was ready, and so were others, better financially equipped, but I could not tell from the tone of your letter whether I should wait for her, or take the initiative. I called up, but it was not until to-day that I finally saw her, on her way to the station; she will tell you how I cooked lunch for her and a French woman, who does plain sewing.[5] I am sorry that there was so little time; [. . .] her conversation is fairly bursting with such sartorial adjectives and nouns as "paradise feathers, sequins, brilliant, tight, black velvet, brown velvet, red fox, dinner gown, Hickon's, Lucille's," etc. I imagine that she puts great faith in the garb that a voice wears. She saw Helen Westley in *Helena's Husband* and seemed impressed. And most of the rest of the time she put in quarreling with George.[6] Once at the theatre she said, "That man's a nance." "What do you mean?" asked George. "It would take too long to tell you. You must read Havelock Ellis," was her reply. "He won't," she said to me, telling the story, "He has no idea that you can spot that sort of thing miles away if you're primed on the symptoms."

The other news which I hope you have not heard yet is Bobby Locher's marriage to Beatrice Howard. It took place in the Broadway Tabernacle last Tuesday. Louise Norton was present. They have gone on their honeymoon to Vermont. I asked Louise if it was a surprise. "Bobby was surprised, I think," she said. [. . .]

Avery Hopwood's *Fair and Warmer* opens tomorrow. We are going with the author, and tonight we are to see Julia Arthur's return to the stage in *The Eternal Magdalene*. Claire Burke is in the cast. We are dining with the rich lawyer friend of Claire's, and after the theatre we are supping with Claire and the author of the play.[7]

Do come back. Fan would send her love to you if she were here.      Carlo

---

[4]Doris Reber was a niece or sister of Edna Kenton's brother-in-law, Neil Reber. Privately referred to as "the family songstress," she spent most of her life studying to make a professional career in opera but apparently never appeared on stage. CVV made several attempts to get hearings for her, and he suggested she adopt "Doris Riebera" as a name more suitable for an opera diva. His letter to Edna Kenton, 30 June 1924, accounts further for Doris Reber's eccentricities. CVV used her as a partial model for the failed singer Clara Barnes in *Peter Whiffle* in 1922.
[5]Marian Dorn, a friend of Fania Marinoff and CVV, later wife of Anglo-American illustrator E. McKnight Kauffer.
[6]George Ramsay, Doris Reber's lover at that time.
[7]Robert McLaughlin.

TO EDNA KENTON                          151 East 19th Street
15 January 1916                         New York City

Dearest Edna, Your lovely letter received, with its blessings, etc. . . . and really I am quite overcome. Look, for instance, upon Mrs. Dawson's Globe approval![8] Could one have hoped for such superb encomiums? Philip Hale (did I write you?) gave me two columns and a half in the Boston Herald. Schirmer is advertising me extensively and I am to have a window, and a poster by [Leon] Bakst, wherever the ballet appears . . . The whole thing is like a fairy tale to me. [. . .] So much has happened during the last few days that I do not trust myself to put it all on paper. Donald Evans has turned up on the Philadelphia Inquirer and he writes that he will never be in New York again. He has covenanted to that effect.

A strange young actress, named Geraldine O'Brien, the outstanding sensation of a failure, *The Devil's Garden,* descended upon us one day last week, divested herself of her corsets and shoes, put cigarettes out by rubbing them against her black satin gown, which in an hour or two was distinctly perforated, found she had too much tea and poured half her cup deliberately out on the piano stool, used the toilet and the telephone indiscriminately and continuously. I think you might have been interested in seeing her. . . . Perhaps you will someday.

As for Louise [Norton] she is waiting for Louis [Sherwin]'s exit from gaol. . . . Allen [Norton] is high-spirited pro tem. Mrs McCutcheon, mère de Louise, has adopted Michael [Norton] . . . Doris [Reber] should be careful of Dal. He gives women babies and he can't marry them because he has a blind wife who won't give him a divorce. [. . .][9]

Fan's masterpiece is *Life's Whirlpool,* with Holbrook Blinn. It is a film version of *McTeague* by Frank Norris. You must see it. She has since done *New York* with Florence Reed, John Miltern, Jessie Ralph, and Forrest Winant.[1]

I am glad you wrote Pitts [Sanborn]; he thought he was being neglected, but I am glad that you wrote me. . . . If you see anything else in any Chicago papers, do be sweet enough to send it on . . . T'would be better if you would bring it . . . Our love to Mabel [Reber], . . . and you.      Carlo

---

[8]CVV's first book, *Music After the Great War,* was published by G. Schirmer in December 1915.
[9]This fascinating figure is not identifiable.
[1]Fania Marinoff made approximately two dozen films between 1912 and 1918; none of them seems to have survived.

## TO GERTRUDE STEIN

151 East 19th Street
New York City

17 May 1916

Dear Gertrude Stein, It's so amusing of you to notice that I wrote there were *Three* in the box. As a matter of fact I left out more than that—a German and his wife—for instance, entirely. Four seemed *too* many somehow. No-one would ever believe so many sat in a box and I think I decided to leave out Florence Bradley's sister . . . and it wasn't the first night of Sacre *[du Printemps]* either, it was the second night. But one must only be accurate about such details in a work of fiction.[2] The real point is that in my own consciousness I am not a bit muddled about the *facts*. I think you will like my new book better—but I am afraid I shall not get over soon my "pleasing enthusiasm." We are always apparently on the way to Spain and then it never happens. Just now, Fan has made a very big hit playing Ariel in Shakespeare's "The Tempest," she is unbelievably lovely in it. I do wish you could see her, one never thought the part could be played before.

You ask about John Reed. He has just published a book about the Balkans, and is writing stories mostly about Broadway *grues*. He's just the same, leading the Washington Square life with an Irish girl,[3] who is interested in the Irish Republic. I never see Mabel [Dodge] any more—but I meet ton frère, Leo,[4] every now [and] again scowling in galleries at manifestations of modern artists, and *talking* but never to me. He seems to be quite certain that he doesn't like me. Why, I don't know. Muriel Draper is here. She is divorcing Paul and working in an interior decoration shop and running about with Nijinsky, who is more marvelous than ever. The ballet sailed for Spain without him.

I am also unpublished—in regard to a book *not* on music—which has been ready ever so long. When it appears I have dedicated one thing to you which you said once you liked—Marsden [Hartley] gave an exhibition of very *pro*-German pictures—and Lee Simonson has done some good stagy decorations. All hail to you and Miss Toklas. Fania said love—      ever—
Carlo Van Vechten

---

[2]In *Music After the Great War,* CVV described what he claimed to be the first performance of Stravinsky's *The Rite of Spring,* from a box shared with three women unknown to him. Actually, at the second performance, he had sat with Gertrude Stein and Alice Toklas with whom he had dined a few days earlier. Stein perpetuated this hoax in *The Autobiography of Alice B. Toklas* in 1933.
[3]Louise Bryant, American radical socialist.
[4]Leo Stein, American writer, Gertrude Stein's brother from whom she had been estranged for several years.

TO WALDO FRANK                                    151 East 19th Street
19 January 1917                                   New York City

My dear Frank, Your note came this morning and astonished me considerably I must confess.[5] I certainly had no intention of "sneering" at Walter Kramer and Horatio Parker. I have the friendliest admiration for Walter Kramer, although I know very little about his music, and I put his name in the list solely on that account, because any mention of a man's name anywhere, no matter by whom, [is] of some value to him. The idea I intended to convey was that as American composers are seldom heard in "classic" surroundings the moving picture bands might really help them out. As the whole article is written to show the importance of the moving picture concerts I can't understand your interpretation of the phrase, expressly as I intended him with Grieg, Tschaikowsky, Liszt and Mendelssohn! However, if you have misunderstood so may others so I've inserted two other names which suit the purpose equally well.

As for the catalogue on page 4 it is a matter of complete indifference to me whether it is omitted or not, although I feel that it [is] the most amusing passage in the article! At any rate the sense is complete without it and there you are! I have indicated the elision.

I hope this will prove satisfactory.       very sincerely,    [unsigned draft]

TO GERTRUDE STEIN                                 151 East 19th Street
[5 April 1917]                                    New York City

Dear Gertrude Stein, Almost everything is happening here, besides our going to war. Sarah Bernhardt has been operated on at the age of seventy-three and had several kidneys removed. A day or two after she sits up in bed and eats spinach, a vegetable which had been denied her for two years previously. She plans to begin another farewell tour of America in August, and is really intending to put on the whole of *L'Aiglon* . . . The Romanoffs, I gather, are lucky if they get spinach. We are hoping that the Hohenzollerns will soon be in a similar predicament.

Isadora Duncan is dancing the Marseillaise and Tschaikowsky's Marche Slav, with a symbolic reference to the Russian revolution, to packed houses. People—this includes me—get on the chairs and yell. Then Isadora comes out slightly covered by an American flag of filmy silk and awakens still more enthusiasm. It is very exciting to see American patriotism thoroughly awakened—I tell you she drives 'em mad; the recruiting stations are full

---

[5]CVV had submitted "Music and the Electrical Theatre" to *Seven Arts* for which Frank was editor. It appeared, with severe cuts, in the May issue.

of her converts—by someone who previously has not been very much interested in awakening it.[6]

Then there is the Salon des Independents (so to speak—at least), which has already had two scandals. The first concerned the rejection by the board (which is not supposed to have the power to reject anything) of an object labelled "Fountain" and signed R. J. Mutts. This porcelain tribute was bought cold in some plumber shop (where it awaited the call to join some bath room trinity) and sent in. When it was rejected Marcel Duchamp at once resigned from the board. Stieglitz[7] is exhibiting the object at "291" and he has made some wonderful photographs of it. The photographs make it look like anything from a Madonna to a Buddha. The exhibition itself is pretty tiresome but there is one picture, The Claire Twins, which you may hear of again. It will probably be bought by the Prado. It belongs in Spain.

Fania has been appearing in [Frank] Wedekind's "The Awakening of Spring." At least she appeared in it once. Then the police stepped in and now all concerned are awaiting a decision from the bench of the Supreme Court.

I am writing. My new book is finished [Interpreters and Interpretations], but it will not appear until fall. We do want to see Paris again soon. I have a feeling that the war will last a very long time; everybody is so anxious that it should stop, but it won't. I should like to see you run a FORD. Perhaps I will yet.     all felicitations and salutations to you both from us,

    Carlo V. V.

Oh yes, Valentine de Saint Point is here too. She gave an exhibition of métachorie (gratis) at the Metropolitan Opera House, about which people are still talking. She has two boys and a monkey with her . . .[8]

Did you ever know Paulet Thévenaz?[9] He is here too.

Ever so many are here . . . but few are chosen!

I never see Mabel [Dodge]. Does she write to you?

Mina Loy (Mrs. Haweis) has a wonderful primitive (sort of Cimabue) in the exhibition.

Do write me soon, and vibrantly!

---

[6]CVV to Bruce Kellner, 19 March 1963: "Fania and I were walking home from the Greenwich Village Theatre. We encountered Frank Conroy, Mrs Lewis, who built the Theatre, and later we ran into Isadora whom all of us knew. Mrs Lewis invited us all to her apartment and it was there I danced with Isadora. (I even carried her in my arms!) And Isadora related how she had rolled around in the damp gutter with a sailor the night before, which she remembered in the morning when she discovered her white lace dress was all blue."

[7]Alfred Stieglitz, see List of recipients.

[8]*Festival of Metachorie*, dances performed to poetry, both by the choreographer.

[9]Paul Thévenaz, French portraitist.

TO NEITH BOYCE                                        151 East 19th Street
22 April 1918                                          New York City

Dear Neith, Vous avez juré. . . . and "old publisher" or not you must let
Knopf see the mss. first . . . I implore this of you. And if he does publish
you you will not be sorry. As for the plays he would publish those or
anything else you wanted him to, after the novel. Of this I am sure; that
is if he liked you and the novel well enough to publish it. But I don't think
it's a good thing to offer him the plays first, nor, perhaps, the Mabel novelette. Of the latter, of course, I cannot judge, not having seen it; it's only
that the subject does not sound like your best *genre*. All this sounds rather
hysterical and vague, I'm afraid. I wish I could talk to you . . . God knows
you are mystic and evasive enough when you are present; in absence and
on letter paper you become positively evanescent . . . Is it enough to say
that I have set my heart on Knopf's seeing the new novel; and I hope you
will not disappoint me in the matter. Of course you are not bound to let
him publish it even if he reads it. . . . any more than he is bound to like
it. I am finishing up a book myself;[1] consequently very restless, very feverish,
very snappy and taciturn, and very very glad to be interrupted! The telephone has not rung once this morning.      yours in the bonds, Carlo

TO FANIA MARINOFF                                    151 East 19th Street
[9 June 1918]                                         New York City

Dearest Baby, I'm afraid I have enough work now to last me for forty years.
Freddo Knopf called me up yesterday and presented me with Underhill's
emendations and suggestions for my Spanish book.[2] As a result the back
room looks like a factory. I was to have had lunch with Louis [Sherwin]
but he never appeared or called up and I suppose, having finished his scenario, he got drunk and overslept. I had lunch alone at the Spanish restaurant
and dinner alone at the Russian rest[aurant]. By the way I understand
ordering there now; you can have alternatives for the dishes in the dinner.
Instead of peach cake blintzes, instead of pea-soup cold borscht, etc! Have
you ever had bitok with smetenye? Otherwise I worked all day and all
evening. Today I'm going out to the Stettheimers';[3] they have Rupert
Hughes's[4] place at Redford Hills! I'm sorry you are not here to go too.

---

[1]*The Merry-Go-Round,* 1918.
[2]John Underhill, editor for *The Music of Spain,* 1918.
[3]Carrie, Florine, and Ettie Stettheimer, wealthy art patrons (and themselves artists). See List
of recipients.
[4]Rupert Hughes, a popular magazine writer and novelist.

Marcel[5] and Avery [Hopwood] and that sculptor, whose name I can't remember,[6] are invited. [. . .]

By the way Phil [Moeller] tells me that Tamara Swarskaia's Baroness, you remember her, is interned as a German spy! Of course it was always rumored that she was.[7]

Much love to you! I hope I'll have some of this work done by the time you return, but good God, it begins to look hopeless. I'll have the dummy of "The Merry-Go-Round" in about a week. If it is anything like the samples it will be by far the prettiest book I have ever had. "The Music of Spain" is to be bright orange printed in red!     Carlo

TO FANIA MARINOFF                    151 East 19th Street
[11 September 1918]                   New York City

Dear Marinoff, You must know that your letters are perfectly maddening; they tell me nothing at all and there is so much that I want to know and so many questions that people ask . . . You are opening Tuesday night now,[8] which is a good thing because Otis Skinner and "An Ideal Husband" open Monday, so you will have time to do something Monday or Tuesday. [. . .] I am invited to Avery [Hopwood]'s to spend the night and think I will go! I am absolutely out of my mind now that my index is over,[9] waiting for news from you and none comes. I don't see how you can be so aggravating. Nothing about your health or whether you have a maid or what your hopes and chances are, nothing but those glorious notices and you haven't sent me any extra ones. [. . .] I'll never let you go away again alone. I didn't realize how terrible you could be in the way of silence. I know you are nervous and tired and everything but you could pencil a line or two from rehearsals which would tell me something and you haven't said a word about anything but your clothes . . . I'm awfully sorry for you, but I'm awfully cross with you, and overjoyed (and not surprised) that you've evidently made a hit.     all my love, baby, Carlo

Edna Kenton comes tomorrow

[5]Marcel Duchamp, a French-born Dadaist painter.
[6]Elie Nadelman, German-born sculptor.
[7]There was other war news as well: CVV to Fania Marinoff, 5 June 1918: "The government is expecting aeroplane raids on New York soon, the aeroplanes to be launched from submarines. So last night, as a trial, all lights were ordered out. There are also suggestions about seeking out the cellars in the morning papers. I think we may expect an air raid in a month or so at the latest."
[8]Fania Marinoff was acting in "The Walkoffs" by Frederick and Fannie Halton.
[9]*The Merry-Go-Round* was the first of CVV's books to carry an index.

TO RALPH VAN VECHTEN                         151 East 19th Street
7 February 1919                              New York City

Dear Ralph, Your letter of advice received. But it isn't advice that I need just now. [. . .] The point is that I have determined to be a writer, not a journalist or a scribbler but a writer. This does not as a rule make money; it usually takes it. Bernard Shaw tells us in one of his prefaces how he threw his mother into the struggle and forced her to make a living for him until he got on his feet. George Moore once told me that he never made enough money off his books to pay his rent. (He does now by the way!) Fortunately for George, a noble Britisher gave him an annuity of £7,000 so that he can write what and how much he pleases.

The kind of writing I do requires time for reflection, it requires going about and meeting a great many people, it requires travel, and buying books and other expenses. It may or may not some time bring in an adequate return. At present it certainly does not. However, to succeed, I am to a certain extent forced to keep my mind free and my pen unsullied. I have started writing books at a somewhat advanced age. If I were younger I might be able to work on a newspaper and write books too. But I am just beginning to get over the bad effects of newspaper work, i.e., the hurry produced by the demand for copy makes one fall into routine expressions which eventually spoil a style. It is one thing or the other for me, either to settle down to a career of a mediocre journalist or to strive for something better. The first does not content me and I have decided (I decided some time ago and told you so, but not at this length nor in detail) to make no compromises.

Curiously enough if I had no income at all I should be much freer to do this. [. . .] Even at the present time I could get plenty of money if I wanted it. Fania's brother[1] never sees me without asking me if we don't need some money, and he can ill afford to give it to me. The point is that I don't feel right about taking money from people like that which I see no possibility of returning immediately; perhaps I could never return it.

My stocks serve to pay the rent and that is about all. By themselves they are quite useless to me. When Fania is working she helps a great deal but I don't want her to work except when she can do her best. Within the month I advised her to turn down a part because I thought it would be bad for her career to accept it. But there is no reason why Fania should

---

[1]Jacob Marinoff, poet and journalist, and editor of the Yiddish weekly, *Der Grosse Kundes.*

suffer for the exigencies of my career, especially because she has frequently helped me very much, and because it is especially necessary that she should be much better dressed when she is not working than when she is working. [. . .] You speak of "cutting down expenses." This is really funny. If you had any idea of how we lived. You spend as much money on one dinner for us when you are here as we spend in a fortnight on food. I spend no money on clothes. As I say Fania is obliged to, and I am obliged to spend money on books. That is our only extravagance, and that is necessary if we are to progress.

In three years (my first book appeared in Dec. 1915) I have issued five books. This month I have had an offer to translate a book of mine into French;[2] Havelock Ellis, George Moore, and James Huneker, have all written warmly congratulatory letters on my latest output; and I have had requests for biographies from three biographical dictionaries. This does not seem to me to be a bad beginning. At any rate I am determined to go ahead. Going ahead is expensive. I have two books in mind which I have not been able to start owing to petty financial annoyances, but one of them I shall start next fall; it may take two years to write. I also intend as soon as possible to go to Spain to write a book. Now at present we are absolutely without money. There is the rent to be paid; there is food to be bought (my January interest all went to pay back accounts) and we have been living since then on driblets from one source or another. [. . .]

This is the situation in a nutshell. I may or may not spend all my principal. At present there seems to be no alternative to spending a little of it, except dropping my career (and for what, for a life of silly drudgery which would mean nothing to me) or borrowing more money from people who would sell their principal to lend it to me. What I am doing now undoubtedly costs more than it brings in; and is likely to do so for some time. I am looking facts squarely in the face as I always do . . . You may have a fear that when my money is gone (and I do not anticipate that it all will be for years to come) I may turn to you. Don't be afraid of that. I shall never ask you for a penny. And you having warned me can have a perfectly clear conscience if I end up poor in ten or fifteen years. [. . .] I am perfectly capable of earning my living, indeed, in a dozen different ways at the present moment. But my intention and desire is for something else and until I have failed at that I wish you would not add to my list of worries. [. . .]     yours with love,   [unsigned carbon copy]

[2]*The Music of Spain*, 1918.

## TO JAMES BRANCH CABELL
[circa 11 March 1919]

151 East 19th Street
New York City

Dear Mr. Cabell, Aside from a bit of prose which Knopf prints on the wrappers of my books I have, unreasonably, but unmistakably, passed by your house without knocking . . . until recently after an unsuccessful encounter with an automobile I was lying on my back one day when Hergesheimer[3] came in and asked what books I wanted to read. Of course I thought at once of Ella Wheeler Wilcox's autobiography[4] but he thought of *Beyond Life* and sent it in the next day . . . with the Wilcox. I chose you and read through the book with a sort of bewildered awe of your ironic art, and a great delight in your artful irony. You roused my curiosity to such an extent, indeed, that once able to hobble about I sought the old book dealers for *more*. I have since devoured The Rivet *[in Grandfather's Neck]* and The Cream *[of the Jest]* and Cords of Vanity and The Line of Love are at hand. I am by the way, indeed, of having a Cabell debauch, and my spies have been commanded to bring me in all your books they can lay hands on. . . . If I had known what was in store I should have reserved the bacchanale until July 1. Indeed The Cream and The Rivet are as intoxicating as anything alcoholic I've ever met . . . Of course Joe was very naughty to send me Beyond Life first. I shall revert to it later with even greater pleasure. Not that it explains but it makes the mystery still more delicate. And by the way I am not sure that Mencken[5] and Follett[6] are any more right about you than those delicious morsels in the back of Beyond Life. You ought to write your own reviews      [unsigned draft]

## TO H. L. MENCKEN
17 May 1919

151 East 19th Street
New York City

My dear Mencken, I have just finished reading your extraordinary book on the American Language,[7] which glides into the consciousness as smoothly as cream cheese glides into the stomach. Of course a new edition will be called for presently and so I am taking advantage of the invitation in the preface to make a few suggestions. I find no reference to the sky words which are all very vivid. Sky-piece (for hat), sky-scraper, etc. Sky

---

[3]Joseph Hergesheimer, American writer. See List of recipients.
[4]*The Worlds and I*, noted for its persistently idiotic optimism.
[5]Henry L. Mencken, American social critic. See List of recipients.
[6]Wilson Follett, American writer and editor.
[7]*The American Language*, 1919.

pilot is probably not American, but I don't know . . . Then there is the verb "to sky" (used of pictures at an art exhibition). Probably this did not originate in America, but I have a theory that it was invented by American art students in Paris. And you do not explain the dropping of the definite article before streets and avenues which bear ordinal numeral names. For example we always say Fifth Avenue or Eighth Street, but in Henry James's *Washington Square* (1880) you may find "the Fifth Avenue" and "the Second Avenue." Probably this is an English variation, and it may still persist for all I know. Also in giving directions to an elevator boy we say, "Third floor" or simply "Third," but if you ask me what floor I live on I answer "On *the* sixth."

Really I can think of nothing else to add to your monumental work;* you seem to have thought of everything important . . . I'm trying to write American already, but what can we poor American authors do when Alfred's printer turns "color" into "colour" with a single turn of the screw?[8]      sincerely, Carl Van Vechten
*There is also the American use of "Knocked up" to compare with the English. And who's looney now? should go into the collection of proverbs!

## TO CHARLES DUANE VAN VECHTEN  151 East 19th Street
## 4 September 1919        New York City

My dear father, Today, I think, is your birthday and I wish you all the comforts and joys of life. I think few people, on the whole, have derived so much happiness from life as you.

The Actors' strike is magnificent! If it still continues Fania is to appear in a bill of one act plays next week, a continuation of the Equity policy to open new theatres each week, when it can secure them. Of course she is playing for nothing. The receipts go towards the strike fund. The last meeting of the Association, attended by over 3000 members in the Lexington Theatre (the last opera house Oscar Hammerstein built before he died) was the most thrilling event of the kind I have ever witnessed. I wish you could have been present to hear the wonderful speeches, to see the wonderful enthusiasm, to hear the cheers, to see them all standing on their chairs waving handkerchiefs and hats! There are indications of an early settlement. The managers have had a meeting which with slight lapses for meals and sleep has already lasted two days. They stand, it is an open secret, 36 to 6 for recognizing the actors, but under the present disgraceful conditions

[8]Alfred Knopf was publisher for both Mencken and CVV. He frequently affected English spellings, though inconsistently. CVV insisted on them.

when *two* men, and only *two* control almost all the theatres in this country, what can thirty-six or even forty do against them? Still I hope for early news.    we both send you both much love, Carlo

TO FANIA MARINOFF                              151 East 19th Street
[31 December 1919]                             New York City

Dearest Baby, I am so sorry for you; I know how horrible it must be to rehearse every day without doing anything definite. However, I think from what I hear that things are not as bad as they seem.[9] [. . .] [Michel] Fokine was terrible last night. The house was packed and I understand no seats were given away. $7.70 a seat. People were terribly sold. He simply can't dance at all any more and he never was a great dancer. His wife [Vera Fokina], too, is mediocre. [. . .] I think you had better [. . .] send me $100 to get things out of pawn. They can go back if necessary. Then I will send you your watch. If you get paid extra for Sunday you will have enough, I think, but, of course, do as you think best about these matters. I am much obliged for the cheque which came this morning. I haven't received a single dividend cheque yet[. . .]. Phil [Moeller] just called up to tell me we are going to "Bronx Express"[1] Friday night. I'm dining with Pitts [Sanborn] tonight. His aunt is out of town. He has in a French cook and is going to have a *goose*. Fannie Halton asked me to a party tonight, but I wouldn't go on a bet. The damned old bat said she didn't think the [actors'] strike was dignified. "It wasn't artistic," she asserted. "Not an artistic but a financial success," put in Freddie.[2] [. . .]
    I hope you are coming home very very soon, darling baby, and so does the boodles.[3]    Carlo
I shall finish the first draft of my book *The Tiger in the House* today!

TO VINCENT STARRETT                            151 East 19th Street
21 March 1920                                  New York City

My dear Mr. Vincent Starrett, Just at present I am thinking so little about Spanish music that I should not have been more astonished had your letter contained a query on the subject of a suitable diet for housemaid's knee. I am naturally the more sorry that I am not familiar with the song you mention; it would be very nice to [be] able to write you all about it in an

---

[9]*Call the Doctor*, 1920, by Emery Pottle, was in rehearsal with Fania Marinoff.
[1]*Bronx Express*, 1919, by Ossip Dymow, in Yiddish.
[2]Frederick and Fannie Halton, American playwrights.
[3]Feathers, the cat: Boodles and Poo were Fania Marinoff's pet names for all cats.

offhand professional way, indicating that I had a complete catalogue of Spanish tunes ticketed in my brain! Moreover I have asked several Spaniards, musicians themselves, without result. The nearest approach to a clue seems to be *Pensares del Alma* by V. Alvarado. However this does not mean that *Alma Perdida* is not the favourite air from the most famous Iberian opera; it only means, that in this instance at least, I am but a poor ignorant sinner. [. . .]

Naturally I am much pleased with your charming paper about me in Reedy's Mirror,[4] and also with your essay on Arthur Machen.[5] I hope, if you come to New York, that you will be good enough to look me up.      sincerely, Carl Van Vechten

TO ALFRED A. KNOPF                      151 East 19th Street
17 May 1920                             New York City

Dear Freddo, My fears were groundless, and the English publishers would have saved themselves much cursing had they sent the book earlier.[6] The reviewer in the London Times simply did not like my book. However, the typographical errors he refers to occur in Morales's portion, which is abominably proofread; I have not yet discovered any typographical errors in my section. Aside from the format, which is hideous, I am delighted with the book. Morales's introduction is the best criticism the work has yet received, and while I do not agree with him at all points, I am more than pleased with what he has written, and hope you will read it. Indeed, if another American edition is called for, I hope we may be able to incorporate this introduction. Call Blanche's[7] attention to the fact that all the world will know now who "Blanchette" is!      always, [unsigned carbon copy]

TO MABEL DODGE STERNE                   151 East 19th Street
18 June 1920                            New York City

Dear Mabel, I was forty years old yesterday—and suppose I still am today. It's middle age, I suppose but the biological change has not yet set in.—I do hope you'll think up something more attractive (to me) than a brig.

---

[4]"Carl Van Vechten" *Reedy's Mirror,* 8 January 1920, pp. 29–30.
[5]Arthur Machen, English mystic writer, whose American career CVV fostered through dust jacket blurbs, essays, and reviews.
[6]*The Music of Spain* was published in England by Kegan Paul, Trench, Trubner & Co., in 1920, with a preface and notes by Pedro G. Morales.
[7]*The Music of Spain* was dedicated to Blanche Knopf.

You know I'm always sick at sea—and I feel nervous on islands. To be perfectly free—& to be completely myself I must live in cities—where I can see people always. I *don't* see them, of course, but I *can*. It is wonderful writing up in my garret, looking over the rooftops & knowing they are all there. In the country, at sea, & all those places, I am seized with panic. I feel shut in—*compelled* to go through with something—all the things another person feels in the city. But your letter thrilled me—and you always thrill me. I worship vitality—I adore it. And that is why, I suppose, I don't grow old—and never will, and I'm not sustained artificially by Dorian Gray's picture either. [. . .]

The proofs [for *The Tiger in the House*] have gone back but they will rejoin me soon—and I want to make an index. Proofs are strange things. You feel that you have had an operation & that the doctor is returning the cut-off organs. They seem to belong to you but you don't seem to want them any more[. . . .]

Ducie is seeking her husband[8] in all the jails—as a possible haul-in by the U.S. government as a spy or an embrusqué or something. He went across a lake in a boat & was supposed to have been drowned but perhaps not, thinks Ducie. Others—some others—prefer to believe that marriage appalled him & that he has disappeared.—Ducie says that Florence is all wealth & gaiety—tea-dances & jazz on every corner—& everything very Chicago. You might like it again. It sounds to be like a delicious confusion of epochs. [. . .]      Keep the secret & The *Secrets*. Carlo

TO ALFRED A. KNOPF                    151 East 19th Street
[28 October 1920]                     New York City

Thank you, dear Alfred. . . . At last I have seen the [*Boston*] Transcript notice. . . . It doesn't seem very interesting to me. Some day it will occur to somebody that it is possible to write a review of this book *[The Tiger in the House]* without mentioning the word cat. Also no one yet has spoken of the *footnotes*. Well I have done my best, and you have done your double best and it may occur to some reviewer to emulate our example. There were days when I was writing it when I really wondered if it were about cats at all. But this aspect seems to have struck no newspaper person—although certain customers have written me very wise letters.—The Borzoi

[8]Ducie: Mina Loy, English poet whose work CVV had attempted to popularize in America, married to the artist Stephen Haweis.

de luxe is lovely: I was even a little jealous at first—but The Tiger is still more beautiful I think—[9]    Carlo

## TO MABEL DODGE STERNE
3 November 1920

151 East 19th Street<br>New York City

Dearest Mabel, What a bully, marvelously bully, letter from you about cats![1] I wish the book would get a review like that but it won't, unless you write it, because no one else will understand. They haven't yet begun to come in, but I know what they will say: Mr. Van Vechten has covered his material with infinite patience, or This is the ultimate book for the lover of cats, or The book is amusingly written, but the subject, of course, is trivial, or The Tiger in the House is a beautifully bound, beautifully printed, beautifully illustrated book, which will make an ideal Christmas gift. Columns of this sort of thing will be printed, but if anything real appears, like your letter, I shall be very much surprised. You ask if I have to get out of myself to write. I would say, No. It is rather giving than getting out of, getting rid of the unessential, peeling off, like a cat shedding superfluous hair, leaving more of the real self behind. But if you saw the hair of a cat, you would say, "That is a cat's hair," and you would know what it came from and all about it, so some perspicacious people—one, anyway, look at the superfluous matter I peel off and know all about me! Don't you think there is some truth in this? Not that I have become a complete cat yet. It takes many years to be a complete anything, but I am on the way, and I am glad you are on the way too. Neith Boyce is almost a complete cat, but she has never been anything else, and so she doesn't know how wonderful it is, and doesn't enjoy it as you and I will, when we compare it with our dog and horse and humming-bird days.    love, Carlo

## TO FANIA MARINOFF
16 February 1921

151 East 19th Street<br>New York City

Dearest Baby Marinoff, I was so blue yesterday that I nearly died; it seems so silly to be *here* and you *there;* I missed you so much, and everything went wrong, and nobody seems to want my work [. . .]. Don't worry about

[9]For its contributors, Knopf issued 100 copies in special bindings of *The Borzoi 1920,* a small volume written by and about the authors whose work he had issued during his first five years in publishing. In his own postscript, he referred to the first edition of *The Tiger in the House*—2,000 boxed copies bound in gold-flecked blue Inomachi boards and linen spines—as "quite the handsomest of all my books."

[1]Mabel Dodge's letter, written in response to *The Tiger in the House.* In 1922, CVV incorporated this verbatim as the spoken observations of Edith Dale, a character based on Mabel Dodge, in *Peter Whiffle: His Life and Works* (pp. 178–80).

the bugs. You imagine you were bitten. There are none in the bed now, and I think I have them under control. I didn't find one yesterday or today, and the whole room was doused again this morning. Didn't you get my valentine? I saw the notices last night! It is very discouraging. I wish road newspapers would appreciate my baby a little more, but judging by the things they write about the others in the cast, it doesn't matter very much.[2] Caruso appears to be dying this morning.[3] God, the world is melancholy . . . But there are bright spots: Mrs Lawrence Gilman, whom I don't know, sent me a Valentine and a few very warm words about The Tiger *[in the House]*, and I had a letter from Mary Young,[4] to whom I sent In the Garret.[5] She had bought The Tiger since, and was reading it, but the lovely thing about the letter was that it was simply addressed Carl Van Vechten, New York City, and I got it the next day! [. . .] The Poo[6] is going to have her name changed to Peck's Bad Boy. When I remonstrated with her for pawing the flowers last night, she made a flying leap right into the center of the cluster, and came out with most of them in her claws or her mouth! This morning I found she had chewed up a Smart Set last night. She seemed to set special store by Mencken's article!     all my love, Carlo

## TO FANIA MARINOFF

[3 March 1921]

151 East 19th Street
New York City

Dearest Baby Marinoff, [. . .] Well I had dinner with Mabel and the Indians last night.[7] They have made themselves well-beloved aborigines and they do war dances in the salon of this little country hotel every evening, to the admiration of all the old ladies and bright young men. The old ladies knit bags for them and the young men present them with gold ornaments and new blankets. We had a special seance of medicine songs, appeals to the gods of water, fire, etc. in Tony [Luhan]'s room. Mabel and I sat on the bed, while Tony and John in their full Indian regalia, banged tom-toms, shook gourds, and sang. Mabel is priceless. Nobody but she could pull a thing like this at a country hotel. She'll be having a Zulu chief at

---

[2]Fania Marinoff was appearing out of town in *Call the Doctor*.
[3]The popular operatic tenor Enrico Caruso died 2 August 1921; CVV's obituary for him—actually an essay assessing his whole career—appeared five days later in translation in the Yiddish newspaper *Die Zeit*.
[4]Mary Young, American actress.
[5]*In the Garret* by CVV, 1919.
[6]The Poo: Fania Marinoff's name for Scheherazade the cat.
[7]Mabel Dodge Sterne had moved to Taos, New Mexico, in 1917, and by the time CVV wrote this letter she had identified herself with the Indian culture there and taken as her lover a Taos Pueblo Indian, Antonio Lujan. They were married in 1923. CVV dined with them in Piermont, New York.

the Biltmore with her before she gets through. Her own cabaliere, Tony, is an injun about fifty years old. His face is a perfect mask. The other, John Marquis (he has a brother named Don!) is about twenty-seven and is very beautiful. They both have very long hair (to the waist) which is bound in two long braids of different coloured braid. The blankets of this tribe are of two colours with a stripe of white down the centre. This stripe outlines the body in almost any position. They are utterly lacking in self-consciousness and are very dignified. I approve more of this affair than of any other Mabel has had.

I am waiting patiently for Sunday. I'll be *so* glad to see you!

all my love, Carlo

TO FANIA MARINOFF                                       151 East 19th Street
[26 March 1921]                                          New York City

Dearest beloved, I was delighted, of course, over the *[Boston]* Transcript.[8] And your Easter card. [. . .] Edna, Dasburg,[9] and Ettie are coming to lunch tomorrow, and I have asked Marsden [Hartley], Demuth,[1] Marcel [Duchamp], Mabel and Neil [Reber], and Ida Rauh[2] to come in after! I can't have Marguerite[3] on Tuesday because she is singing Wednesday night, so I think I'll just have Emily [Stevens] and Phil. For lunch tomorrow I'm having anchovies, veal kidneys, peas and mushrooms, sour cream salad, cheese and jelly, and coffee! Also I have five magnificent calla lilies! I had dinner with Ralph and Duane[4] and the girl she is stopping with last night on Spring Street. Duane and her papa had an awful row. They never get on too well. It was nice when it was over. But Ralph seems to be taking a real interest in a privately printed book, of which more anon.[5] Duane is here for two weeks. I have asked her to lunch at the tearoom on Monday. Pepe [Joseph] Schildkraut and Lee Simonson[6] have had their first grand row, and with quite exceptional tact, Eva LeGallienne[7] mixed up in it, taking Pepe's side!! She may not be so willing to do this later. Of course

[8]A review of Fania Marinoff in *Call the Doctor*.
[9]Andrew Dasburg, American painter.
[1]Charles Demuth, American painter.
[2]Ida Rauh, Mrs. Max Eastman.
[3]Marguerite D'Alvarez, Peruvian contralto, as Claire Madrilena, a character in CVV's novels.
[4]Duane Van Vechten, adopted daughter of Ralph and Fanny.
[5]CVV offered his brother the manuscript for a collection of short pieces titled (after his second—never published—book) *Pastiches et Pistaches*. Nothing came of this.
[6]Lee Simonson, American scenic designer, founding member of the Theatre Guild, working with Schildkraut on Ferenc Molnar's *Liliom*.
[7]Eva LeGallienne, English-born actress, also cast in *Liliom*.

he is trying to gain all the cohorts he can. I don't think there is a bug in this house. I haven't seen one for days. Today I swept and scrubbed and dusted. Cat hairs an inch thick everywhere. She was a sweet poo last evening. Stayed beside me and purred while I petted her. I am going to ask Mabel Reber if she won't take her to the country but I don't think she will. I'm dining with the Stettheimers tonight (Seligman[8] asked me to dinner, too) and Ettie tells me that Avery [Hopwood] sailed on the Aquitania so he went back to his George. I see that Gertie's Garter[9] gives Thursday matinees. I wish you would see it. I can't begin to tell you how much I miss you and how much I am looking forward to seeing you; I wish you were going to be here tomorrow.     all my love to you, darling, Carlo

The last four books have come from the binder. They are in English prints and look *wonderful*.[1]

## TO FANIA MARINOFF
[31 March 1921]

151 East 19th Street
New York City

Dearest Baby, Bach's St Matthew Passion was too much me; I heard Marguerite [D'Alvarez] sing one air, and the chorus for half an hour or [so] and then I came home. I had dinner home alone, scraps from the Stevens banquet, including hot boiled potatoes, in oil and vinegar dressing prepared for artichokes the night before! Just as in the morning I gave Mabel and her boys [Tony Luhan and John Marquis] the remains of the cocktails. Tomorrow night I am going to hear a lecture on Dadaisme and either dinner or supper with the Stettheimers [. . .] Hugh Sherwin[2] is an old fluff. Louis was good to him for two years, long after everybody else Louis knew couldn't stand him. You remember that. The tragedy is that Louis will be just like him in a little while. I have always said that and I am more convinced than ever that it is true. Like his father, Louis's only connection with life is through sex. This is all very well when one is young, but an older man has got to have money to pull it off. But old man Sherwin goes on complacently believing he is still attractive to women, and moans when they don't fall for him. Louis will do likewise. The Poo [Scheherazade] is adorable; I am loving her more every day. She is a most difficult Poo to

---

[8]Edwin A. R. Seligman, Columbia University Professor of Economics, a Stettheimer cousin.
[9]*Getting Gertie's Garter,* a play by Avery Hopwood.
[1]It was CVV's habit—even before later wealth easily allowed the luxury—to have manuscripts and books with worn bindings bound in colorful cloth boards or put into slipcases.
[2]Hugh Sherwin, critic Louis Sherwin's father.

get to know and she is slow in forming her own conclusions but I think she will be a masterpiece when she finally arrives. [. . .]

All my love to you, Carlo

## TO FANIA MARINOFF
[22 April 1921]

151 East 19th Street
New York City

Beloved, blessed baby, Claire [Burke]'s party was a saturnalia. I stayed until ten o'clock and left everybody on the floor. Even Edna Kenton passed out, and Reg[3] was pie-eyed. Only Willard[4] and I retained our sobriety. General DuPont was there but he left before the general passing-out. [. . .]

Alfred had lunch with me yesterday and he is crazy about the idea of Peter Whiffle. I was rather amazed because he has had so little luck with my books that I wouldn't have been surprised if he had dropped me off his list. He wants some sort of synopsis to take to London, as he may arrange for the London publication. And he has put it on his spring list for 1922. Of course he may not like it at all when he reads it, and it won't be done until he returns in August. I am working madly at it. And I hope to send Pastiches et Pistaches to Ralph [Van Vechten] tomorrow. [. . .] I've turned down invitations to the Pollocks and the Hapgoods. I must get this book done so that I can hurry to my dearest baby's side. Mabel [Reber] and I are going out to Long Island tomorrow.     all my love, Carlo

## TO FANIA MARINOFF
[24 April 1921]

151 East 19th Street
New York City

Dearest Beloved Marinoff, [. . .] I won't send clothes, because I shall arrive in Chicago either May 3 or 4, at least I shall start out on one of those days. *Pastiches et Pistaches* went off to Ralph today . . . and I can see the end in sight of Peter Whiffle. But it means working very hard next week. [. . .] Andrew Dasburg had to go to Woodstock over Sunday and so Louise [Norton] has postponed her dinner until next Wednesday. Emperor Jones and Gilpin,[5] and Suppressed Desires[6] and Ida Rauh are going to London on July 17th!

---

[3]Regina Wallace, American actress, Fania Marinoff's closest friend.
[4]Willard Schermerhorn, Claire Burke's husband.
[5]Charles Gilpin, who had played successfully in Eugene O'Neill's *The Emperor Jones,* was scheduled to repeat the role in London; black actor-singer Paul Robeson replaced him in the part, however.
[6]*Suppressed Desires* by Susan Glaspell, American playwright.

Send the list of things you want soon, and don't make it too long. Read notices coming on; your name is correctly placed. (Enclose a few) Saw Tallulah[7] last night at the Algonquin [Hotel]. She *is* blooming. She talks of nothing but her Lesbianisms. Went to the Capital to hear Percy Grainger. He sat at the duo-art piano, and played the first movement of Tschaikowsky's E minor concerto with orchestra, letting the duo-art play his reading occasionally, and occasionally turning it off and really playing. It was quite a thrilling stunt, but he followed it up with his variations on Turkey in the Straw which were simply too marvelous, especially *there;* of course all music sounds better in moving picture houses where the lights are right.

[. . .] Going to Phil's tonight for a party & *working all day*. I *must* get through quickly to get to Chicago to see my baby whom I miss more every day.      all my love, Carlo

Arnold [Daly] doesn't like He, The One Who Gets Slapped.[8] He doesn't think it is commercial enough.

## TO ARTHUR DAVISON FICKE      151 East 19th Street
## 2 June 1921                            New York City

Dear Davenporter,[9] Donald Evans died Sunday. I bought a New York Times in Albany Monday morning and read an ambiguous obituary. Among other things "an excellent newspaper man and a promising poet." The janitor smelled gas, called the police, and broke into the apartment. All the gas was turned on; besides Donald had taken an overdose of chloral. He was unconscious; they took him to Bellevue where he died. You are aware, perhaps, that he was divorced a few weeks ago; and Esther[1] is pregnant again. A friend of Donald's, who attended the funeral in Philadelphia, reports that he recognized nobody. Perhaps, now Donald may become famous.      Carlo Van Vechten

[7]Tallulah Bankhead, flamboyant American actress.
[8]*He Who Gets Slapped,* by Russian playwright Leonid Andreiev.
[9]Arthur Davison Ficke was born and reared in Davenport, Iowa, not far from CVV's home in Cedar Rapids.
[1]Esther Evans, Donald Evans's wife.

## TO JAMES BRANCH CABELL
29 September 1921

151 East 19th Street
New York City

Mon cher maître, My principal sensation this morning is that I have received a letter from James Branch Cabell in which he refers to a paper of mine as "very beautiful." For the present I ask nothing more. When Miss Clark[2] wrote me that you were considering serializing this paper made up of memories and mists, I was, I admit, a bit terrified, but your suggestion of dichotomy has relieved me. It seems, indeed, to divide very neatly. By all means, end "The Tin Trunk" with the phrases from Page 10. . . . And, of course, omit these phrases from the subsequent paper—as it seems to read all right without them.[3]

When, I wonder, am I to meet you? Joe [Hergesheimer] has promised me this pleasure for years, and his easy, delightful talk of you has become an aggravation, since the promise has not been kept. Do you ever come to New York? And when you do, could you find time for a lunch or a dinner—or a goblet of sacramental wine?          sincerely, Carl Van Vechten

## TO ARTHUR DAVISON FICKE
24 December 1921

151 East 19th Street
New York City

Caro Jap, Come, of course! You *must!* There is nothing to be afraid of. Edmund Gosse is librarian of Parliament and Walter Pater was a Fellow at Oxford and Huysmans[4] was even worse, if you want precedents . . . I could go on, for Rimsky-Korsakoff[5] was a ship captain and . . . but why? . . . All this is not selfish, of course . . . Jamais, jamais, do I ever do anything that is not selfish, but it's good advice all the same. I am beginning to realize what a fine team we should make, cooking up strange broths and raising Eblis generally! Starting hare-hunts and bootlegging monkeytricks, making James Whittcomb Riley or whoever famous and what not! Your

---

[2]Emily Clark founded *Reviewer*, a literary fortnightly, with other young Virginians in Richmond. Margaret Freeman was its business manager; she later became the second Mrs James Branch Cabell. Hunter Stagg was its literary critic. Emily Clark was its editor. Together they coerced many published writers to contribute to the magazine, among them James Branch Cabell, Joseph Hergesheimer, H. L. Mencken and CVV. In turn, CVV arranged for work by Ronald Firbank, Gertrude Stein, and Hugh Walpole to appear in the *Reviewer*. The contributors were not paid.
[3]"The Tin Trunk" and "An Old Daguerreotype" appeared in the November and December issues of the *Reviewer,* 1921.
[4]Gosse, Pater, and Joris-Karl Huysmans (the latter a strong influence on CVV's *Peter Whiffle*) were all well-known literary figures who had taken employment to supplement their income from their writing.
[5]Nikolai Rimsky-Korsakoff, Russian composer whose memoirs CVV was then editing for Knopf.

monotonous life in Cambridge will be relieved by telegrams from me . . .
and trips to New York and I *will* actually visit you there. I've always hated
Boston and now you can take the curse off, just as another took the curse
off London for me. Your letter has excited me so much that I haven't been
able to work for two days and mss. and proofs are piled to my chin in all
directions. I'm so afraid you won't do it, and you must. Burn all bridges!
It is a rule of my life, learned after some experience, never to make moves
of my own accord; I make them when they come *from outside!* Perhaps
you are like that, I fancy you are. If you are not one who moves from
internal initiative, never neglect opportunities *from outside.* [. . .] As for the
Japanese Print book, I am overcome with delight. As for the inscription,
you *are* nice. You shall have presents directly yourself. It won't be long
before Peter Whiffle (there are two ffs please!) bursts forth. He certainly
has his moments . . . If the book sells, your seals will go up in value immediately (and then I'll stop sealing letters!) as Leda is immortalized therein.[6]

    Telegraph me that you are coming.      tout coeur, Carlo
I am beginning to regret that I haven't met the Davenport fast set.

## TO MABEL DODGE STERNE

27 December 1921

151 East 19th Street
New York City

Dere Mabel, Yes, the Indian work-basket arrived, and the silks to mend
my pyjamas, also. You are sweet. As they came without postage, in tissue
paper, I expected to see you the next day, but I was doomed to disappointment. Bobby [Robert Edmond] Jones came to breakfast one morning
. . . and Andrew Dasburg, who always charms me is back, senza Ida [Rauh].
I can't tell you the thrill that your letter gave me: on the minute, I decided
to outlive you! Save everything and I will reconstruct periods in forty volumes. Posterity must be amused. Yes, I have decided to reminisce from
now on: I have reached middle age, and les jeunes humble me! No more
present or future for me but only the past. In 1950 I shall be writing blithely
about 1930 . . . I am keeping my eyes open. My job as always is to be
amused . . . and more people laugh *after* than *before;* you know what I
mean.

[6]Leda and the Swan was the subject for an amethyst intaglio ring Fania Marinoff had given
CVV in 1912. In *Peter Whiffle* it belongs to Peter; in Mabel Dodge Luhan's 1936 memoir
*Movers and Shakers* the ring identifies CVV: "He wore a merry intaglio depicting Leda and
the swan, set in a gold ring, an emblem of his attachment to *scabreux* subjects rather than to
any ancient, half-forgotten truth, and his neckties came from Fifth Avenue shops"(16).

Je suis un peu fed up with Lawrence . . . He is too consistent.[7] . . . and too serious, sort of a creative and artistic Walter Lippmann.[8] Nevertheless, Women in Love is great. . . . When are you going to begin on Melville: I wish you could read his Pierre!! Such a book for 1851. It has never been republished. Moby Dick will give you thrills, but not quite such good ones. I am writing about Ouida[9]. . . . I shall gradually work up to 1921! The past is always so amusing in terms of the present: psychoanalysis applied to Ouida and Melville, etc. etc. I'll send you my Melville paper when it appears.[1] Read Weaver's new biography of Melville: not so good. . . .[2]     love, Carlo

## TO RONALD FIRBANK
12 March 1922

151 East 19th Street
New York City

Dear Mr. Ronald Firbank, I am very sorry to be obliged to inform you that I think there is some danger of your becoming the rage in America. J. C. Squire,[3] queried at a recent dinner, declared he had never heard of you, with the result that everybody present rushed into bookshops the next morning to demand your complete works. I have done what I can to stem the rising tide by writing a paper about you, a copy of which I shall, of course, send you when it appears. But more must be done. Can't you write me some facts about yourself, *so that* I can publish them injudiciously, *so that* people may be kept misinformed about your incredibly delightful books to the last possible moment.[4]     sincerely, Carl Van Vechten

## TO ARTHUR DAVISON FICKE
17 April [1922]

151 East 19th Street
New York City

Caro Arturo, I screamed over your letter. But do not begrudge the $7.89.— Just put the books aside & in six months you will be able to sell them for $12.00 apiece. In the meantime, perhaps, your mind may regain that purity

---

[7]D. H. Lawrence, the English novelist, had become Mabel Dodge Luhan's latest obsession, and less than a year later she had persuaded him to move to Taos.
[8]Walter Lippmann, American social critic, who with CVV had been a frequent guest at 23 Fifth Avenue, Mabel Dodge's pre-war salon in New York.
[9]Ouida: Marie Louise de la Ramé, English author of florid romances.
[1]"The Later Work of Herman Melville" was published in *Double Dealer,* January 1922.
[2]*Herman Melville: Mariner and Mystic* by Raymond D. Weaver, 1921.
[3]John Collings Squire, English poet and editor, founder of the London *Mercury.*
[4]"Ronald Firbank," *Double Dealer,* April 1922. CVV to Bruce Kellner, 15 February 1952: "Almost all of Firbank is quaint reading and enough to make your hair, even pubic hair, stand on end once you understand it."

and poise whereby you will be enabled to detect the subtle virtues of Valmouth.[5]

Peter [Whiffle] is getting astounding reviews, which are amusing me very much. I am even considering writing a review myself after it is all over, just to make it more mysterious. Peter has been praised as a great religious mystic & he has been damned for a cad. He has been identified with my subconscious mind, & with the satirical heroes of Max Beerbohm![6] I am very content, of course. And if, in my review, I tell the whole truth, no one will believe it, because I will only be repeating what I have already said in the book—for those who have eyes.     Salute, Carlo

## TO MABEL DODGE STERNE          151 East 19th Street
## 20 May 1922                          New York City

Dear Mabel, This is a nice letter from me. I think I was nicer then than I am now. I wonder who said "nothing is so necessary as a gay new idiot"? I wonder if I did. But I have put it in quotes. It is *very* profound. Is [D. H.] Lawrence a "gay new idiot"? His letter amused me and I will keep his secret. So he is coming to Taos! Firbank is a gay new idiot. I sent you my paper about him. You will *love* Firbank. He lives at Fiesole and writes me letters in purple ink. I send you more clippings. Please return. The picture was in Lord & Taylor's—with books (all colours!) & the two pages which refer to it photographed & enlarged & a title "The Portrait of Edith Dale" by Andrew Dasburg.[7] Now it is in Frank Shay's window in the Village. Andrew said he would send you Henry McBride's write-up. I haven't a copy. I saw Stieglitz. He is mad about the book—says it is a perfect study of the period. "It's all there" he exclaimed & he said that he had never known before how that International Exhibition had been pulled off but now he realized it had been done over your table. [. . .] What a funny idea Lawrence has of America! America is just like any place else: a good deal of this & a little of that. You & I are *the others:* democratic, free, aristocrats: or aristocratic democrats. Everything to somebody—& nothing to nobody. What a quaint man he is to be sure. Doesn't he *know* these things *yet?*

Ettie Stettheimer says that Ida [Rauh] is Peter Whiffle! & Maurice Sterne told her he had not read Peter Whiffle—but I don't believe him. Neith & Hutch are selling their house (if they can) to go to Italy to live cheap.

---

[5]*Valmouth,* a novel by Ronald Firbank.
[6]Max Beerbohm, English fin de siècle satirist.
[7]The first edition of *Peter Whiffle* was bound in batik boards of which there were 97 color-variations. These, with Dasburg's portrait of Mabel Dodge, were used in advertising displays.

Waldo Frank has a baby. Have you read *Ulysses?* The Irishmen (Boyd,[8] Colum,[9] etc.) tell me that it isn't symbolic or anything like that at all— That it's a sordid *realistic* catalogue of everything & everybody in Dublin— done à la Zola.     love, Carlo

TO RONALD FIRBANK                        151 East 19th Street
20 May 1922                              New York City

Dear gay genius, The first American paper about you was published in The Double Dealer (New Orleans) for April. The second (also by me) in the Reviewer (Richmond, Virginia) for May. Both have been sent to you. The first to Italy, the second c/o Grant Richards,[1] together with sundry clippings which they have evoked. In case, however, that they have perished in passage—like constipated rabbits—I have just mailed you two more copies. Unfortunately, all the newspaper clippings are not available again, but I have found one of them. The prospect of receiving a Japanese vellum copy of Odette[2] sustains me without food until it arrives.—Nay, shameless, I ask for something else. I hear rumors of portraits of the master by Augustus John.[3] Have these been photographed. Could I? Might I? Will you? I should be grateful. My impatience to read The Flower Beneath the Foot[4] exceeds all powers of imagination. To say that you are a sensation in New York is to speak modestly. All the world is reading you, quoting you, *buying you,* admiring you. You are almost a "best seller." One shop cannot keep you in stock at all. They are sold as fast as they come in. I think you are at least as famous in New York as Anatole France. Certainly more than [Max] Beerbohm. Mais, pour quoi pas?     Salute, Carl Van Vechten

TO CHARLES DUANE VAN VECHTEN[5]          151 East 19th Street
[circa May 1922]                         New York City

Dear Father: You ask me to tell you the meaning of Peter Whiffle, but there are so many! To begin with, it may be taken as a picture of certain phases of a period, & a very faithful picture. Then to go a step further, it is certainly

---

[8]Ernest Boyd, Irish-born literary critic.
[9]Padraic Colum, Irish poet, novelist, and playwright.
[1]Grant Richards, Firbank's English publisher.
[2]*Odette D'Antrevernes,* Firbank's first book, privately printed in 1905, had a large paper edition of only ten copies, printed on and bound in Japanese vellum lined in silk moiré. CVV's copy is now in the Berg Collection of the New York Public Library.
[3]Augustus John, the English portrait painter, sketched Firbank circa January 1915.
[4]*The Flower Beneath the Foot,* 1923, by Ronald Firbank.
[5]CVV's father copied this letter out in long-hand for his brother.

a satire of those schools of authors who make a fetish of methods arguing about romanticism & realism, etc. The point is made that there are only two schools, bad writers & good writers, & good writers are not greatly concerned over method, but write what they feel in the way they feel it.

There is another, still deeper meaning: Peter seeks self-realization through experience, learning in the end what he should have known all along, that the self is a mystic entity which may be studied better in contemplation than by searching contact with the world. Much, really, only causes disturbance.

The book is, of course, a moral document of the highest value, but fortunately for its prospective sales it is also amusing & may be (& has been) read by people who find it delightful. Indeed, up to date, you are the only one who has not been immensely pleased with it & it has been said many times (a few times in print, already) that it is a great advance in thought & style & form over any of my previous work. Aside from any of the inherent meanings I have advanced above, the book has a purely factitious interest for those who know the people in the book. Edith Dale is, of course, Mabel Dodge, in at least one aspect.     [unsigned transcript]

TO HENRY BLAKE FULLER                 151 East 19th Street
6 June 1922                           New York City

Mon cher Maître, Having warmly admired your work for many years, I have long had it in mind to pay it some kind of public tribute. That tribute, as it has developed, does not altogether satisfy *me* and, probably, if you are moved by it at all, it will make *your* hair stand on end. Nevertheless, as it is highly probable that this paper,[6] with certain modifications and additions, will someday go into a book, I hope you may permit yourself to ejaculate a few suggestions. It is with some such idea in mind that I have caused this paper to be printed first under somewhat obscure auspices, not too obscure, I hope to reach certain eyes. Yesterday, I added Under the Skylights to my collection, which is now complete but for the Stanton Page[7] edition of The Chevalier *[of Pensieri-Vani]* . . . I am not hopeless regarding that. With this letter I am sending the June issue of The Double Dealer.     very sincerely yours, Carl Van Vechten

[6]"Henry Blake Fuller," *Double Dealer,* June 1922.
[7]Fuller published his first novel under the pseudonym Stanton Page. Subsequently, it was issued under his own name.

## TO HENRY BLAKE FULLER
24 June 1922

151 East 19th Street
New York City

Thank you, dear Mr. Fuller; in a week or so, I may come to a period, but at present I must continue to threaten you with semi-colons. You speak of The Cliff-Dwellers having been a novelette; was it published in this form and where? And Miss Walker writes my brother that you wrote a story about her cat which appeared in the Chicago Tribune. I am extremely desirous of possessing a copy of this; are there any available? You ask me to throw Stanton Page on the rubbish heap; that would be a difficult undertaking as I have never even seen a copy. When I do see one, it goes into a slip-case, and into a safe, if I have one! [. . .] Ernest Boyd, interested by my paper to dig out a set of your works, has become one of your warmest admirers, but no warmer, I hope, than     Carl Van Vechten

Have you, by the way, another novel started or finished? That is really what I am writing to ask you!

## TO RONALD FIRBANK
12 July [1922]

151 East 19th Street
New York City

Dear Gay genius, Merci, mille fois, for the splendid Odette, bound in baby-skin or so I would imagine, so ivory and tender it appears, and I am very much touched by your sending me your own copy. Rose[8] shall have your messages when I see him, but no birds are flying up and down Fifth Avenue, no birds at all. I'm sorry you haven't photographs—you don't say you haven't—of *all* the paintings you describe. I should like to see you in all your moods. As for your picture of deserted bars, it is a romantic one. There is more drinking than ever; only the old bars have been turned into soda fountains and pastry shops, with the old bar-keepers as attendants, while the old pastry shops and soda fountains have been metamorphosed into bars. Tomorrow, when I go up town, I will ask Knopf to send you my newest book—now a little over two months old.[9] It has been so long since I read it that I find difficulty in remembering whether or no there are subterranean passages; if there are, you will find them! In the book I am writing now there are none, I know. Everything is so clear that no one will understand it. I have lost fifteen pounds in wondering how soon The Flower

[8]Stuart Rose, American bibliophile and, later, editor.
[9]*Peter Whiffle.*

Beneath the Foot will appear. Please do not cause me to lose fifteen more; I am quite thin enough. Do have a picture taken with Mrs. Hurstpierpoint[1] and send it to me!     Carlo Van Vechten

## TO RONALD FIRBANK
## 25 October 1922

151 East 19th Street
New York City

Dear Ronald, You promised to write me from Jamaica and you didn't, and you didn't send me your address or tell me how long you were going to stay, else I should have cabled you to come up at once as New York suddenly became *very* brilliant—so brilliant that I broke my arm at a party[2]—but it was soon bandaged up and I continued to go to parties and saw a man shot at one of them—or shortly after. He lay in the street quite bloody. Do not read *any* of my other books—especially in Rome. My *new* book—nearly finished—might amuse you, however. It will not be published until the fall of 1923.[3] I have mailed you a Reviewer with some more silly notes. I wonder if someday you would send me something for The Reviewer? It is run by an amusing woman who looks like a Toulouse-Lautrec portrait of the Grand Duchess Anastasie—quite more curious than anything ever seen at Polangre's.[4] Do write something for her. Send it to me & I will send it to her & she will be only less happy than the readers of The Reviewer. Of course, we *all* give her things for nothing.

   I am really sorry I didn't urge you to come up—but when I wrote you it was especially unamusing. However, I may go to London or Rome or Spain this winter—if some one will take care of my cat. In the meantime you might answer some of my prayers for your picture.     tout coeur,
Carlo Van Vechten

## TO ARTHUR DAVISON FICKE
## 21 November 1922

151 East 19th Street
New York City

Dear Arthur, Life is too amusing! Wallace Stevens drank a pint of my best Bourbon yesterday and then told me how much he disliked me . . . and today you get a divorce! I suppose you are getting married again. Permit me to congratulate you on both ceremonies. You see you are the only one

---

[1]Mrs Hurstpierpoint: a character in Firbank's novel *Valmouth*.
[2]In merriment, Horace Liveright threw CVV off a piano bench.
[3]*The Blind Bow-Boy.*
[4]Emily Clark.

of the principals I know, but it seems to me that you also are the only one that will get *all* the thrills. So naturally you are the one to be congratulated. I have noted a highly emotional (not to say hysterical) tone in your Cambridge letters, and have been expecting excitement for some time. So I was not surprised. A new portrait has been painted of me.[5] It is simply unbelievably wonderful. I never saw it at all before today, when it was finished, and I turned cart-wheels of admiration. You will be very envious when you see me sitting placidly in my bed of roses surrounded by chaud-froid, merry-go-rounds, cats, pianos, books, theatres, wives, and other devilments and pleasures, and as decadent as you please. I may use it for the wrapper of a book . . . You must come over.      love to you: single or double. Carlo V. V.

## TO THEODORE DREISER        151 East 19th Street
19 January 1923        New York City

Dear Mr. Dreiser, I saw the man I spoke to you about today, and gave him your name. So, when you want something, telephone him, mentioning my name:

  His is   William Linehan
              Kingsbridge 1228.

Over the telephone one is discreet and calls gin: *white* . . . mention the number of bottles you want. Scotch is *gold.* If he isn't in, leave your name and number and he will call you. I hope we may get together again soon.      very sincerely, Carl Van Vechten

## TO MAX EWING        151 East 19th Street
19 January 1923        New York City

Dear Max Ewing, I am very much amused and a little bit jealous. Why couldn't it have been *your* paper about *me* which caused the faculty to cut buck and wing capers and turn handsprings?[6] However. . . . Of course, it's all your (speaking collectively) own fault. You have no business to be going to college, and in college you have no business to be thinking for yourselves. Rubber-stamp opinions were de rigueur in institutions of the higher learning in my day, and it is pleasant to observe that times have not changed. Does

---

[5]By Florine Stettheimer. See List of recipients.
[6]In an earlier issue of the University of Michigan newspaper, Max Ewing had written an extensive article on CVV. Both he and the rest of the newspaper staff came under fire from the administration for later printing material judged too salacious for the eyes of students.

the faculty belong to the K[u] K[lux] K[lan] and will any one be lynched? If so telegraph me and I will come out to see the fun. Naturally, I am delighted with your very flattering paper. If a few people had seen it, doubtless I should have received many love letters, after being called a "perfect dear" by M[ary] G[arden]. If you can dig me up one or two more copies I would be overjoyed. And do send the clippings from the Detroit papers and a statement of the case to H. L. Mencken, care of The Smart Set. Tell him I told you to. It will amuse him vastly.     with all salutations, Carl Van Vechten

## TO GERTRUDE ATHERTON
23 January 1923

151 East 19th Street
New York City

Dear Gertrude, You are much too young to be called Madame Zatainny any longer . . . and hereafter I propose to treat you like the contemporary you are . . . Congratulations on your book! You have hit on a novel (and perverse) idea and have treated it with the vitality and glamour of which you . . . and only three or four others . . . have the secret.[7] Vitality is the great thing in writing . . . as it is in everything. It is the secret of Sarah Bernhardt's prolonged success, and doubtless Queen Victoria and Disraeli possessed it! You have it in abundance. Black Oxen should be a pronounced success, and you will be receiving letters from every dowdy frump in the country demanding the address of that doctor in Vienna! The irony of it is that you are the only woman in the world who will never need to go to him! Some day soon you must write something indiscreet in your latest book.     my love to you, Carl Van Vechten

## TO JANE COWL
7 February 1923

151 East 19th Street
New York City

[. . .] There is no such thing as "realism" in the theatre, at least not in any good theatre, just as there are no photographs in the National Gallery. Stanislavsky knows this just as well as you and I do. He does for The Cherry Orchard exactly what you have done for Romeo and Juliet. He produces a play in the way it should be produced and so do you . . . It is, perhaps, a feeling for the play spiritually realized: these things are very difficult to explain . . . In any art the three essentials are vitality, glamour, and imag-

---

[7]In *Black Oxen,* Gertrude Atherton's middle-aged heroine is rejuvenated to youth with secret injections.

ination. Shakespeare projected all of these in his great tragedy, but there are ways of presenting this tragedy which obscure these qualities. Your production has magnified them. This result cannot be achieved by turning a spot light on the star and asking the other characters to mumble in the dark, especially if the star has no idea what she is talking about. In any great play every character is important and must appear to be so. There was a maid servant who answered the bell in The Three Sisters who never spoke a line, but I shall never forget her. Your Juliet is very fine, so fine, indeed, that it is unlikely that any one else will equal it in our generation, but you have not been content to leave it there. All the characters live; the pace, the tone, the colour all match the poet's intention . . . and the result charms and entrances everybody. During the potion scene while you stand silent, not a cough is heard, and this during a season when most of the theatres suggest that they were built to harbour tubercular patients. This is true not only because you play the potion scene magnificently but also because, through your cast and production, you have roused the audience up to the point where they forget everything but the play. . . . I think I may honestly say that I have never seen a performance of Shakespeare that delighted me so much, STRAIGHT THROUGH, and I have seen Ellen Terry as Portia, Modjeska as Lady Macbeth, and my own wife's adorable Ariel. May I hope for more? You can't stop here. After seeing the Russians, I am unalterably opposed to translations. Actors cannot realize alien rôles. But do give us some more Shakespeare: Antony and Cleopatra, The Taming of the Shrew, As You Like It, and Twelfth Night, Much Ado About Nothing are all in your best manner; after you have done one or two more performances like your Juliet, some modern playwright will create a great play for you.     [unsigned draft]

TO MABEL DODGE STERNE                      The Colonial Inn
22 February 1923                           Fairhope, Alabama

Dere Mabel, This is a single tax—socialist—theosophist—Christian Scientist community where I fit in very nicely. There are pine trees, & roses, & Mobile Bay, & mocking-birds & my father. I shall stay for a while—(two or three or four—or five days) without cocktails secure in the belief that it is doing me good. The Chatelaine of the Inn won me completely by telling me that other authors had been here: "Not very good ones"—Sherwood Anderson,[8] Waldo Frank, Upton Sinclair.[9] [. . .]

[8]Sherwood Anderson, American novelist.
[9]Upton Sinclair, American novelist.

I am seeing lots of Joseph Hergesheimer, Hugh Walpole,[1] Theodore Dreiser, Scott Fitzgerald,[2] Ernest Boyd, & Gertrude Atherton, but not together. Aren't you coming East this winter?     Carlo V. V.

## TO FANIA MARINOFF
[23 February 1923]

The Colonial Inn
Fairhope, Alabama

Dearest Baby Marinoff, I hope your shoulder is better. I think about you all the time. If you were here I might like it better. It is warmish—Roses are blooming and I go everywhere without a hat or overcoat. This morning I dressed in a room with the windows wide open. I saw Babbitt[3] on the shelf in father's room last night & happened to say that I knew him. This led to details. After dinner last night when the convoy of senescent dotards had gathered round the fire in the lounge I was horrified to hear Addie exclaim, "Just think, our son knows the author of Main Street." Since then I have been asked to describe him, etc. I have set limits on my stay—Next Wednesday is the day of my departure. So don't send any mail after Saturday. But write me on Sunday & it may get here. This will bring me home on Friday. My cough is no better but I'll take my chances on pneumonia & Dr Livingston in New York. This probably will be the last time I'll ever go anywhere.

How is the pookins?[4] I love you so much, blessed baby, & I'll be so glad to see you again.     Carlo

Emily Clark writes & begs me to stop off in Richmond, promising a lunch with Cabell, etc. but I don't think I'll be up to it.

## TO SINCLAIR LEWIS
8 March 1923

151 East 19th Street
New York City

Dear Hal, Recently, while freezing my ears on Mobile Bay, I belatedly read Babbitt. Is it impertinent of me to tell you that it completely bowled me over? It is, I fancy, one of the finest books America has yet produced. Quite apart from the ironic picture of the kind of people I spend my life avoiding, presented with great gusto, the whole thing has a vitality, and sweeping rhythm, accentuated towards the end by the sympathetic doubts which assail Babbitt, and terminating in a touching coda—that magnificent last page!—which place it, in my mind, at least, safely far above any similar

[1]Hugh Walpole, English novelist. See List of recipients.
[2]F. Scott Fitzgerald, American novelist.
[3]*Babbitt,* 1922, a novel by Sinclair Lewis.
[4]The pookins: either Scheherazade or a new cat named Ariel; they overlapped.

works in our language. It is not, of course, as I had been told realism; it is not, as I had also been told, burlesque. It is simply a great book, and, like all other great books, a symphonic pattern woven from living themes. Bravo!     [unsigned draft]

## TO FLORINE STETTHEIMER                    151 East 19th Street
[circa spring 1923]                                     New York City

Dearest Florine, Miss Glasgow,[5] before Ettie, reiterated that she would like to buy your flowers, but she doesn't buy them, and I suddenly realized that I didn't want her to, that I couldn't bear the idea of their departure, and, as certain sums of money have come to me lately, I asked myself: why shouldn't I buy them?—Dear Florine, I can't remember the details of your priceless price list, but if I am in a modest enough class, I shall be delighted to forward you a cheque by return mail. Please let me know at once.[6] [. . .]     our love to you all, Carlo
I can't send *all* the books to you, but a book went to Ettie, Gertrude [Stein]'s which you will probably like more than she does.[7]

## TO HUGH WALPOLE                          151 East 19th Street
[May 1923]                                            New York City

Dearest Hugh, You never disappoint me and so I was by no means surprised that you appreciate [Henry Blake] Fuller. He is one of the very best of our writers. I have two more extra copies of his books, which I am sending you. The Chevalier *[of Pensieri-Vani]*, his first book, was his greatest success, and The Last Refuge is almost my favourite of the lot. After these, try to get his realistic Chicago novels, With the Procession and The Cliff Dwellers. Both published by Harper's and both, probably, out of print. You will find a complete list of his books in Bertram Cope*['s Year]*. I do not seem to have a copy of my paper on Fuller (published rather obscurely two years or more ago) by me. Besides I don't want you to read it *now* because it contains my only other (the one you saw occurred in the review of M*[aurice]* Guest) silly dig at you, when I was naively trying to attract your grand

[5]Ellen Glasgow, American novelist. See List of recipients.
[6]CVV purchased this painting of a bowl of zinnias, which had been hanging in his apartment on loan from the artist. By his will, it was bequeathed to the Museum of Modern Art in New York.
[7]*Geography and Plays*, 1922.

Gertrude Atherton, 1935

Sinclair Lewis, 1937

Arthur Davison Ficke, 1932

Hugh Walpole, 1934

attention, having made up my mind that I would meet you in one way or another. That time, happily, is past; we are indelible and permanent friends, and now I can love you and your books until death do us part![. . .]

Now that I have read The Purple Cloud I am with you on Shiel.[8] We are going to make Children of the Wind go, so that we can revive the others. The Purple Cloud is immense, and so, with reservations, is Cold Steel. I even like the ones I didn't like better now that I understand Shiel better. He has imagination, glamour, vitality, style. He lacks balance, rhythm, suspense, even in his best books. His endings are all bad. (I mean that they could be improved.) But rhythm is the great thing in a book: you will remember that I think The Cathedral has it to an extraordinary degree. The lack of it will often make a book a failure. He has too much talent, he is careless and redundant. I doubt if the man has ever taken pains. Nevertheless he is a fine man and I am going to do what I can for him. [. . .] If you can send me any particulars regarding him do, please, because I intend perpetrating a paper sooner or later (which will begin with your name, invoked, pleasantly, like that of Mercury, this time!)

The [Blind] Bow-Boy is nearly out; the damned illustration is holding up advance copies.[9] The original is so subtle that none of the reproductions have yet satisfied me. I am to see another this morning. Grant Richards is to bring it out in England almost immediately after (say, September). I hope the English will like me again. I'm over half way through the second draught* of The [Tattooed] Countess, and I think there is a great possibility that I shall dedicate it to you, but I never am sure until I finish a book. If not this, another. [. . .]

I haven't seen Joe [Hergesheimer]. But he spent two days with my brother on his way to Wisconsin. He couldn't stand Wisconsin and came back after two days more there, and then went fishing in Canada. Now, I believe (Mencken came up the other evening) Joe is working on The Magnetic West, a terrible opus that no one wants him to publish. Mencken started to tell him so, but Joe's face registered anger, so Henry desisted.

I do miss you very much, and long to talk with you. One or two amusing things have happened. Write me often all about yourself, and believe me        affectionately yours, Carlo V. V.
*milieu, mood & style are all quite different from anything you know of me.

[8]Matthew Phipps Shiel, English novelist. See List of recipients.
[9]The frontispiece for The Blind Bow-Boy was painted by Robert Locher.

## TO H. L. MENCKEN
[circa 24 August 1923]

151 East 19th Street
New York City

Cher Herr Doktor de Musique, Of course a mechanical piano can wail a quarter tone off key. I know three that do constantly. I'll introduce them to you if you can stand it. This detail, like all others in my book has been carefully documented. In a realistic work one cannot take too many pains.[1]

It is very kind of you to ask me to contribute to the new magazine[2]—I have already congratulated Knopf on his splendid selection of editors[3]—but the only work I have in sight is my new novel of which I shall finish the third draught along in October or November. The title is The Tattooed Countess. I call it a "romantic novel with a happy ending." Place: Iowa. Time: 1897. I hardly think it is suitable for a family paper . . . even if you consider running serials.     bien à toi, Carl Van Vechten

BOOK COLLECTOR'S NOTE: I wonder if sometime you will drop in and sign seven thousand of your books for me (perhaps you'll sign my Herman Melvilles too). Name the hour and you may have any drink you will demand in advance (or at least any label).

## TO HUGH WALPOLE
[circa 25 August 1923]

151 East 19th Street
New York City

Dearest Hugh, Well, you were right. The book *is* a sensation—four editions and it has only been out ten days. They simply can't keep copies in the office. It has already gone over 10,000. A good deal of this I owe to you—that splendid send-off in the International.[4] Then you witnessed The [Blind] Bow-Boy contract (Luck, that, I calls it!) and finally you sat on a tripod and predicted great things. I am sending you some of the reviews. All are good *selling* reviews but nobody has written anything about the book yet, although one or two hover around it. Of course, it is a tremendously serious book with a sardonic approach. The line, "It is not good to say fountain, out of your basin I will never drink" explains one phase of it—but Campaspe sums the whole thing up. However, I don't care what they say just so long as they don't proclaim me the "great American novelist"—. It's so hard to continue to be that—& I leave that struggle for Joe [Hergesheimer]. The

---

[1]Mencken had written CVV to chide him for including a piano that played quarter notes in *The Blind Bow-Boy*.
[2]*The American Mercury*.
[3]H. L. Mencken and George Jean Nathan.
[4]"Six Best American Novels of 1922: An English Critic's View" (in which Hugh Walpole included *Peter Whiffle*), *International Book Digest*, January 1923.

large paper copies only arrived today & one went off to you immediately. But I cannot make out your address & so I shall continue to send to the Athenaeum Club. Vanity Fair's Bad Books was a triumph. The clippings have cost me as much as a set from your lecture tour would have cost you. Every paper in the country commented & [Alexander] Woollcott stops me in the Algonquin Lobby & demands what I mean by including Barrie.[5] I'm dying to see The Red-hair Man.[6] I'm sure it's immense. It came to you so easily. Don't you think a red-haired man should know a tattooed countess? The third draught I begin as soon as The Bow-Boy excitement somewhat subsides. I'm naturally delighted that Melchior[7] is doing so well. I had dinner one night with Knobloch[8] & we talked of him and you.

Have you heard of Knopf's new magazine, January 1, 1924: The American Mercury—Editors Mencken & Nathan. The Smart Set died, I hear. You'll hear from me again soon. I wish I might see you. Don't forget me!    Love, Carl Van Vechten

TO H. L. MENCKEN                                        151 East 19th Street
27 August 1923                                          New York City

Dear Henry, [. . .] You ask when you may emblazon my books, just as if you lived around the corner and I could say, as I would be delighted to, come to lunch today. As it is, you must say when. You are invited to dine or lunch as soon as you like (come armed, the street is dangerous). Telephone me (6041 Gramercy) when you are in town and proclaim the national holiday.

Joe [Hergesheimer] came up yesterday. He says he has spent all his money on making over his house (this means his $100,000 inheritance from his mother, $760,000 for the motion picture rights to The Bright Shawl, $340,000 for the screen rights to Java Head, $11,432,569.23 from The Saturday Evening Post for The Magnetic West, and divers smaller sums for stud rights, etc.) and has no money to buy coal. I suggest therefore that you assign him to write the first three numbers of The American Mercury at his usual rates to put him on his feet again.    Love, as always,
    Carl Van Vechten

[5]In "The Ten Dullest Authors: A Symposium," *Vanity Fair*, August 1923, CVV had included James M. Barrie, English author of *Peter Pan*, as well as (among others) Sigmund Freud, James Joyce, and D. H. Lawrence.
[6]*The Red Haired Man*, 1923, a novel by Hugh Walpole.
[7]Lauritz Melchior, Danish heldentenor.
[8]Edward Knobloch, English playwright.

## TO HUNTER STAGG
[16 September 1923]

151 East 19th Street<br>New York City

I was very glad, dear Hunter, to get your letter. Of course, send *all* my books up that aren't already written in, as soon as you will, & please send a photograph too. (*Not* one of mine!) I've started work on the third draught of The Tattooed Countess & so for a time I shall be occupied—Not a word from Joe about the trip to West Chester—but I hear that none of his furniture fits the house & that he is distracted.[9] [. . .] Neysa McMein,[1] by the way, asked at Putnam's for The Blind Cow-Boy & a customer at a shop in Evanston, Illinois, demanded The Blind Bow-Wow. [. . .]

Have you started work on your newspaper yet? When you do please send me some of the pages, & I hope you've done something for the Westminster—I am naturally lying awake waiting for the October Reviewer. The account of the meeting with John Powell[2] amused me. I now find that people who don't like niggers bore me,—but I hate propaganda of whatever nature.[3] Rascoe was here last night—the second time he has been in the house. So you may expect almost anything in The Daybook[4] next Sunday. I think it would be nice if you would walk in this afternoon.

au revoir, Carlo

## TO ALFRED A. KNOPF
3 October 1923

151 East 19th Street<br>New York City

Not for my sake (although certainly to my deep enjoyment), not for [M. P.] Shiel's sake (although I hope to his future profit), but for *your* sake (and both your profit and enjoyment, perhaps), dearest Alfred, I have now read nineteen of Shiel's twenty-one books with growing enthusiasm. Even his less good work has a certain interest after one gets the hang of his mad and brilliant manner. Consequently I retract the substance of our last conversation on the subject: Shiel is, to my mind, much more than a commercial proposition. He is an artist, and in his strange way an important one. He is, I should think, properly presented, sure of at least some popular success, but he is just as sure, in the end, of critical success, too. His faults,

---

[9]Joseph Hergesheimer restored an 18th-century Dower House in West Chester, Pennsylvania, and proposed inviting various literary friends down for a weekend.
[1]Neysa McMein, American fashion illustrator.
[2]John Powell, conservative book reviewer.
[3]In 1923, CVV was—like most white people—still in ignorance that this epithet was offensive.
[4]"The Bookman's Daybook," a kind of literary gossip outlet in the *Herald Tribune* by American critic and reviewer Burton Rascoe.

such as they are, would never interfere with his popular success, and in his best work it would be very difficult for a severe critic to find any very important faults, granted the critic has any idea what the man is trying to do. He has glamour, imagination, and a brilliant style. The man can certainly write when he sets his mind to it. And there is a certain grandeur about his manner, about the utterly magnificent way he permits his imagination to work, which reminds me of no one else but Herman Melville. One of his favourite subjects (he has treated it in several books) is the conquering of the world by the overman . . . and then his defeat. He treats this subject, as befits it, in the grand manner. [. . .] Shiel is a peculiar man; he is a recluse, sees few people, seems to have no public address, and throws postmen out of the window because he dislikes men in uniform. He is very religious and takes great pride in the health and strength of his body, hence taking thirty mile walks before breakfast. He also thinks he is the greatest writer of all times. You can see, therefore, that a letter to him must be couched in peculiarly soothing terms and, if one is written, we might discuss this later. I think this is a good bet. What do you think?

[unsigned carbon copy]

Better preserve this letter for reference.

TO ALFRED A. KNOPF                    151 East 19th Street
20 October 1923                        New York City

Dear Alfred, Thanks for the beautiful Lost Lady[5] which arrived today. I am extremely glad to have it. Your books seem to get handsomer every year, which means, thank God! that mine do too. [. . .] After our splendid and extremely satisfactory talk yesterday I was reminded that during our eight years association we have never had a quarrel or even a serious argument, or even a disagreement (one of us always gives in at once if the other wants something badly enough). That is one of the fifty reasons why you are the only publisher to whom I sign myself,        permanently yours,

    Carl Van Vechten

I finished the last draught of The Tattooed Countess this morning, as I had thought I would. If you can find *two* old copies of The Merry-Go-Round and *two* of In the Garret, I can paste them up and it will save me considerable trouble in making revisions when I get around to rewriting my past. I have old copies of Music and Bad Manners and Interpreters and Interpretations.

---

[5]*A Lost Lady,* a novel by Willa Cather.

## TO RONALD FIRBANK
30 October 1923

151 East 19th Street
New York City

Dear Ronald, Well, it is all settled and Brentano's will send you your contract today. I am delighted. Now, you will be put over in America in good shape, and the cheques you crave will presently begin to arrive. It is the present plan to bring out not only the new one (which, I think, is one of the best!) but several of the old ones which are out of print. I hope you control the rights to these. If not, get them. I have been asked (and desire) to write an introduction to the first; I hope you won't object to this. Also after reading this delightful opus, I suggested that Prancing Nigger would be a better title, and they all agree to this.[6] This change, however, would, of course, not be made without your consent. I may say, however, that beyond a doubt the new title would sell at least a thousand more copies. They are planning to bring the book out as closely as possible in the format of the English books, and they will get Bobbie Locher, who did mine, to do the frontispiece. But you will hear of all these things from them. Rose, I think will write to you himself.

I don't know what to think about The Blind Bow-Boy. I mailed him to you *three* months ago. Is he lost in the mails? He was *registered*. Let me know, because if he is you must have another. I can't have you reading the English edition (which has just arrived and which has a most amusing drawing) because it is expurgated.[7]

You will have heard from me e'er now about the charming photos.

I have finished my new book, The Tattooed Countess, but it will not appear until August, 1924.

It is quite possible that I may go to London or to Italy or somewhere a little later. I *do want* to see you!     bien à toi, Carlo Van Vechten

## TO HUGH WALPOLE
7 November 1923

Jefferson Hotel
Richmond, Virginia

Dearest Hugh, Jeremy & Hamlet was misdirected & only arrived on the day before I set out on my grand tour. So I took it along & read it on the

---

[6]In England, Firbank's novel was published as *Sorrow in Sunlight;* the phrase "prancing nigger" appears in the text.
[7]Grant Richards insisted on deleting from CVV's novel a character's motto, "a thing of beauty is a boy forever" (actually an observation popularized in 1915 by Allen Norton); a reference to chrysanthemums looking like "geese's bottoms"; and a longer passage recounting one schoolboy's making "a curious request" of another; also, the verb "whip" was changed to "kiss," rendering a passage meaningless.

way to Philadelphia—and, of course, loved it. Jeremy is adorable—& so like you—and I can never get enough of him. I am waiting for the red-haired feller with all my breath bated![8]

Starting out a week ago with a luncheon given in Philadelphia for Cabell, Joe [Hergesheimer] et moi, my life has been a succession of entertainments. Spent five days at Dower House—not only the Cabells were there but several others. Joe has almost ruined Dower House by making it so perfect. It really requires Puritan costumes. It is very austere and correct. Personally I prefer things more hit-or-miss, *comfortable & personal,* but, of course, I would not tell Joe that. We went to one such house—which was nearly perfect—to a hunt-breakfast. Joe and I came down to Richmond yesterday, Joe to start work on Bale Hundred, his new Virginia novel,[9] and me in search of adventures! We are going out to the Cabells this afternoon.—I shall write you more about Cabell later. He is *very* difficult but on the whole we got on better than I expected. Frank Harris's book is vraiment a scream—a naïf one at that.[1] Have you read Miss Cather's new book?[2] It is the first work of hers I have admired. I am liking travelling so much—you know I so seldom leave New York—that I shall probably go lots of places—my new book is done![3]—I am even thinking of running over to London for a couple of weeks. I *do* want to see you. You don't pay any attention to my questions I ask. So I still don't know what your address is.     Love, Carlo

I'm going to Baltimore from here & then home in about 10 days.

TO ALFRED A. KNOPF                          The Jefferson Hotel
12 November 1923                            Richmond,
                                            Virginia

Dear Alfred, I've received a charming letter from [Matthew Phipps] Shiel—who, by the way, lives in London & is a friend of Arthur Machen [. . .]. So when I get back we can go to it—if you want to.

I've had a marvelous time here & almost cried when I said good-bye last night to a lot of them. Cabell, who has not yet received The High Place,[4] told me to tell Guy Holt that he was barking like a Borzoi.—Joe

---

[8]The references are to characters in at least three of Walpole's novels.
[9]*Balisand,* 1924.
[1]*My Life and Loves,* 1922.
[2]*A Lost Lady,* 1923.
[3]*The Tattooed Countess,* 1924.
[4]*The High Place: A Comedy of Disenchantment,* 1923, a novel by Cabell. Guy Holt was his editor at Robert M. McBride and Company; for some time CVV had tried to persuade Cabell to publish with Alfred A. Knopf (who used a Russian wolfhound as an insignia on all his books).

[Hergesheimer] hasn't done any work yet, but says he begins today—now that I am leaving. By the way I was amorously assaulted in the lobby here by a Miss Williamson, one of your ex-stenographers.

Dinner in Baltimore tonight with Mencken—I shall be with David Bruce[5] at the Maryland Club for a few days. Home the end of the week.

Love to you & Blanche.    Carlo

TO ALFRED A. KNOPF                          151 East 19th Street
21 November 1923                            New York City

Dear Alfred, [. . .] A letter from Gertrude Stein puts her on record as entirely sympathetic, nay even enthusiastic, about our plan of sounding out the dealers by circulars before we go ahead. She deplores the condition of the first volume; it seems the corrected copy was lost; this is the first typewritten copy. The other volumes are better.[6] [. . .]

The Review of Love Days in The New Republic is very gratifying. The book may not sell (although I hope it will) but I don't want you to feel that I am entirely an ass when it comes to the selection of literature![7]

By the way I told Mencken that no other man in the world would have thrown away a complete translation without argument or discussion after it was paid for simply because it was bad; no other except you.[8] I am delighted to see that you are by no means uncertain to reap your reward.      love, as always, Carlo

The box for The Presbyterian Child arrived and I am grateful.[9]

TO H. L. MENCKEN                            151 East 19th Street
26 January 1924                             New York City

Dear Henry, I hope you will forgive me for turning you out of the house the other night. When I emerged and found it snowing I could think of nothing but the two orphans; so far as I know you and Boyd are buried

---

[5]David Bruce, minor American writer, a member of an old Virginia family.
[6]CVV had tried unsuccessfully to place Gertrude Stein's *The Making of Americans* in America. Although Knopf had agreed to issue a brochure, he later contended that none was ever printed.
[7]*Love Days*, 1923, a novel by Ettie Stettheimer, published under the pseudonym Henrie Waste, that CVV had persuaded Knopf to issue.
[8]CVV to Fania Marinoff, 7 April 1922: "After a conference with Alfred, he decided to throw Nardony's translation of Rimsky [Korsakoff] into the fire, and start afresh. This was my advice. And I can't tell you how relieved I am to have the damn thing off my mind for a while."
[9]*The Presbyterian Child*, a memoir by Joseph Hergesheimer, was issued privately by Knopf only in a limited, boxed edition.

under some snowdrift at this very minute. Well, the opportunities to attend Kosher weddings with a Brooklyn blonde are too rare to be passed up. I shall never forgive myself if you and Boyd are dead from exposure, but I feel that, in the circumstances, I would do the same thing again. I should have written you this letter yesterday, had I been able to write yesterday. [. . .] And will you please write your autograph on a separate card for Channing Way, Jr. I am getting a grand collection for this twelve year old West Chesterian. In the meantime command me in any way you see fit (save writing an article for The *[American]* Mercury; of course, any amount of work would not keep me from doing this if I found a suitable idea; for the present nothing occurs to me). You will find me very versatile.

Q.B.S.M. Carl Van Vechten

TO EMMA GRAY TRIGG 151 East 19th Street
26 February 1924 New York City

Dear Emma Gray, Your letter was as usual enchanting, but it disheartened me somewhat to hear that Billy is going to church. I hope this will not have a permanent dampening effect on his character.—I am sorry you were so bent on visiting theatres when you were in New York. Otherwise, we might have amused ourselves at greater length & in broader fields. Will you always go too often to the theatre when you come to see us? Joe [Hergesheimer] was here for a week, *resting,* which means that he saw from twenty to thirty people an hour & went home a wreck. I went back with him to attend a birthday in his honour at which the guests were invited to arrive as characters from his books. *Everybody* came as La Clavel.[1] I've never seen so many bright shawls. I am working very hard still, but am *beginning* to see my way through. If Joe doesn't come in April would I be welcome without him?      salve, Carl Van Vechten
The picture goes to you tomorrow. I had a splendid letter from Delia. I wish you would present a lot of nice messages to her, Dick & Billy—[2]

---

[1]La Clavel, a character in Hergesheimer's novel *The Bright Shawl.*
[2]Richard and Delia Carrington, Richmond gentry; William (usually Billy) Trigg, Emma Gray's husband.

## TO EDNA KENTON
16 March 1924

151 East 19th Street
New York City

Dearest Edna, Salutations to your enduring charms, on this most happy day. I hope you noted the Hopwood engagement in the morning prints.[3]
[. . .]   Love, Carlo
I am sending you the [Sinclair] Lewis clipping because you said you'd thrown yours out. I advise you to save this—oh! and a long letter from H. B. Fuller in which he tells me he is taking a youth from the University of Illinois abroad in June. He describes him as an Indiana Methodist. Edna Millay has not yet sailed.[4] Marinoff & three others are leaving the cast of Tarnish[5] in two weeks.

## TO EDNA KENTON
1 April [1924]

Jefferson Hotel
Richmond, Virginia

Dearest Edna, Gertrude Stein writes "I'm glad your book is about Iowa. Iowa is different. It was different even when it was a doughboy." Ford Madox Hueffer[6] starts *serial* publication of The History of a family in the Transatlantic for April.[7] If he prints it all the magazine will keep going a long time. Gertrude's birthday book with Picasso's illustrations is nearly done. And she is also publishing Portraits & Prayers. The April Reviewer will contain my *new* portrait which is to go in this book.[8]

The enclosed interview will show you how tasteful I can be when it's time, but one line in it almost disrupted my relations with the author of Cythera.[9] We are dining with Ellen Glasgow (whom I have not yet met) tonight, & Thursday at the Cabells. Elinor Wylie arrives tomorrow and Emily Clark is giving a dinner for her, Joe, me, Cabell & Miss Glasgow. The Knopfs arrive Thursday. Cabell says it reminds him of an Elks' convention. [. . .]   Carlo

[3]As a publicity stunt, Avery Hopwood and the dancer Rose Rolanda pretended they were going to be married; some time later Rolando married the Mexican caricaturist Miguel Covarrubias.
[4]Edna St. Vincent Millay, American poet.
[5]*Tarnish*, 1923, by Gilbert Emery.
[6]Ford Madox Ford, English novelist.
[7]*The Making of Americans* appeared in monthly installments, April through December, in *The Transatlantic Review*.
[8]*To Do: A Book of Alphabets and Birthdays* remained unpublished until 1957 when it appeared (without Picasso's illustrations) as the seventh volume of the Yale Edition of the Unpublished Writings of Gertrude Stein; *Portraits and Prayers*, with "Van or Twenty Years After," remained unpublished until 1934.
[9]Joseph Hergesheimer, CVV's entré into the Richmond literary circle.

Again, I took a trunk. This time it is full of J. B. C[abell]'s books for inscription. The initials of this hotel (designed by Stanford White) are identical with Joe's & they are plastered on every column & all the silver. I was desolate until I discovered the Confederate Veterans of Virginia.

TO EMMA GRAY TRIGG                    151 East 19th Street
8 April 1924                          New York City

Dear Emma Gray, I promised your splendid mother to look into the matter of Scotch whisky for her, and it was the first thing I attended to upon my return. My excellent bootlegger assures me that he sends packages all over the place—St. Louis, Chicago, where not—and that there has never been the least difficulty. He packs the bottles in excelsior, puts them in a barrel or something that doesn't look like a case, labels them preserves or tanagra figures, and sends them by express. The price for a case of Scotch (12 bottles) is $60.00 which includes packing charges. If your mother wants this done she might prefer to have the case sent c/o Billy. Cheques should be made out to Jack Harper. Of course, he can get you *anything* from champagne to bacardi.

What a splendid time I had with you dear people and how much I love you all. Please convey my warmest appreciation & affection to Delia, Dick, & Billy—*more* even to your blessed mother. You were all so good to me. And, to you, dear Emma Gray, I bow my lowest.      Carl Van Vechten

I expect to see Billy in May—& you & Delia later—in New York. Marinoff wishes to be remembered to you. She is leaving tomorrow for a week at Atlantic City.

TO ELLEN GLASGOW                      150 West 55th Street
9 April 1924                          New York City

My dear Miss Glasgow, One of the principal reasons for my trip to Richmond was to meet you, a reason richly satisfactory in results. Do let me thank you for your great kindness to me—and do let me hope that we shall soon meet again. If you come to New York please let me know. Will you present Miss Bennett[1] with my best wishes, and to you my lowest bow.

very sincerely, Carl Van Vechten
Scheherazade sent Jeremy her photograph yesterday.[2] Tomorrow I shall write to Hugh [Walpole].

---

[1] Ann Virginia Bennett, Ellen Glasgow's companion.
[2] Scheherazade was CVV's cat; Jeremy was Glasgow's dog.

## TO GERTRUDE STEIN
## 13 April 1924

151 East 19th Street
New York City

Dear Gertrude, I am delighted to hear the news about The Family [*The Making of Americans*]. I think this will be an excellent way to get some public reaction to this work and also will furnish it with a lot of splendid publicity. I hope it will enable Knopf to make up his mind about it. I have asked him to return Volume III to you; if it doesn't arrive within a reasonable period let me know.

I have given my portrait, Van After Twenty Years, to The Reviewer. There were about fourteen editorials about The Indian Boy and they were overjoyed to have the new one.[3] When I was recently in Richmond I was asked more questions about you than about any one else.

A bookseller friend of mine wishes to know if copies of the birthday book are to be on sale, and, if so, from what publisher or dealer in Paris they can be ordered. Will you let me know about this.

Mrs. [Arthur] Acton is all wrong about Mr. Wu, but almost everything else has happened.[4] D. H. Lawrence has returned to Taos, and according to a recent letter, beer and jazz records can only be brought out after he has retired. His scorn, it seems, is feared.[5]

I think you will like Prancing Nigger by Ronald Firbank. It is published by Brentano's in this country and you can probably get it at Brentano's in Paris.     saluti, Carl Van Vechten

## TO EDNA KENTON
## 30 June 1924

150 West 55th Street
New York City

Dearest, Doris [Reber] arrived on Saturday (or should have; I haven't seen her) for two weeks in New York before Europe. Like the late George Atherton[6] she will probably sail the seas pickled in rum. Coincidental with this arrival I have been rearranging my letters and have reread yours: the

---

[3]Over the protests of the editors, CVV insisted that the *Reviewer* print work by Gertrude Stein. "An Indian Boy" appeared in the January 1924 issue, and "Van or Twenty Years After, a Second Portrait of Carl Van Vechten" appeared in the April 1924 issue.
[4]*Mr. Wu*, circa 1920, a play by H. M. Vernon and Harold Owen, or *Mr. Wu*, circa 1920, a novel based on it by Louise Jordan Miln.
[5]CVV to Gertrude Stein, 13 June 1924: "D. H. Lawrence & his big German wife Frieda, are living in a cottage on Mabel's estates. Mabel and The Indian are living at the big *house*. Every morning at 7—Mabel hurries up the hill, gets breakfast for D. H. & *Frieda*, washes pots & pans etc. [. . .]Aren't you happy to see Mabel functioning so nobly."
[6]George Atherton, Gertrude Atherton's husband.

whole, screaming Doris histoire is there, from beginning to end. Some matters offer topics for discussion. For instance, after she took what she took, and Eddie the Mutt[7] withdrew, Doris departed for New York on April 27, 1916. You may have forgotten how time flies. Figuring on the basis that she had studied at least one year before this (and it may have been two [. . .], you will now perceive that Doris has been preparing for her opera career for *nine years*. Well, Columbus did not set out with the intention of discovering America. Eddie seems to have been a good prophet. Again and again he remarked, "You'll never sing in *Grand* Opera. You ain't got it in ya." Another detail of still more importance rises. I had always blamed myself for the Louis [Sherwin] episode, but I discover that it was you who suggested it. In October, 1915, Doris came to New York with George Ramsay, putting up at the Astor. On October 24, 1915, you wrote informing me of that fact, and you continue, sweetly, subtly, with devilish innuendo, "I have always seen these two meeting." In June, 1918, Ida Reber, enraged because Louis has shut her out of the bathroom, making her suffer "ten thousand hells," and has walked off with all her sofa cushions, emerges as a hierophant, writing Doris: "There is a black side that will show itself one day. In his own heart he knows it is there now. A man without a conscience or honour can never succeed for long at a time." [. . .] Oh, yes, there is a Sinclair Lewis theme, too. Every year or so there is a reference to Hal's[8] second or fifth attempt to bring you and Grace [Hegger Lewis] together, so that she may like you. From the beginning you have written invariably, "I have always been willing." [. . .] The heat and the fact that I am in a hell of a mess in the middle of a book have put me in a bad way. Marinoff is spending the Fourth and ensuing days till Monday at Sag Harbour. [. . .] I wonder if it will amuse you to come up one of those lonely holiday nights [. . .] and make raspberry shortcake. I may be going through a change of life [. . .]. At any rate I feel that (for the fiftieth time) I am on the verge of knowing some new people. Somehow, at these transition periods, I never fail to think tenderly of you!     with every wish for your continued good health, with rosemary and pansies, I remain,

    Carl Van Vechten

Seventeen years ago yesterday (Saturday was the day of the week) I married

---

[7]Eddie the Mutt: Doris Reber's early lover, always referred to by this appellation and otherwise unidentifiable.

[8]Sinclair Lewis was called "Hal" at least since he and CVV had lived in the same rooming house in 1906.

an innocent little Iowa girl in London.[9] I have been reading Donald Evans's letters too. Do you think this is mere morbidity, or an outbreak of the castration complex?

TO PHILIP MOELLER                                      150 West 55th Street
15 July 1924                                           New York City

Dear Philip, How nice of you to write me all about Ronald![1] Hunter Stagg says that you have caught him on paper for all time! I thought you might write again after the dinner—but you didn't. He did. However, without descriptive details, & *thanked* me for sending you, and another youth wrote me that he had dined with Firbank "the day after Mr. Moeller." I think you will like our new house. It is pretty well settled but there is no place to sit down. I am constantly reminded of the wail of the old gentleman in Trelawney of the Wells: "Cheers, Cheers. Have we no cheers?" Across the street is a mosque, with a façade of effulgent tiles, cupolas, gilded [?] windows, moorish arches, & a dome surmounted by a scimitar & crescent. Soon, funny, fat men in fezzes will run in & out. Down the way is a Venetian palazzo with a painted façade. This, then, is my environment. We have no cook now but we did have a splendid one.—and doubtless we shall have another. But the gem of our collection is Marinoff's new old Boulle dressing-table. There is one exactly like it in the Palais at Versailles. I am about through another novel: The Tattooed Countess will be out in a week & I shall reserve your copy for you. I hope you are reserving my copy of Fata Morgana[2] for me. Have you heard what has happened to Helen [Westley]? Her young man simply couldn't stand it in Europe without her & he has *returned* to her arms & her apartment where they are living in absolute bliss. I hope you are coming back soon.      Poppies & corn flowers to you, Carlo

---

[9]CVV married Anna Elizabeth Snyder on 29 June 1907; Kenton had known them both in Chicago before that.
[1]CVV to Hunter Stagg, quoting Philip Moeller on Ronald Firbank, 21 June 1924: "No one but he could have so deliciously seemed to get behind himself. [. . .] I thought at any moment his leg would lift in wriggles and get about his neck. I've never seen any one seem to droop so in fifteen different ways and still stay standing. [. . .] He seems to be delightful but my only impression so far is that if he suddenly stood still, I don't think he would be there."
[2]*Fata Morgana,* by Ernest Vajda, translated by James L. Burrel and Philip Moeller.

## TO FLORINE STETTHEIMER

151 West 55th Street
New York City

15 July 1924

Dear Florine, Thanks for your pretty postcards & thank Ettie for her amusing letters. Also tell Ettie that I changed my belt for three beautiful ties. I wish I could see the window you "trimmed." Some window! I'll bet. We have been doing our own work for some time. Our faithful Eva left suddenly one day to go to the bedside of a dying father. This was the second relative she killed in three weeks. Life is very quiet but I am working very hard on a new novel. I shall write a chapter a day until the first draught is completed. Shall I send *you your* copy of The Tattooed Countess to the Greylock? It will be ready early in August. Instruct me, as Ettie speaks of going to Cape Cod. The weather here has been affreux but our apartment is cool & I dress very much like Beatrice Wanger[3] & manage to keep comfortable. Carrie has not written to us & we feel this deeply. Is she busy looking into the little dishes?

with our warmest salutations, Carl Van Vechten

## TO THEODORE DREISER

150 West 55th Street
New York City

15 August 1924

Dear Dreiser, When I telephone Chelsea 2163 an evil Jap answers and tells me you don't live there. Have I the number wrong? I thought it was what you gave me. In regard to the manuscript, I am not your man. I don't take the slightest interest in such discussions & besides I loathe reading manuscripts. But I can make a helpful suggestion. Last night Robert Morss Lovett (one of the editors of The New Republic & a professor in the University of Chicago) came to see me & I discussed this matter with him. At once he said to advise you to send the manuscript to John M. Manly at the University of Chicago. Manly is, I think, head of the English department. At any rate Shakespeare is his major interest. He has read everything on the subject & wants to read more. And he is in a position which will make it possible for him to get anything he recommends published. Lovett says that if *you* write him a letter asking him to examine the mss. that Manly will be flattered to death & will be delighted to do so. Of course, mention Lovett's name.

I'm glad you liked Powys but I knew you would. See if his brother hasn't

---

[3]Beatrice Wanger, niece of Florine, Ettie, and Carrie Stettheimer, noted for diaphanous high fashion.

a copy of Soliloquies of a Hermit (*not* published by Knopf).[4] This is his *spiritual* (?) autobiography & the real *goods*. It is a denial of practically *all* the excuses discussed so far for existence. I think you will regard this opus with favor.

I enjoyed our talk on the Hudson as I always enjoy talking with you. If you will send me the correct version of your telephone number (perhaps, after all, it was Central who gave the wrong number & connected me with the evil Jap) I shall try to persuade you to grant me another audience.     Goldenrod & edelweiss to you, Carl Van Vechten

TO ARTHUR DAVISON FICKE                    150 West 55th Street
30 August 1924                                      New York City

The musk-melon seed velvet collars, dear Arthur, were very real. Well, I remember my sister sitting on the front porch, a bunch of dried seeds by her side, a strip of black velvet ribbon in her lap, composing a design for a masterpiece. There were even attempts at embroidering whole dresses in this fashion . . . And the title *[The Tattooed Countess]* is *in* my *third* manner. One of the reasons for it is that the Countess was certainly full of pricks. Anyway you are a duck to like my little opus so much—and I hope Gladys had pleasant reactions too.

I should certainly like to see you on a horse. Myself, I should prefer a camel. I rode a donkey once—at Vallombrosa—but my legs dragged on the ground, so that thrill was neither danger nor delight.—A fair amount of dignity was achieved, however.

When are you coming back? You must come right up. The house is "fixed up" enough—but I need about 5,000 dollars more for embellishments. Perhaps I'll get it through the Countess. I was published on August 15, & in two days I was the best seller in Chicago, and am now in the 5th edition.

I am writing another called Firecrackers. Is this a *third* manner title?

I am looking forward to the possession of the prints you bought for me in Paris.

Marinoff & I send cornflowers & poppies to you & Gladys.[5]     Carlo

[4]Llewelyn Powys, The English writer visiting his brother John Cowper Powys in New York, attended Theodore Dreiser's celebrated (and frequently described) literary soirée, at which nothing was served to drink, and later wrote about it in *The Verdict of Bridlegoose*, recalling CVV "like an aging madonna lily that had lost its pollen and had been left standing in a vase which the parlor-maid had forgotten to refill with fresh water." A third Powys brother, Theodore Francis, wrote *The Soliloquy of a Hermit* in 1916, published in America as *Soliloquies of a Hermit* two years later.
[5]Gladys Brown Ficke (Mrs Arthur Davison). See List of recipients.

TO EDNA KENTON                           150 West 55th Street
[August 1924]                            New York City

Dear Miss Kenton, Thanks for your grand letter. The Stettheimers, en masse, on the way to another hotel, stopped in last night *with* mother. They have been to *four* and Tuesday Ettie is taking mother to the Ritz in Atlantic City. Florine and Carrie remain in New York, each at her little apartment. Mother likes hotel life so much that they are thinking of giving up the house for the winter and travelling from place to place. Mother is very healthy and I think a trip abroad will be the next thing she'll want. When she decided to go home last evening, after a call of the proper conventional length, her daughters attempted to persuade her to stay, "just for a glass of lemonade, mother." She just got up and swept the whole brood out of the place.

I am enclosing the Chicago reviews which it may interest you to read. Please return them. The other Tribune clipping is an editorial.* The *[Tattooed]* Countess went to the printer for the *fifth* time last Monday. She is now in her nineteenth thousand, and out only two weeks tomorrow.

Walter White, the author of The Fire in the Flint,[6] spent two hours with me the other day. He speaks French and talks about Debussy and Marcel Proust in an offhand way. An entirely new kind of Negro to me. I shall, I hope, see something of these cultured circles. Being a great deal whiter than Waldo Frank he does not travel in Jim Crow cars. He relates with glee his experience with a Georgia cracker who boasted he could always tell a nigger. "They always have a purple streak in their finger-nails," he explained, pointing to Walter's hands without the streak.    with much love, Carlo

In case of death, I hope it can be arranged for Bobby [Locher] and James Keating to lie together, so that Helen [Westley] may sprinkle tube-roses in a wholesale way.

*Harry Hansen writes me that this will drive Fanny [Butcher] after her own review, mad, as she always stands for Correct Behaviour. Sinclair Lewis is in *this* week's number of the Saturday Review

[6]CVV to Hunter Stagg, 21 June 1924: "It is a fine book and sensational to any degree. Blacks call Georgia crackers 'white bastards' and there are chapters about the K[u] K[lux] K[lan] that Mencken might have written if Mencken wrote in Blood and giggled simultaneously."

## TO MABEL DODGE LUHAN
[summer 1924]

150 West 55th Street
New York City

Yes, dear Mabel, you told me years ago that all your letters and papers were to come to me. Do not change this clause in your will—on any account. However, I have scant hope of ever seeing these documents except, perhaps, when I am too toothless, withered, & palsied to care whether I do or not. I have a strange feeling that you & I will outlive each other. [. . .] Why don't you let Firbank write his own books? He has written about a dozen & if I wrote them & my own, too, think of the labour. I'm glad you liked my [Tattooed] Countess. To her personally I am devoted, although in real life she would be a person not to know. Ida Rauh, who sees *you* in all my books, sees you even in this! Well, *we* don't, do we? There will be, I think, a flickering glimpse, like a flashback in a motion picture, of Edith Dale in the book I am writing now. [. . .] I am causing to have sent to you soon a novel, The Fire in the Flint, written by a Nigger. It is some document & I want you to talk about it & write intriguing letters around the world about it. I was thinking the other day that if *all* your acquaintances read a book that it would sell out *three* large editions. If you have a Santo you are tired of I have a spot on my wall where I would love to hang it.[7]   Love, Carl Van Vechten

## TO GERTRUDE STEIN
8 September [1924]

150 West 55th Street
New York City

Dear Gertrude, Thanks for your nice letter. I'm glad you found my Iowa gentle. In Iowa they seem to take the book that way but in the east they seem to regard it as a vicious attack. I have written Firbank that you want to see him & I hope he will call on you someday but he is described by those who have seen him as excessively shy.

Mabel [Dodge Luhan] dropped into New York unexpectedly the other day & came up to see me. Avery Hopwood happened to be here a little drunk. He was amusing. The next day Mabel wrote me a letter saying she couldn't come to my house again, that she didn't like to see people in that condition. "You know," she wrote, "that one of the modern conventions that I can't conform to is the continual public catharsis" etc. etc. etc. O, such a long letter! "I like *you* very much" etc. etc. I was very much amused. I cannot keep Avery sober—and I don't want to keep him out of the house when he wants to come. And some people like to see him just as much as they like to see an Indian chauffeur, drunk or sober—so I just haven't

[7]Santos: Mexican religious statues carved of wood.

70

answered Mabel's letter—I can't think of anything to say.     Mignonette
& pansies to you and Miss Toklas.   Carl Van Vechten

## TO JAMES BRANCH CABELL
29 September 1924

150 West 55th Street
New York City

Dear James, I am infinitely delighted to possess an inscribed copy of the new edition of From the Hidden Way. I must confess to you that poetry says as little to me as you admit books on music say to you—but as an added feature of my collection it has a distinct value to me.[. . .] I am finishing the third & final draught of a book called Firecrackers which I have decided to send into the world as "a realistic novel"—How splendid if [M. P.] Shiel had thought of doing that for The Lord of the Sea! Firecrackers has afforded me so many difficulties, so many tiresome days, so much real perplexity, that—on the eve of setting down finis—I am inclined to regard it with reasonable scorn.     Goldenrod & asters to you & Priscilla,
    Carl Van Vechten

I am urged by the Knopfs to attend a "book fair"—whatever that may be—in Richmond during the week of September 10. Having been highly diverted—not to say amused—by the last class reunion of authors in the ancient capital of the South, I am considering this plan with some seriousness. I presume that Emily will find it convenient to defer her nuptials until after this event.[8] . . .As I write these lines a clipping from a Richmond paper arrives—[. . .] Louis Bromfield ha[s] already accepted! I quiver with impatience!

## TO MABEL DODGE LUHAN
8 October 1924

151 West 55th Street
New York City

Dere Mabel, Thanks for your lovely letters—at least there were so many enclosures that I felt there were at least *three* letters—and all of them scarlet. I do not care so much for Change of Life as I do for the Pansy Bed but I like it, and Johnson's portrait of you has the same fault that *all* portraits of you have, that it has succeeded in making the artist self-conscious while you elude him.[9] That is all artists but me, because I am modest and when I do you—as in Peter Whiffle—I attempt only the faintest one-dimensional portrait, and so make that much richer than if I had tried to get you down in three dimensions, to say nothing of four.

[8]Emily Clark had announced her engagement to Edwin Balch of Philadelphia, thereby terminating her association with *The Reviewer.*
[9]Spud [Willard] Johnson, who had written about Mabel Dodge Luhan in his little magazine, *Laughing Horse,* for which Luhan in turn had contributed several pieces.

And, of course, what you say about me and sex is perfectly foolish. I *never* invent stories. I always select a classic theme and write modern variations around it. Peter Whiffle is Elektra or Hamlet; The Blind Bow-Boy is my version of The Pilgrim's Progress; and The Tattooed Countess is Phaedra. My new novel, Firecrackers, nearly complete, is, I should say, Parsifal or, more probably, Savonarola! My intention in writing is to create moods, to awaken unconscious echoes of the past, to render to shadows their real importance. I don't think I ever think of sex at all. It plays around here and there, but that's not what my books are about. They seem to me to be books about a man who is alone in the world and is very sad.

I hope you will be in New York soon!　　Love, Carlo

What did you think about The Fire in the Flint?

TO HUGH WALPOLE　　　　　　　　　　150 West 55th Street
18 October 1924　　　　　　　　　　　New York City

Dear Hugh, Thank you for your adorable letter and for The Dark Forest— The Old Ladies have not yet put in an appearance, but I run to the door every time the mailman arrives and clamour for it![1] I think you are quite right in everything you say about The *[Tattooed]* Countess, that is everything but the catalogues. The period *is* done as everybody in the middle-west recognizes and catalogues are part of my interesting temperament. As so many people object to them I know that they must be an essential part of me. But, of course, The Countess is not as *done* as The Blind Bow-Boy, nor anywhere nearly so difficult to do. I met Maugham,[2] at last, the afternoon before he left for Honduras, and three days later, from New Orleans, I received a perfectly amazing letter from him about The Countess, which he had taken with him. He literally stopped at nothing, ending by admitting that he had never read The Bow-Boy. I sent that off to him to the City of Mexico. [. . .] In spite of a series of most incomprehending reviews—good and bad, none of the men seem to have any idea what I was driving at, assuming that I have contrasted the sophistication of The Countess against the naiveté of a small town, when I should think it would be obvious to any fair intelligence that the Countess is merely a worldly, sex-beset moron, seduced, for purposes of his own, by a ruthless youth whose imaginative sophistication transcends all of the Countess's experience; Maugham wrote me: God help the Countess when she gets Gareth to Paris: I have been

---

[1]*The Dark Forest* and *The Old Ladies,* novels by Walpole.
[2]W. Somerset Maugham, English novelist.

there with him, and I know! or words to that effect—my Countess has already gone over 20,000. The English publication is not yet arranged. Richards wanted her, but I thought this would be an excellent opportunity to part company with him. He had never sent me any royalty reports, until, when he cabled for The Countess, we thought this was an excellent opportunity to suggest that he repair that omission, and contrived to drag £100 out of him before we refused to let him have it. I am going West next week, for the first time in three years; so that England is probably postponed at least until Spring. When I return I *may* write an opera, for the music of George Gershwin. He has an excellent idea, and I am tempted—a serious jazz opera, without spoken dialogue, all for Nègres! He has unlimited funds to produce this. By the way, I had Ernest Newman[3] here the other evening to listen to Gershwin, an historic occasion![. . .] By the way, I have a piano again now[4]—again having room for one, and a phonograph. So, to some extent, I am going in for music again, but jazz, toujours jazz!     with my love,   Carl Van Vechten

TO FANIA MARINOFF          Chicago and Great Western Railway
[23 October 1924]          [enroute]

Dearest Baby, [. . .] excuse writing. I am not ginny but the roadbed is punk. This is the same train that Ella Nattatorrini[5] took in 1897—& I share all her feelings. Everything is just the same. I've been thinking more about the opera & I have more ideas—but I'm sure Gershwin wants something different, and nothing will come of it. In that case I think I'll write a Negro novel.[6] [. . .] *Hold* all mail in New York after Saturday until I telegraph you when & where to send it to Chicago. I can't have you forward it to Minnesota because I haven't any idea whether I'll be there one day or four until I see what it's like. But in case you have to reach me my address there will be % Mrs. Walter Douglas, Walden, Excelsior, Minnesota.[7] You can telegraph if anything important comes up. [. . .] I hope you & the Poo are well—     All my love, Carlo

---

[3]Ernest Newman, music critic and historian, most notable for his studies of Richard Wagner.
[4]Having no space for it in her apartment, the actress Marie Doro gave her Knabe grand piano to CVV.
[5]Ella Nattatorrini, the title character in *The Tattooed Countess*, 1924.
[6]This may be CVV's first reference to *Nigger Heaven*, begun a year later.
[7]Mahala Dutton Benedict Douglas, widow of Quaker Oats mogul Walter Douglas who went down on the Titanic. CVV had known her since his youth in Cedar Rapids. She was in part the model for Ella Nattatorrini.

## TO FANIA MARINOFF
[11 December 1924]

Jefferson Hotel
Richmond, Virginia

Dearest Babykins, I spent nearly the whole day yesterday with [James Branch] Cabell alone. It's the only way to get to know this strange man. They did not have a fire in the house, however, & as it had turned colder I thought I should come away with pneumonia. And last night I dined alone with Ellen Glasgow & we talked together until ten-thirty. We supped rather than dined—It was a regular Richmond supper. First fruit cocktail, then—all at once—partridge, tomatoes, baked apples, beans, and *eight* kinds of hot bread, including waffles & batter bread. Then salad & ice-cream. At ten-thirty we went on to a dance given by the richest & most powerful social family in Richmond, for Miss Glasgow's niece from London.—There are, I can assure you, very few Southern beauties here now—and the men all look like aenemic Tom Smiths.[8] But it is interesting to watch the frumpy respectability of it all.[9] Miss Glasgow's niece, dressed in London, looked smart in comparison with most of the belles.[. . .]      all my love, Carlo

## TO SCOTT CUNNINGHAM
[circa January 1925]

150 West 55th Street
New York City

Dear Duke, Thanks for your nice letter. By the way, I wore your tie all the time I was signing copies to send away. For *your* sake I am not going to let you see proofs of Firecrackers. I see small chance of my getting away very soon: New York is too amusing. Saturday night, for instance, at a party here, Adele Astaire danced, Marguerite D'Alvarez and Mary Ellis sang Gershwin songs, Gershwin played—all of the Rhapsody, among other things.[1] Also seven Negroes were present, all of them interesting in one way or another: Paul Robeson singing spirituals is really a thrilling experience [. . .]. Several minor celebrities were present, such as Zuloaga,[2] Covarrubias, and Otto Kahn. The latter offered unlimited funds for the

[8]Tom Smith, American editor and publisher.
[9]CVV to Florine Stettheimer, 22 February 1923: "Travelling is uncomfortable & it annoys me to watch roses bloom in February under dusty rusty trees. The tropics are nothing to me. The dilapidation & sordid splendors of the South do not awaken my sympathy."
[1]CVV to Bruce Kellner, 13 June 1963: "Before he actually finished the rhapsody [*In Blue*] George played it one night chez nous, 150 West 55th Street. He was there most of the night. [. . .]"
[2]Ignacio Zuloaga y Zabaleta, Spanish painter.

74

establishment of a Negro theatre as the result of the evening. Nevertheless, I want to see you! [unsigned]

I am half way through Excavations. It will be a very long book. Publication date: January 2, 1926. The galley proofs of Firecrackers, ripped to pieces, have gone back to the office. Did I tell you that I have written a piece about Gershwin for Vanity Fair: March number, I think.

## TO FANIA MARINOFF
[19 February 1925]

150 West 55th Street
New York City

Dearest Babykins, [. . .] We had a grand tea party yesterday: Gertrude, Ralph [Van Vechten?], Mahala [Douglas], Avery [Hopwood]. Gertrude was in great form and lit into the Liverights. She called Otto a slimy little worm and Horace a mass of obvious and cheap sensuality. She says that Horace awakens all her sadistic impulses and that she treats him like the devil.[3] [. . .] I am lunching with Carrie [Stettheimer] tomorrow. Mahala has just asked me to a party Saturday. Tonight Donald [Angus] is coming to dinner, and Countée[4] is giving me my first lesson in the Charleston, after dinner. All day, as usual, I work. After dinner last night I went to Ettie's party: [. . .] I managed to break a fruit dish and a cup and saucer without arousing Ettie's ire. [. . .] Blanche threw all discretion aside last night, and told me she was tired of sleeping with Alfred. What is the world coming to?

all my love to you, dearest Baby, Carlo

## TO HUGH WALPOLE
29 April 1925

150 West 55th Street
New York City

Dear old Hugh, [. . .] Maugham is a duck. He has been saying the most splendid things about me, in and out of print, and it is good of him to continue doing so in London. *You,* of course, have been an angel in this respect and I hope you will always continue to be one. I am glad to hear the splendid news about Melchior. I haven't been inside the Metropolitan [Opera] for four years, but his advent may lead me there once. [. . .]

I haven't yet met Michael Arlen. He is mostly in moving picture circles. His play, The Green Hat, with Katharine Cornell, is playing in Chicago to about $19,000 a week and he is making lots of money. Also I hear that

---

[3]Horace and Otto Liveright were Gertrude Atherton's publishers.
[4]Countee Cullen, black American poet. See List of recipients.

he is being paid $25,000 to write a scenario for Pola Negri.[5] Joe [Hergesheimer] has been in Cuba and Mexico and I have not seen him for two or three months. He called up on his return last week, but we were unable to arrange a meeting. Ellen Glasgow's new book [*On*] Barren Ground, is splendid, and has been warmly received. She is coming to New York again in the middle of May.

In a couple of months I shall be sending you my new novel, Firecrackers. I can't hope that you will like it much. It is a modern treatment of the Parsifal theme . . . I have also arranged a book of literary papers (all old) under the name of Excavations which will be published in January 1926. [. . .] No one, save Grant Richards, wanted to publish my [*Tattooed*] Countess in England. Just as well, perhaps, from what you tell me in regard to the reception of American novels there. Yet I count two English novelists among my warmest admirers. I have written a paper about Ernest Newman for Alfred's Borzoi Book commemorating his tenth year as a publisher, and I have written prefaces to two books of drawings, one by Alastair (with seven illustrations for The Blind Bow-Boy)—which, by the way, Maugham likes less than the Countess), the other by Covarrubias, the Mexican caricaturist. These last three are scheduled for the fall. I am pretty well cleaned up, therefore, and presently expect to start work on a subject that has obsessed me for some time, a novel about Negroes.

Well, dear old Hugh, I'm very fond of you. [. . .] And it is great news to learn that you will be over next year. I make plans to go to London occasionally, but lose my nerve. I want to see *you*, and one or two others, but, aside from that, I don't want to go at all.     love, Carl Van Vechten

## TO FANIA MARINOFF
3 May [1925]

150 West 55th Street
New York City

My dearest Angel, I miss you more and more and the poo has gone back to a slight attack of leukorrhea on account of your departure.[6] Nothing serious, and no blood. She eats like a horse and prances like a zebra but she discharged a couple of drops on Irene's[7] chair. Nothing very serious has happened; and nothing very important, except the Opportunity dinner and the events which followed it. Everybody went to the dinner, except the Walter Whites, even James Weldon [Johnson]. Fannie Hurst[8] was there

---

[5]Pola Negri, Polish film star, later in 1925 in *A Woman of the World*, a wildly inaccurate movie based on *The Tattooed Countess*.
[6]Fania Marinoff had sailed for Europe with Regina Wallace.
[7]Irene Marinoff, Fania Marinoff's niece.
[8]Fannie Hurst, American novelist. See List of recipients.

and Bob Davis[9] and the Van Dorens.[1] Langston Hughes received the first poetry prize and Countée Cullen the second; and Eric [Walrond] received the third short story prize. After dinner Rita,[2] Eric and I went to Mrs Walker's[3] apartment and about 1 o'clock we went on to the Y.M.C.A. dance, smaller but more amusing than the N.A.A.C.P. dance. Among other things there was a Charleston contest. Then, as guests of a party we went to Bamville. At 4.30 Rita, Eric, and I went to the Comedy Club. A large supper for forty was being served for Miss May of the Cotton Club who is leaving for Chicago and I cannot begin to tell you how marvellous it all was. The band from the Cotton Club was there and the performance was continuous, spontaneous, and thrilling. At a quarter of eight I drove Rita home through the sunlit, flowering park, where ladies and gentlemen were riding. As I walked in the door John [the doorman] was sorting the mail. A moment later a man came to tune the piano and so I decided not to go to bed at all. [. . .] Langston Hughes came to see me yesterday and I had dinner alone and went to bed. He is coming again this afternoon on his way to the train. He lives in Washington. Tonight we are all going to the Robeson concert and then to a party at Winold Reiss.[4] Tomorrow night Rita, Eric, and Louella Tucker[5] are coming here to dinner and then we are going to a party at A'Lelia Walker's. I am trying to finish up a paper on spirituals for Vanity Fair and Lawrence[6] wants me to do a paper for the Theatre Magazine on Paul Robeson. Ella has been very good. She does everything I tell her without a murmur. On Friday she made a good start on my robe.

Remember me to Reg[ina Wallace]. AND ALL my love to you! Have a good time.     [unsigned]

If I write my Negro novel, and sometimes the difficulties frighten me, I am going to dedicate it to you. Lawrence wants to go to Harlem before he sails. Langston Hughes is one of the most interesting persons I've met. I paid your Equity dues.

[9]Robert James Davis, Australian photographer.
[1]Irita and Carl Van Doren, American writers. See List of recipients.
[2]Rita Romilly, American dance instructor and longtime social patron for black artists and writers.
[3]A'Lelia Walker, black heiress—her mother had perfected the hair-straightening process—and social arbiter in Harlem. See List of recipients.
[4]Winold Reiss, German-born painter best known for his portraits of celebrated black Americans and as teacher of several prominent black artists.
[5]Louella Tucker, black intellectual whose apartment at 580 St Nicholas Avenue in Harlem (which she shared with Ethel Ray Nance and Regina Anderson Andrews) served as a Harlem Renaissance salon for young black artists and writers.
[6]Lawrence Langner, co-director of the Theatre Guild.

TO H. L. MENCKEN                                    150 West 55th Street
29 May 1925                                         New York City

Dear Henry, [. . .] Your letters on music interested me profoundly—and despite the fact that I disagree with most of the opinions expressed I believe it to be as sound as any musical criticisms. I am more & more convinced that above a certain level—and not always even is this true—feeling for music is a personal taste and emotion even in what are regarded as the best critics. Myself, for example, am more moved by Debussy than by Strauss. Ernest Newman falls lower & hoists the Union Jack over Elgar & Hugo Wolf (whom he places above Schubert, almost haughtily, too). Newman also has a word of lusty praise for Berlioz. He once told me that Les Troyens was the greatest of modern operas. I must say that I applaud your opinion of Berlioz. When we come to a man like Finck,[7] the argument becomes absurdly axiomatic—Finck shrieking for Grieg, MacDowell, Wyat [?], Massenet, and even Rubinstein, & deriding Strauss and Brahms. But I daresay he has as much right to his personal taste as the rest of us. The fact is that writing men—and critics are writing men—seek a sort of Nirvana in music, a species of nervous excitement or the exalting of the nerves. Now, each of us being constituted differently each of us reacts differently to applied stimuli. I am therefore interested to see that you and I agree on certain fundamentals, certainly about Schubert's genius, about César Franck & Bizet. Elektra is my favorite of Strauss, but not Tod & Verklärung. I put Til Eulenspiegel next. This seems to me the epitome of Strauss's puckish perversity—with his faults left out. Beethoven, I would naturally regard as one of of the greatest composers, but his music has little to say to me. I prefer Gluck & Mozart. The Barber of Seville, which you no doubt detest, I consider a masterpiece. It is the one opera I never tire of. I could say almost the same for Gluck's Orfeo. I could no longer sit through a performance of Meistersinger: I appreciate its greatness, but I have heard it too often.

Well, a long letter—and about music, which, as is well known, is my discarded mistress. Jazz, the blues, Negro spirituals, all stimulate me enormously for the moment. Doubtless, I shall discard them too in time—at any rate, believe me your devoted admirer—and ora pro nobis.

Carl Van Vechten

I might add that I have secured an extra copy of my vicious songs, Five Old English Ditties—100 copies printed in 1904—for *you*. It is too unwieldly to mail with safety, but if you will make a rendezvous for lunch, dinner,

---

[7]Henry Theophilus Finck, American music critic.

H. L. Mencken, 1932

Langston Hughes, 1936

or cocktails for your next New York visit—any time will do, if you notify me a week ahead—I will present it to you officially. But perhaps you don't want this tautological specimen!

TO LANGSTON HUGHES                    150 West 55th Street
[May 1925]                            New York City

Your letters are so very charming, dear Langston, that I look forward every morning to finding one under the door. I have been lucky during the past week! The poems came this morning and I looked them over again. Your work has such a subtle sensitiveness that it improves with every reading. The poems are very beautiful and I think the book gains greatly by the new arrangement and title [*The Weary Blues*]. Knopf is lunching with me today and I shall ask him to publish them and if he doesn't some one else will. Would you permit me to do an introduction? I want to. [. . .]

I've never even heard of the Little Savoy; I wish I had been with you that night. I have never, in my experience of twenty-five years, seen a fight in a Negro cabaret; on the other hand I've never been in a white place when there wasn't one. The difference, I suppose, is that white people almost invariably become quarrelsome when they are drunk, while Negroes usually become gay and are not inclined to fight unless they want to kill some one. I'm going on a Harlem party tonight; if you were here we'd take you with us. [. . .]

You will find your name, by the way, in the note I have written about Countée Cullen in the June Vanity Fair, not yet out.

Will you do something for me? I want you, if you will, to write me out the story of your life—detailing as many of your peregrinations and jobs as you can remember. Is this too much to ask?

I'll let you know about your book as soon as possible. In the meantime, please don't forget     Carl Van Vechten

TO GERTRUDE STEIN                     150 West 55th Street
30 June 1925                          New York City

Dear Gertrude, I'm sorry that you and Fania could not connect. She is passing through Paris again along the middle of July. Perhaps something will happen then. She had at least one evening with Avery [Hopwood] in Paris . . . The Knopfs, it seems, are not going to Paris at all. Their route embraces London, San Sebastian, and Poland: God's truth! Nobody has ever made this tour before. It has something to do with AUTHORS!

I am so excited about *all* your new books and hope they will soon be coming along. I shall soon send you Firecrackers. At least two pages of it are sure to amuse you. I am reading proofs on Excavations, which is to come out in January, and when I have finished reading proofs, I shall start on my Negro novel. I have passed practically my whole winter in company with Negroes and have succeeded in getting into most of the important *sets*. This will not be a novel about Negroes in the South or white contacts or lynchings. It will be about NEGROES, as they live now in the new city of Harlem (which is part of New York). About 400,000 of them live there now, rich and poor, fast and slow, intellectual and ignorant. I hope it will be a good book. One of my best friends, Paul Robeson, goes to London in September to play The Emperor Jones. He is a great actor and when he sings spirituals he is as great as Chaliapin. I want you to meet him. If you are going to London in the fall let me arrange it. I can send you a letter or give him a letter or you can just collide.      with much love, Carlo

## TO ARTHUR DAVISON FICKE

3 August 1925

150 West 55th Street
New York City

Dearest Arthur—I had wondered what had become of you until I saw your name in Benét's[8] column—And so I was not too surprised when your letter with its unpleasant information arrived. Fortunately, a prominent physician told me, no longer ago than last Friday, that tuberculosis is no more dangerous nowadays than a bad cold. But you will probably be dreadfully bored—and anything I can do to alleviate that condition I'll be glad to. I shall begin, rather unpropitiously, by forwarding your copy of Firecrackers which has been ready for you since July 4. Also 4 French books—en suite— which may amuse you. At any rate they will cause no rise in temperature.

In response to your query I would reply that if I were a chameleon my colour would now be at least seal-brown. I see *no one* but Negroes—This accounts for my not having seen more of you—and presently I shall begin work on my Negro novel.

Marinoff got back from three months in Europe last Thursday—She does *all* my travelling for me now. I rarely if ever leave the house, but my life can scarcely be described as sedentary.

You do not mention Gladys, but I venture to send her my love—and believe, dear old Arthur, that I send *you* a lot of that.      Carlo

---

[8]William Rose Benét, American poet and critic, and *New York Evening Post* literary columnist; husband of Elinor Wylie.

TO LANGSTON HUGHES               150 West 55th Street
[early August 1925]                  New York City

Dear Langston, The histoire de ta vie[9] was so remarkable both as regards manner and matter that I hesitated for some time before deciding what should be done with it. It seemed absurd for me to write a preface about you when you had written such a beautiful one yourself, but another idea has dawned which seems even better. I have discussed the matter with Mrs. Knopf and she agrees with me fully. As I wrote you before I think you are a topnotch writer of prose: in this biography you have an amazing subject. Treat it romantically if you will, be as formless as you please, disregard chronology if you desire, weaving your story backwards and forwards, but however you do it I am certain not only that you can write a beautiful book, but also one that will *sell.* There will be in it not only exciting incident, vivid description of character and people and places, but something more besides: the soul of a young Negro with a nostalgia for beauty and colour and warmth: that is what I see in all your work. Now this is why the book will have an enormous appeal, because hundreds of young people, nay thousands, have this same nostalgia but they do not know how to express it, but they react to it emotionally when it is expressed. What I want you to do, therefore, is to *write this book.* It may be as long or as short as you please. I know it is hard to write a book with all the other things you have to do, but *I am sure you can do it.* What I am going to suggest to you is that you *make yourself* write a little every day: say 300 words. You will find this method hard at first and very easy after a week or two. In fact, some days you will want to write 2,000 words, but however many words you have produced on a certain day make yourself write the stipulated 300 on the next. [. . .] I shall be very happy when you write me that you have begun this book. Be as digressive as you please—when anything reminds you of something else, another experience, another episode, put it down. Try to be as frank as possible, but when your material runs a little thin, don't be afraid to imagine better material or to put down someone else's experience as your own. [. . .]

I hope Vanity Fair will like your poems as much as I did; but if they don't, remember that that will not destroy their beauty. I can recall the time, not so very long ago, when a paper of mine would come wandering back refused by eight or ten magazines. Off I would shoot it to another

---

[9]At CVV's urging, Langston Hughes wrote a short autobiographical memoir, "L'Histoire de ma vie."

and eventually it would usually be accepted. You have caught the jazz spirit and the jazz rhythm amazingly; some of them ought to be recited in stop-time!

Firecrackers is my new novel. In it appear characters from all the old ones. I hope soon to start work on my Negro novel, but I feel rather alarmed. It would have been comparatively easy for me to write it before I knew as much as I know now, enough to know that I am thoroughly ignorant! [. . .]     pansies and marguerites to you!   Carl

TO SCOTT CUNNINGHAM                    150 West 55th Street
16 August 1925                                      New York City

Of course, it is too delightful, dear Scott, & you are a *lamb* and an *angel.* It looks even better in the Post than it did in manuscript, and I believe it all![1] To my amazement Firecrackers apparently is going to be my best seller. It has already gone to 15,000.

As soon as I have finished reading page proofs of Excavations I shall settle down to my great work for which I have found so good a title—at present undivulged—that I feel it should be very easy to write the book.[2] I have not yet discovered a record of My Daddy Rocks Me for you, but you should know that I now have this ballad rendered viva voce chez moi.[3] My Harlem intimacies continue unabated, although, in certain quarters, alarm is beginning to be shown—caused by a justifiable fear that I will leave some one out of the book, and so, of course, I shall. The Robesons have gone to London, but his records will begin to appear in September. I think you will like Any Woman's Blues—Columbia 13001D & Sinful Blues—Columbia 14052D. Perhaps you have seen my paper on the Blues in the August Vanity Fair. In the September number I introduce Langston Hughes to the world. In the October number I have a paper on the Negro Theatre—largely unfavorable. There will be a picture of Clara Smith, than whom who is greater?     Remember me affectionately to yourself,
    Carl Van Vechten

---

[1]"Yellow Jackets," a review by Cunningham of *Firecrackers* in the *Chicago Evening Post,* 14 August 1925.
[2]*Nigger Heaven.*
[3]Nora Holt, the glamorous black singer and musician who became one of CVV's closest friends as well as the model for Lasca Sartoris, the steamy courtesan in *Nigger Heaven,* included this scabrous number in her regular repertoire.

## TO ELINOR WYLIE
7 October [1925]

150 West 55th Street<br>New York City

Naturally, dear Elinor, I thought it strange that you had not even written me to tell me that you did not like Firecrackers, and your inscription in The V[*enetian*]. G[*lass*]. N[*ephew*]. was extremely algid, but your note makes up for all. It is a very charming note . . . I hope you are finding some time for writing. You should have all the time & leisure in the world for your undertakings because you are one of *the* most important of living authors & I expect great things of you & get them. Moreover, I feel that your next book *will sell*. Do not, therefore, be too dramatic. Shirk as many responsibilities as possible, & devote your strength & beauty & charm to your *art*. You were never made to devote them to anything else. I hope when you are in town again that we can meet. For the first time in years I have no book finished—save a book of essays to appear in January. I have not even begun my black novel as I want to be free to go to Sicily or Spain or Cuba, if I can ever succeed in persuading myself that I shall like it as well as New York. [. . .]

I bow thrice and waft you a damask rose.     Carlo Van Vechten

## TO HUNTER STAGG
[16 November 1925]

150 West 55th Street<br>New York City

Well, dear Hunter, the concert last night was a sensation; but I couldn't go; the doctor had put me to bed the day before and said I must stay there. Anyway the concert was sold out; many were turned away. And at the end no one budged. Johnson and Gordon added four more songs, and could, doubtless, have sung till dawn.[4] The audience was a very brilliant one and included many celebrities. In fact it was made up of Jews, Negroes, and celebrities, and some were two of these. Afterwards Irita Van Doren gave a party. Emily Clark was Irita's guest at the concert and went to the party and so she has now met the James Weldon Johnsons, the Rosamond Johnsons, and Taylor Gordon, with what result I don't know, but she is coming to lunch with me tomorrow.

My health has been so shattered that I must plead that as my excuse for not having written to you before. [. . .] I have had a series of indigestions, colds, and coughs, and at last the doctor discovered (hence putting me to bed) that I had [. . .] a species of blood poisoning and he is already discussing

---

[4]Taylor Gordon, a black countertenor, and J. Rosamond Johnson, the composer-brother of James Weldon Johnson, had begun a series of recitals of Negro spirituals.

the possibility of removing my tonsils, my teeth, and my ovaries. You may see me some day, however, alive and well again. [. . .]

Did I write you that Gertrude Stein gave a large party for Paul and Essie [Robeson]? And Hugh Walpole writes me that he likes Paul better than almost any other American he has ever met. And the Revue Nègre in Paris is a sensation and having packed the Champs Elysées for six weeks has moved to another theatre. Such papers as the Figaro devote two serious columns to it, comparing the music to Stravinsky and the dancing with the Russian Ballet. And Josephine Baker, the leading woman, is now the best kept woman in Paris with a house on the Avenue du Bois de Boulogne! She was a chorus girl in the original production of Runnin' Wild. Well, life is dramatic.

I hope you are happier and that you are writing, if you want to write. Somehow, I can't care much what you do or what you don't do. It's all the same to me where my affection is concerned.     Carlo

TO LOUIS UNTERMEYER                    150 West 55th Street
28 November 1925                         New York City

Dear Louis, I'm sorry you couldn't come in to see Countée Cullen yesterday. Tuesday, December 1, Langston Hughes is coming up from Washington and I am giving a party for him that evening any time after nine. Will you and Jean Starr [Untermeyer] come? There will be Spirituals and don't dress and will you let me know?     ever, Carl Van Vechten

TO HUNTER STAGG                        150 West 55th Street
[early December 1925]                    New York City

Dear Hunter, No, I am not sick. I have never been quite so well, but I write all day and go out every night. The first draft of my novel is nearly complete and it is to be called "Nigger Heaven." I don't know yet quite what I think of it, but I've never found it easier to write anything and that is usually a good sign with me.[5] There are seven or eight things to do every night; often I content myself with going to bed at eight o'clock with a nice book. Did I tell you about my new Charleston teacher? Everybody asked me to find a Negro teacher and I dug up Charles Davis who put on "Shuffle Along." In his girls' class which has been running three weeks are Mary

[5]On November 30th, however, CVV wrote to H. L. Mencken, "At present I am in the midst of labor on a new novel which I expect will lay me low. I wish you'd give me an hour or two when you next come up: I need your optimistic Americanism. Ain't it hell to be a Nordic when you're struggling with Ethiopian psychology?"

Boland, Marinoff, Leonore Ulric, Anita Loos, Blanche Knopf, Helen Hayes, Rita Romilly, Regina Wallace, Helen Mencken, Phoebe Foster[6] . . . The man's class (with *me*) starts on Tuesday . . . I think you will find the motion picture version of "The Tattooed Countess" sufficiently amusing. I did. It is certainly sufficiently vulgar. [. . .] I gave a party for Langston Hughes who was up here for two days last week and I have promised one to Countée Cullen who is coming up for Christmas. I am invited to Ashville N. C. for Christmas, but of course I can't go anywhere just now. I am afraid you are using your excellent critical sense to too great effect on your own work. Probably anything you would do would be above the average. At any rate, you are *you*, whatever you do or don't do, and that is sufficient for people who like you . . . Emily [Clark Balch] is here tomorrow and has invited me to lunch with DuBose Heyward[7] . . . Langston, by the way, has written some really extraordinary Blues. He is going to do a book of Negro folk songs, some Spirituals, and some work and convict songs. Vachel Lindsay,[8] recently in Washington, has taken him up heavily.    cornflowers and appleblossoms to you!    Carlo

[J.] Rosamond Johnson & Taylor Gordon give their *third* concert at Town Hall on Dec. 27. Paul [Robeson] gets back next week and Walter White is giving a party for him the night he arrives.


TO COUNTEE CULLEN                           150 West 55th Street
11 December 1925                            New York City

Dear Countée, Let us make the party Wednesday evening, December 23, from nine o'clock, and, if you don't mind, informal, as I hate evening clothes. Will you let me know, please, by return mail if this is all right, as I must invite people right away if I expect to get any one here during Christmas week.

I read your review of Porgy[9] with great interest and approval. I, too, had not read this book when I made my statement about Jezebel.[1] Only one of your statements I would challenge—although heaven knows you know more about it than I do. I think, perhaps, it is a little excessive to make such an arcanum of the Negro mind. I believe all races to be more or less human, and susceptible to what are known as human reactions—I am

---

[6]The Charleston class was made up entirely of theater performers of the period except for Anita Loos, whose novel *Gentlemen Prefer Blondes* was currently popular, and Blanche Knopf.
[7]DuBose Heyward, American novelist and playwright best known for *Porgy*.
[8]Vachel Lindsay, American troubador poet.
[9]*Porgy* by DuBose Heyward, 1925.
[1]*The Wooings of Jezebel Pettyfer* by Haldane McFall, 1925.

speaking quite generally and include the Japanese and the Malays. In each case, however, these human reactions are modified by conditions (from within or without) which produce superficial differences in reactions. Thus conditions have created certain subtle differences in reactions between white Americans and American Negroes. On the other hand the Irish (or the Hindus) react in almost the precise manner that American Negroes do. I may be wrong; I often am, but I cannot help feeling that the distinction between white and colored psychology has been overstressed. I go into this a little in my review of The New Negro, which, on the whole, I think, is a superb book.[2]

Mrs. Knopf is forwarding you proofs of Langston [Hughes]'s book and my preface.[3] It is splendid of you to review it. I shall never cease to regret that we did not publish Color,[4] but that was not my fault, you will recall. However, if you want to send your next book to Knopf, I think they will be only too delighted to welcome it.

I look forward to seeing you at Christmas time.     always sincerely,
Carl Van Vechten

TO ALFRED A. KNOPF                    150 West 55th Street
20 December 1925                       New York City

Dear Alfred, I have the honour to announce that I have completed the first draft of "Nigger Heaven." The final manuscript will be ready late in March or early in April. Will you kindly, therefore, definitely schedule this book for August 15. I have already asked you to announce this book in your "Latest publishing arrangements." Further, I would suggest (if my argument meets with your approval) that you include such a line as "in preparation, NIGGER HEAVEN, a novel of contemporary Harlem life, by Carl Van Vechten" whenever you print the Negro list we spoke of the other day, and also, quite possibly, in connection with "Excavations." Ordinarily, I quite agree with you that books should not be advertised so long in advance, but this book is different. It is necessary to prepare the mind not only of my own public, but of the new public which this book may possibly reach, particularly that public which lies outside of New York. If they see the title, they will ask questions, or read "The New Negro" or something, so that the kind of life I am writing about will not come as an actual shock. To

---

[2]*The New Negro,* ed. Alain Locke, 1925.
[3]*The Weary Blues* by Langston Hughes, 1926.
[4]*Color by Countee Cullen, 1925:* Cullen had refused Van Vechten's offer to try to place the manuscript for *Color* with his own publisher, Alfred A. Knopf, choosing instead to place it with Harper.

that end, as you know, I have during the past year written countless articles on Negro subjects (I have one in the [*Herald*] Tribune today and two more are in proof chez Vanity Fair) and I have seen to it that as many outof-towners as possible saw enough of the life themselves so that they would carry some news of it back to where they came from.     with these words I beg to remain your humble servant and devoted author, Carlo

## TO H. L. MENCKEN
[circa 1925]

150 West 55th Street
New York City

Dear Henry, You overwhelm me with your kindnesses! And as a pamphleteer you are beginning to surpass the prolific eighteenth century fellows. In regard to Hal [Sinclair] Lewis, he called me on Saturday, asking me to join a party of dukes, princes, & archduchesses—what he called "extremely sophisticated middle-Europeans." I was not up to this in the heat—and passed it by.     Bien à toi, Carl Van Vechten
I was out last night with the Sheka of Harlem [Nora Holt]. She looks like Mary Garden & her trail is strewn with bones, many of them no longer hard. Her last husband[5] had the restaurant privileges in the Bethlehem Steel Works. He settled $50,000 on her when she married him. Soon thereafter she began to operate on so extensive a scale that Mr. Charlie Schwab became alarmed and demanded that her husband divorce her so that she could be removed from Bethlehem.

## TO H. L. MENCKEN
9 February [1926]

150 West 55th Street
New York City

Dear Henry, [. . .] I am decaying rapidly: senility is setting in. I hope to live long enough to finish Nigger Heaven. Then perhaps I can have a coloured Masonic funeral—with the sky lit by flaming crosses set up by the K.K.K.—In the meantime is anything scientific known about pyorhea (I haven't enjoyed it long enough to learn the spelling) at Johns Hopkins?

Guy Johnson (co-author of The Negro & His Songs) of the University of North Carolina was here last week. He has the skeleton of a fine article on the Blues (with a new idea). I advised him to send it to you, when complete. Also, he is working on a paper concerning the songs & legends connected with John Henry, the famous black [. . .] hammer driver. I once spoke to you about him. I think you would do well to write to the professor

---

[5]Nora Holt's fifth husband, Joseph L. Ray, had been preceded by musician Sky James, politician Philip Scroggins, barber Bruce Jones, and hotel owner George Holt.

(or his partner [Howard] Odum). They are not very lively writers, but they have collected more of the working, social, & whore-house lore of the Negroes than any one else. By the way, they have turned their entire collection (including tunes) over to Rosamond Johnson for setting.

I hope you will come to see me before I die.     Evergreens & balsams to you! Carlo V. V.

TO LOUIS BROMFIELD                                150 West 55th Street
4 March 1926                                      New York City

Dear Louis, I loved your letters and the picture of you and Mary out for the hunt. I think I shall send it to Vanity Fair or the New Yorker. You would have heard from me long ago—although you neglected to furnish me with an address in your first letter,—had I not been occupied up to the hilt—this sounds like a Jurgenism[6]—with my new novel, Nigger Heaven. I have worked on this for the past five months, sometimes as much as twelve hours a day. Writing letters afterwards was too much of a task. Now, however, the damn thing is finished and you know the feeling of helplessness that comes after.[7] I just don't know what to do. I might even go to Paris! Pourquoi pas, mon vieux! Everything has changed very much, as it always does in New York. Every year one knows new people and goes to unfamiliar places. Now that I have thoroughly explored Harlem, I think I shall take up the Chinese.     Fania and I send orchids, sapphires, zebras, and chocolate ice-cream to you and Mary! Carlo

TO HUNTER STAGG                                   150 West 55th Street
[21 May 1926]                                     New York City

Dear Hunter, The bibliographical description of [Herman Melville's] Omoo is much too long to quote to you, but the book was issued in 1847. It was reprinted four times that year and there is some argument among collectors as to which is really the first. The colour of the binding is unimportant, as in that period publishers were accustomed to use any cloth that happened to be around the place, and one edition might have fifty bindings . . . I heard at last from Nora [Holt] Ray. She sailed on Saturday on the France.

---

[6]Jurgenism: from James Branch Cabell's fantasy, *Jurgen*, 1919, notable for its sexual euphemisms.
[7]CVV to Alfred Knopf, 18 March 1926: "Believe me I shall hesitate before I enter into any more artistic race riots and orgies: the future is in the hands of my dear public. I can foresee no more than you what the result may be, but I shall always be grateful to you for pointing out the perils in advance."

I didn't see her. But I shall put certain persons in Europe in touch with her . . . Last night Elinor Wylie gave a dinner for Aldous Huxley.[8] I found him very long and he has queer eyes. Otherwise I can't think of anything to say about him. Probably you know him . . . James [Branch Cabell] writes me that he is dedicating The Music Behind the Moon (his new romance) to me. That, of course, is nice for me . . . Emily [Clark Balch] came over for the week-end and Margaret [Freeman] gave a party for her and I took the gals to dinner at a marvellous Japanese place I've just discovered where the food is cooked on the table before your eyes and under your grateful nose. Alice [Clark] is due in Philadelphia today and I think I shall run down next week to meet Sir Toby Belch [Edwin Balch] . . . I have finished reading page-proofs of Nigger Heaven, and I suggest that you refrain from reading it at all. It is *rotten* . . . Did you ever get Shake That Thing?[9]        many blossoms to you! Carlo

## TO JAMES WELDON JOHNSON                    150 West 55th Street
## 7 September 1926                           New York City

Dear James, I thought you might like to see a few more [reviews of *Nigger Heaven*]. You will particularly enjoy, I should think, Time and Dr. Hubert Harrison's[1] vivid report. The Baltimore Sun review is typical of the Southern reviews. Curiously enough, they have all been wonderful so far, and I've had them from Texas, Kentucky, West Virginia, California, and other states. Burton Rascoe writes for a syndicate and his review appeared in at least a hundred newspapers: I've had one of his clippings from Knoxville, Tenn. I thought Grace might like to read Charles S. Johnson's[2] letter which the Pittsburgh Courier printed. I'm sorry I haven't a copy at hand of the editorial in the Age. A lot of rotten characters who come to a bad end, is Fred Moore's[3] report: hence a fine book. The N.Y. News (colored) says that any one who would call a book Nigger Heaven would call a Negro Nigger. Harlem, it appears, is seething in controversy. Langston [Hughes], the other night in Craig's,[4] suggested to a few of the knockers that they might read the book before expressing their opinion, but this advice seems to be re-

---

[8]Aldous Huxley, English writer whose early novels, *Chrome Yellow* and *Antic Hay*, were frequently compared with CVV's.
[9]"Shake That Thing," 1925, a scabrous song by Papa Charlie Jackson, popularized by Ethel Waters and quoted (without permission) in *Nigger Heaven*.
[1]Hubert Harrison, black sociologist who passionately condemned *Nigger Heaven* in the *Amsterdam News*, 9 August 1926.
[2]Charles S. Johnson, President of the National Urban League. See List of recipients.
[3]Fred Moore, black owner and editor of the New York *Age*.
[4]A popular Harlem restaurant.

garded as supererogatory. Will you please return to me (as soon as possible) the Transcript, Courier, Rascoe, Baltimore Sun, and Tattler. The others you may keep, if you like.

Painters are all around and over us, but they shall be through by the end of this week. We send our love to you and Grace.     affectionately, Carlo V. V.

TO GERTRUDE STEIN                           150 West 55th Street
10 December 1926                             New York City

Dear Gertrude, Nora Holt writes "I went to tea at Gertrude Stein's and adored her. She is a great person," but I've heard nothing from you about her. She is now singing at Monte Carlo. I like the Hogarth Press edition of Composition as Explanation and have taken an especial fancy to the one about Jean Cocteau.[5] Did you ever know Germaine Tailleferre,[6] by the way? She has just married my friend Ralph Barton, three weeks after they met. Useful Knowledge (among Negroes) is simply stupendous and would help with white people too.[7] And I learn that the Bonis are to do Three Lives.[8] Hurray for our side! . . . I have a bad cold and don't feel that I can ever write again . . . and I haven't written a line since March 1, and do you think I'd like Antibes? Mrs. [Carolyn Dudley] Regan is trying to put on another Révue Nègre, here, this time, and she wants Nora Holt among others. New York has gone almost completely native and soon we'll be all mixed up, but those that are born already can never be any darker or lighter. Nora wrote me that you had written her: "You write Holt and Carl writes Ray." "Well," added Nora, "Rose is a rose is a rose!" Mabel [Dodge Luhan] is still in New Mexico, or should I say *yet*.     hortensias and mimosa to you! Carlo V. V.

TO FANIA MARINOFF                           [Taos, New Mexico]
[8 January 1927]

Dearest Baby, Here I am at Taos where the weather is 15° below zero—Last night I slept under *four* blankets & all the Navaho rugs in my room,

[5]*Composition as Explanation,* 1926, included a word portrait of French writer Jean Cocteau.
[6]Germaine Tailleferre, French composer, with Milhaud, Poulenc, Auric, Honnegger, and Durey, one of "Les Six." She married Barton after a three-week courtship following his divorce by Carlotta Monterey.
[7]"Among Negroes," in *Useful Knowledge,* 1928, a word portrait of entertainers Josephine Baker, Maud de Forrest, and Ida Lewelyn, singer Paul Robeson and his wife Essie.
[8]*Three Lives,* Gertrude Stein's first published book, in 1909, reprinted by Albert and Charles Boni, 1927, with a CVV dust jacket blurb.

with the windows tightly shut.—But the place is beautiful, marvellously beautiful, & in these mountains Mabel [Dodge Luhan] has fashioned one of her luxurious atmospheres with everything from bathrooms to Italian furniture. We stopped a few minutes in Santa Fe before driving out here— seventy-five miles up the canyon of the Rio Grande—and saw everybody there at Ida Rauh's.[9] Arthur Ficke looks very sick. There is no one at the house now but Tony—who has been an angel—''Brett,'' D. H. Lawrence's deaf secretary & a boy from Albuquerque—a painter, but next week Mabel has invited Dorothy Henry,[1] the Dasburgs, Hal [Witter] Bynner, & the Fickes—Gladys said that Arthur couldn't take the long drive but she might come with Hal . . . I haven't heard a word from you yet, but the telegraph station (30 miles away—they telephone messages) was closed Jan. 1—& today, of course, being Sunday, I hope I'll hear tomorrow. Also I should get some mail from you tomorrow . . . If you don't hear from me any day, don't be amazed. Mabel is talking of driving to Zuni for some dances. That means a day & a half across the desert.—But even to mail letters here I have to walk half a mile & in a blizzard that is difficult. Mail is brought here (to Taos) once a day by stage from Santa Fe.     all my love, Carlo
    Regards to Meda[2]


TO FANIA MARINOFF                    Ambassador Hotel
19 January [1927]                    Los Angeles, California

Dearest Baby, [. . .] This hotel is extraordinary. It is like living in London. You need a guide. I am in one of the cottages on the grounds—& Scott [Fitzgerald] is in another just opposite me. The hotel Lobby is about two miles away. I have the cottage that Pola Negri used to live in. The Fitzgeralds are here because he is writing a scenario for Constance Talmadge. I had great fun with them yesterday afternoon. The hotel is immense. The room clerk recognized me at once & it was he that sent over the Fitzgeralds. Also they were followed by a huge basket of fruit from the management.— These attentions will doubtless cost money! While I was registering Pepe [Joseph] Schildkraut called up to arrange about a luncheon for Reinhardt.[3] I talked with him & he asked me to dinner tonight.—This morning I am being interviewed. Scott arranged that—Blanche [Knopf] is coming to

[9]Ida Rauh, formerly married to Max Eastman, then to painter Andrew Dasburg.
[1]Dorothy Henry, Witter Bynner's secretary.
[2]Carlmeda Randolph was the Van Vechtens' cook-housekeeper in 1927; CVV memorialized her in his introduction to Taylor Gordon's *Born to Be* in 1929.
[3]Max Reinhardt, European theatrical producer-director.

lunch.—Aileen Pringle,[4] by the way, lives fifteen miles from here & my taxi fare over last night was 5.50!—This, the Fitzgeralds assure me, is a short trip. They went nearly 80 miles to dinner one night! Fortunately Cedric Gibbons[5] drove me home.—Aileen Pringle hasn't worked for five months, but she suddenly gets a job & started the day Blanche arrives, so that Blanche is on her own day times. Maybe Blanche and I will go back to New Mexico next week—Hal Bynner wants her to stay with him. My last day in Santa Fe—the drive in the Harvey car to the little Mexican village of Chimoyo—was one of the sweetest of all.

We are going to two *huge* movie teas—one at Lois Moran's[6]—on Sunday, where, Aileen promises, I can meet everybody. [. . .] I telegraphed you yesterday to send mail here till further notice. The Ambassador is in *Los Angeles*—not Hollywood, but I don't think that'll make any difference. I can't begin to tell you how wonderful everybody in Santa Fe was to me— and I think I'm going to enjoy it here, but I miss *my baby.*

all my love, Carlo

I haven't been away so long as this since we went to the Bahamas. I wish you had sent me a copy of Opportunity.[7] If it isn't too late when you receive this, please send me one. [. . .] I hope your cold is better. Naturally I am delighted that Bertha & Frank[8] are coming.

TO FANIA MARINOFF            Ambassador Hotel
[24 January 1927]            Los Angeles, California

Dearest Baby, Last night I suddenly became struck with the possibilities of this place for fiction. There is, to date, only Jarnegan[9]—and that is not *IT* at all. If I decide to do it I'll stay here a couple of months, because it requires as much intensive study as Harlem. It is queer. There is nothing else like it on earth that I know about.—I won't know for sure for several days what I am going to do—but if I decide to stay I'll probably take a small

---

[4]Aileen Pringle, film-actress who had become the mascot of the literati, notably Joseph Hergesheimer whom she knew in Hollywood, Henry L. Mencken with whom she had a serious and amorous alliance, and CVV of whom she became an intimate friend from 1925 until his death.
[5]Cedric Gibbons, costume designer, Aileen Pringle's current companion.
[6]Lois Moran, film actress who wanted to make a movie based on CVV's *The Blind Bow-Boy.*
[7]*Opportunity,* publication of the National Urban League. The January issue carried an announcement of the Van Vechten Award, a $200 literary prize that CVV had established.
[8]Bertha and Frank Case, owner-managers of the Algonquin Hotel in New York, celebrated for its literary gatherings.
[9]*Jarnegan,* 1926, a Hollywood novel by Jim Tully.

house & you must come out. This is all private & confidential—and I'll let you know in a few days.

In the meantime I am swimming among movie stars. A quiet day yesterday—Saw something of Zelda & Scott [Fitzgerald], & Gilmore Millen of the [Los Angeles] Herald came to lunch [. . .] The fun began about 5 when I went to a party at Lois Moran's, where I met Lillian Gish,[1] Jim Tully,[2] Joan Crawford,[3] and Florence Vidor.[4]—Lillian Gish pretended she remembered me from Good Little Devil days.[5] This I don't believe . . . Then to Betty Haines[6] for another party. There was an orchestra & untold amounts of food & drink & I talked mostly to King Vidor & his wife Elinor Boardman. He is an angel. Goosing, by the way, I discover, is the principal Hollywood pastime. Tell Reg[ina Wallace] that she can get a job with Doug Fairbanks any time—as he will engage anyone who is goosey! He loves to hear 'em scream.

Well then, Aileen [Pringle] & Cedric [Gibbons] who were carting me around took me to a very swanky dinner at Marion Davies,[7] about thirty guests including [. . .] Elinor Glyn, Pola Negri & God knows how many others. Mrs Glyn drove me home & I am seeing Pola tomorrow. I heard her last night—as she lives in my bungalow—across a narrow court. After she returned she had a terrible row with her lover & snarled and snapped and growled and howled for an hour.—Mrs. Glyn is more priceless than ever. I hazard peradventure she is the biggest idiot I have ever met. She is giving a special showing of Three Weeks (with Aileen Pringle) for me on Friday. I told her I had never seen it.[8] [. . .]

How wonderful of you to read Peter Whiffle[9] & write me glowingly about it! I miss you terrible & your letters are grand. I hope your cold is better. I haven't been drunk since I've been here—so there!        all my love, Carlo

Scott is more or less on the wagon because he is working but he & Zelda have fallen off a couple of times.

---

[1]Lillian Gish, American actress.
[2]Jim Tully, American writer.
[3]Joan Crawford, Hollywood starlet, later a film star.
[4]Florence Vidor, film actress.
[5]A Good Little Devil, 1913, by David Belasco, a play.
[6]Betty Haines, film actress.
[7]Marion Davies, film actress, mistress of William Randolph Hearst.
[8]Elinor Glyn, inventor of "It" and author of many florid romances, had been interviewed by CVV in Paris in 1908 when he was New York Times correspondent there. Her best known novel, Three Weeks, was modernized for a movie in 1927.
[9]Knopf reissued Peter Whiffle in 1927, with a slightly revised text, illustrated and boxed.

Ambassador Hotel
31 January [1927]                                      Los Angeles, California

Dearest Baby, I was overjoyed to get the news that you were better—I think *I* am getting one of the celebrated California colds I have heard so much about—from motoring over 150 miles last night in the night air. [. . .] Tia Juana is the most amusing place I've *ever* been. We motored to San Diego Saturday, Donald,[1] Pauline,[2] et moi—in Pauline's car, Donald driving.—We [. . .] had dinner at the Hotel del Coronado at Coronado Beach & about eleven the next morning we motored over to Mexico—which is fifteen miles. Tia Juana is simply incredible—nothing but *bars, dancehalls,* gambling halls, races, cock-fights & prostitutes—tough as hell. Everybody comes nevertheless, and about 5000 Americans poured into this. I have never seen a whole town drunk before—This one was by three in the afternoon. Even staid Rotarian ladies of sixty were lying in the gutters.—These mixed with the grandest swells in Rolls-Royces. [. . .][3] Well, I'll describe it more fully later. I was perfectly sober. I drank a great deal but was too astonished to become intoxicated, and the trip back! You see you have to cross the border before six or you can't get back & there is no place to stay at Tia Juana.—Cars lined up for miles—four abreast on the road. You see everybody has to go through the customs—so that liquor won't be carried back. It took us over an hour to go half-a-mile. Donald Freeman is leaving here Thursday & will arrive in New York next Monday. He will tell you about it. I am doing a series of articles—or have promised to—for Vanity Fair. Please preserve enclosed photograph for me. This was taken by a street man—Donald took others. Isn't Pauline pretty. Donald wants to marry her, but she apparently does not take this suggestion seriously. Today I lunch with Jesse Lasky[4] at the Paramount—& tonight I am going [. . .] to a theatre party to the opening of The Miracle.[5]

all my love, Carlo

---

[1]Donald Freeman, an editor for *Vanity Fair* magazine.
[2]Pauline Starke, film actress.
[3]CVV to Bruce Kellner, 15 February 1952: "I drove there from Hollywood circa 1930. [. . .] Everybody was drunk; prostitutes were legion and one place advertised the longest bar in the world, of which you could scarcely see the end. I went into the John and discovered the pissoir was like a trough. In this was lying, extended at full length, an extremely young boy (a Harvard or Yale type), very well dressed, as soused as they make 'em. However he managed to look at me and to say very disconnectedly, 'Just pee . . . on me. I'm all wet anyway.' The sordidness of Tia Juana was its charm, like the world of Toulouse-Lautrec."
[4]Jesse Lasky, film producer and director.
[5]*The Miracle,* Max Reinhardt's celebrated European theatrical pageant.

## TO IRITA VAN DOREN
[early 1927]

150 West 55th Street
New York City

Dear Irita, These new Blues I think will prove to you that Langston is improving along the lines we spoke about, i.e. he is getting deeper into a real *racial* idiom. It is the first time, I think that an American Negro has attempted to imitate the actual folksongs of his race; certainly the first time he has done so successfully. I am sending you the nine that have not been sold for publication. Take your pick and return the others *to me.* Cheque should be sent to Langston Hughes, Lincoln University, Pennsylvania. If you publish any of them [in *New York Herald Tribune Books*] it should be stated in a note that these are selected from a forthcoming book bearing the title, "Fine Clothes to the Jew."

It was more than a joy to see you again yesterday.     apple-blossoms and mignonette to you! Carl Van Vechten

## TO LANGSTON HUGHES
25 March [1927]

150 West 55th Street
New York City

Dear Langston, thanks a lot for what you say about *me.* Thanks a lot for your paper which I think is *superb.*[6] The situation is *easy* to explain: You and I are the only colored people who really love *niggers.*     Avocadoes & Navajo jewelry to you! Carlo

## TO LANGSTON HUGHES
11 May [1927]

150 West 55th Street
New York City

Dear Langston, I know something (a great deal in fact) about all the parties you write of, but I was laid up and didn't go to any of them. I did go to the Opportunity Dinner,[7] however—first to a cocktail party at Dorothy Peterson's. The principal excitement at the Dinner was our late arrival, slightly soused, about which there was much unfavorable comment, and the presence of Paul Green[8] who made a speech. Also as I went out William Pickens[9] caught my arm to ask me who the "young man in evening clothes"

[6]CVV was referring to the manuscript for "Those Bad New Negroes," a two-part article that appeared in *The Pittsburgh Courier,* 9 and 16 April 1927; largely devoted to young black writers of the Harlem Renaissance, the article praised both *Nigger Heaven* and CVV in its second installment.
[7]The Urban League sponsored a banquet for winners of the *Opportunity* magazine literary contest.
[8]Paul Green, white American playwright whose play about southern blacks, *In Abraham's Bosom,* had just won the Pulitzer Prize.
[9]William Pickens, black educator and field secretary of the NAACP.

was. It was Bruce Nugent,[1] of course, with his usual open chest and uncovered ankles. I suppose soon he will be going without trousers. Through Walter White a great deal has already happened to Allen.[2] He has taken Taylor Gordon, Rosamond and James Weldon Johnson, Walter, Dr. DuBois[3] (who is running a piece about him in the Crisis), A'Lelia [Walker . . .], and others are arranged. I think Walter arranged Ethel Waters last night. I shall be photographed as soon as I am handsome enough. [. . .]

laurel and peach-blossoms to you! Carlo
Douglas's drawings for God's Trombones are simply hors de concours.[4]

## TO H. L. MENCKEN
[circa 21 May 1927]

150 West 55th Street
New York City

Dear Henry, Sorry to miss you in Baltimore, but as Sara's[5] beauty and charm grow more potent I probably should have looked your way seldom, had you been there. On our return we stopped at the Fitzgeralds and found that young man with two black eyes, one a bleeding mass, discreetly covered by a towel. He had hopefully attacked the bouncer in the Jungle, a New York cabaret, on the previous Friday. When he was completely sober: an unheard of occurrence. In Philadelphia we met a certain Mrs. Godfrey (whose name would be perfect if she changed the Y to an E) who informed me graphically that Aileen [Pringle] had snatched you from her yearning bosom (or words to that effect). Aileen has asked that I forward the enclosed to you. Before the winter is over Aimée[6] will be sending Aileen violets.    Marinoff sends you her burning passion and I shake your hand warmly, Carlo Van Vechten

## TO FANIA MARINOFF
[24 May 1927]

150 West 55th Street
New York City

Dearest Babykins, Henry Mencken, Margaret Freeman, Blanche and I saw Alfred off last night on the Columbus and I liked the boat so much that I wouldn't mind sailing on the North German Lloyd. Consider this line on

---

[1]Richard Bruce Nugent, Bohemian black free spirit of the Harlem Renaissance, author and illustrator of willfully and cheerfully decadent material.
[2]James Allen, black American photographer.
[3]W. E. B. DuBois, greatest black American activist of the century, editor of *The Crisis,* publication of the NAACP, author, educator.
[4]Aaron Douglas, black American artist, had supplied drawings for James Weldon Johnson's book of verse-sermons *God's Trombones,* 1927.
[5]Sara Haardt, short story writer who in 1930 married Mencken.
[6]Aimée Semple McPherson, popular evangelist of the 1920s.

your return.[7] We all dined at the Knopfs and Henry and I played piano duets after dinner: truly a pretty picture. Rosamond [Johnson] and Taylor are sailing on Friday (May 20) on the Rochambeau. [. . .] Do see that Taylor Gordon meets Tallulah and people like that. [. . .] You will be amused to know that Doris Reber is back and living with Louis [Sherwin . . .] I learn [. . .] she is looking for a backer so that she can return abroad and complete her studies. Two more years, she says, will fit her for an operatic career. The Swedish translation of Nigger Heaven has arrived. [. . .] I am so sorry you have felt rotten. I cabled you last Sunday. I hope it reached you. Probably you are better by now. Your Paris life must have been pretty strenuous. I think it was extremely sensible of you to make straight for the country.    *All* my love to you! Carlo

TO FANIA MARINOFF                    150 West 55th Street
27 May [1927]                        New York City

Dearest Babykins, [. . .] We had a wonderful time at the Fitzgeralds. They have a marvellous yellow plaster house on the Delaware with iron balconies and endless space—about fifteen bedrooms and a drawing room nearly a hundred feet long. Chestnut trees bloom on the lawn. Negro bands came in in the evening and the numerous retainers danced. [. . .] Monday I went to Baltimore and saw Donald [Angus], and Mencken, and Edwin Knopf's stock company which is superb and a great success, strange as that may seem. [. . .] Edwin says he is to have Chanin's Theatre next season to produce in and he wants The Blind Bow-Boy for Douglass Montgomery and says he is cabling Noël [Coward] to ask if he will dramatize it. We shall see what we shall see. Donald was not acting in the current bill, but he is acting as stage manager. I only stayed there a day; I had intended to stay several but it was too hot. New York is cold and it is raining every day. [. . .] I am terribly excited about Lindbergh: I don't believe anybody before has ever done anything so thrilling. And he has behaved so beautifully since.[8] [. . .] I understand about how difficult it is for you to carry out your plan in London, and of course you must take your time, much as I miss you. And when you need money let me know. And please stop scolding me, because scoldings across the Atlantic upset me frightfully and you must know how much I love you.    all my love, and Meda sends hers, Carlo

[7]Fania Marinoff was on another European holiday.
[8]Charles A. Lindbergh had just crossed the Atlantic in The Spirit of St. Louis.

## TO BLANCHE KNOPF
30 July [1927]

150 West 55th Street
New York City

Dear Blanche, I have just received the enclosed letter which would seem to indicate that it is not too late to stop publication.[9] Well, if it is not too late, STOP IT. However, as you are on the ground I leave such matters to your discretion. On the other hand, if they go ahead I want them to understand that they do so with my strongest disapproval. This letter places the blame for the cuts on the length of the book. Well, they knew how long the book was when they accepted it. Fifty pages out of any book as closely knit as Nigger Heaven would completely destroy the sense. The cuts they have indicated completely murder my intention and misrepresent me before the French public. In a letter addressed to the office [. . .] they give an entirely different reason for the cuts. They state that the French public wouldn't understand certain things in the book. Well, you know and I know that they would understand them quite as well as the English or Americans, to both of which publics the strange background was the principal interest. There are, so far as I can discover, no cuts of any importance in the German version. From the nature of the cuts I have gathered that the real reason for them is a fear of what the French Negro colonies will make of the book. At any rate, under the circumstances, I am absolutely opposed to the French publication. I am not answering Soupault's letter because I don't know what you have done already in the matter. So will you please answer it or see him and *please return his letter to me.*

much love to you and Alfred, Carlo

(What a letter to write on a lamb's birthday!)

I have sent you songs from Ethel [Waters]'s show which is a knockout. Aaron Douglas is now doing new sets. Taylor [Gordon] writes that he and Rosamond [Johnson] are at the Coliseum for two weeks.

## TO PHILIPPE SOUPAULT
1 September 1927

150 West 55th Street
New York City

Monsieur, When, through my American publisher I received your list of cuts you wished to make in the French translation of Nigger Heaven, I instructed Mr. Knopf to cable you at once that I refused to authorize these cuts.[1] I have since that date put all letters received from you immediately in his hands. I have just received from him in Europe copies of your cor-

---

[9]The French writer Philippe Soupault had translated *Nigger Heaven* but with substantial cuts.
[1]*Le Paradis des Nègres* was published in November 1927, without CVV's permission, deleting over forty pages.

respondence. My decision remains unchanged. I have no desire to appear before the French public in the mutilated version that you propose. You write that the French public would be unable to understand the conditions about which I write. The English public, to whom the book was presented in its entirety, have understood them so well that the book there has gone into nine or ten editions. The German version, likewise, is integral. The book depends for what effect it may make far more on its background than it does on its plot. You have succeeded in removing, through your proposed cuts, many of what I consider the most important passages in my novel. Under these circumstances I must continue to refuse to sanction the French publication of my novel.    Very truly, Carl Van Vechten

## TO WITTER BYNNER
4 October 1927

150 West 55th Street
New York City

Dear Hal, I want to know all about the Santa Fe jail for something I am writing.[2] Will you be an angel and tell me about it: where it is, a swift description of the interior; are the guards Mexicans? Are the prisoners allowed to roam about or are they locked in cells? And is there a sheriff at Santa Fe or a Chief of Police? And anything else about it, briefly, that you can recall. I feel sure you must have been in it some time; if not will you inquire of some of your criminal friends? I'll be grateful if you can send me this right away.

Ethel[3] has made a sensational début at the Palace since your departure and now she is to be the hostess at the Club 300 on Fifty-fourth Street.    Mignonette and petunias to you! Carlo

## TO DOROTHY PETERSON
[11 January 1928]

150 West 55th Street
New York City

Dear Dorothy, What a lamb you are to send me the Bound Ebony & Topaz[4] & I never told you I didn't like it. Anyway much love & thanks. I am working now on the third draft of a novel called Spider Boy, which is *not* about Marcus Garvey.[5]—And I still have a cold. Tell Sidney[6] for God sake to cut his hair.    Yours in the blood of Jesus, Carlo V. V.

---

[2]A chapter in CVV's novel *Spider Boy,* 1928, takes place in Santa Fe.
[3]Ethel Waters, popular black singer. See List of recipients.
[4]*Ebony and Topaz,* a collection of articles, stories, poems, and drawings by members of the Harlem Renaissance, edited in 1927 by Charles S. Johnson of the National Urban League.
[5]Marcus Garvey, militant black leader prominent during the early 1920s, notable for his "Back to Africa" movement.
[6]Sidney Peterson, M.D., Dorothy Peterson's brother.

TO FANIA MARINOFF                           Drake Hotel
21 February 1928                            Lakeshore Drive
                                            Chicago, Illinois

Dearest Baby, A very terrific scene this morning at the lawyer's when Duane
learned that she was never legally adopted [by Fannie and Ralph Van Vech-
ten] & so has no interest in her mother's property as Fannie left no will.
This must be entirely under your hat as trouble is likely to ensue if it gets
out for reasons I'll explain later. Duane will, of course, be plenty rich enough
through the money she inherits from Ralph. [. . .] I'm arranging about
money & I'll send you a cheque tomorrow. God knows you'll have enough,
I should think, from now on.[7] Duane's name, by the way, was Censolina
Harper. This strikes me as funny.—Please send me address of Opportunity.
You'll find a copy on my desk. I am going to renew my prize offer.[8]

   [. . .] I worry about you—all the time—your cold etc. Please go to Atlantic
City or somewhere & get over it. I am all right. *Don't worry about me.* Why
don't you take Reg[ina Wallace] to Atlantic City? She took you to Europe.     All my love, Carlo

TO FANIA MARINOFF                           Ambassador Hotel
2 M[a]rch [1928]                            Los Angeles, California

Dearest Baby, [. . .] Well, Aimée McPherson came to dinner. The waiters
almost dropped dead, & so did Aileen [Pringle] & I believe—without warning she brought her manager & his wife and her daughter. Well we managed
by using some spaghetti & family holding off. Mrs [Jesse] Lasky came too.
Aimée is marvellous! What a personality! What pep!—I enjoyed every moment. Afterwards we went to the Temple, where she baptized 75 people
among other things—total immersion & very beautiful with a stage set—
pool—colored lights & Aimée in the centre of the pool letting them down.
I got Frank & Bertha [Case] seats too & afterwards Aimée took us all over
the Temple—an amazing experience. And when we were all worn out she
was fresher than ever. [. . .]     All my love always, Carlo

---

[7]By the terms of Ralph Van Vechten's will, his wife inherited his estate; on her death, two-
thirds passed to his foster daughter Duane, one-sixth in trust to his sister's son Van Vechten
Shaffer and one-sixth in trust to CVV. The total estate was in excess of six million dollars.
[8]See note 7, 19 January 1927.

TO FANIA MARINOFF                          Ambassador Hotel
[8 March 1928]                             Los Angeles, California

Dearest Woojums, Met Jack Dempsey[9] last night & I'm crazy about him.
I woof-woofed[1] and everything. (By the way woof woof has become the
sensation of Hollywood.) He has promised to look me up in New York.
Tonight I'm asked to dine with the Pickfords[2] but it is my last night &
Aileen [Pringle] is coming to dinner—It is, as a matter of fact, a very busy
day—I'll write you more later.

    Tomorrow I leave for Santa Fe.    All my love, Carlo
Days before your letter arrived I had already bought you some Chinese
pyjamas at a much sweller place than Gumps.

TO ELINOR WYLIE                            150 West 55th Street
[spring 1928]                              New York City

Dear Elinor, To attempt to tell you adequately how entranced and captivated
I am by Mr. Hazard is somewhat of a task. Perhaps I can best convey my
enthusiasm by admitting that I like the book as much as—perhaps more
than—Jennifer.[3] I read it at one ecstatic sitting & I heard birds sing & gods
laugh. Elinor, what a lovely book! I am envious & proud.

    You should have heard from me before, but I have been in California
&, returning, buried under proofs of Spider Boy. It was only now that I
could give myself the supreme pleasure of meeting your Mr. Hodge.

    Purple parrots to you, Elinor, & shagreen boots! Carlo

TO H. L. MENCKEN                           150 West 55th Street
[13 June 1928]                             New York City

Dear Henry, The crabs sound tempting and you always are, but my time
is entirely taken up reading letters from persons who want money. Personally I never was more poor. I have traced these rumors to your tongue
and curse you heartily. No wonder you are in trouble. I am sending you
my favorite photograph. Will you hang it in the Maryland Free State? Marinoff sails on the France on Friday, although under what name God only
knows. Also we are cleaning house. The slaves make succulent spare-ribs

---

[9]William H. Dempsey, heavyweight boxing champion during the 1920s.
[1]Woof-woof: CVV barked a lot to demonstrate his enthusiasm; also he bit people, a practice
that had a brief vogue among his friends.
[2]The Pickfords: Mary Pickford and Douglas Fairbanks, royalty among Hollywood film stars.
[3]CVV mounted a personal publicity campaign to insure some modest success for Elinor Wylie's
first novel, *Jennifer Lorn*, in 1924. Her fourth and final novel, *Mr Hodge and Mr Hazard*, was
published in 1928.

and sauerkraut for themselves, but refuse to make any for us. The tempting odors are driving me out into the storm. The doctor tells me there is nothing the matter with me, but I am taking pills.      my regards, Carlo V. V. The annual octoroons' ball is being turned into a farewell party for Marinoff on Thursday night. I hope you can come.

TO FANIA MARINOFF                                            150 West 55th Street
[20 June 1928]                                               New York City

Dearest Angel, Thanks for your sweet cablegram which didn't arrive till the day after. [. . .] I had a quiet, but lovely birthday—aside from missing you—party at Alfred [Knopf]'s. It was a lovely day, and he had some people out. Lots of telegrams came. Jim and Grace [Johnson] regretted their house wasn't ready for a party this year. The Stettheimers sent a large chocolate cake with a spider and web on top! In the evening Donald [Angus] had dinner with me at Claremont and then we went to the opening of the endurance dancing contest at Manhattan Casino. It was amusing and we saw Walter [White], Bledsoe,[4] Bill Robinson,[5] and many others. [. . .]

I had a bad attack of indigestion yesterday. [. . .] The doctor gave me calomel. He says it's nothing chronic or organic but something like hay fever or asthma. Something disagrees with me. Now he thinks it's fish. Well, I'm keeping a diary of what I eat now and how it affects me. Go to Jac Auer's [health spa] three times a week and had my best day today. I have no intention of getting a house in the country *yet.* I don't want to clutter up my life with more servants and taxes until I know exactly what I want to do. The more I think on it, the more free we are the less we change our mode of life. Heaven knows what is happening to the estate. One day I hear one thing and one day another. There will be enough to live on simply in any case.[6] I am going to get a passport next week, so that I can come abroad if everything breaks right. I'll let you know by cable if I am coming in plenty of time to cancel your sailing. In the meantime look up the price of motor trips as I have asked you. There are others I may prefer—such as to the Black Forest and Baden-Baden, or the Austrian Tyrol. In case we go alone we shan't need so big a car although we must carry some baggage. In case we take somebody with us*—as is possible we shall require a large touring car. It may be cheaper to buy a car, and hire a chauffeur, and sell the car at the end of the trip, but I don't think so. Well,

[4]Jules Bledsoe, black singer, first to sing "Old Man River" in *Showboat,* 1928.
[5]Bill "Bojangles" Robinson, celebrated tap dancer.
[6]CVV had not yet learned he had inherited a million dollars in trust from his brother's estate. See note 6, 21 February 1928.

any way get all the details. If I come over you'll have about six weeks more after you planned to come home, and you'd better plan to go to the country somewhere. Don't get wild with the five hundred I sent you till we see how things are going to turn out. You'll have plenty of time to buy things later. On the other hand don't stint yourself. Get the Persian earrings at once. I only write the above because so much of this depends on how much money I get and how soon I get it. [. . .] In getting escargot things remember you want small picks as well as the clamps.

I am going to the Langners Sunday.　　All my love & Meda sends hers—
Carlo
*Say Avery [Hopwood] and Nora Holt!!

## TO AVERY HOPWOOD                    150 West 55th Street
[June 1928]                          New York City

Dear Avery, Woof! Woof! Woojums! I hope you received the cowboy shirts. I sent them to you ages ago, but the post office department was not hopeful. They could *not* be registered. Anyway it was a lot of bother, and I loved doing it. Maybe I'm coming over in September; so don't come back too soon. I thought maybe you and Nora [Holt] would join Marinoff and me in a motor tour of the principal cities. Gertrude [Stein] writes: "We did see a bit of Avery and he is sweeter and more delightful than ever." And so he is, bless him!　　love always, Carlo
There's quite a bit of the all right turning up over here in God's country.

## TO JOSEPH HERGESHEIMER              150 West 55th Street
3 July [1928]                        New York City

Dear Joe, Ralph died a year ago on June 28, and almost exactly on the anniversary Quiet Cities arrives with moving dedication and its cool grey-stained cover. Of the dedication I know how much it would have pleased Ralph as would the book itself. Fannie, of course, lived long enough to foresee the dedication.[7] This matter of death! Avery Hopwood's death has shaken me terribly.[8] It is my first experience with the death of an intimate contemporary and it is frightening. I was as fond of him, I think, as one human being could be of another, and I had known him for seventeen years.

[7]Hergesheimer dedicated *Quiet Cities* to CVV's brother. Ralph Van Vechten's widow died less than a year after her husband.
[8]Avery Hopwood died of a heart attack while he was wading in the Mediterranean at Juan-les-Pins.

Quiet Cities, dear Joe, together with Linda Condon and Tampico, has immediately slipped into a very high place in my attention, toward the top of the list of my favorites of your books. Its qualities have enlisted your greatest charms and your highest powers. I read a part of it first in the [*Saturday Evening*] Post, then all again in the small paper. Now the rich vellum [edition] does its part in framing your words appropriately. You have succeeded, as no one else, in creating a past which lives with all its varied environments and characteristics.

I shall probably join Fania in Europe in September. Perhaps you and Dorothy will find it convenient to let me pay you a short visit before then.

my love to you both, Carlo

TO FANIA MARINOFF                                    150 West 55th Street
20 July [1928]                                        New York City

Dearest Baby, I spent all day yesterday (she had to wait over a day for a train) with Julie[9] and I think in some ways Avery's death is a relief to her. Now he belongs to her completely and she doesn't have to worry about him. I now have the whole story and it is too horrible that the poor woman got into the hotel at Juan-les-Pins and was told by the management. [. . .] But the facts of his death are reassuring. He died of heart disease instantly in front of Otis Skinner's[1] house in two feet of water. The Skinners saw the whole thing and he was fished out immediately. There was not a drop of water in his lungs. This might have happened anywhere. [. . .] You will be interested to know that Tallulah [Bankhead] sent no word of any kind, whereas Rex McDougall[2] who is not at all indebted to Avery was with Julie every minute and attended to every detail of the troublesome red tapes necessary to get a body out of France. Lots of Avery's things were stolen and everybody tried to do Julie. By will she receives all of Avery's property in trust. After she dies it is dispersed. John then gets $10,000 (it is a will Avery made in 1922).[3] When Julie heard this she said she had wanted to die before but now she wanted to live forever. She knows how much I loved Avery and how much he loved me and she has been very sweet and sympathetic. [. . .] Did I tell you that decorators will be here all

[9]Julie Hopwood, Avery Hopwood's mother.
[1]Otis Skinner, American actor.
[2]Rex McDougall, an English friend of Hopwood and CVV since 1912.
[3]John Henry Floyd, actor and playwright, Hopwood's lover. He received $10,000 in trust and $10,000 in cash by the will, in addition to an outright gift of $250,000 several months prior to Hopwood's death. Fania Marinoff and CVV each received about $40,000 by the will.

next week? You see I am getting everything ready for our return, doing all *the* dirty work. I hope you won't go to London till I get over. I want to do this last and sail from there. If I finally decide on Vienna, Prague, and Buda-Pesth as places to go, you'll have to get visas for Austria, Hungary, and Czecho-Slovakia. I'll cable you if I decide. In the meantime please take a rest in the country. You write as if you were all tired out. Why don't you go to some quiet place on the Normandy coast? Antibes is no place to rest. I want you to meet me in Cherbourg and then we'll go to Paris for a few days. It isn't necessary that we should live at the Ritz—although I don't mind if it's not too expensive—but I want a room with a bath—one room with two beds is all right, and I do not want to live in the Montparnasse Quarter. I hate it. At any rate we'll probably only be in Paris a few days.     all my love, Carlo

TO VIRGIL THOMSON                    S. S. Ile de France
16 Août. [1928]                      [at sea]

Caro Virgil, It was sweet of you to write to the boat, but you are always sweet. Anyway I shall miss you—and your little ways—and our strange excursions & adventures very much. I hope you meet & like my Spanish friends. [. . .] A pat on the head for El Grosser[4] and . . . I kiss your hand, Madame!     C.

TO CARRIE, ETTIE, AND                R. M. S. Mauretania
FLORINE STETTHEIMER                  [at sea]
6 September [1928]

Dear Three Sisters: Your rhythmic communication from the cherry orchard of Tarrytown touched the seagull very deeply. I wish you might have seen my departure! Thanks to a little influence I am occupying part of the Royal suite and doing it proud. Hundreds, including the fascinating Nora Holt, came to do me hommage and to lap up as much champagne as they could decently imbibe. I think you might have enjoyed it. The sea is calm today, but as usual I have gastritis. I won nine games of parcheesi on the afternoon of my departure to my opponent's one, and among my presents was a splendid board with elaborate pieces and die in precious stones.

My best to you always, Carlo

---

[4]Maurice Grosser, American painter and designer, scenarist for the Virgil Thomson-Gertrude Stein opera, *Four Saints in Three Acts*, 1927–34.

## TO GERTRUDE STEIN

27 November [1928]

Carlton Hotel,
London SW 1

Dearest Gertrude—Well, the doctor permitted me to go to Paul [Robeson]'s party if I promised not to drink & directly after went to bed for the week. So I promised & this is the next day & I am in bed . . . Paul & Essie, & Mrs. Goode, Essie's very distinguished mother & the baby have taken a large, late-Victorian house in St. John's Wood—there are cockney servants & in the dining room large oil paintings of *turks*. Elsewhere whatnots, porcelain glass & various knick-knacks. The party was lovely. There was a great deal of food & much champagne. All the distinguished Negroes in London were there: Layton and Johnston, who sang, Leslie Hutchinson, and some very socially distinguished . . . Also Mrs. Patrick Campbell, Lady Ravendale (Lord Curzon's daughter), Lord Beaverbrook, Lady Laski, Hugh Walpole—most of the stars of the English stage: Fred & Adele Astaire, Cathleen Nesbitt, Jeanne de Cassilis, [Alice] *Delysia*—who sang, Nicholas Hassan, Constance Collier, Athenée Scyles, etc. Paul sang & was a lamb. It was their first party & a great success. I think you should come to London to go to a party at Paul's. And I'm sure he would give one for you.

I don't understand why it's so difficult about the Tonny drawings.[5] Why couldn't [Virgil] Thomson just slip them between his shirts? Anyway I'll get them later—but don't make me sign papers & things. Couldn't they just be handed to me simply? You don't know the bother that I'll have to go through if I have to get them out of customs. So have *somebody* smuggle them in. Because I *quote* 6 ms & I don't want any bad feelings transferred to the pictures.

I am having such a nice time in bed. I wish you & Alice would come to London. Marinoff is combing her hair & I am awaiting a luncheon guest . . . *Don't* forget me!     Carlo
*The channel seems to be rough.*


## TO BLANCHE KNOPF

[May 1929]

R. M. S. Mauretania
[at sea]

Dearest Blanche, It turned out that I just adore the passport letter of credit holder & never can do without one again *ever* anywhere & Marinoff wants one so badly I am getting her one in London. So you are always right. Our

---

[5]Kristians Tonny, Dutch-born artist whose work Gertrude Stein had begun to support. CVV had agreed to attempt to sell some of his drawings in America.

Eddie[6] is the belle of this very social boat. Some ladies stole the handle of his phonograph because he played so late at night, but he recovered it & last night (Monday) played Ethel Waters records for opera singers in the lounge till all hours. [. . .] The carnations were long, the lilies were lovely, & so is Blanche.     Love to Alfred, Carlo

TO FANIA MARINOFF                              Brackenburn, Manesty Park
[June 1929]                                        Keswick, England

Dearest Baby, I am sitting in a room with a fire looking down a terrace of columbines & lupines across the pine trees at the lake surrounded by mountains. It is cold—very far north. The house is modern but very attractive & it is not necessary to bring books. Hugh [Walpole] has here his collection of English novels—first editions—from the beginning to modern times. It includes every important work. The house is small. There are two houses, servants besides the chauffeur & gardener. I am not drinking & I think three or four days of this will be very good. Hugh works in the morning. In the afternoon we may drive or walk,—or talk or read. We are miles & miles from anything but country-people—in the midst of the Lake District. I am planning to go back to London Thursday & probably will dine with Emilie [Grigsby]. Then—unless something spectacular promises—I shall go to Paris on the Golden Arrow on Saturday—but I'll telegraph you definitely when I decide, and you can arrange about rooms at the Bristol & *meet* me. I'll be so glad to see you. There is much to tell you—about how Rebecca [West] slapped my face *resoundingly* in King Street—and how I have discovered the great place for china in London—and nearly *went mad*—there is a Wedgewood dessert service, but never mind!

All my love—I shouldn't think you would get this much before you hear from me by telegraph—but I can't help that. This is very far away, on the border of Scotland.     Carlo

TO MURIEL DRAPER                                              [Spain]
29 July 1929

Dear Muriel, I am getting letters from all over asking if I am a socialist. It seems Gilbert Seldes[7] has written an article. Dear Muriel, am I a socialist?     Love, Carlo

---

[6]Edward Wassermann (who changed his name to Waterman), heir of the Seligmann banking family, a longtime CVV acquaintance, later a Paris art dealer, Catholic convert, drug addict.
[7]Gilbert Seldes, American writer. See List of recipients.

TO ALFRED A. KNOPF                          150 West 55th Street
24 August [1929]                            New York City

Dear Alfred, Today, I have sent to J. G. Wilson of Bumpus four books for
the Prince [of Wales], *tall paper* copies of Nigger Heaven, Firecrackers, The
Blind Bow-Boy, and The Tattooed Countess. He now possesses all my novels. Will you please, according to our conversation, write Wilson that I
shall be delighted to offer these books to the Prince. In case he insists upon
paying for them quote him the original price in each instance. This matter,
you will understand, is profoundly confidential. Under pain of death in
the Tower, court martial, and shot as then came the dawn, there must be
NO publicity. I think, however, that sooner or later, we can worm some
out of it. For instance, "Mr. Van Vechten, the American novelist, is spending
two weeks next summer at Windsor Castle, the guest of, etc."

Mr. Grognet[8] was superb, but next time I am going with a coupla black
boys. I got very tired and the chauffeur grinned. My favorite wines are
unobtainable, but I got the next best. I am nearly all unpacked and am
almost ready to go to Berlin.      love, Carlo

TO ELLEN GLASGOW                            150 West 55th Street
10 September [1929]                         New York City

There is no good telling you, dear Ellen, that you will get over it because
you won't.[9] I know that. Always when I think of Scheherazade[1] there is
that dull pain at the back of my heart. That is the permanent comfort that
animals give us, the power to *remember* & feel. I understand, dear Ellen,
but I cannot help you.      with my affection, Carlo

TO ELLEN GLASGOW                            150 West 55th Street
14 September 1929                           New York City

I have just laid down They Stooped to Folly, dear Ellen. What a book you
have written! [. . .] Your wit always amazes me—and you have not been
sparing of it in your miraculous dedication—but more often, in this book,
I found myself near tears, for you have created a mood of timeless melancholy—like that of the final scene of Der Rosenkavalier. In short, I not
only congratulate you, I also envy you the sureness of your pen. The mas-
terful manner in which you put down what most of us are only permitted—

[8]Knopf's bootlegger.
[9]Ellen Glasgow's Selyham terrier Jeremy had just died.
[1]CVV's most recent (and last) cat.

108

so fragile are our talents—to suggest vaguely.    Ich kusse ihre hand, Madame!   Carl Van Vechten

## TO WALTER WHITE
13 December 1929

150 West 55th Street
New York City

Dear Walter, I heartily concur with you that Clara Smith would make an outstanding success in the "white" music halls. Of all the Blues singers she is the one most fitted, I believe, to carry this gospel into the alien world. She represents something that is fast going: the primitive old Southern Negro, and when she sings "Prescription for the Blues" or "If you only knowd" she epitomizes the tragic moments in the love lives of those people. But she is expert in her delineation of comedy songs too. Personally, as you know, I consider her an important artist. In an article entitled "Three Blues Singers" published in Vanity Fair for March 1926 I have more to say about her.      sincerely, Carl Van Vechten
Of course you are at liberty to use this letter in any way you like.

## TO JAMES WELDON JOHNSON
[1929?]

150 West 55th Street
New York City

Dear Jim, Experience has taught me that it is dangerous to make unqualified statements like the one you propose to make about Lulu Belle.[2] Some grey-beard will rise to confute you. So far as I know, you are correct. [. . .] However, I do not remember whether The Dreamy Kid was laid in Harlem or The Rider of Dreams. I never saw Goat Alley or Roseanne. Or The Gold-front Store, and I think the Ethiopian Art Theatre did another modern Negro play. Of course there was the case of Bert Williams and the Follies, but his scenes were with one or two white men at the most. Show Boat and Golden Dawn came after Lulu Belle, I suppose.

   four pink dolphins to you! Carlo
Certainly from the point of view of importance & influence you are correct.

---

[2]For his study of Harlem, Black Manhattan, notable for its history of black theater, James Weldon Johnson proposed Lulu Belle, 1926, by white playwrights Charles McArthur and Edward Sheldon, as the first play to employ a cast of black and white actors. The other plays referred to might have done so: The Dreamy Kid, 1920, an early one-act by Eugene O'Neill; The Rider of Dreams, 1917, by Ridgely Torrence; Goat Alley, 1921, by Ernest Howard Culbertson; Roseanne, 1923, by Nan Bagby Stephens; The Goldfront Stores, Inc., 1924, by Caesar G. Washington. The Ethiopian Art Players staged The Chip Woman's Fortune by black playwright Willis Richardson in 1923. The black comedian Bert Williams did appear onstage with white performers in various editions of Ziegfeld's Follies until his death in 1922. Otherwise, Johnson was correct about Lulu Belle.

Was Uncle Tom ['s Cabin] ever done with colored actors? If not what a chance for an impressario!! Robeson as Uncle Tom—Clara Smith as Topsy, and mammoth chorus of spiritual singers!

TO FANNIE HURST 150 West 55th Street
12 February [1930] New York City

Dear Fannie: The time has now come to tell you that
Chief Long Lance[3]

Hugh Walpole ⬚ Carl Van Vechten

Theodore Dreiser
lunched together at the Crillon today.
Believe it or not. C.

TO FANIA MARINOFF 150 West 55th Street
15 February 1930 New York City

Why, my precious lamby van Poo, how you do run on! You certainly aren't spending much time in New York this winter,[4] and next winter, after I get my book out, I expect to be away a lot. Perhaps we'll go to Egypt. And, of course, I can't imagine living anywhere you don't live, so, of course, I won't do anything about Bill's[5] house, although I don't think I ever liked anything so much, and I think it could be got superbly cheaply, and, of course, I'll live in California if my baby wants to or anywhere else she wants to. And that's that. I'm feeling so much better because my book is coming along better now, and I am working all day. Next Monday the Knopfs will send the following broadcast to all the papers:

> If you happen to meet Carl Van Vechten these days or nights at gatherings where cocktails are served, at large dinners, or suppers, it is likely that he is working rather than enjoying himself. He is engaged at present in writing a novel called "Parties" which Alfred A. Knopf will publish next autumn. This will be the first book Mr Van Vechten has written since "Spider Boy."

---

[3]Chief Long Lance, a Blackfoot Indian, popular during the 1920s for his personality as well as for his native dances.
[4]Fania Marinoff had taken a cruise down through the Panama Canal and up to Hollywood to make screen tests for talking motion pictures which had just caught on.
[5]William Seabrook, American writer, whose country house CVV had considered buying.

I wish you wouldn't write me anything more about Eddie [Wassermann]. It merely irritates me. I am so delighted to have him out of town. [. . .] Nora [Holt] is dining with me tonight and then we are going to a party given for James Weldon Johnson—so times change. She thinks she will leave New York next week. Edna Kenton was here for dinner last night: she doesn't want Europe for another year, as she is working.[6] You seem to have sent Joe [Hergesheimer] a telegram on Eddie's birthday! Today, the fifteenth, is Joe's.     Very much love, I miss you terrible, but stay as long as you are happy, Carlo

Thanks for your swell valentine and I's askin' you everything. Random House is publishing my pamphlet about Feathers[7] in the Spring. Please tell Aileen [Pringle] I want some *blonde* photographs subito.[8]


TO FANIA MARINOFF                          150 West 55th Street
19 February [1930]                          New York City

Dearest Babykins, I'm so glad you heard Aimée [Semple McPherson] at last. She is remarkable for vitality, efficiency, and versatility. Anything she undertook she would do remarkably. It is just as well she confines herself to religion. If you go again—and you must see a baptism—try to meet her. I think she would remember me, and after services one of her people would take your name back and she would show you her temple and herself, etc. Don't sit so close next time. It's really better in the balcony, because, unless she knows who you are, she is likely to rope you into going on the stage and getting you to sign your fortune away. The temple is exactly the kind of place the people who go there feel at home in, and she deals with that kind of people because it's easier to get money out of them with less effort. If you meet her, give her my warmest regards. [. . .] Miguel [Covarrubias] came in yesterday with what he had done for Nigger Heaven and the drawings were terrible and I am actually relieved he is out of it.[9] I

---

[6]CVV to Edna Kenton, 28 August 1929: "How soon do you think you will be sufficiently free to undertake a trip to Europe? Whenever you are I want you to give me the pleasure of sending you. Whenever you are ready to make definite plans I shall be delighted to put into your hands a cheque sufficient to cover a three month voyage (at last)."

[7]Feathers, CVV's cat, 1919–20, about whom he wrote a memoir, published as one of six prose quartos, boxed, by Random House, with others by Theodore Dreiser, William Rose Benét, Louis Bromfield, Conrad Aiken, and Sherwood Anderson.

[8]Aileen Pringle, customarily a flaming redhead, had bleached her hair temporarily.

[9]Alfred Knopf planned to issue a deluxe edition of *Nigger Heaven* with an introduction by James Weldon Johnson and illustrations. Eventually the American-born English illustrator E. McKnight Kauffer was engaged, but he delayed too long, and with the weak market for expensive books during the Depression, the project was cancelled.

never thought he could do it anyway. I don't know where we'll turn now
. . . I am working steadily on *Parties*. I think the trouble before was that I
didn't have a title. It's so much easier to work with a title. I opened the
enclosed invitation by mistake, but it's just as well. *You* answer it from out
there, and don't mention me, as it will be too late for me to go then anyway.
I hope you are still enjoying yourself, and I think of you all the time.

all my love, Carlo

TO FANIA MARINOFF                          150 West 55th Street
28 February 1930                           New York City

Dearest Baby, It is certainly wonderful the way you begin to write about
coming home just when I am beginning to ask you. Our letters cross as
usual. I hope you'll plan to reach here for your birthday [20 March] but
I do think you should stop at Santa Fe. Apparently Mabel [Dodge Luhan]
won't be there, but Hal Bynner will, and [Andrew] Dasburg, and probably
others that you know. Now about money write me exactly how much to
deposit for you—you know what I mean by exactly, i.e., so that you will
have enough, not too little, too much if anything—or if you want to move
more swiftly telegraph me. I don't wonder you're tired of it out there: I
don't see how you've been able to stand it so long, and apparently you
stay up and drink and misbehave in a way you never do at home. I may
have the second draught [of *Parties*] done by the time you get here and if
not you will have to be very good day times and at present I do not stay
out late nights. Let me know what you decide and the sum of money will
cover it. [. . .] Lawrence [Langner] is raging about the success, tremendous,
of Green Pastures.[1] He is almost ready to resign from the [Theatre] Guild.
You know how much he wanted to do that play. [. . .] Edna Aug[2] is really
not a nice person. Thank God she is leaving these parts. [. . .] She talks
endlessly about her own troubles and she is a mess, just a mess. Still I am
glad I gave her some money (which she insists she will pay back). As
Thornton Wilder[3] says in The Woman of Andros: "The mistakes we make
through generosity are less terrible than the gains we acquire through cau-
tion."

Hal Bynner was here for dinner last night, with Nora [Holt] and Nella[4]

---

[1]*The Green Pastures,* 1930, by Marc Connelly, a play with an all-black cast based on *Ol' Adam
and His Chillun* by Roark Bradford, retellings in black folk idiom of Old Testament stories.
[2]Edna Aug, American actress with whom CVV had conducted an extensive correspondence.
His letters to her are apparently lost.
[3]Thornton Wilder, American novelist and playwright.
[4]Nella Larsen, black American novelist.

and after dinner the very pretty Nina Mae McKinney[5] came in with Lewis Cole,[6] and he says he will be back in Santa Fe by the 8th of March. [. . .] A nice time was had and everybody talked for hours on end about The Green Pastures. Indeed, no one talks about anything else. Don't worry about Europe. Something may happen to get us there earlier and if I can't go I'll send you off anyway. Now that we are talking of your returning I get more and more lonesome for you and can hardly wait.

all my love, Carlo

I am taking Carrie [Stettheimer] to the Philharmonic this afternoon. Toscanini returns. A beautiful picture of Carlotta [Monterey O'Neill] taken by the Baron de Meyer just arrived.


TO BLANCHE KNOPF                            150 West 55th Street
28 February 1930                            New York City

Dear Blanche, Welcome home! As to Nigger Heaven, I think [E. McKnight] Kauffer is swell, and am quite willing to have him do it (but his *must* be in color) if he wants to.[7] This afternoon I got an even more brilliant idea: Picasso! If Bradley[8] went after him, I could get Gertrude Stein to help. He likes Negroes and of course the originals would belong to him, and if Picasso did it, why he wouldn't have to do more than five or six (although more would be pleasant). These foreign matters must be settled by cable, I think, or they will take forever. In the meantime I have told Mr. Anspacher to tell Helene Johnson and Elmer Campbell,[9] both of whom have done one interesting drawing, to go ahead and try another (in competition) on their own responsibility, if they want to. We promise them nothing, but Kauffer and Picasso may both refuse or ask too much money, and so there is a chance for these Americans. Aaron Douglas[1] is out, apparently. He has not replied to my letter asking if he would reconsider, and I have seen him several times since.

Did you know that Spider Boy is running as a serial in French in the Revue Hebdomadaire? Are we getting anything for it? If not, *please don't*

---

[5]Nina Mae McKinney, black American actress in films, earlier a chorine in black revues.
[6]Lewis Cole, sometimes Louis Cole, black American dancer.
[7]See CVV to Fania Marinoff, 19 February 1930, note 6.
[8]William Aspenwall Bradley, American literary agent in Paris.
[9]Helene Johnson, black artist and writer of the Harlem Renaissance; E. Simms Campbell, black artist later celebrated as a cartoonist for *Esquire*.
[1]Aaron Douglas, black artist of the Harlem Renaissance, who designed the advertising illustrations for *Nigger Heaven* in 1926 as well as dust jackets for other novels of the period.

*make trouble* because the thing was arranged by a friend of mine, Robert de Saint Jean who is also a friend of Julien Green.[2] [. . .]

If you care to you may quote me as follows in regard to The Maltese Falcon:

> It is with unusual eagerness that I open the pages of each new book by Dashiell Hammett. It seems to me that he is raising the detective story to that plane to which Alexandre Dumas raised the historical novel. It is in his drawing of character that this romancer excels, and the characters of The Maltese Falcon are as odd a lot as he has yet turned out.     C.V.V.

I send you seven knitted afghans and a pair of siamese twins, and advise you to see The Green Pastures as soon as you are able to sit up. What about publishing this? It is the best evening I have ever spent in the theatre.

*Please file* this letter in case—     [unsigned]

I'm glad you like Langston [Hughes]'s book, but "Not Without Laughter" is an *awful* title: Like "Smile, boys, smile," I shall die if it is used. [. . .]


TO ALFRED A. KNOPF                          Carlton Hotel
19 June [1930]                              London SW 1

Dear Alfred, Thanks, thanks for the flowers. We arrived in London in the middle of a violent thunder storm (which struck a thunderbolt through Emilie Grigsby's[3] cottage) and they were welcome as beauty relief. [. . .] G. B. Stern[4] is in Villefranche. John Van Druten[5] is away. Hugh [Walpole] is in Cumberland. And it has rained all the time. But I have been to a few "parties" and saw Paul [Robeson]'s Othello last night. He is magnificent, unbelievable, but the play is not a success, on account of Maurice Browne's miserable Iago. He has retired and there is a swell Iago now, but I'm afraid it is too late. The Robesons had supper with us at the Carlton and afterwards drove me in their town car to my party at Berkeley Square. I have the same rooms at the Carlton on the first floor that I had when you were here and the waiters are all the same and the footmen and the concierges and the elevator boys (now nearing ninety). The porter met us at Paddington and took all our baggage for us, and it was like coming home . . . I think

---

[2] Julien Green, American-born French novelist.
[3] Emilie Grigsby, an English acquaintance through Edward Wassermann.
[4] G. B. Stern, English novelist.
[5] John Van Druten, English playwright.

we shall go to Paris at the end of the next week, but I shall of course cable you.      love to you both, Carlo

The Mauretania trip was simply extraordinarily successful. My old friend Mahala Douglas was on board and she ordered all the meals in advance and nobody else on board had *anything*. The weather was swell and I read all the books of Charles Pettit[6] with real pleasure.

I shall try to think of a blurb for Langston [Hughes]'s book [*Not Without Laughter*], but at the moment my mind is on higher things. As usual we go to the Caledonian Market tomorrow in Emilie's Rolls and we are going to the country at Doris Keane's[7] over Sunday.

TO ALFRED A. KNOPF                          Carlton Hotel
28 June [1930]                                    London SW 1

Dear Alfred, [. . .] I have been very well in spite of the weather which is worse than usual, a great deal of rain and either too hot or too cold. I have had a swell and very satisfactory visit. [. . .] I've seen a lot of Paul [Robeson] and Epstein[8] and Rebecca,[9] and done a lot of things unnecessary to mention.

A fabulous luncheon at Lady Cunard's and a cocktail party at the Bryan Guinness's in which she received with baby at her breast and an Irish wolfhound as big as a colt at her feet. [. . .] Ethel Mannin's Confessions and Impressions is the talk of the town, but I don't think it's much good for America. You might take a look at it. The first edition disappeared at once and it can't be bought until they reprint . . . Going to Paris Tuesday, I should think. Marion Dorn is making pyjamas for Marinoff and a velvet robe (African) for me. I'm invited to Elinor Glyn's country party for Marion Davies and William Randolph Hearst . . . We may go to Greece or the Balearic Islands, but I think a motor trip to the south of France is indicated.      much love to you both, Carlo

TO A'LELIA WALKER                                    [Paris]
10 August [1930]

But, dear A'Lelia, what would I do with a house?[1] I am always away all summer. And where *do* you think I'd get all that money. A'Lelia behave!

---

[6]Charles Pettit, early twentieth-century French novelist whose books (usually on fantastic Chinese subjects) were being published in translations by Lady Una Troubridge in New York.
[7]Doris Keane, English actress known primarily for a six-year run (in America and then in England) in Edward Sheldon's popular *Romance*, 1913.
[8]Jacob Epstein, English sculptor whose bronze head of Paul Robeson CVV purchased.
[9]Rebecca West, English novelist.
[1]A'Lelia Walker had invited CVV to purchase the Villa Lewaro, her fabulous palace at Irvington on Hudson.

Saw Lloyd and Edna[2] yesterday. I hope to see you early in September when we return. Best wishes to you & Mamie [White]!     Carlo

## TO MARY GARDEN                                    Le Bristol
5 September 1930                                      Paris

Dear Mary, This will introduce you to my great friend, Virgil Thomson who—with Gertrude Stein—has written an entirely new kind of opera—on the subject of Santa Theresa that I am sure it would interest you to hear.[3]     with affection and admiration, always, Carl Van Vechten

## TO JAMES WELDON JOHNSON                           S. S. Paris
[15 September 1930]                                   [at sea]

Dear Jim! Yesterday was the roughest day I have ever spent at sea. The boat leapt in the air & came down with a bang. So I stayed in Bed and reread *Black Manhattan*—all the way through with a great deal of pleasure also *looking for errors*. Now, usually books of this sort are really *full* of errors. It is almost impossible, when you are stating so many facts, to keep them out. I can't find any, however—not *one*. Besides, I must say that I enjoyed the second reading even more than the first. There are depths to your irony that do not always pierce the ears at the first jab of the needle! I love the parts about the churches & Marcus Garvey & the classes in Harlem & I adored the Garland Anderson story[4] [. . .]. Of course, it will be a great source book for a long time to come as was the autobiography [*of an Ex-Coloured Man*] & no one—absolutely no one, except Defoe, can write prose like you.

I shall mail this from New York, so you will know we are back & I hope that we shall see you & Grace soon. If you are in town please call up at once. For a couple of weeks we shall be mortared & painted & polished but after that we expect to be right pretty. Wait till you see our new dining room chairs![5] I have some new photographs for you which I think you will like. It is surprising how many Negroes there are in famous paintings. Some day I think it would be lovely to collect them all in a large volume.     Much love! Carlo & Fania

---

[2]Lloyd Thomas and his wife, black actress Edna Lewis.
[3]*Four Saints in Three Acts* was not produced until 1934, and then with an all-black cast.
[4]Garland Anderson, black playwright who toured his play *Appearances*, 1925, across the country from San Francisco to Broadway.
[5]CVV and Fania Marinoff purchased eight backless stools, the bases of which were carved wood blackamoors holding the seats on their heads.

## TO VIRGIL THOMSON

150 West 55th Street
New York City

[29 October 1930]

Dear Virgil: Mary Garden gave a Debussy concert with Gieseking[6] at Carnegie Hall & I went & tried to see her after, but she went when she got through & left her flowers on the stage with Gieseking. Anyway Muriel Draper is talking with her about the OPERA [*Four Saints in Three Acts*], but I am afraid she is not being convinced. You must remember that leopards do not change their spots. However we shall see. We have been doing our apartment over & have had no cook, but now we have a French Valentine & a Black Edith.[7] New York is more incredibly lustrous than ever. I have only been out a few times, but every time I go out I faint from sheer excitement. A coupla nice people have arrived from Spain & England & parts unknown. Florine [Stettheimer] talks about you a great deal & IS PAINTING YOUR PORTRAIT. This may be a secret, so don't mention it till you hear from her. I have not seen it yet, but hope to this week. I hear that Louis Cole has got a silver racing car. Please kiss the dear boy for me, should you see him. Nigger Heaven is in Italian now, but I hear that all the dear colored orchestra boys have been driven out of Paris. Man Ray has done me a photograph of the Service Rapide sign. I haven't done anything on [George] Hugnet's poems yet, but hope to some day. If you could see my desk now! Will I ever get settled. I do love to be with you & wish you were in New York.     best butter dolphins to you! or whatever. Carlo

## TO ALFRED A. KNOPF

150 West 55th Street
New York City

18 November [1930]

Dear Alfred—[. . .] The English notices of Parties are almost as violent as those directed against Jude the Obscure. But, unlike [Thomas] Hardy, I shall probably write another novel some day.

7 best buttered dolphins to you! Carlo

## TO MABEL DODGE LUHAN

150 West 55th Street
New York City

8 December 1930

Dear Mabel, "Lorenzo in Taos" arrived and I read it at once and I think it is as good as your first Buffalo volume.[8] Maybe I think it is better. Anyway

---

[6]Walter Gieseking, German concert pianist.
[7]In the long catalog of CVV's servants and domestics, Edith Ramsay was the first to stay for any extended period, 1930–36.
[8]*Intimate Memories: Background*, 1933. CVV refers here to Mabel Dodge Luhan's books in manuscript. *Lorenzo in Taos* was not published until 1932.

this is as high praise as I could give any book, because nothing (of its kind) could be much better than your first Buffalo volume. I think you get down a period of turmoil & excitement and a kind of primitive fighting for supremacy between a lot of he & she women, and through it all one thing remains as rooted in reality as an oak, and that is Tony [Luhan]. I think the background is amazing & Jaime[9] & Clarence[1] and the others amusing & delightful contrast. And when it is all over I think Lawrence[2] remains the same enigma that he is in his own books & that he obviously was in life & so I think you have done him well, because I think if you had completely explained him that would not have been Lawrence & no one would have recognized the portrait. Mabel, I think this is a fine book you have written, & I send you laurel wreaths in bulk & wholesale.

I don't know what to write you about ourselves, except that our apartment is larger (we broke through the wall & added another one), that we have a sweet late Victorian room which came out of my mother's piano quite naturally, that neither of us is working. I'd love to join you in Mexico, but I got so sick of travelling this summer that I don't want to go places right away. [. . .]

Willa Cather[3] is here & will have the book presently. Several others want to read it. I shall be very careful & return it to you in Taos in due course.

I am getting very wonderful reactions to Parties from a *very* new audience. [Alfred] Stieglitz, Henry McBride, [Charles] Demuth, find it a creative masterpiece & a step in advance for me—"wholly lacking in the photography" which some times lurks in my novels, if you know what they mean. Gertrude [Stein], too, thus construes it.

Muriel [Draper] has a very pretty house—wood—with a great white drawing room & gilt chairs upholstered in grey & a *throne* for her & Gurdjieff.[4] Gertrude's (and Virgil Thomson's) opera [*Four Saints in Three Acts*] is going to be published. They want Mary Garden to sing it! Thus, in the end, all our acquaintances & friends come together—like the gathering of principals at the end of a comic opera.

I salute you, dear Mabel. You have always had at your centre a great &

---

[9]Jaime de Angulo, French-born medical student turned cowboy who studied anthropology in Taos, New Mexico.
[1]Clarence, an androgynous visitor from New York who fell in love with both Mabel and Tony Luhan, identified only by his first name.
[2]D. H. Lawrence, subject of *Lorenzo in Taos*.
[3]Willa Cather had spent time in Taos as early as 1912 and visited Mabel Dodge Luhan there in 1925.
[4]G. Gurdjieff, Russian mystic who founded the Institute for the Harmonious Development of Man in Paris.

enduring charm, and now you are learning to use your great gifts to some purpose.     My love as always to Tony     Carlo

## TO ALFRED A. KNOPF
7 February [1931]

150 West 55th Street
New York City

Dear Alfred, Lorenzo in Taos is so good that you ought to persuade Frieda [Lawrence] to permit it to be published. If not, you should persuade Mabel to rewrite it as a novel, which it perfectly well could be with a few changes of names, etc. Willa Cather and Ettie [Stettheimer] share my enthusiasm.

It has also occurred to me that W. J. Henderson[5] might do a swell book on the great singers and virtuosi from Patti on—he has heard them all— à la Chorley,[6] before he dies. This probably would not sell but it would be authentic and valuable.

Booth Tarkington in a recent interview said that this was a country-club age and that the public had practically ceased to read, owing to radio, talking pictures and what not. He added that when television in the home was practical no one would ever open a book. I am inclined to agree with him. I also think that the rapid strides of science (Einstein, etc.) and geographical changes, owing to wars, etc., and ethnological changes will soon make all books out of date, and so I have decided sooner or later to write another, especially since I ran across the following (from Emerson) this morning: "The disadvantages of any epoch exist only to the fainthearted."

We are giving a buffet luncheon on Lincoln's birthday [. . .], and we wish you and Blanche were here. Well, anyway, love to you both, AND 143 royal purple dachshunds with silver legs to you!     Carlo

## TO VIRGIL THOMSON
24 February 1931

150 West 55th Street
New York City

Dear Virgil: Your news is breaking me down—as we say "en nègre."[7] And your letter is both amusing & sad-making. I wish you could be in New

---

[5]William James Henderson, *New York Times* music critic, librettist.
[6]H. Fothergill Chorley, nineteenth-century British critic and widely travelled writer.
[7]Virgil Thomson had asked CVV to write a preface to a collection of his songs to texts by Gertrude Stein and French poet George Hugnet; then he and Stein decided to have CVV write a preface to *Four Saints in Three Acts* instead, when publication of the opera became a possibility. The "amusing & sad-making" news was Stein and Hugnet in disagreement over the size of the typeface in which their respective names were to appear on joint publications, apparently on Thomson's music (for which Stein had put up the major sum, although she acknowledged Hugnet's financial contribution) as well as on her translation of Hugnet's *Enfances* (1933). Thomson's account in his autobiography *Virgil Thomson* (1966), Stein's account in "Left to Right" (1933), and Thomson's letters to CVV at the time are at minor variance.

York this winter. I have indigestion & alcohol-poisoning & a cold, but I go right on for fear I'll miss something. I do not know whether we'll come to Paris. Probably not. Loved the program you sent me.      Le tentchass Carlo

## TO MATTHEW PHIPPS SHIEL                    150 West 55th Street
## 14 March 1931                              New York City

My dear M. P. Shiel, Of course I was thrilled and delighted to receive The Black Box[8] and dipped straight into it and raced through its vivid pages to the ripe conclusion, an amazing example of your skill in construction, and the lustiest example of your superb prose to come from your pen in some time. The phrases are actually painfully pleasurable: whole pages arousing long forgotten brain cells to cry out with applause. My niece[9] finds you her favorite author and she shall be the next to read.

I don't know whether we shall be coming to England this year or no. It may be California instead. I am not working very seriously, but expect to prepare a book of short sketches between now and June. Parties got bad reviews and sold badly, but I hold it in great esteem.      435 Laurel wreaths with gold tips to you! Carl Van Vechten

## TO JAMES WELDON JOHNSON                    150 West 55th Street
## 30 April 1931                              New York City

Dear Jim, Last night was another historic occasion. I have long contended that a Negro ballet, along the lines of the Russian ballet, would be a sensation. Last night saw the beginnings of such a group[1] and it was far from unpromising. It was indeed so original and so good that I predict a very speedy realization of a great African ballet with a symphony orchestra etc. The tiny Chanin theatre was packed to suffocation last night and many were turned away. The program is to be repeated in a larger theatre. I suggest that you look into the next performance. I might add that the enormous Majestic Theatre in Brooklyn has dusted up the S.R.O. sign and is using it for the first time in weeks. The GREAT Ethel Waters has at last come into her Kingdom.      always with affection, Carlo

---

[8]*The Black Box*, 1930, a novel by M. P. Shiel.
[9]Elizabeth Hull, daughter of Emma Van Vechten Shaffer.
[1]The New Negro Art Theatre, sponsored by white doyenne of modern dance Ruth St. Denis, presented a recital based on African themes and Negro spirituals.

## TO GILBERT SELDES

150 West 55th Street

4 May 1931

New York City

Dear Gilbert, Of course you are right about the gigolo songs, but I suspect that worse is yet to come. Now that the sobsong is at the height of its rage—Handy[2] and his St. Louis Blues probably fathered and mothered the breed—I am waiting for pleas to pity the painted pansy, to sob with the forsaken snowbird, or to give heed to the cares of the hapless bootlegger. There may be a croon or two devoted to the overworked columnist. Let the torch-song writers get busy and wring as many tears as possible from willing eyes before the reaction sets in. About the only subject that doesn't seem to demand a decent dirge nowadays is a Lindy Hop dancer.[3]      yours, Carl Van Vechten

## TO FANIA MARINOFF

150 West 55th Street

20 May [1931]

New York City

Dearest Baby, Carlotta [Monterey O'Neill] called up this morning bright and early and she and Gene are coming to lunch tomorrow and I asked them to dinner on Friday May 29, because you are to be back then and they will only be here next week when Carlotta is going to California etc.[4] Let me know at once if you will be back for that dinner.[5] Of course they don't want anyone else in. Carlotta says they want to see nobody except old friends, and she says she is afraid to cross the street in New York. [. . .] Two letters came from you this morning and I am delighted that you are having such a nice time. Don't worry about the girls.[6] They are getting along all right. There is still a good deal to do, but I guess we will get it done. I mailed Van [Vechten Shaffer] one of the [Berenice] Abbott photographs [of CVV] yesterday. I am wondering if you will like the Lachaise head.[7] I think it is going to be grand and he seems absolutely confident about it, but posing is so very tiresome and God knows when he will be

---

[2]William Christopher Handy, black composer.
[3]CVV makes use of current slang, some of which continues its currency: Pansy = homosexual; snowbird = drug addict; bootlegger = illegal liquor salesman; Lindy Hop = popular black dance.
[4]Eugene O'Neill and his wife had just returned from France, where CVV and Fania Marinoff had visited them the summer before.
[5]Fania Marinoff was visiting her in-law-relatives in Cedar Rapids, Iowa.
[6]CVV's cook Edith Ramsay had been joined recently by a housekeeper—Pearl Showers—who remained in CVV's employment until 1953.
[7]Gaston Lachaise was sculpting a head of CVV. Later, CVV gave the bronze cast of it to the Chicago Art Institute.

121

through with me. I am dining with Reg[ina Wallace] tonight.

all my love, Carlo

If you want to buy any shoes etc. in Chicago you have two cheques of your own.

I was interrupted in the middle of the last sentence by Mr Wassermann at the phone to tell me that Ralph Barton killed himself this morning. That seems to justify so many of the things he has done, if he felt that strongly about things. You will doubtless read this in the papers before you read it here. You will remember Tom Smith said he had tried to do this last winter.—And Carlotta coming to lunch tomorrow. I wonder if she will have any feeling about this.[8]

TO FANIA MARINOFF                    150 West 55th Street
22 May [1931]                        New York City

Dearest Baby, Well, last night Carlotta [O'Neill] telephoned again and she was feeling better and I am to see them today at lunch. Gene had an appointment yesterday to see the reporters at the [Theatre] Guild and he decided to go through with it and the result was very dignified and, as the [*New York*] Times announces this morning, Ralph [Barton] was already forgotten: nobody called to see him; there were no flowers. I think the O'Neills were lucky. He hated Gene and was crazy enough to kill him . . . Lachaise went a step back yesterday. He says he is at the point now, however, when he may finish any second. He wants "life" to come in. Texas Guinan's[9] farewell party on the Paris last night was a riot. It began with a buffet dinner for fifteen at Eddie [Wassermann]'s and there must have been two hundred on the boat. She gave her show. Dwight Fiske[1] gave his, there was a band and dancing and a supper. I recognized a few stewards. Everybody was introduced, of course. I followed Chevalier[2] and Primo Carnera[3] and said:

---

[8]Tom Smith, an editor with Horace Liveright for whom Barton had made illustrations for Balzac's *Droll Stories,* had reported Barton's suicide attempt by a drug overdose during one of his increasing periods of depression. Carlotta O'Neill was Barton's third wife; she had left him in early 1926 because of his infidelities. Following a fourth failed marriage—to French composer Germaine Tailleferre—Barton shot himself, leaving a note to declare his despondency over his inability to complete further drawings and over his having lost Carlotta. CVV to Fania Marinoff, 21 May 1931: "This, I think, was his most completely rotten act. [. . .] Ralph has always been furious because she married a man more famous than himself. He knew she was in town and he saw a good way to make trouble for her, inasmuch as he was killing himself anyway."
[9]Texas Guinan, popular speakeasy hostess.
[1]Dwight Fiske, nightclub singer of raunchy songs.
[2]Maurice Chevalier, French chanteur.
[3]Primo Carnera, Italian boxing champion.

Je t'aime, cherie,
Bonne chance à Paris!

I had a nice time with Judith,[4] Ann Andrews,[5] Muriel [Starr], Zena,[6] etc. Eddie had Jean Malin[7] and his boy friend and of course Jean did a lot of entertaining. Also had a lovely time with Jay Brennan[8] and Helen Morgan.[9] You're getting back just in time for Eddie's series of farewell parties. A cablegram from Paul [Robeson] today reads: No injury voice away long rest love . . . Haven't had a letter from you today. If you haven't already written me telegraph if you will come back for O'Neill dinner next Friday,     all my love, Carlo
Practically everything around the house is done now. The final touches will be put on tomorrow. The girls have been splendid.

TO HUNTER STAGG                                    150 West 55th Street
[8 August 1931]                                    New York City

Dear Hunter, How chatty we seem to be getting in our semi-senility! Anyway your new typewriter seems to inspire you to write lovelier letters than ever and I *am* pleased to get them. [. . .] You should also be categorically informed that I have given up drinking *for ever* . . . This is because I am tired of drinking, having exhausted every phase of it, and want the new sensations that perfect sobriety can give me. Some of these I have already experienced, enough to realize that I have received a mystic message of approval. Anyway, as happens so often with me—every seven years or so—I seem to be entering into a new period, and will probably engage in some new activity. It is strange, but the fact that I have stopped drinking is already having an uncanny effect. Last night four young men here all solemnly refused to touch a drop of anything, although, naturally, the house was as full of booze as ever. They all eventually became very gay and lively on water! Anyway I am sick of the taste of liquor, sick of its effect, and the new sensation promises to be very enlivening. My plans are very indefinite [. . .]. I am working a little. I suppose in the end I shall give up writing! Well, I can scarcely call it renunciation after thirty years of inebriety!     176 rosy wishes to you! Carlo
What do you mean by thermometerizing your charm? You big stiff, you!

[4]Judith Anderson, Australian actress.
[5]Ann Andrews, American actress, one of CVV's warmest friendships.
[6]Zena Naylor, American actress.
[7]Jean Malin, female impersonator.
[8]Jay Brennan, American actor, partner to the transvestite entertainer Bert Savoy.
[9]Helen Morgan, American torch singer and actress.

## TO ARTHUR DAVISON FICKE

150 West 55th Street
7 December 1931                    New York City

Dear Arthur, My life is precisely like yours. I don't drink. I eat a great deal
& I lie in bed most of the time. I have entirely given over parties. Your
book[1] is being given an ever-widening circulation and is much admired,
& so are *you*!     Love, Carlo

## TO MAX EWING

150 West 55th Street
[25 December 1931]                New York City

Dear Max: Ettie S[tettheimer] is mad about a movie star—one Warner
Baxter (whom I have never seen). She even has him on a cover of her box
of cascara pills. I hope you can do something about this. She said he is a
bad actor, but the muscles of his mouth are irresistible.     Aff. Carlo

## TO FANNIE HURST

150 West 55th Street
[1931]                             New York City

*Dear* Fannie: How can you go like this? I haven't seen you since I read
Back Street, which completely broke me down. A fine & *unforgettable* per-
formance. Well, have a swell time and come back soon. You *do* move fast.
I just got through reading* that you were motoring in Canada with Z[ora]
Neale Hurston![2]     I kiss your hand, madame! Carlo
*in the Tattler

## TO MURIEL DRAPER

150 West 55th Street
1 January 1932                     New York City

Dear MaDraper! Didn't you tell me [Vladimir] Horowitz was your favorite
pianist? After today, I am with you, body & soul! Happy New Year & love
always.     PaVechten

[1]*The Hell of the Good,* 1931, by "Edouard de Verb," of which "twenty-two" copies were printed,
Arthur Davison Ficke's semi-pornographic "theological epic" in verse. Probably many more
copies were printed, despite the limitation note. See CVV to Donald Gallup, 9 December
1947.
[2]Fannie Hurst had employed the black writer Zora Neale Hurston as her chauffeur and secretary.

Muriel Draper, 1934

Fannie Hurst, 1932

Donald Angus, 1932

## TO MAX EWING

150 West 55th Street
New York City

18 February 1932

Dear Max: [. . .] I practiced photography with lights last night & blew *all* the fuses out, but I'll be ready for you soon.[3] George Lynes[4] took me today listening to a sea-shell through spectacles, and I took him. I also saw Shanghai Express[5] & thought it had loads of atmosphere.

My compliments, C.

## TO DONALD ANGUS

150 West 55th Street
New York City

[circa May 1932]

Mrs. [Gertrude] Atherton bought a dress chez vous. Did you see her?—A man at 136 W 55 has a live fox on a chain which he carries in his arms. Anna May's film is perfectly blank.[6] No one can imagine what happened— except it was April 1. Paul's is marvellous.[7] A German band is playing Auf Wiedersehn, my dear, outside. I am very melancholy & about to kill myself on account of Anna May's film. I am convinced the lousy bastards exposed it to the light. What shall I tell Anna May? How can I get that angel to come again?     [unsigned]

## TO PRENTISS TAYLOR

150 West 55th Street
New York City

[16 June 1932]

[. . .] Langston [Hughes] was here and took everything but *Negro Mother*[8]— because he had some of these. He hoped to find time to write you, but he had only a day here and I saw him only a couple hours before sailing. In case he writes later I told him to address you care of me . . . I asked him about his reddishness and he said that he thought such organizations as the N.A.A.C.P. were no good any more, that the subject wanted dynamiting. But he hasn't joined the Communist Party because if you do, they own you body & soul & can dictate. I asked him if he didn't think this moving picture in Russia was a racket, and he grinned & said he guessed he'd go

---

[3]When Miguel Covarrubias returned from Europe with a Leica camera CVV bought one, in February 1932, and began his long career as a photographer.
[4]George Platt Lynes, American photographer.
[5]*Shanghai Express,* 1932, a film by Joseph von Sternberg with Marlene Dietrich.
[6]Anna May Wong, the Chinese American film actress was the first photographic subject CVV developed and printed himself. It was the failure of this first sitting that motivated his installing full equipment in a darkroom in his apartment, probably in May 1932.
[7]Paul Draper, Muriel Draper's son.
[8]*The Negro Mother and Other Dramatic Recitations,* 1931, by Langston Hughes with illustrations by Prentiss Taylor.

anyway.[9] And I told him probably *all the others* would have to walk back.—
I printed Helen Morgan last night & they are swell. You will get some later.
And with Donald [Angus] I'm printing Ethel [Waters] tonight. Paul [Draper]
came after his pictures last night & raved. *PLEASE WRITE MORE PLAIN-
LY*     [unsigned]

TO HUNTER STAGG                                  150 West 55th Street
[15 August 1932]                                  New York City

Dear Hunter, In your day, and out, you have done many sweet things, but
I must especially thank you for sending Mark[1] along. A delightful person
of whom I have grown very fond. He is returning today and will indeed
be in Richmond when you receive this letter. He has the photograph you
asked for and another which I thought you might want if you saw it. It
is, I think, my authoritative portrait of this epoch: I mean the one by Ber-
enice Abbott. As these are very expensive I have had very few of them
made, but however few there should be one for you if there was a desire
on your part for one, and I am sending it to you on the chance there may
be.

Also I have presented Mark with Blair Niles's new book: Strange Brother,
already known hereabouts as Condemned to Manhattan. I have asked him
to let you read this at once. It isn't issued until the 13th. Mark, it appears,
had not heard much about Blair, who, as you know, is from Richmond,
but of course you know enough about her so that this book will completely
break you down. It is very pro-pederast, and sentimental, and in fact a riot
and to cap the climax (to coin a phrase) the hero's name is Mark.* I need
not add that it is not literature.

I have decided to buy Leslie Bolling's[2] large head for myself. It is now
very well placed and everybody likes it. So I am enclosing a cheque which
please see that he gets pronto. That I have sold none of the others means
nothing, because no one has seen them since that day Lachaise was here.[3]
It has been too hot to have people in and the right people to buy aren't
in town anyway. Don't have him send any more on unless I ask for them,
but I wish he would keep you informed if he has anything new or striking.
Langston Hughes has seen them and is very enthusiastic.

---

[9]The Meschrabpom Film Corporation engaged a group of black Americans to appear in a
Russian-made movie called *Black and White* about life in the southern United States. The
project was never realized.
[1]Mark Lutz, Richmond, Virginia, newspaper reviewer. See List of recipients.
[2]Leslie Bolling, black Richmond sculptor.
[3]CVV had been trying to find buyers for this black artist's work.

In the meantime believe that I am deeply appreciative of your loyalty and your generosity and your friendship, and I send you 444 white and purple orchids with silver chalices!     Carlo
*He is not a bit like Mark from Richmond, needless to say.


## TO FANNIE HURST
23 August [1932]

150 West 55th Street
New York City

Dear Fannie, For the second time in my life I saw a Manx cat yesterday. In fact I saw two Manx cats. The first time was in Cincinnati in 1896 when I was 16. I am getting to be quite zoological.     Pats & purrs to you! Carlo


## TO ELLEN GLASGOW
29 August 1932

150 West 55th Street
New York City

Dear Ellen: There is a kind of "They couldn't help it" implication to every page of "The Sheltered Life" which makes it the most human and (hence) the most pathetic of your books. The characters lead their disordered (and sheltered) lives under the spell of their doom. I think never have divided natures been more skilfully & subtly presented.—Jenny Blair really loves Eva and in her passion for George there is no thought of hurting Eva. Of course George really loves Eva too—completely—and in his philandering he has no intentions of hurting her. And they suffer. And Eva who believes that nothing can be divided, that *feeling* must be *one* and steadfast, suffers still more, first because she is afraid she will lose the object of her steadfast feeling, and second because she is afraid she has lost it. I have seldom read a book that so mercilessly exposes the sadistic nature of God and you have never before written a book which is rooted so deeply in the inexplicable torments & impulses of earthly creatures.

Sheaves of cornflowers & poppies to you from your admiring     Carlo


## TO PRENTISS TAYLOR
[16 September 1932]

150 West 55th Street
New York City

Chiaroscuro has got me at last and I am working it to death. I hope I'll soon be through with this sordid phase.—I do not know Langston's cable address. The only address I have is the [Meschrabpom] film Co. which you have too. But I don't see how cabling would do any good. He knows you want the money . . . and he hasn't got it & probably has no chance of getting it under current conditions. You've done enough business with that printer so that he should be reasonable.[4] But all these upsets & downsets are part of an artistic career. As you can discover by reading Savage Messiah.[5]—I am going to use *Blue* lights now, you big stiff you!

Many happy returns! C.

TO DONALD ANGUS                    150 West 55th Street
1 October [1932]                   New York City

[. . .] That great Shakespearean scholar, Gene Tunney,[6] attended Troilus and Cressida last night. I inspected him carefully in the lobby, on our way to the EXIT, after. Max [Ewing] went to Eddie [Wassermann]'s yesterday, set up a tripod & lights & took pictures. Now, really!!    [unsigned]

TO THEODORE DREISER                150 West 55th Street
18 October 1932                    New York City

Dear Dreiser, It was delightful of you to think of me in relation to the American Spectator, but I have not written a line (beyond that or this contained in letters) for six months and do not propose to do so *until I feel a very strong urge.* In the meantime (and how!) I have become the slave of photography which I have taken up very seriously and it has become very important to me to have you sit for me as soon as you can conveniently. I was therefore very pleased to learn that you had agreed to do so. If possible, it would be better to telephone me (Circle 7–3399, *not* in the book) as I am obliged to arrange for an electrician to assist me, several days in advance.    sincerely, Carl Van Vechten
Of course, if the spirit moves me to write something I'll communicate with you at once.

TO BLANCHE KNOPF                   150 West 55th Street
14 December [1932]                 New York City

Dear Blanche, I am delighted to be able to report at once that I find myself tremendously enthusiastic about Langston's book from its splendid title[7] straight through to the end. All of it is good and some of it, I should think,

---

[4]The Golden Stair Press published two pamphlets by Hughes and illustrated by Taylor: *The Negro Mother*, 1932, and *Scottsboro Limited*, 1933.
[5]*Savage Messiah*, by Harold Stanley Ede, 1931, a biography of French sculptor Henri-Gaudier Brzeska.
[6]Gene Tunney, world heavyweight champion, notable as well for his lecture on *Troilus and Cressida* before Professor William Lyon Phelps's Shakespeare class at Yale University.
[7]*The Ways of White Folks*, 1933.

is great. I had read three of the stories in magazines and admired them. Something has happened to the lad; he has grown up, I guess. Anyway, this collection of stories is a step ahead of Not Without Laughter, his best work up to date. They are also written from a new formula, the complications that ensue between black and white lives, from the colored point of view. I am glad to feel this way after my reaction to that communist poetry book . . .[8] Incidently, he says there are two more stories. I think he ought to put 'em in.      congratulations, Carlo

P.S. I have long believed that Ethel Waters and Langston had more genius than any others of their race in this country and I think Langston will in the end have as wide a success as Ethel. This boy grows under your eyes. The manuscript is waiting here for you.

I started the book right after dinner tonight & my eyes were *glued* to the pages till I had finished it.

TO MAX EWING                                    150 West 55th Street
[1932]                                          New York City

Dear Max, I have read Going Somewhere[9] (at last) with real delight (and also extreme annoyance). Delight, because it seems to me a diverting book with negligible faults, some of which can be rectified. Annoyance, because if you had brought it to me in the first instance, as I suggested, it would have been an extremely simple matter for me to get it published. It is not so simple now. I have written Blanche [Knopf] a *warm* account of it, and this will help, but it may not get the book published. You see, nothing is selling at the moment and it is a particularly bad time for a first book by an unknown author. There is also the fact, well-known, of course, as such things get about, that this book has been rejected elsewhere. I do not lay too much stress on this last, however. And let us hope that the book will make a strong enough impression on the readers at A[lfred] A. K[nopf] so that they will suggest publication in spite of real or fancied obstacles. I am praying for you. [. . .]      anyway with rosemary and jasmine to my dear Max! Carlo

---

[8]See CVV to Blanche Knopf, circa 20 March 1934, and to Langston Hughes, 20 March 1934.
[9]Manuscript of a novel by Ewing, subsequently published (1933).

## TO JOSEPH HERGESHEIMER
[circa January 1933]

150 West 55th Street
New York City

Dear Joe, Thank you so much for the very handsome tall paper copy of Tropical Nights [i.e., *Tropical Winter*].[1] I am delighted to possess it . . . The book itself I devoured over the weekend before this tall paper copy arrived and two days ago I wrote Blanche about it with the warmest enthusiasm. I think it is a complete success, this performance, and I said so to her in very certain tones. I am also saying so to the world in a very loud voice. Of course, the obvious things are all true: you have captured a place and a period, made it and its people a part of your imagination and creative skill, evoked a remembered atmosphere and given it permanent form. Of course, you have also written a book which is bitter, critical, and ironic. As that, it gains as a work of art. May I confess that I loved the book chiefly because it is so entertaining. In these days when I scarcely read at all and most books I touch seem poisonous, I found it entirely impossible to lay this charming volume down. I read it at a sitting. It has another quality usually separable from books of short stories; there is a kind of unity which holds it together. This is more than a unity of place. There is a sort of community of feeling as if all these people actually knew each other. Thank you, dear Joe, and congratulations. This is my favorite since Tampico. When will you make an appointment to come over to be photographed? It would be quite surprising for me to give an exhibition without your countenance. Do telephone me and let us arrange something of the kind.

love to you and Dorothy from both of us, Carlo

I adore that Gloriana Bader who subdues English novelists & scraps with them in the pantry! Where are we going to get the *complete* Meeker Ritual?[2]

## TO FANNIE HURST
[circa January 1933]

150 West 55th Street
New York City

Dear Fannie, It's not quite as simple as that. You see, if they were broadcast to newspapers they would be mutilated, distorted, misrepresented, and even retouched! So, I must draw the line there. Further, if I arranged for one of the lordlier magazines to print your picture—which I hope to—they would be discountenanced to see it appear elsewhere. What can be done

---

[1]For many of his authors—and inevitably for CVV and Hergesheimer—Knopf issued limited editions of their books, usually printed on expensive paper and bound in vellum or decorated boards, boxed, numbered, and signed.
[2]References to incidents in Hergesheimer's book.

about this: if a worthy occasion arises (or ten worthy occasions arise) to print one of your beautiful photographs where it will be well reproduced *intact*, if my permission is asked I will furnish a suitable print and my blessing. Otherwise, let them confer their honors on lesser artists! Yesterday I printed some more pictures for your private use which you will have in a little while. On being shown your pictures last night, Kit Cornell exclaimed rapturously: "But isn't she too divinely beautiful!" She says she doesn't know you.     I kiss your hand! Carlo

I hope to see you at Rover's party on Sunday.[3]

TO BLANCHE KNOPF                    150 West 55th Street
[circa January 1933]                New York City

Dear Grand Duchess Cunegonda Wilhelmina Schwartz,

Tropical Nights [i.e., *Tropical Winter*], it seems to me, is one of the most entertaining books Joe [Hergesheimer] has written. I read it with really a passionate interest and I recommend it to all and sundry.

Thank you for the information about Myra Hess.[4]

If you have time, drop into the exhibition of Beautiful Women (photographs) at Bergdorf-Goodman's.[5]

Ninon Vallon[6] is really very fine. You should hear her.

Please tell [. . .] the enclosed young gentleman (Nathan Sherman) that he certainly cannot use "two or three pages of Peter Whiffle" in any play of his. This is a new species of nerve, and quite tremendous, I would say.     a night-blooming cereus to you, and my love, Carlo

[3]In December 1932, CVV acquired "Rover," "6 feet of black gopher snake with a red belly. Very handsome & a sweet disposition" as a Christmas present, so he wrote to Fannie Hurst the day after.
[4]Dame Myra Hess, British concert pianist.
[5]CVV exhibited his photographs for the first time in this show, including his pictures of actresses Ina Claire, Judith Anderson, and Lynn Fontanne, and novelist Fannie Hurst.
[6]Ninon Vallon, French soprano appearing in New York.

TO FANIA MARINOFF                          150 West 55th Street
26 June 1933                                New York City

Dearest Babykins, [. . .] I hope you liked the boat till the end.[7] Claire Luce[8]
[. . .] came for her photographs Saturday afternoon, and was really sent.
I have rarely seen anyone so enthusiastic. [. . .] I saw her again at the
Cotton Club[9] Saturday. I finally did go. Ethel [Waters] got me a ringside
table without difficulty, because she is a POWER just now. The place was
jammed and they just love her and applaud and applaud. She came to
dinner on Thursday and brought Pearl Wright her accompanist and so when
we weren't photographing she was singing. She sat in semi-darkness and
never moved and sang away, Sleepy Time Down South, Stormy Weather,
etc., and were we entranced! Edith [Ramsay] came in to listen. [. . .] By
the way her ears are pierced and I think she deserves some swell earrings.
Also I have promised her a small party (just her old white friends, like Rita
[Romilly] and Eddie [Wassermann]) after her first night.[1] Eddie will tell
you about his farewell party. I found it very dull and cannot go the people
he and Blanche [Knopf] are at present associating with, riffraff nobility,
etc. But one's interest in people varies with the years I have discovered
and doubtless I have known many worse. I sat in a corner and talked with
Alfred till it was 10 o'clock (we didn't have dinner till 9) and then came
home. [. . .] There is a Hagenbeck-Wallace Circus—they feature Clyde
Beatty with his lions and tigers—in a tent in the Bronx and I have already
been twice. Edith has been cleaning out the china closets and kitchen closets.
She will finish up this week no doubt and next week I may go away. By
the way, I had Pearl [Showers] go over all the old things wrapped in tar-
paper in the Chinese chest in the living room and she found moths in my
old steamer rug. She'd better go through all your shawls, etc. sooner or
later. And somebody—it must have been at the birthday party—dropped
a lighted cigarette end into the couch. It did not burn the brocade or the
cushion but went right through to the hair. I don't see why we weren't
all burned up alive. However, it smouldered and went out. It is hot again,
you will be glad to hear, seeing you are not here: I love it! [. . .] Have a
swell time—I know you will—I don't think Europe will be safe for travel
in many years more and I am delighted you are seeing Greece while yet
you may. I doubt if I ever want to travel much again—except a few airplane
journeys around America. Now that San Francisco is a few hours away

---

[7]Fania Marinoff was off on another cruise, this time to the Mediterranean.
[8]Claire Luce, American actress.
[9]The Cotton Club, a Harlem nightclub catering almost exclusively to white patrons.
[1]Ethel Waters was about to open in Irving Berlin's musical revue, *As Thousands Cheer.*

everything seems simple here. You really don't have to pack to take a trip.    All my love to you, dearest Baby and I'll write again next week. I'll send you a radiogram today. Carlo

TO FANIA MARINOFF                                    150 West 55th Street
[15 September 1933]                                  New York City

Dearest Babykins, I was very glad to get your letter and if it isn't very cheerful, probably the next one will be more so. [. . .] The O'Neills came to dinner and loved it and are mad about the photographs. Gene says they are the only photographs he has ever had taken he recognizes. He wants me to do the title page of his book.* And he may have a frame at the [Theatre] Guild. Carlotta wrote one of her letters—too marvellous—when she got home. It was in the mail this morning. She thinks you will be better if you relax and she sends you much love and hopes you will be fine soon. They have invited us to the opening night [of *Ah Wilderness!*] [. . .]. It rains all the time. I had lunch and went to the movies with Donald [Angus] today. I haven't quite decided whether I'll go to Philadelphia tonight or early tomorrow. Tomorrow (Sat.) I shall probably be in Doylestown visiting the Bucks County Museum (unless it rains), But when I come back to Phila I'll be at the Barclay. Sunday I'm going out to Merion to see the Barnes Foundation pictures. I have succeeded in getting an invitation from the old gentleman.[2] [. . .]    All my love, Carlo
*The play after Ah Wilderness [*Days Without End*]

TO ALFRED STIEGLITZ                                  150 West 55th Street
27 September 1933                                     New York City

Dear Stieglitz, Your letter naturally pleased me *very much* & also scared me a little—for is not praise from you almost an accolade & am I not in danger of believing I have become a maestro?[3]—It is very hard, but I have hit myself & told me that I'm not good enough even yet! . . . But please you & O'Keeffe[4] come & be photographed when you come back to N.Y! You would be the pinnacle of the collection!—    best buttered dolphins to you both. C. V. V.

[2]Albert Coombs Barnes, the wealthy Philadelphia pharmacist-inventor who exhibited his extensive and impressive private art collection—primarily impressionist but also African primitive—only at his own whim.
[3]Alfred Stieglitz to CVV, September 1933: "If I wore a hat I would take it off before your photographs. [. . .] They are damn swell. A joy. You are certainly a photographer. There are but few."
[4]Georgia O'Keeffe, American painter, Alfred Stieglitz's wife.

## TO LOUIS BROMFIELD

[circa 1933]

150 West 55th Street
New York City

Dear Louis, Thanks for The Farm. I was sorry (for my sake, glad for yours) it was a ninth printing. But even a ninth printing with your lovely writing in it is a good deal. I will read it next time I take a tour which is the only time I read nowadays, as otherwise I am too busy in the DARKROOM. I took a tour yesterday, for instance and read [Robert Coates's] Yesterday's Burdens, [Ernest Hemingway's] Winner Take Nothing, and Ring Lardner's Roundup. I am sorry. Ring Lardner, for instance, I had never read, but everybody shouts so loud for him I thought I oughter. But, with his laboriously work-up-to trick endings he seems very like O. Henry, with more knowledge of vernacular, of course, and much too much knowledge of Bridge, Baseball, and Golf. All such games bore me and reading about them bores me almost more . . . This isn't at all the vein in which I'll write about The Farm . . . eventually.     151 mulatto gals with red hair and blue silk panties to you! Carlo!

## TO GERTRUDE STEIN

8 February 1934

Heublein Hotel
Hartford, Connecticut

Dear Gertrude, Four Saints, in our vivid theatrical parlance, is a knockout and a wow. I cabled you when I got home from the invited dress rehearsal last night (I mean you were invited to buy seats). It was a most smart performance in this beautiful little theatre. People not only wore evening clothes, they wore sables and tiaras. Henry McBride[5] sat just in front of me.* I haven't seen a crowd more excited since Sacre du Printemps. The difference was that they were pleasurably excited. The Negroes are divine, like El Grecos, more Spanish, more Saints, more opera singers in their dignity and *simplicity* and extraordinary plastic line than *any* white singers could ever be. And they enunciated the text so clearly you could understand every word. Frederick Ashton's rhythmic staging was inspired and so were Florine [Stettheimer]'s costumes and sets. Imagine a crinkled sky-blue cellophane background, set in white lace borders, like a valentine against which were placed the rich and royal costumes of the saints in red velvets, etc. and the dark Spanish skins. The wedding funeral in the third act was like an El Greco. The manager who is taking it to New York expects it to be a success and I am sure it will be something. I'll ask Virgil [Thomson] today if he is sending you programs etc. and if he isn't I'll send you some

⁵Henry McBride, American art critic and early Stein endorser.

of this kind of thing when I get back to New York. I suppose your clipping bureau will attend to the rest. But I enclose a couple of samples and the coupons from our two seats. Now, please let me write this preface.[†6] I really think you should see, hear, and feel Four Saints. Maybe you and Alice can be persuaded to try it out. Dollars go farther here too now than they do there and perhaps you would escape the revolution.[‡]     love always, Carlo

*& was really wild with delight
[†]I have to send it in *today!*
[‡]& be photographed *officially.*

## TO JAMES WELDON JOHNSON

150 West 55th Street
New York City

25 February 1934

Dear Jim, I was prepared to thoroughly agree with They Shall Not Die[7] and to be much moved by it. I came away completely unmoved and disliking the play very much. I think it will react against the purpose for which it was written. It is a bad play, the point of view is often false, and the interpretation of the facts is so obviously inspired by hate that often you are forced to admit to yourself you just don't believe the author. The attack on the N.A.A.C.P. is childish and Lucy Wells's (Ruby Bates) love affair with the travelling salesman is enough to turn a strong stomach. The Southerners against whom the play is directed will, of course, never see it. Other Southerners will not find it important enough to answer. I should add, by the way, that the Negro boys are quite beautiful and the face of the one in the courtroom scene very haunting. But no play in which all the dice are loaded can be very convincing. Even in Uncle Tom's Cabin there were some good Southerners, some Negroes who escape the lash. But not in this opus. Hugh Walpole, who was with me, agreed with my judgment and so did that eminent radical, Emma Goldman, a member of the same audience.

I should say that the performance of Four Saints [*in Three Acts*] by a Negro cast was much more important to the Scottsboro cause and to the history of the Negro stage in general (in which it is one of the big milestones). I should say the success of Ethel Waters in As Thousands Cheer and the grand tour of The Green Pastures are adding to the respect and

[6]For the souvenir program distributed during the New York run of *Four Saints in Three Acts*, CVV wrote ''How I Listen to Four Saints in Three Acts,'' and when Random House published the libretto, he supplied a preface.
[7]*They Shall Not Die*, 1934, by John Wexley, based on the Scottsboro Case.

recognition which is being given to the Negro. Add to these Along This Way,[8] Langston's new book, The Ways of White Folks, and Zora Neale Hurston's Jonah's Gourd Vine (which Lippincott's in Philadelphia will presently publish with Fannie Hurst and C.V.V. leading the cheering) and there is very much more REAL SOLID evidence of a "Negro Renaissance" than there was in 1926–27. I think, for instance, that Miss Waters does more in Supper Time[9] to awaken the torpid imagination to a realization of what may happen to those boys in Scottsboro than any number of silly, unbelievable dramas like They Shall Not Die.

By the way, I think it is highly important you should see Four Saints and They Shall Not Die, even at some expense and the risk of a few other broken engagements.

Love to both from us and a special kiss to Grace on Tuesday the 27th when she will be sixteen!    Carlo!

TO HUGH WALPOLE                                    150 West 55th Street
15 March 1934                                       New York City

Dear Hugh, By this post I am sending your photographs to you registered. I like some of them a lot and I hope you will, but I itch to take you again. A couple are scratched (this sometimes happens, on a tiny film, and is unavoidable) but I am sending these anyway. And I am sending duplicates of several. If you want any more copies, please ask for them. I'll be delighted to send them to you (or to any one in America you may want them sent to). At any rate, please tell me which ones you prefer. You will find them all clearly numbered. [. . .]

You will have my letter [of introduction] to Miss Stein by now. Your letter from the boat arrived yesterday on the Majestic with Miss Grigsby! It is amusing that you should say about Three Lives the very thing Gertrude wrote me about it, after she had read it in the Modern Library reprint edition for the first time in fifteen or so years, that it is sentimental. But so is a good deal of your beloved Dickens. And so is Carlo when he thinks of Hugh! It is one of my greatest disappointments that I can't write a sentimental book* which is very astonishing when you think how sentimental I really am.

[. . .] We have another new play which is really beautiful: Yellow Jack, of which mosquitoes in test-tubes are the principal protagonists.[1] They Shall

---

[8]*Along This Way*, 1933, James Weldon Johnson's autobiography.
[9]"Supper Time," a song by Irving Berlin in which a black woman mourns her husband who has been hanged, from the musical revue, *As Thousands Cheer.*
[1]*Yellow Jack*, 1934, by Cryssie A. Hotchkiss.

Not Die is deservedly a flop. The Shining Hour[2] is a success. But I am getting tired of seeing the company at parties. They seem to go together in a body everywhere!

Please give my best regards to Harold[3] and tell him I won't be satisfied till I photograph him. [. . .]     love, dear Hugh! Carlo!
*I may manage this yet!

## TO LANGSTON HUGHES
20 March 1934

150 West 55th Street
New York City

Dear Langston, In looking over your volume of poems again I find I like them even less than I did last year.[4] In fact, I find them lacking in any of the elementary requisites of a work of art.* This opinion has nothing to do with the opinions expressed therein. I find myself violently at variance with the opinions expressed by Diego Rivera's flaming frescoes in the Workers' School on Fourteenth Street, but I am drawn back to them repeatedly by his vital and superbly imaginative painting. I think A Good Job Gone[5] is 100 percent [stronger] propaganda for the Negro (here an artist is working who exhibits a Negro character arrogant with a white character) than the whole book of poems which I find, as art, as propaganda, as anything you may care to mention, Very Very Weak. Doubtless I am wrong. At least you can rely on my being frank with you. If you are interested at all, I could say a lot more (would that you were here so we could talk), but doubtless you are fed up with the subject already. [. . .]

*This is a little too sweeping, I am speaking "generally." There are certain poems in the book that are very good indeed, only less good than your best work in this form.—But nothing sufficiently novel or strong to rate as "first class." I think your public has a right to demand only the "first class" of you after "Not Without Laughter" & "The Ways of White Folks."     768 white penguin feathers for 76 black swans to you! (and an owl)   [unsigned]

---

[2]The Shining Hour, 1934, by Keith Winter.
[3]Harold Cheevers, Hugh Walpole's companion, chauffeur, houseman.
[4]See CVV to Blanche Knopf, 14 December 1932.
[5]"A Good Job Gone," story in The Ways of White Folks, 1934.

## TO BLANCHE KNOPF
[circa 20 March 1934]

150 West 55th Street
New York City

Dear Blanche, There seem to be some slight changes in this Langston manuscript,[6] but that does not alter my opinion of the book as a whole. I think the revolutionary poems are pretty bad, more revolutionary than poetic; all this has been done a million times better. And the centre part of the book is not nearly as good as Langston's other books of poetry. I think, as a matter of fact, that he has gone as far as he will ever go as a poet and, except for casual magazine appearances, he might be well advised to leave this Muse alone henceforth. Of course, there can be no talk of his going elsewhere with the book. He should be written that of course you will print it if he insists upon it. I think stress should be laid on the fact that he has another book coming out and that it is impossible for a publisher to do justice to two books at once and that it is advisable to put this off for a time. And that if he still wants to publish this next year, why of course you will do it. If further arguments are necessary, it might be brought forward that it is bad policy to publish a book which is such a letdown from his previous work in this direction, that communists do not buy books and few others will want to buy a book in which the communistic sentiments are stronger than the art. If he wants to let his radical friends know how he feels, he has already done so when these verses have appeared in magazines.

However, at all times, it should be stressed that you will print the book, of course, if he wants it done. Langston is never unreasonable and I don't think he will be in this case. However, as you are going away, you'd better talk the situation over pretty thoroughly with Alfred, as many letters and telegrams may go through about this.

Thank you for letting me read Avery [Hopwood]'s Diary. I do not see anything in this for you, but it was immensely interesting to me.

All these manuscripts are awaiting your boy, who may have them happily with a spoon![7]      789 white heron's feathers in a silver basket to you! Carlo!

---

[6]Some of the poems from Hughes's manuscript were published four years later, by the International Workers' Organization, as *A New Song;* others awaited posthumous publication, in 1973, in *Good Morning, Revolution.*

[7]"Having happily had it with a spoon" was a line from Gertrude Stein's *Four Saints in Three Acts,* popular at the time because of the recent stage success, and widely quoted.

Alfred A. Knopf, 1935

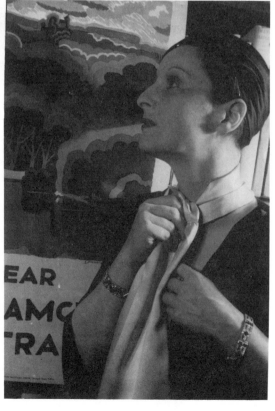

Blanche Knopf, 1932

James Branch Cabell, 1935

James Weldon Johnson, 19

## TO ALFRED A. KNOPF
11 May 1934

150 West 55th Street
New York City

Dear Alfred, The enclosed [letter] from Claude McKay[8] arrives just as I am leaving.[9] If you don't want to do anything about it, will you please write and tell him so. But maybe you'll take a peep at this manuscript. I think he is good, sometimes very good indeed, and maybe you can get him to turn out something special. He is better (so far at least) on the West Indies or the Riviera than he is on Harlem, but there is no objection to that. Please return this letter to me.      with l and k! Carlo!

Langston [Hughes] writes he has sold his Soviet story to the Woman's Home Companion![1] Good God, he'll be in the Ladies Home Journal next! What a boy!

## TO FANIA MARINOFF
[31 May 1934]

Hotel Vier Jahreszeiten
Munich, Germany

Dearest Babykins, Flying across the North Sea above the clouds to Amsterdam for lunch is quite an experience. And after lunch came on to Munich arriving around 4, stopping briefly at Cologne, Frankfurt, and Nuremberg. I sent you a wire at once & got your sweet reply. You needn't worry. By the time you receive this I won't be flying any more. Going on to Venice Saturday and to Rome next Wednesday. I am *very well* & sticking as closely to Hay[2] as possible, but sometimes you get fooled by the food,— excellent everywhere, by the way. Munich is sweet as ever & the shops are full of the *most* fascinating things. I suppose people are poor & have sold things.—Anyway I'm not buying much. Going to [*Das*] Rheingold tonight at the opera & Wiener Blut (Johann Strauss) tomorrow at the Gartnerplatz Theater. This morning, just after dawn, saw a stupendous religious procession from the Cathedral to the Maximilian Strasse. The Cardinal himself was in it, all sorts of rosy cheeked girls with wreaths on their hair & flowers in their hands. It is much warmer here than in London. [. . .] I hope you are having a grand time.[3] This is about the last letter I can get

---

[8]Claude McKay, black poet and novelist. See List of recipients. He had written to ask CVV help him place *Banjo* with a publisher.

[9]CVV and Mark Lutz flew to England, Germany, Italy, and then travelled by train to France during a six-week holiday together.

[1]"In an Emir's Harem," *Woman's Home Companion*, September 1934.

[2]The Hay Diet, a popular plan of the period for weight reduction. By 1934 CVV had ballooned to over 250 pounds.

[3]Fania Marinoff was in Hollywood on vacation.

off to you with any hope of its reaching you. But I will cable frequently.—
When I get to Paris I may go down to the country to see Gertrude [Stein].
She has asked me to & they have a bath room now!—Well, I'll be seeing
you soon, and it will be grand. I love you very much.      all my love, Carlo

I haven't received *any* letters from America except the one you wrote
me from Panama.

TO JAMES BRANCH CABELL                    150 West 55th Street
1 October 1934                                        New York City

Dear James, I feel more and more obligated as your handsome books continue to come to me and I continue to have none to send to you! You see
I have given myself so wholeheartedly to photography (in which I can be
my own publisher, printer, and binder!) that I have almost forgotten that
I ever was a writer, although perhaps some day this consciousness may
return to me! At any rate, for the moment, I have no books of my own to
send you. If it would amuse you I could substitute volumes by Gertrude
Stein or it might be that you would like one of my photographs of Radio
City or Pompeii. What I would rather do than anything else is to make
some portraits of you and I hope you will give me that privilege before
long. In any case, feel free to command me. As for Ladies and Gentlemen[4]
I had already sampled its delights in The Spectator and elsewhere and so
I returned to the charge with enthusiasm. It is, I think, an exciting and
delightful book. And I thank you.      most sincerely, Carl Van Vechten

TO GERTRUDE ATHERTON                      150 West 55th Street
19 October 1934                                      New York City

Dear Gertrude, I do not think G[ertrude] Stein is going west of Iowa City,
but I don't know what eventually she may decide to do if her lectures at
Columbia, Princeton, etc. are a success. She is arriving on the Champlain
October 24 and will stop at the Algonquin Hotel: so why don't you write
her yourself? I think you are marvellous to have thought of having her
and I am sure her personality and presence would delight the Californians
who had the pleasure of attending the dinner.[5] [. . .] It was so grand to
hear from you after this long silence. Please remember me most warmly
to Mrs. Russell.[6]      with affection from Fania and Carlo Van Vechten

---

[4]*Ladies and Gentlemen: A Parcel of Reconsiderations,* 1934, by James Branch Cabell.
[5]Gertrude Atherton had offered to entertain Gertrude Stein and Alice Toklas if they came to
California during Stein's October 1934–May 1935 lecture tour.
[6]Muriel Atherton Russell, Gertrude Atherton's daughter.

TO BENNETT CERF                                          Drake Hotel
[circa 5 November 1934]                              Chicago, Illinois

Dear Bennett, It gets wilder & wilder—Greta Garbo in her palmiest days
never had such a tour!—G[ertrude] S[tein] loves flying, but she will tell
you all about that. In the meantime here are a few stories to console you
& Donald[7] for having secured such an unpopular author!!!      14 Siamese
cats & a green parrot to you! Carlo


TO GERTRUDE STEIN                               150 West 55th Street
[10 November 1934]                                      New York City

Dear Gertrude, [. . .] The party for 9 P.M. November 18 is shaping magnificently. I hope you will have it happily with a spoon.[8] It has occurred
to me that that blessed St. Therese No. 1 will be back and I am going to
ask HER.[9]

We flew back in four and a half hours (a half hour early!) without a
jolt, and flying at night is very wonderful.[1]

[. . .] Please call me up when you get up to say hello. I want to go to
the Cosmopolitan Club on Tuesday if it is a different magpie: You must
tell me.[2] Whenever you want to go to Florine [Stettheimer]'s, let me know.
Whenever you want to do anything, let me know.

I am going to make you both Ladies of the Royal Order of Woojums,[3]
and you will go out with medals after this instead of orchids and gardenias.      567 white hyacinths in jade pots to you both! Carlo!
May I give one of your pictures to Mrs. Charles B. Goodspeed?[4]


[7]Donald Klopfer, Bennett Cerf's Random House partner.
[8]See CVV to Blanche Knopf, circa 20 March 1934, note 7.
[9]Beatrice Robinson-Wayne, American soprano who was singing a leading role in *Four Saints in Three Acts.*
[1]CVV had flown to Chicago with Gertrude Stein and Alice Toklas to see a performance of *Four Saints in Three Acts.*
[2]A "different magpie": a different one of the six lectures (of which CVV had heard only two) Gertrude Stein was offering during her tour. "Magpie" occurs frequently in the most popular aria from *Four Saints in Three Acts.*
[3]CVV fancifully named Gertrude Stein "Baby Woojums," Alice Toklas "Mama Woojums," and himself "Papa Woojums." These affectionate nicknames endured until their deaths. Orig-inally, *woojums* was an address of enthusiasm CVV had now and then used for others, and during the 1920s it was the name of a lethal cocktail. See CVV to Donald Gallup, 9 December 1947 for the recipe.
[4]Bobsie Goodspeed, later Mrs Gilbert Chapman, was Gertrude Stein's Chicago hostess.

## TO GERTRUDE STEIN
[1 December 1934]

150 West 55th Street
New York City

Dearest Gertrude, Your letters about the Dance Marathon and the Squad Car are pretty cute and Thornton Wilder has got me down with jealousy.[5] Don't go and like him BETTER, PLEASE! . . . What I mean by schedule is, how long can I write you at the Drake, and where do I write you after that? So please ask Alice to let me know. *All* your letters are here, including one from Alice addressed to 150 West 50th street, so the heart of the post-office is in the right place. Did Alice write Mrs. Walter Douglas, Wayzata, Minnesota? PLEASE DO NOT MISS THIS. Address Muriel Draper, care of the American Embassy, Moscow and it will reach her (in time for Christmas). Marie Harriman sent me a telegram (which I am looking for this minute and cannot find) asking me to ask you to be the guest of honor at the opening of the Rose Show (Sir Francis and not the "is a" kind) on Friday.[6] I telephoned her and told her you wouldn't be back till the holidays. Beau Broadway in the N Y Telegraph says spies have discovered you call each other Lovey and Pussy. No one he says has yet reported on what you and Alice call C. V. V. (so Woojums is still inviolate! Don't you go calling T[hornton] W[ilder] a woojums! I will bite him!). Tell Alice I never got her letter from the Plane, so where was this sent? (Oh yes, I remember I did get two serial cards!) Did you get Arthur Griggs obituary?[7]

I spend all my time in the darkroom crying for my beautiful pair of Woojums who are TRAVELLING in the WEST.     LOVE, LOVE, to you BOTH! Fania and Pearl and EDITH send LOVE! Carlo

## TO JAMES WELDON JOHNSON
[1934]

150 West 55th Street
New York City

Dear Jim, Robert Hatch of the Viking [Press] has sent me the sheets of your new book yesterday, and it had not been in the house many minutes before I had read it through.[8] That is a fine line you've got in the foreword about the ofays![9] They'll eat it up. Anybody faintly interested in the Negro

[5]Thornton Wilder, the American writer who acted as Gertrude Stein's literary host in Chicago. The police there gave her and Alice Toklas a brief tour.
[6]Sir Francis Rose, minor English painter in whose career Gertrude Stein had developed an interest. The Marie Harriman Gallery mounted an exhibition of his work, for the catalog of which Gertrude Stein wrote a preface. The "is a" kind, of course, refers to Gertrude Stein's best known line, "Rose is a rose is a rose is a rose."
[7]Arthur Griggs, the American-born writer living in Paris, had been trying to arrange for a French production of *Four Saints in Three Acts*.
[8]*Negro Americans, What Now?*, 1934.
[9]Ofay, black argot for a white person, pig-latin for foe.

"question" is bound to read it and I think it should do more to convince those who do not believe there is any Negro "question" than anything that has yet been published. In the first place, you have never written in so superbly simple a style: as English it is a little masterpiece. Then you are so temperate, so reasonable, so logical that it would be difficult for any reader to resist your line of argument, certainly any white reader. It is more difficult to predict the effect of this book on the colored man. Will he read it at all? There is a passage that seems to fear that he won't. If he does read it will he support the NAACP or will the church and press work hand and glove with that organization? It hardly seems likely. And yet if the Negro put up a united front he could have what he wanted probably within the month because the forces against him for the most part are nourished only by an ignorant prejudice. Like you, however, I feel hopeful that *something* is bound to happen soon because so much already has happened. A little bit more here and a little bit more there and the dam will break and the waters no longer be segregated.

My congratulations!     Love to you both, Carlo

I have written Hatch!

It is significant, I think, that the time has come when you can address *the race* rather than the other race!

You are probably a Woo Jums!

## TO FANIA MARINOFF
[3 February 1935]

Monticello Hotel
Charlottesville, Virginia

Dearest Babykins, On a lovely morning, warmer, with the sun rising over the mountains & I'm just up. We got in last night at a quarter of eight & [. . .] were met by the President of the Raven Society (they are the club who invited Gertrude) who looks like Scott Fitzgerald *used* to look, & two professors, and I was in bed by 10. The trip down was very amusing. I opened a book once for ten minutes & the rest of the time G. S. talked. At Washington a whole carful of Sweet Briar girls invaded the train & that perked G. S. up no end! Today we are visiting Ash Lawn, James Monroe's house, Monticello, Carter Hill. where Amelie Rives Troubetzkoy lives, the university [of Virginia] and lunch, at the Farmington Club. Besides G. S. is going to write a couple of syndicated articles before her lecture tonight.[1] Tomorrow we go to Richmond. [. . .] G. S. was *entranced* with her birthday gifts!     all my love, Carlo

---

[1] CVV travelled south with Gertrude Stein and Alice B. Toklas for a part of the lecture tour. Amélie Rives, American novelist and playwright married to Prince Pierre Troubetzkoy.

## TO FANIA MARINOFF

[5 February 1935]

Jefferson Hotel
Richmond, Virginia

Dearest Babykins, [. . .] The ladies are *most* insistent that I accompany them to Charleston & New Orleans & are all having such a lovely time of it I am tempted, but I think it is more likely I will return to New York early next week after they have departed. [. . .] Gertrude's lecture last night, before a general audience at the Woman's Club, went better than any I have ever heard before. They loved her & she was a wow. At the end they kept her reading and reading from Portraits [*and Prayers*], frequently interrupting with applause.—Nobody got up till she left the stage. Today we go to Williamsburg to lecture & to Yorktown, because it is Yorktown.

all my love, Carlo

## TO ELLEN GLASGOW

[6 February 1935]

Jefferson Hotel
Richmond, Virginia

Dear Ellen, Everything was perfect last night.[2] You look better than ever, it was good to see you, and I am sure your house is the most beautiful house in the world. I *always* say so. What I am really writing for is to tell you the ham has been ordered. I do not know if we will get it, but I am trying. The supply is limited. Tennessee hams are not cooked like Virginia hams, but instructions should arrive with the ham. Some time today also I am leaving Miss Stein's Portraits & Prayers for you, suitably inscribed. As I did the photograph on the cover and/for the book is dedicated to me, & as it includes a [word] portrait of me, I am taking the liberty of signing it too (tho obscurely).      1001 happy flamingos to you! Carlo Van Vechten

I am very much excited about your memoirs. "A Virginia Lady" would be a perfect title.[3]

## TO FANIA MARINOFF

[9 February 1935]

Jefferson Hotel
Richmond, Virginia

Dearest Babykins—So you are going away on Thursday![4] Well, I am leaving the ladies *Monday*, when they start from Sweet Briar to Chapel Hill & so I will be in N.Y. (the train leaves here at 12.10 P.M.) about 7.30 or 8 or

[2] Ellen Glasgow gave a small dinner for Gertrude Stein and Alice Toklas at CVV's request, followed by a large eggnog reception.
[3] Withheld from publication until nine years after Ellen Glasgow's death, her memoirs appeared as *The Woman Within*, 1954.
[4] Fania Marinoff was in rehearsal for *Times Have Changed*.

Mabel Dodge Luhan, 1933

Alice B. Toklas and Gertrude Stein, 1934

maybe a little earlier (I haven't a time-table handy) Monday night. [. . .] Yesterday we motored to reconstructed Williamsburg (really beautiful) & had lunch in the President's house, built by Louis XVI!! and then G[ertrude] S[tein] lectured in a very hot room & I'm afraid it didn't go very well—it was one of her more difficult lectures—and then she began to read & they *loved it* and were mad about it & were *entranced* & she read on & on & they loved it and afterwards they all but kissed her. [. . .] I'm sure your rehearsals will be all right. Anyway don't worry. It doesn't matter. If this is No Good there will be something else. I have a feeling you are getting a better reputation as an actress than you've ever had before.

    I'll be seeing you Monday night & all my love    Carlo
I should get a special delivery from you tomorrow (Sunday)

TO GERTRUDE STEIN AND ALICE    150 West 55th Street
TOKLAS    New York City
[16 February 1935]

Dear Mes! dames Woojums (Baby and Mama) Your New Orleans address for tomorrow couldn't possibly reach you (I just got it today) and so I am sending this to the Algonquin. Ed Wynn, a comic, who performs on the radio had it the other night that his aunt's phonograph got stuck on a record of a song and it went on repeating "a rose is a rose is a rose." She was enraptured, thinking it was Gertrude Stein. [. . .] Charleston and its dismal swamps sounds most appealing, and I am sure New Orleans will be all fanlights, magnolias, and soft-stepping, sweet-voiced blacks. DO MEET HUEY LONG![5] Be kind to Republicans everywhere, but I think if you would run on the ticket (Baby Woojums for President) it would pull through. [. . .] I think I shall give a garden party for you (in some apple orchard). So get out your organdies. New York will be hot as hot in that sweet month.[6] You have forgotten how hot! I don't need to remind you, dear Mama, to wear your rubbers any more. This sweet tour is drawing to a close. I shall cry for days when you sail!    love, love, love!

    Carlo (Papa Woojums!)
The Virginia pictures are mostly developed but not printed. You will like 'em.

---

[5]Huey Long, American politican demagogue, governor of Louisiana.
[6]Gertrude Stein and Alice Toklas were scheduled to return to France in May.

## TO MABEL DODGE LUHAN

[circa February 1935]

150 West 55th Street
New York City

Dear Mabel, Of course I'm not "mad." It didn't seem very important to me to write you about the book[7] because I don't like it and I didn't see any sense of telling you that! You seem to belittle every character in it including yourself* . . . and the characters I know I would hardly recognize from your dealing with them, but maybe that's the way you see it and feel it and maybe you are right. I suppose "truth" can always be no more than one's own point of view . . . In the circumstances I wonder if telling the "truth" is what Miss Loos's blonde[8] would call "educational"? Permit me to prefer (and love) Winter in Taos,[9] and, of course, I'm not "mad."      love to you and Tony! Carlo!

*I constantly had the impression I was looking at life through the *big* end of the opera glasses.

## TO FRANCES LEIGH WILLIAMS

[spring 1935]

150 West 55th Street
New York City

Dear Frances, [. . .] It is most saint-like of you to offer to get me a plate of ice cream in Japan. What I am always looking for is a new and spectacular background [for photographs] and a cotton print at five cents a yard often makes a very good one (I usually get two yards). Or maybe you might see a banner or a poster. If you brought home a trunkful of such pretties and dumped them in my lap it wouldn't displease me. See motto above![1] Anyway, your letter pleased me *very very* much and so do you!

167 white and silver flamingos and 768 purple dolphins with gold fins to you!      Carlo Van Vechten

## TO FANIA MARINOFF

[16 June 1935]

Hotel Ritz
Barcelona, Spain[2]

Dearest Babykins! I am writing this mostly so it will get to you at the boat as there isn't much especially to write now. Anyway it will be the last letter

---

[7]*Movers and Shakers* by Mabel Dodge Luhan, 1936, read in manuscript.

[8]Lorelei Lee in *Gentlemen Prefer Blondes* by Anita Loos, 1925.

[9]*Winter in Taos,* 1935, a memoir by Mabel Dodge Luhan.

[1]Some of CVV's stationery was engraved with a small circle of print in the upper left hand corner reading: "A little too much is just enough for me." He had used this—in French, attributed to Jean Cocteau—among the epigrams for his novel *Firecrackers,* 1925. Cocteau in turn, according to CVV, had appropriated it from Chief Long Lance.

[2]CVV and Mark Lutz took a second European holiday, travelling by ship to Spain, Morocco, and Italy.

146

Papa Poo will write before he steps off the boat in N.Y. Míro[3] has been wonderful. Nobody with a mere letter of introduction has behaved so sweetly. Last night he gave a dinner in a wonderful fish place, in the fisherman's quarter, and also a Señor Gomez and his beautiful french wife & another couple. It was very sweet & after dinner we all went into the public Square to watch the people dance the Sardanes, the popular dance of Catalonia. This was wonderful, the music, the dancing, the people. Anybody that dances—In fact the ladies in our party did—with street boys they had never seen before. The whole thing was sweet and naive. I am amazed at Barcelona. I thought it would be another big city & it has more local color than about any other city of its size I can recall. I also went to Montserrat yesterday. This is the mountain of the Holy Grail where Parsifal takes place & all day, pilgrims from various towns were trudging up the mountain bearing crucifixes (life-size) from their churches to be blessed. I made (I am sure) some wonderful photographs, and this morning the beach of Barcelona & this afternoon to a bullfight.

Well, I'll be seeing you in a minute & I will be gladder than you are. I am dying to see my baby, and hope you'll get to feeling better in N.Y. where you *should* get some sleep. I'll walk in on you Sun. but of course I'll wire you from the boat and before. Please send me a wire from *your* boat after you sail. If you don't get an address by wire better send to Hotel Excelsior, Florence & if you don't get another wire changing address wire me there when you land but I think I'll be back in Genoa before then. I don't think I have bought even as much as you, but perhaps I have one or two amusing things.     all my love, Carlo

The black madonna at Montserrat is very *sending!*
A very sweet letter came from you last night!

TO R. W. COWDEN                              150 West 55th Street
25 December 1935                             New York City

Dear Mr. Cowden, I had already heard from Gertrude Stein about what good work you are doing with the Avery Hopwood awards[4] and I was

[3]Joan Miro, Spanish painter.
[4]See CVV to Channing Pollock [February 1943].

prepared and glad to hear from you. There is but one portrait of Avery, but that is not only an excellent portrait but also an important work of art by one of the most important of the contemporary American painters, Miss Florine Stettheimer. [. . .] She was an intimate friend of Avery's and is interested in the project. She suggests that for the present she loan it to you. Later, if you feel that you want to have it hang permanently in the Memorial Library I think you can come to some agreement with her. [. . .]

sincerely, Carl Van Vechten

## TO MATTHEW PHIPPS SHIEL          150 West 55th Street
11 January 1936          New York City

Cher Maître, Some time ago I received The Invisible Voices, "with compliments" [. . .]. Anyway last night I at last found time to get into the book (I knew if once opened I would have to finish it before I laid it down!) and I must compliment you. It is one of your best, I think. Full of that verve and excitement and ECSTASY that only you, among current novelists, appear to be complete master of. They SING, these invisible voices . . . As for me I do nothing but take photographs at present. I hope when I return to London you will permit me to take yours!     all good wishes to you, dear Mr. Shiel!     Carl Van Vechten

## TO BLANCHE KNOPF          150 West 55th Street
[circa January 1936]          New York City

Dear Grand Duchess, I've told Miss Cather repeatedly she may come any time of day, even at dawn. (I haven't used Donald [Angus] for years.)[5] I suggested dinner and photographs as a comfortable and painless method. Please tell her she may set her own hour, but that I'd like to take her while America is still Royalist. P.S. I think she would like Edith's cooking!     1789 red orchids and flocks and swarms and budgets of lemon butterflies to you! Carlo!
I'll bring some duplicate examples of Pat [Alfred A. Knopf, Jr.] to you one

[5]CVV suddenly stopped seeing Donald Angus in 1933—after nearly fifteen years of intimate friendship—without explanation. Although Angus continued to see Fania Marinoff regularly, he was *persona non grata* until 1943 when, suddenly and without explanation, CVV began to see him again, and they remained afterward as friendly as they had been in the past. Meanwhile, Mark Lutz began helping him with lighting for his photography, although Lutz later said this never amounted to much labor nor required any talent.

day. I am experimenting again with framing & may have an idea you'd like to try later.

TO H. L. MENCKEN 150 West 55th Street
9 March 1936 New York City

Dear Henry, In order to get the full flavor of it, bad and good, I sat down last night to read Sara's Southern Album[6] at a sitting and I must say it was an easy thing to do. You know the way it is with most short stories—every time you begin again and sometimes you read on for pages before your interest is reawakened. This is not at all true of these stories because they are all bathed in the really loving personality and presence of Sara herself and this personality gives at times an almost unbearable poignancy to her intention. It seems to me, had she lived, with her critical faculty and her sense of humor hovering over her real knowledge of and love for the deep south, she might have written that masterpiece that Stark Young[7] tried to write. And what she did write is no mean tribute to her skill. I cried a little at the beginning and the end—at your very touching preface (I do not recall anything quite so good or so repressed in feeling in this line save William Allen White's tribute to his daughter) and at her own summing up of her own feeling in Dear Life. You describe Sara as languid but has it ever occurred to you that she accomplished more actual labor than many another young man or woman with 100% vitality! In fact, her health being what it was, she accomplished miracles. Fania is reading Southern Album and you will hear from her. And we would be delighted to have you dine with us whenever you come to New York.      Thank you, dear Henry    Carl Van Vechten

TO FANNIE HURST [150 West 55th Street
[15 March 1936] New York City]

Dear Fannie, Marinoff & I went to see Ponselle in Carmen last night, & my dear, Mary Garden & O[lin] D[ownes] do not exaggerate. She is magnificent. Rarely, if ever, have I seen a Carmen I liked so much. A consistently

---

[6]Following Sara Haardt Mencken's early death, her husband arranged for a book of her stories to be published, *A Southern Album*, 1936.
[7]Stark Young, American novelist and drama critic.

planned & splendidly executed performance. I am the more amazed because I don't remember Ponselle particularly hitherto as an actress.[8]

151 white doves to you, Carlo

TO FANIA MARINOFF                                       150 West 55th Street
[23 May 1936]                                            New York City

Dearest Baby-Mama, Dr. Livingstone gave a startled exclamation yesterday and began tugging at something in the middle of my back with tweezers. Seemingly he pulled the skin out about an inch but whatever it was wouldn't budge. He assured me it was alive and wiggling and buried head first in the skin. It took a knife to dislodge and was as big as a small fly. I suppose I collected this on the beach in Georgia.[9] So please ask the natives what it is. The funny thing is it didn't hurt and I was entirely unconscious that anything like this was going on, being completely aware my shoulders were peeling. They are okay, by the way . . . Tom Mabry[1] came to dinner and we went to [Gluck's] Orfeo, done after the manner of [Rimsky-Korsakoff's] Coq d'Or with the singers in the pit and the ballet on the stage. It was pretty terrible, but there were those who liked it. [Pavel] Tchelitcheff was the inspirer of this completely camp production. Florine [Stettheimer] gave a party after. [. . .] Absolutely nobody has telephoned today and there is no mail or news. No letter from you even, yet.      All my love, !Carlo!

Gene [O'Neill] said something about some records one day. The gramophone was upstairs & we didn't go up to hear them, and, hélas, afterward I forgot.

TO CHANNING POLLOCK                                    150 West 55th Street
30 July 1936                                            New York City

Dear Don Quixote, You are a holy knight but you are tilting at windmills, and so I continue to love you and enjoy your prose while I disagree with it.[2] The conditions you describe in your panygeric on aristocracy have ceased to exist, and forces have been released which are beyond control. Another

---

[8]Rosa Ponselle sang her first *Carmen*, 27 December 1935. In the *New York Times*, Downes wrote: "We have never heard Miss Ponselle sing so badly, and we have seldom seen the part enacted in such an artificial and generally unconvincing manner." CVV regularly disagreed with most other music critics and always preferred interpretation over vocal purity.
[9]CVV had just returned from a visit with Eugene O'Neill and Carlotta Monterey at Sea Island, Georgia; Fania Marinoff had stayed on.
[1]Thomas Mabry, young southern American educator who had been fired from his university teaching position because of his integrationist views.
[2]*Adventures of a Happy Man*, 1935.

depression & democracy is gone forever. In the meantime why wail? Life seems pleasanter under FDR to me than it has ever been before.

Love dear father! Carlo. Buddy.[3]
and love to the ladies!

## TO FANIA MARINOFF
[1 August 1936]

Providence Biltmore Hotel
Providence, Rhode Island[4]

Dearest Baby & Mama! Three letters here from you and I read the wrong one first! Which was very upsetting. I mean I ended with the BAD letter! I hate to upset you in any way and when you are upset I get upset too. Please don't get upset because things between *us* have never been better. [. . .] You have been *wonderful* this summer, but you are always wonderful (except when you're bad) and that is why I love you! [. . .] NOW: I thought I told you I'd be away five weeks & you suggested if I wanted to spend part of that time in N.Y. I could. I'd rather spend next week in NY than travel any more but I could find somewhere to go, I suppose, if you are tired of Montauk[5] and want to go home yourself. Will you please telegraph me *here* if you get this in time (I'll be here at least till Thursday morning) what you want to do. If you are staying another week I would land in NY about Sunday & spend a week there. This vacation of mine will END July 15 definitely & I'd expect you back that night or Sunday the 16th. Or if you plan to go home yourself I will be home on one of those days. [. . .] Please don't be unhappy or cross or anything. I love you very much and we'll have a grand time moving[6] and I haven't been away very long and I'll soon be back!     All my love, blessed Pandikins! Carlo

## TO GERTRUDE STEIN
24 March 1937

101 Central Park West
New York City

Dear Gertrude and Baby Woojums, [. . .] The Philharmonic, under [Artur] Rodzinski, recently gave some performances (in concert form) of [Richard] Strauss's Elektra. As rehearsal time approached the lady engaged to sing the title part fell ill and Rosa Pauly of the Vienna Opera was brought over to take her place. Pauly turned out to be just about the greatest singing

---

[3]"Buddy" was CVV's nickname circa 1900–10, a period during which he had first known Pollock.
[4]CVV was on a tour of New England with Mark Lutz.
[5]Fania Marinoff was taking a holiday at a resort in Montauk, New York.
[6]A parking garage had opened on the ground floor below Fania Marinoff's bedroom window, facing West 54th Street, and the noise made it imperative that she and CVV move. In September, they took an apartment at 101 Central Park West.

actress this town has ever seen or heard and we all went wild. It was like the old days come back. People always think that middle aged people are exaggerating about the triumphant performances of the past until something like this happens and then they are just bowled over. I am glad to say that I hear Miss Pauly is Jewish (she is from Prague) and there is even a chance she has some Arabian blood. If she ever sings in Paris, pawn your jewels and attend to her! [. . .] Anyway Fania and I send lots of love to you and Mama Woojums and I hope you are wearing your rubbers these damp days!    !Carlo!

Madame Gaston Lachaise has really turned up the most amazing painter, a Negro cleaning woman in Boston. She sells her works for 50 cents a piece and soon or late I'll be able to get an example for you. They are done in colored pencils and the background is always the same: a picture of the Virgin, a grand piano, a palm in a POT and a divan. In front of this, one or two principal figures. I thought they were grandes cocottes or maybe grues in houses of Joy. But no, says Isabel Lachaise, Mary Bell (such is her lovely name) is very religious. Rather they are saints. Saints then in ratted hair, blonde, black, and titian, and every kind of WRAPPER, in design color and lace trimmings most complicated. Sometimes a Suitor. Something like [Henri] Rousseau, but O so different. What an artist![7]

Love and let love!

## TO GERTRUDE STEIN
22 June 1937

101 Central Park West
New York City

Dear Baby Woojums, At LONG LAST, Bennett [Cerf] let me read the manuscript,[8] over a weekend as the Atlantic had to have it back, and it seems to me that Everybody's Autobiography is one of your finest works. It is not as amusing or as gossipy as the Alice B Toklas opus, but it is much more of an integrated work of art and much more in line with the rest of your work. Don't you agree with me? I think you give the effect of living it as you write it: it all flows with your consciousness and the reader is exhausted* by YOUR vitality. I am sure this work will have a most notable success, whatever the press, which is unimportant. I am pretty sure, however, you can count on a good press! Bennett wants me to illustrate it with photographs. Of course I have hundreds which are suitable, but you may

---

[7]CVV amassed a collection of well over a hundred works by this extraordinary artist, most of which he donated to the James Weldon Johnson Memorial Collection of Negro Arts and Letters at Yale University.
[8]The manuscript was published as *Everybody's Autobiography*, 1937.

not like the idea at all and if you don't PLEASE SAY SO. If you do, I think Thornton Wilder and the Kiddie (I don't even know this number's name)[9] ought to be in it and so if you will tell me where I can find the former and will write the Latter to write to me and arrange to come to NYC some time, maybe with his uniform, that would be swell.

Fania has gone to a Dude Ranch in Montana for a month, the servants are away, and I am alone in the house. I have taken many interesting photographs lately, Thomas Mann, Thomas Wolfe, and Scott Fitzgerald, among others. I told George[s Jacques] (at the Algonquin) he was in the book and he nearly DIED with pleasure.     my warmest enthusiasm and my heartiest congratulations and lots of love to you and Mama Woo-jums.!   Carlo!
*pleasantly!


TO FANIA MARINOFF                       101 Central Park West
[30 June 1937]                              New York City

Darling baby-Mama, Your telegram arrived at five minutes of five last night.[1] I called up Purdy's at once and they close at five. So I will go in this AM. On account [of] the frame, etc. I thought I had better see them. I'll ask them to send them airmail and you MIGHT get 'em Saturday. Anyway you've got to have 'em. When you get back, please get yourself still another pair [of glasses]. It's crazy to travel without at least two pair. [. . .] Of course don't stay out there a minute after you get bored. [. . .] In any case if they aren't doing anything to amuse you come home at once where you will be welcome. On the other hand don't worry about ME if you are having a good time because I have LOTS to do and am not ONE bit nervous in this apartment. I fall asleep as soon as I hit the pillow and sleep soundly till morning. I am even used to the strange noises overhead and in the hall. They haven't given any more parties upstairs. I sent you a LOT of postcard photographs that you haven't mentioned. Didn't you get these? No money yet. When I put some in your bank I'll tell you, of course. Your Monday and Tuesday letters BOTH arrived today in the first mail. [. . .] I went out with Eddie [Wassermann] last night and he is beginning to complain about Blanche [Knopf] again. But he is better tempered than usual. I wish all my relatives would go live in Bali. All [Van Vechten] Shaffers are going

[9]W. G. Rogers, American journalist, nicknamed "The Kiddie" by Gertrude Stein and Alice Toklas when they met him in France during the First World War as a doughboy.
[1]Fania Marinoff had broken her reading glasses during her stay at the Montana Dude Ranch and had wired frantically for a replacement.

to be here the night of the 26 (Angevine's sister is getting married the next day). I say we go to Detroit to spend the day. Langston came to see me the other day. He is going to Madrid, the International writers congress, as the American delegate [. . .] . He says Nora Holt intended to go back to China but she has just passed the school examinations in Los Angeles so brilliantly (for teaching music in the high schools—she has been doing this part time) that she is going to stay in LA. [. . .] If glasses have to be adjusted bend the stems very carefully yourself *but do not break them*. It has to be done with PATIENCE and DEXTERITY. On reading your letter over I see you DID get the PIX postcards.[2] In the first reading I missed an inside page. Georgia O'Keeffe is at Lake George, N.Y. Just like that and you spell it with two ffs. Write immediately as she asked you to let her know right away as she might go back to Taos.[3] The Stettheimers are thinking of going to Santa Fe and I am encouraging this as I think they would love it. Witter [Bynner] is here at the moment, but I haven't seen him.     all my love, Carlo!

## TO FANIA MARINOFF
[4 July 1937]

101 Central Park West
New York City

Darling Babykins, The radio is on every minute in an effort to learn that Amelia Earhart[4] has been saved. It is terrible to realize we may not hear what has happened to her for weeks and months. [. . .] And here is our old friend Muriel [Starr], on the air twice a week in It's a Woman's World! I went to the Algonquin last night to dine alone and who should walk in but Miss Starr. She said she had had a card from you but it was all blobbered over with postmarks and so she asked for your address. You might even hear from her. [. . .] Mark [Lutz] got in after dinner and we went to Room Service[5] which is funny but not nearly as good as Brother Rat[6] or Three Men on a Horse.[7] But it seems to be the biggest hit [George] Abbott ever had and people laugh their heads off. I see by the Times this AM that his next venture is called Home, Sweet Harlem, and our TOPSY [Ethel Waters] is to be in that.[8]     all my love, dearest baby-mama, Carlo

---

[2]It was CVV's habit to print up his photographs on postcards to send out to friends and for brief correspondence.
[3]Fania Marinoff had proposed returning to New York by way of New Mexico for a visit with O'Keeffe.
[4]Amelia Earhart, American aviator, lost at sea.
[5]*Room Service*, 1937, by John Murray and Allen Boretz.
[6]*Brother Rat*, 1936, by John Monks, Jr., and Fred F. Finklehoffe.
[7]*Three Men on a Horse*, 1936, by John Cecil Holm and George Abbott.
[8]Apparently this show never materialized.

TO FANIA MARINOFF                        101 Central Park West
[28 July 1937]                           New York City

Dearest Baby-Mama, This being Saturday. I guess there'll be no mail from
you, hélas! It is a nice day but I am in pasting my scrapbooks up. I just
had lunch: turtle soup (jellied), and roquefort cheese with guava jelly and
a bottle of Ballantine's ale! [. . .] I went [. . .] to see The Cradle Will Rock,
the WPA (originally) show about the steel strike by Marc Blitzstein. Well,
the WPA wouldn't let 'em do it so Orson Welles and John Houseman are
giving it at the Venice Theatre on their own and Equity wouldn't let 'em
do it this way if they did it on the stage; so Blitzstein plays the piano on
the stage and the actors are in the first rows and boxes. Like everything
Welles does it is tremendously effective and his speech at the beginning,
explaining what it's all about, is one of the best things in the show. The
house was packed but John Houseman was in the box office and he got
us in. The audience too was tremendously responsive and became part of
the show. Sometimes Welles says they get into scenes. "Keep out of the
script, tonight, please," he advised this audience. Ladies are riding past on
the bridle path in the park[9] and I am wondering if you are going to do
this when you get back!     All my love, Carlo

TO GERTRUDE STEIN                        101 Central Park West
1 August [1937]                          New York City

Why, my wonderful Baby Woojums, how did I ever give you that idea?[1]
I must have written some very clumsy English. It would be marvellous if
we could do it, but I would have to print night and day for eight or nine
months and I would have to print over 40,000 photographs and it would
cost thousands and thousands! So everything is just where it was: i.e., your
original idea is the right one, as it includes Thornton W[ilder] and Lord
Berners[2] etc. etc. and if Bennett [Cerf] argues with you remember he argues
with me too, as this idea of having Papa W illustrate the book was his,
and you must have the book exactly as you like it and so I tell him and
[you] tell him. After your sweet cable came I didn't feel sure of exactly
what you meant till your letter came and then I couldn't cable you as you

---

[9]101 Central Park West faced Central Park, affording spectacular views around the calendar.
[1]CVV had proposed supplying photographic illustrations for *Everybody's Autobiography;* Gertrude
Stein construed this to mean he proposed distributing original prints with each copy.
[2]Gerald Hugh Thyritt Wilson, Lord Berners, English author and composer who set Gertrude
Stein's *They.Must.Be.Wedded.To.Their.Wife* as *A Wedding Bouquet,* a ballet for Sadler's Wells,
1937.

asked me to because I didn't want to cable I WASN'T going to print 40,000 pictures and I didn't know what else to cable and tell Mama Woojums if we all lived in the same town none of these things would happen.

[. . .] AND a girl named Margery Sharp has written a novel coming out soon (Little, Brown) called The Nutmeg Tree and it is laid in Belley and there is lots about the Pernollet and Landscape and Aix [les Bains], but not a word about Baby Woojums. Do you know this lady? O yes, she has plenty to say about Brillat-Savarin.[3] [. . .]    1001 bright stars to you and Mama Woojums and love from Papa Woojums also known as    Carlo

TO ARTHUR DAVISON FICKE                101 Central Park West
19 August 1937                          New York City

Dear Arthur, This business of putting me in the prize ring with authors had already been thought of. Still I see no harm in our smacking each other's faces with a bouquet of champagne bottles in the Ritz Bar on Christmas Eve. [. . .] It's curious you should speak of my writing. I was very tired last night and ready for bed when the cover of Parties attracted my eye. I took it down and read and read, five chapters in all, EN-THRALLED. I couldn't recall a word of it and it didn't seem to have anything to do with ME but I LOVED IT. I am planning to read all my works.

O Arthur, how can I tell you how I got my musical education? Like all my other educations, it is due to curiosity and energy. I took a few piano lessons when a kid and immediately began to sample masterpieces. Nobody played 'em in Cedar Rapids, Iowa. There was no symphony orchestra, no opera, no radio, no phonograph, but CVV spelled out Schubert and Beethoven and Bizet and Gounod on his mother's Gilbert Square Grand (which I still possess). I recall that when I was about 17 a fifteenth-rate opera singer who was a connection of some Cedar Rapids person bobbed up. I went to see her with the score of Carmen under my arm and asked her to sing it to me. She didn't and I was furious. Now I know she COULDN'T. Anyway Carmen and lots of other operas were an open book to me when I went to Chicago in 1899. Here I played in luck. Theodore Thomas was conducting the Chicago Orchestra. Never an inspired conductor, he was a god-given maker of progams. Hence he played all he could of Debussy, Strauss, and Sibelius almost the moment it was written. I have heard works of Debussy and Strauss there that were played in New York for the first time (after I got here) ten years later! As for Sibelius I have heard music

[3] Jean-Anthelme Brillat-Savarin, early 19th-century French epicure, born and raised in Belley.

of his in Chicago that is being played here for the first time NOW. We had lots of opera too. It was expensive and I "suped."[4] But the Met used to play four weeks in Chicago with the greatest casts, Melba, Calvé, Eames, Nordica, the de Rezskes, Schumann-Heink. Will I ever forget Ternina's first Tosca in the old Auditorium? We had the New Orleans opera company too from the old French opera house, now defunct, and I heard operas like Sigurd and Salammbô that you couldn't hear anywhere now. I went to all the piano and violin recitals and every concert of the Chicago Orchestra for seven years. Moreover I worked on my piano and PLAYED IN PUBLIC with a violinist[5] sonatas by Grieg, César Franck, and Richard Strauss, for violin and piano. Latterly I have laid down somewhat on music but I still have it in me. I was on the music department of the NY Times for years and years and one week, when Hammerstein, the New Theatre, and the Met were all going strong, I heard TWENTY-ONE different operas! Now will you be good? [. . .]     l and k, Carlo

## TO FANIA MARINOFF

[30 October 1937]

101 Central Park West
New York City

Dearest baby-Mama, It is a bright morning, I am feeling fine. Mark [Lutz] is here. The girls[6] are back. We have just opened the grouse and they look lovely and we are going to have them for dinner. No letter from you this AM and no telegram. So I don't know where to send this letter. I'll hold it until late today, hoping I'll get an address, so I can send it special airmail.[7] [. . .] I found a letter from you here yesterday when I got in. I flew from Chicago here in three hours and a half, with a tail wind![8] Did you ever hear of such a thing! It was one of the most agreeable flights I've ever made. And last night went to the ballet, where there was nothing new but

---

[4]"Supers" were supernumeraries, non-singers who swelled the crowds on stage. CVV appeared with most of the operatic luminaries between 1900 and 1907.

[5]Jessie Call, a colleague on the *Chicago Inter-Ocean*.

[6]When Edith Ramsay retired as CVV's cook, Mildred Perkins Thornton replaced her. She remained in CVV's employ—intermittently—until his death. Pearl Showers continued as housekeeper.

[7]Fania Marinoff was appearing in an out-of-town tryout of Shakespeare's *Antony and Cleopatra* with Tallulah Bankhead and Geoffrey Tearle. CVV to Fania Marinoff, 25 October 1937: "Don't worry about the play or whether you are mentioned. I guess that will soon be over and everything YOU *do in it is distinguished and more* and it makes the theatre seem silly to me. But some day maybe you will get with people who really work. [. . .] Tallulah doesn't know that this may be her last chance and she may be sitting on her ass [. . .] next time. [. . .] But maybe, by a fluke, you'll turn into a sensation. The Variety review is annihilating."

[8]CVV had been to Cedar Rapids, Iowa, for his step-mother's funeral.

it was all very nice and I think the dancing is better than it used to be.[9]
all my love,

The performance of Gene [O'Neill]'s one-act plays at the Lafayette Theatre[1] got a bad notice in the Times this morning. [Brooks] Atkinson says justly that the point of these plotless plays was the characters of different nations. A point completely lost in a Negro performance. I am sending the clipping to Gene. Later: Home from seeing Coq d'Or as a ballet which is really lovely and like old ballet times. I wish you could see this, but the ballet is having such a success I guess they'll come back in the spring. [. . .] Sorry Tallulah is sick. Give her my love.     Carlo

TO GERTRUDE ATHERTON                  101 Central Park West
5 January 1938                        New York City

Dear Gertrude, No, you haven't offended Gertrude [Stein]. She admires you enormously and spoke endlessly of you before leaving America. The article you saw was just chopped bits out of her book, Everybody's Autobiography, selected by the editor of the Atlantic [Monthly]. The book has more continuity. If you are not mentioned, neither is Ellen Glasgow, nor Fania for that matter! Often, on account of something she wanted to get in, the least important people are mentioned. Is there anything I can do for you while you are laid up? Anything you want to read or eat? Just as I am mailing this I discovered the enclosed in the Post!     Happy New Year! Carlo!

TO DOROTHY PETERSON                   101 Central Park West
[22 March 1938]                       New York City

Dear Dorothy, Yes, I knew about Sidney's arrangements.[2] He wrote me and I was much honeyficated and wrote him. You must all come here some night. Ariel* HAS been photographed[3] and you will get a copy as soon as they are available which is in a week or TWO. I liked Haiti[4] a good deal. I think it is excellent melodrama and most picturesque, but with the

[9][Vassili] de Basil Ballet russe de Monte Carlo.
[1]The Lafayette Theatre in Harlem had staged serious drama from circa 1916 until 1923, at which time it changed management and became better known as a musical comedy house. It closed down during the Depression but opened again briefly in an attempt to reestablish a black repertory company.
[2]Dr Sidney Peterson was about to be married.
[3]A statuette of Fania Marinoff as Ariel in Shakespeare's The Tempest by black sculptor Richmond Barthé.
[4]Haiti, 1938, by William DuBois.

exception of the leading lady[†] whom I admire extravagantly (who IS she?) I found the ofay actors insufferable, especially that General who should have been played by Dudley Digges. I thought the father-butler and the Toussaint were dignified and excellent and, like you, I worried because Rex [Ingram] was not showing his SHAPE. The costumes, of course, were stolen right out of Macbeth. I did see Shadow and Substance[5] but sat so far back I missed a good deal of dialogue, including the line you mention. I'm going again as I admire the play very much though I didn't know what it meant until Prentiss Taylor told me that None of the characters is entirely Right and Each some right. Sara Allgood completed this [the] same evening when I asked her if the play was pro- or anti-Catholic. "Both," was her prompt response. It is extraordinary to find so much argument and emotion in a play with so much fairness in the point of view.[‡] I'D LOVE to have Langston's book.[6] We went to Pins and Needles[7] last night. And loved it. Have you seen it. Probably for the sake of the idea there is a Negro girl (one) in the chorus. She has nothing personal to do and does what the others are doing as if she might go to sleep at any minute. Next to Stepin Fetchit[8] she is the laziest sepia artist before the public. I'd like to go to Haiti myself but somehow feel as if I'D ALREADY BEEN THERE. I'm more likely to go to Portugal, one of the spots God has left alone.      l and k, Carlo

*and is marvellously (yet not finally) disposed.

†Elena Karam, I think her name is.

‡or maybe it ISN'T extraordinary.

TO FANIA MARINOFF                    101 Central Park West
[29 June–2 July 1938]                 New York City, and Worcester,
                                       Massachusetts

Dearest Baby-Mama, Blanche [Knopf] sails this AM and I am sending her a telegram and ordering flowers for the funeral tomorrow for dear James [Weldon Johnson] for us and Elizabeth.[9] [. . .] I also had a bill for your will and it was $25 which is most reasonable. I guess it costs us $25 apiece. I'll get around to mine soon. JWJ loomed important in the old one.[1] [. . .] I spent the afternoon with [J.] Rosamond and his family. Bertha Randolph was there and others including W. C. Handy who has been wonderful. I

[5]*Shadow and Substance*, 1938, by Paul Vincent Carroll.
[6]*A New Song*, 1938. See CVV to Langston Hughes, 20 March 1934.
[7]*Pins and Needles*, musical revue by Harold Rome.
[8]Stepin Fetchit, black character actor in films, notable for perpetuating an invidious stereotype.
[9]Elizabeth Hull, CVV's niece, daughter of his sister Emma Van Vechten Shaffer.
[1]James Weldon Johnson and CVV had been each other's literary executor.

got a full description of the accident which happened in a fog at a most dangerous crossing where there have been other accidents.[2] Jim was killed almost instantly. It would be a mercy if Grace would die but I guess she won't. She seems to be improving but one side of her face and one eye are mostly gone and her breasts and legs are crushed. The Nails[3] and the R. Johnsons are opposed to cremation. Grace's father is almost hysterical about it. Yet that is what Jim and Grace want. Why can't people let dead people at least have their way? I am an honorary pall-bearer at the funeral and immediately after that (Mark [Lutz] is not going to the funeral) we will be on our way to Boston via Worcester. [. . .]

Thursday [30 June]: Arthur Hays went up to see Grace and reports she will NOT lose her eye. She is progressing very well indeed and with plastic surgery may be as good as new. She sent word down to have any funeral they wanted to. She wouldn't interfere. [. . .] Went to the [Lewisohn] Stadium last night to hear [José] Iturbi conduct Russian music. The Stadium was being picketed as Iturbi is for France and students marched up and down outside shouting "Boycott Iturbi" but the orchestra played better as a result and they and the audience applauded Iturbi more than usual [. . .] Saturday, July 2. This won't go until July 5 but on account of Sunday and the holidays I think I had better mail it today. It will be safer. You should have received a telegram from me at the Azores and another at Ponta Degada which you should receive today.[4] [. . .] Last night went to the Boston Pops concert. Arthur Fiedler conducts the Boston Symphony in popular pieces while people sit at tables. Unbelievably swell. Mary Bell *won't* see me.[5] She is very shy or has false pride or something. Anyway, she just *won't* see me.—So that's that. But it is nice here & a change & cool (for the moment—it rains all the time) and the ladies [Pearl Showers and Mildred Perkins] are away till next week. So I think I'll stay here till they get back—or nearly.

I miss you frightfully & will LOVE to have you back again. In the meantime, please have a grand time!     all my love, Carlo

---

[2]An unlighted train backed into the Johnsons' car while they were driving at night, during a summer holiday in Maine. Grace Johnson was at the wheel.
[3]John A. Nail was Grace Nail Johnson's brother, notable for having colonized Harlem as a black community circa 1905.
[4]Fania Marinoff was off on a cruise to the Azores and Scandanavia.
[5]See CVV to Gertrude Stein, 24 March 1937.

## TO GRACE NAIL JOHNSON
2 July 1938

The Ritz-Carlton
Boston

Dear Grace, what can I write? You know how I feel. Above all else I am grateful we had that June 17th together.[6] Pat [Alfred A. Knopf, Jr.] who is more upset than I could have imagined said he was glad of this too. I sent you a telegram as soon as you were awake and I have been with Mildred & Rosamond [Johnson] on the phone or at the house a good deal.

I can't tell you how many people wrote or called me that didn't even know Jim. They just loved what he was! [. . .]

The funeral was beautiful. The day was fine. The church looked lovely with the banks of flowers, and the music was exceptionally good. Go Down Death was always my favorite of the sermons.[7] Do you remember how often I would ask Jim to read this? And Juanita Hall's choir gave an extraordinary rendering of this. Have you heard them do it? When they sang Since You Went Away, I cried & so did everybody else. Gene Buck[8] was marvellous in his eulogy. I hope somebody made a copy of this for preservation. With the pall bearers I sat between Arthur Spingarn[9] & Rabbi [Stephen] Wise. Theodore Roosevelt [Jr.] & W. C. Handy were adjacent. Could any one else bring out such a strange combination of people in united love?

I hope, dear Grace, you are much better. Is there anything you want done? [. . .] When you come to New York and want to see me, let me know please & I will come at once.       lots of love and Fania would send hers too if she were here. Carlo

## TO ANNA MARBLE POLLOCK
9 November 1938

101 Central Park West
New York City

I think it is ENTIRELY out of character for you to go to Shoreham to vote and I think you must love Channing very much to do this for him. I never vote at all UNDER ANY CONDITIONS because I believe in the long run one course to be as good as another. [. . .] I am reading Mein Kampf [by Adolph Hitler] just in case, and it is making me awfully mad. Please convey

---

[6]CVV, James Weldon Johnson, and Alfred A. Knopf, Jr., had celebrated their joint birthday together, a tradition they had maintained whenever they were all in town at the same time.
[7]"Go Down Death," one of the verse sermons from James Weldon Johnson's most enduringly popular work, *God's Trombones*, 1927.
[8]Gene Buck, ASCAP president, an organization with which Johnson had had been associated for many years.
[9]Arthur Spingarn, lawyer. See List of recipients.

to Channing my very deepest sympathy and you know there is nothing in the world I wouldn't do for any of you.     I love you, !Carlo!

TO GERTRUDE STEIN                              101 Central Park West
2 December [1938]                              New York City

Dearest Gertrude, I am awfully upset about Basket.[1] It seemed to me he was an immortal dog and would be eternal. I always love animals so much more than people and I have a pang whenever I recall any of my dead cats. When they die it is agony and anguish for months. That is why I don't have them any more. There are people who take these things more lightly and get a new dog every time one dies and of course it IS possible to love a new animal, though it never takes the place of an old one. I am so very sorry, sweet Baby Woojums and I know what a heartbreak it is. I shall look into the Boudoir Companion[2] and I am glad The World is Round* is arranged for. Any publisher YOU choose becomes important on that account. Maybe Bennett [Cerf] is more interested in the Spanish War for the moment than he is in literature. I think The World is Round will be a favorite Child's book and can't wait to find out. I shall send copies to all the children I know. I met [Alexander] Smallens on the street yesterday and he asked "What about the opera Gertrude Stein and Berners are doing?[3] I want to conduct it." I told him I didn't think it was ready yet. The world is dreadfully excited by this. We have a love[ly] new picture of St Cecilia charming the animals, painted by Roelandt Savory (Flemish) circa 1600. We got this at an auction. And I think your picking up Hemingway on the Faubourg St H[onoré] will result in literature on BOTH SIDES. I can't wait to see what you write about this. I'm glad you met all the Orientals and liked them![4] It seems to me that since there is so much race prejudice one meets more races than one used to. We had a snow storm the other night with thunder and lightning. Did you ever see anything like that? PLEASE!

    Love to you and Mama Woojums, [unsigned]
*I dote on this!

[1]Gertrude Stein's standard white poodle had died.
[2]*The Boudoir Companion*, 1938, a collection of stories and essays by and about women, contained an "Ida," which anticipated Gertrude Stein's novel, *Ida*, 1941.
[3]After the success of *A Wedding Bouquet*, Gerald Lord Berners proposed an operatic collaboration with Gertrude Stein, "Dr Faustus Lights the Lights," but he was never able to complete the project. Later it was set to music by Meyer Kupferman.
[4]CVV had sent a letter of introduction to Gertrude Stein with Lin Yutang, the Chinese-American philosopher and philologist (he invented an indexing system for Chinese ideographs) and his wife Tsuifeng.

## TO NEITH BOYCE [HAPGOOD]
3 December 1938

101 Central Park West
New York City

Dear Neith, I am flattered by Hutch's request to use the photograph of Beatrix[5] in his Autobiography[6] and he has my permission to do so, but there are two conditions. First, the picture must be credited to me in the book and second, Hutch must send me an inscribed copy! . . . Of course I couldn't be mad at YOU. Why on earth are you mad at me? and why don't you tell me about it? I've never had an inkling. Years ago you promised to write me about a project you had afoot and never did. Then I wrote you an eighty page letter to a Florida address and never heard a word, but I think of you often and night before last was talking about you when somebody brought up Provincetown. Then yesterday we ran into Robert [Morss] Lovett. Of course I am NOT in the country. I am the man who died in a hansom cab[7] and I don't think it is what Mabel [Dodge Luhan] writes about *them* that makes her friends drop off like flies. I think it is something much more obvious and subtle than that. Me, I have never been in the least annoyed with Mabel for anything she has written about ME, but I'm frequently quite embarrassed by what she writes about HERSELF. I guess I feel sorry for Mabel! . . . I don't know if anything we are doing would interest you much. I still see lots of Negroes and I still take photographs and I still have a very warm spot in my heart for the Hapgoods.     Love to you and Hutch, and Fania sends hers too! Carlo

## TO MURIEL STARR
4 January 1939

101 Central Park West
New York City

Muriel, my pet, I saw Gene Autry, thanks to you, and The Citadel thrown in, for 10 cents. This is my favorite theatre and I am mad about G. A. In one of the sequences a man is thrown off his horse, badly bruised, & several bones broken. Gene asks softly, "Shall I send for the doctor, pal?" "No," replies the invalid, "sing for me, Gene, and I'll get well!" Gene does of

---

[5]Beatrix Hapgood, daughter of Neith Boyce and Hutchins Hapgood.
[6]*A Victorian in a Modern World*, 1939.
[7]The reference is probably to CVV's long-standing contention that he never left town because he was afraid he would miss something; that he hated the country; that he intended to die in New York City.

course. Nobody on the screen acts quite so thrillingly, except perhaps Dorothy Lamour![8]    Yours infatuated   Carlo

Ethel Waters I regret is sure to be an anti-climax

## TO ALEXANDER WOOLLCOTT            101 Central Park West
## 9 February 1939                   New York City

Dear Alexander, If you will recall, I told you it would take ages to finish your photographs, but I must report they were finished today just as your amusing letter arrived. They are, I would think, magnificent, but I dare say you won't like them at all. [. . .]

I am sorry to report that I am extremely unlikely to tire of the Frou-Frou. In fact, if I like a picture at all, I am inclined to like it more and more as the years roll by. May I suggest that you may feel quite free to come to look at it any time you like. You mentioned Clairin's Sarah Bernhardt in an affectionate manner.[9] Do you know where this picture is hanging at present? Reynaldo Hahn's "La Grande Sarah" is shot through with references to Clairin and I am at present in correspondence with him in an effort to discover the name of the actress who posed for Frou-Frou. I discover in his book that Sarah doted on Clairin and even built a summer studio for him at Belle-Isle so he could spend his summers beside her, but my informant is wrong, he did not die at Belle-Isle. He died at his sister's in Brittany.     109 scarlet (housebroken) tanagers to you! Carlo V.V.

## TO LANGSTON HUGHES                101 Central Park West
## 1 March 1939                      New York City

Dear Langston, To get a cheque for $100[1] just before the income tax is due is something that doesn't happen to this baby often. Thank you very much. I was even more pleased to hear about all your good luck. The piece of prose you read about my first night in Paris is an early chapter of Peter Whiffle which I certainly thought you had read. A Negro Diamond Lil[2] sounds swell and I hope it comes off that way. A'Lelia Walker could have played that part! I think the greatest break the Negro race has had in a

---

[8]CVV refused to take motion pictures seriously until late in his life. Gene Autry was a popular western star; *The Citadel,* a 1939 version of A. J. Cronin's idealistic novel; Dorothy Lamour, a Hollywood actress notable for her sarongs.

[9]Georges Clairin, French painter whose *Frou-Frou* hung in CVV's drawing room. He willed it to his niece, Elizabeth Shaffer Hull.

[1]Hughes had repaid a loan, one of several made over the years.

[2]*Diamond Lil,* 1928, a play by Mae West.

long time is this BAD PUBLICITY for the DAR and isn't Mrs. [Eleanor] Roosevelt a honey.[3] Edward Robinson[4] in Hollywood has a painting by Grant Wood called Daughters of American Revolution depicting four hatchetfaced old crones looking mean over the teacups. There are postcards of this (I used to have some) but I don't know where they could be found. Why don't you write to E. G. Robinson? ANYWAY I think it would be delightful if all the Negroes in the USA, including CVV, would begin to use this postcard extensively. By the way, I wrote Who's Who. I was surprised NOT to find the names of Marian Anderson and Ethel Waters and it seems (the editor wrote me back at once) they have been bombarding Miss A with questionnaires since 1936 and never had ONE reply. They asked me if I could help. So I am using the influence of the NAACP and Hubert Delany[5] to see if I can get her to send in the required information. The editor also told me [he] had just sent a questionnaire to Miss Waters. So I asked about that and she had already thrown it away. So I got her another one and I am working on that myself. Miguel [Covarrubias] is doing a mural for the Mexican Building in the San Francisco Fair. It is probably finished but I think he is still out there. His address in SF is the Plaza Hotel. Do you see Nora Holt? If you do, please give her my love. I miss her very much and please tell William Grant Still[6] to call me when he comes East as I MUST photograph him. Earle Jones[7] at last accounts was doing Joe Louis[8] in the movies. Tonight the Negro Actors Guild Ball. I have a box and Morris Ernst[9] and his wife and Eddie Wassermann, among others, are going with me. Fania is well and sends love and so do I, with 131 silver (housebroken) dachshunds to you!     Carlo

## TO PRENTISS TAYLOR

[13 April 1939]

101 Central Park West
New York City

Whoever presented you with a typewriter, my dear PT, and taught you how to use it, conferred a great boon on your friends. I can read every word now. And it was very sweet of you to let me know about the Anderson

---

[3]Marian Anderson, the black American singer, had been refused the right to sing in Washington, D. C., because of pressure brought to bear by the Daughters of the American Revolution. Mrs Roosevelt promptly invited Anderson for tea at the White House and subsequently arranged for her to sing on the steps of the Lincoln Memorial.
[4]Edward G. Robinson, film actor and art collector.
[5]Hubert Delany, black New York City tax commissioner, later justice of domestic relations.
[6]William Grant Still, black American composer.
[7]Robert Earle Jones, black American actor, father of James Earl Jones.
[8]Joe Louis, heavyweight boxing champion.
[9]Morris Ernst, Broadway producer.

concert. One thing you don't mention: could she be heard in these great open spaces?* You knew Mrs R[oosevelt] was pinning the Spingarn medal on her in Richmond in June and that she was to sing before the King and the Queen at the White House? E[thel] W[aters] has made some more records, not out yet, but if you really want to curl your hair, try Ray Bourbon's Gigolo, Liberty Music Shop,     Hoping you are the same! C
*and wasn't it cold?


## TO GERTRUDE STEIN
14 May [1939]

101 Central Park West
New York City

Dear Baby Woojums, [. . .] The opening of the new Museum of Modern Art was something! Bobsy Goodspeed, Brancusi,[1] Marsden Hartley, and Anne Lindbergh[2] all in the same room together! Cars were stalled all the way up and down Fifth Avenue as Piccadilly is when there is a Drawing-Room and inside the Museum I discovered that when they are crushed together in a heated room rich people smell a little worse even than poor people. The show begins with [Albert Pinkham] Ryder and [Thomas] Eakins and Cézanne and comes down to Míro, Picasso, and even Dali. The arrangement is good and it looks like a smash hit. Sculpture is in the garden and in the basement is a moving picture theatre (for old films) which is most amusing. On the opening night they were showing Theda Bara in A Fool There Was. Then Dudensing[3] has Picasso's Guernica and when I wandered in the opening day somebody asked me to be photographed and pushed me over next to a nice Spaniard in front of the picture and when it was over we were introduced and it was General Megrin.[4] There are a lotta important shows here on account of the [World's] Fair and I think the two most generally represented artists, curiously enough (I mean in combination) are Picasso and Eakins. I haven't been to the Fair yet but we expect to go tomorrow if it doesn't rain, which it generally does. Everybody raves about the Fair and says it is beautiful and FUN.* The Lin Yutangs are back and were here for a (partly) Chinese dinner one night. And I am

[1]Constantin Brancusi, Russian-born sculptor.
[2]Anne Morrow Lindbergh, American writer, wife of Charles Lindbergh.
[3]Valentine Dudensing, art dealer. CVV and Fania Marinoff were among the sponsors of an exhibition at the Valentine Gallery on behalf of the Spanish Refugee Relief campaign. The show featured Pablo Picasso's chef d'oeuvre, Guernica, for many years afterward on display at the Museum of Modern Art until it went permanently to Spain.
[4]General Juan Megrin, Republican prime minister of Spain.

addressing this letter to Bilignin[5] with the idea that you will be there by the time it arrives!

Lots of love to Baby and Mama Woojums from ton Papa Woojums!     P!

*But it is not yet successful.

## TO FANIA MARINOFF

101 Central Park West
New York City

[2 August 1939]

Dearest Babykins, Yes it is hot here but it is dry heat, which I don't mind and almost cool at night. At the Fair yesterday it was terrific during the day but the evening was cool. Home early. The only new thing I saw was Carmen in the Gas Building and this is not worthwhile. The puppets are so small and handled in such a primitive fashion there isn't the least illusion. They only did part of one act. They give the four act version only at 6.30. In any case it is very much cut. [. . .] Essie Robeson's letter is a knockout and I guess they not only feel guilty but scared. Essie doesn't want Paul to open in NYC with all his friends down on him. Of course any of it doesn't make sense. She says again and again in the letter that Paul never pays any attention to what she asks him to do and then says he refused to appear at the benefit because she wouldn't let him. Further there is no word from Paul that HE is sorry but of course he is conscious of the whole thing because he told her about it, IN DETAIL, as you will see. There is, of course, only one thing to do, if we are to see them again *or if we aren't,* * and that is refrain from flattering them by letting them think we are MAD. So I'm going to write and ask what all the shouting is for, that we understand perfectly that Paul was busy and that certainly we weren't mad, etc., and why did she think we were, etc. Then in the fall it's ALL up to them.† It's pretty obvious that Paul doesn't want to see *us* very much, or *most* of his old friends, and the hardest thing to explain is why he didn't go back stage after Mamba's Daughters.[6] And if he only does pleasant things because Essie makes him, WHY! But I think I'm handling this right. You needn't do anything at all. [. . .] That's all this morning. I hope you are getting lots of sun and rest and when you get bored let me know.[7]     *all my love,* Carlo

*I don't want Essie saying Carl & Fania are *mad* because Paul didn't have time to see them.

†They won't bother us much!

---

[5]In the 1920s, Gertrude Stein and Alice B. Toklas had rented the manor house in Bilignin, a village near Aix les Bains and Belley. They spent fourteen consecutive summers there.
[6]*Mamba's Daughters*, 1939, a play by DuBose Heyward based on his novel, starring Ethel Waters.
[7]Fania Marinoff was taking a holiday in Atlantic City.

TO FANIA MARINOFF                                          101 Central Park West
[4 August 1939]                                            New York City

Dearest Babykins, The heat is terrific; the hottest days we have had. Last night was incredible. I am dripping at the moment. O dear, couldn't there have been some mistake about this medicine and Dr Livingston? If I can't trust him, where am I? Just in the dust heap *probably* and ready for an operation! And so I want to trust him, but I'm afraid I can't if you have understood him correctly and then I'll have to change too and it will be a great nuisance and as I say the next Doc will tell me I'll have to have an operation and people always die of prostate operations. [. . .] The point about Paul [Robeson] is that he only wants to talk about himself and how he's improving and how he is working on new songs and he can't talk to his old friends that way because they've heard this story so long: so he hunts up new ones to listen. But as I wrote you there is no earthly use in going into all this because it is a matter of indifference whether we see him or not. So I am writing Essie exactly what I suggested. Then if they want to call up and come round in the fall, why let them. I don't think they will bother us much. Essie's whole idea is to keep us from getting sore, because she knows that would do Paul harm, but the other people he has treated like this will do him more harm. [. . .] I got a card from Ettie [Stettheimer] this morning and she evidently hates A[tlantic] C[ity] N[ew] J[ersey] and you don't seem to be caring for it much. As soon as you decide what you are going to do, let me know and then I'll let you know what I'm going to do and write the gals [Mildred Perkins and Pearl Showers]. [. . .] I DO MISS you, my lamby, very much indeed and I love you to bits and send you all my love,      Carlo
I can't find the Bara recipe! Did you decide to keep this? Are you writing to thank her? The stuff hasn't come yet.[8]

Myra Kingsley in Life predicts an American Revolution in 1942–43 (when our lease runs out).

---

[8]The silent film actress Theda Bara had invented a recipe for "Garlic Ice Cream," a frozen salad dressing served in avocado halves, calling for a California spice mix called "Cowboy's Delight" and available, apparently, only on the west coast. It became a staple at subsequent Van Vechten parties, and its recipe was included in *The Alice B. Toklas Cookbook*, 1954.

## TO H. L. MENCKEN
12 September 1939

101 Central Park West
New York City

Dear Henry, Thanks for your interest. Naturally, I was terrified, but the Medico who attended me, after pushing a rubber hose up one end of me and his fist up the other, began to laugh and pronounced it a slight congestion which he assured me treatment would do away with in a month. I'm afraid this is [an] anti-climax, but a happy one.

I am on my way to a birthday luncheon for Alfred and I wish you were going to be here to celebrate your venerable years. I shall wash your health down in some of Alfred's valuable Hungarian tokays.

My respects and thanks, Carl Van Vechten

## TO DOROTHY PETERSON
[3 December 1939]

101 Central Park West
New York City

Dear Dee Pee, [. . .] Tonight Swingin' the Dream.[9] Butterfly McQueen was in that schoolboy play that George Abbott did a couple of years ago and did I love her! She had about three lines and the audience always applauded her ten minutes after she spoke them. I heard Miss [Maxine] Sullivan on the radio Sunday and was she corny! She speaks her lines like a sophomore in drag in a Mask and Wig show and if you've never seen one of these I advise you [to] take one in next year! You will have a chance to admire Harold Cromer in the new DuBarry Show,[1] which is so dirty that Ethel [Waters]'s old songs, Shake That Thing etc., sound like songs for innocents in comparison. In the Morning, NO, is perhaps the dirtiest. [Luigi] Lucioni's Ethel Waters, by the way, got the vote at the Carnegie Show at Pittsburgh as the most popular picture in the show and my scouts tell me (tho it is still a secret) that the other 5 Scottsboro boys will be pardoned before Christmas. [. . .] With great pleasure I spit on Russian sympathizers who thought it was so dreadful to bomb women and children in Spain [during the Civil War there]. Their sympathy does not extend to the Finnish. Whatever your feelings, my blessed Dee Pee, I exclude YOU from my wrath. O yes, a long letter from Noel Sullivan who says he wants to keep Langston on his farm FOR EVER. So maybe you were right about his not coming to NYC.     l and k, Carlo

---

[9]*Swingin' the Dream*, 1939, a black musical version of Shakespeare's *A Midsummer Night's Dream* by Jimmie Van Husen and Eddie De Lange.
[1]Harry Cromer, black entertainer, in *DuBarry Was a Lady*, 1939, by Cole Porter.

TO HUTCHINS HAPGOOD                    101 Central Park West
13 December 1939                       New York City

Dear Hutch, Nobody could read A Victorian in the Modern World² without
loving you, or, if they already loved you, without loving you more. I have
just finished the book and that is what I feel and I'm sure Neith will bear
me out in this. By the way if you will glance at the references to me on
pages 381 and 433 you may note (as I did) they are so placed and worded
(and you say so little) that the average (ignorant) reader will read between
the lines and gather that Neith and I have been carrying on together for
ages! [. . .] Neith and your children, it seems to me, never emerge from
the shadows at all. This may have been intentional on your part. In any
case, I, who have known all of them, had a hard time piecing them out
into personalities. You leave Charles hanging in the air,* so to speak, after
page 469, and that is a bad place to leave him. [. . .] I wish you had written
more, and more personally, about Mabel [Dodge Luhan]. I have heard you
say things about her that you have not put in the book. I think you are
decidedly unfair to Gertrude [Stein],† but that is a strange word to use in
connection with you, because fairness‡ dominates your whole personality
to such an extent that it would be impossible for you to throw yourself
utterly into any movement, be it Communism or Economic Royalty: your
sense of fairness and your knowledge of the truth on the other side would
prevent you from swallowing unadulterated propaganda. And I'm inclined
to believe that your interest in prostitutes, laboring men, thieves, etc (I
don't necessarily group these categories together, save for convenience) is
a little like François Villon's. These are the people who are most congenial
to your habits and general state of mind. And it is always easier for you
to cast your sympathy to the weak rather than the strong, but it is difficult
for me to think of you as one who is interested exclusively in social bet-
terment for the race, perhaps for reasons given by Neith, in your book, for
her non-acceptance of others who work for "causes." What you write about
your brothers, particularly Norman, is fabulously good. But more than
anything, the book is a pretty complete portrait of yourself, and a loveable
portrait if there ever was one. This portrait is assuredly your masterpiece
and if your work is to live, I think, dear Hutch, it will live by this book.
[. . .] Fania and I send our love to you both and if you will stop off§ in the
spring you must dine with us so we can talk about the whole damn business!     [unsigned]

---

²A Victorian in the Modern World, 1939, an autobiography.

*Boyce is better, of course, but the "feeling" in that seems to be transmitted from Neith's book.[3]
†So unfair I think you may try to correct this impression some time. Even if all the things you say are true, you utterly ignore her picturesque personality, her charm, etc.
‡Sometimes your fairness is mere perversity. I understand you better, perhaps, because I am somewhat this way myself.
§It would be helpful if you would write us when to expect you.

TO WALTER WHITE                    101 Central Park West
14 December 1939                    New York City

Dear Walter, It is all excellent as far as it goes, I think.[4] And you certainly are a fast worker when you get started. I would say "symbolic figures atop the pedestal" instead of the singular "figure." He [Richmond Barthé] plans to make at least two and maybe three. I think you should add a short paragraph stating that the idea of the [James Weldon Johnson Memorial] committee was to glorify the Negro and encourage the Negro sculptor as well as to provide a monument for Mr Johnson,* as at the moment there is no Negro monument in New York City, although several exist in other cities in America. [. . .] I think the letter of invitation should be withheld until you are able to give the name of the Treasurer with advice as to how money is to be sent and to whom cheques are to be made. This is important as many will send in a cheque with their acceptance. [. . .]

I see Paul [Robeson] has come out in favor of Russia against Finland in the Philadelphia Record (quoted in The Daily Worker and the New York Amsterdam News). This is very bad business, indeed.      hearts and flowers to you! Carlo!
*Of course, this is the kind of monument that would please *him* most.

TO NOEL SULLIVAN                   101 Central Park West
13 February 1940                   New York City

Dear Noel, Thanks for the letter and the cheque, which I have turned over to Colonel Theodore Roosevelt. Later I will send you a leaflet concerning the [James Weldon Johnson] Memorial. [. . .]    Am I to gather from your letter that Langston turned against the USSR. If so, I am overjoyed. One-

---

[3]Charles and Boyce, sons of Neith Boyce and Hutchins Hapgood.
[4]Walter White had joined CVV in an effort to organize a Memorial Committee for James Weldon Johnson and, through it, to raise subscriptions to finance a piece of statuary in New York City. See CVV to Walter White, 24 September 1941.

third of America may be enslaved, but everybody in Russia is a slave, with no hope of ever climbing out of it. Here there is that possible chance for any one . . . A long time ago I learned that politics, no matter what kind, were invariably the steppingstone whereby unscrupulous men seize POWER. The country with the fewest laws is therefore the safest. Occasionally too by some lucky chance a country gets a benevolent ruler, like Wilhelmina of Holland, like, I believe, Franklin Delano Roosevelt, who perhaps will be more appreciated in the future. But, in the last analysis, the only person one can improve* is oneself. Few people ever learn this axiom, or, having learned it, act upon it. I consider *you* one of the notable exceptions.

And, if you don't mind, I send you my love, Carlo!

*or help *in any way!*

## TO DOROTHY PETERSON
[15 April 1940]

101 Central Park West
New York City

My pretty Dee Pee, [. . .] I want to photograph Katherine Dunham[5] but just haven't got time at the moment. I never have been so busy. I think you'd like Rebecca[6] if you haven't seen it. There is a terrific movement on foot amongst influential ofays to get Marian Anderson into the Metropolitan Opera House, via Erda in Siegfried, or Fricka in Das Rheingold.[7] I think it most likely that D Maynor[8] will get in ahead of her, tho'.

curds and whey and my affections to you! If the Germans take Brooklyn I hope you'll have a sense of humor about it!      Carlo

## TO HUGH LAING
[8 June 1940]

101 Central Park West
New York City

Dear Hugh, Antony's[9] tender, wistful, nostalgic, poetic, mystical, heartbreaking Jardin aux Lilas knocked me over again last night and I wept at its beauty! It was better done, I thought, even than at the City Center, tho' it seemed marvellous there too. It is by far the best thing I have seen *you* do and you are magnificent in it: exactly right* (or better!) The lighting, as always, at the [Lewisohn] Stadium, was terrible, and I've always disliked

[5]Katherine Dunham, black American dancer-choreographer.
[6]*Rebecca,* 1940, an Alfred Hitchcock film of the Daphne DuMaurier novel, of interest largely to CVV because of Judith Anderson's performance as Mrs Danvers.
[7]Marian Anderson was not invited to sing at the Metropolitan Opera House until several years later, and then she made her debut as Ulrica in *Il Trovatore.*
[8]Dorothy Maynor, black American contralto who was then appearing as soloist with the Chicago and Philadelphia orchestras.
[9]Antony Tudor, English dancer-choreographer.

the set. I discover that Antony looks like Swinburne in this ballet. Was that intentional? It was a pleasure to see this fragile ballet which you would think only suitable for a small hall, grip the vast audience at the Stadium more completely than anything else. That is because when it was created it was TRULY FELT. [. . .]

About Thursday morning. If it is sunny and nothing has happened to you in the meantime, I will stop for you in front of the Windsor about 11.10 AM[†] It would be nice if you could be downstairs. At any rate we won't have much time.[‡] Bring your kit with makeup and red pants etc. In case of dubious weather or rain, please call me up. Sometimes it clears as the morning goes on,[§] so better wait until 10 AM for this. We will lunch at the Langners before going to work and I'll have you back in town before dinner.[1] [. . .] If it DOESN'T rain tonight, maybe you could come Friday, Saturday, or Sunday night (or even Thursday if it was the only night available, tho I think we will be pretty tired) but IF YOU CAN I would be grateful if you would telephone me tomorrow Wednesday morning to set a night before I get booked up in any way. Next week wouldn't be good for me at all.     Love and congratulations to you both, Carlo

*charming, romantic, tragic, & with just a dash of diablerie. Incredibly handsome, of course.

[†]Wednesday

[‡]I will bring [Alexander] Juante *with me.*

[§]Or vice versa!

I am printing you & Juante (June 8) today. Some of these will startle anybody!

TO BENNETT CERF                    101 Central Park West
4 August 1940                      New York City

Dear Bennett, After it gets going, [Walter Van Tilburg Clark's] The Ox-Bow Incident is pretty terrific and stays in the memory like the lash of a whip across the face.[2]

I think you made a mistake not to get Mr Clark to change his name. THAT is impossible to memorize. I rather favor Tilburg Clark,* but Walter Van Tilburg wouldn't be bad.

Do you ever see Lancelot Hogben (There's a fine name for an author!)?

---

[1]CVV had arranged to make nude photographs of Hugh Laing and black dancer Alexander Juante in natural surroundings at the Westport, Connecticut, estate of Lawrence Langner and Armina Marshall.

[2]Random House used CVV's line about *The Ox-Bow Incident* in its advertising campaign.

If so, I'd like to photograph him. And won't you *please* arrange about Faulkner some day?³      our best to you, Carlo

*or vice versa

When is Isherwood going to have a *new* book?⁴

TO GERTRUDE STEIN                              101 Central Park West
11 September 1940                              New York City

Dearest Baby Woojums, I write and write and cable and cable, but nothing seems to get through. Maybe this will [John] McCullo[ugh] had TO DO⁵ only one night (he borrowed my copy as his never got through) when he wrote his report to you. So now he wants to go over it again and have some children read it. But I agree with him that it is not a child's book (we both, as he says, may be wrong) especially as you say letters M and N are unlucky and half the children who read it will be named Nathan and Mary. It is too bad he can't talk this thing over with you but that seems impossible just now and you must realize that you are only receiving a very tiny percent of the mail that is being sent to you . . . Bennett [Cerf] is getting married to a Phyllis Fraser on Sept. 17. We have not met her yet but she is coming here to be photographed with him tonight.

In view of changing conditions, I am considering presenting your first editions, inscribed, and the periodicals with papers by you to some institution where they would be *kept safely* in vaults. Also, *if you don't object,* your letters. Write me when you think of this. Perhaps you would like to see these in Yale, where your Mss are, but perhaps the N Y Public Library which makes equal provision for their care and preservation would make the collection more available to students.⁶

I do hope this letter reaches you. W. G. Rogers writes you don't get his letters either.      Love to you both, Papa W.

---

³In expanding his catalog of photographs of artists and writers, CVV counted on his friends to supply the subjects. William Faulkner was a Random House author, but CVV did not photograph him until 1954, and then not through Bennett Cerf. See CVV to James B. Meriwether, 24 May 1962.

⁴Christopher Isherwood, English-born novelist living in America.

⁵*To Do,* subtitled "a book of alphabets and birthdays," was finally published in the seventh volume of the Yale Edition of the Unpublished Writings of Gertrude Stein in 1957.

⁶CVV gave all of his Stein material to the Yale Library.

## TO VIRGIL THOMSON
[20 October 1940]

101 Central Park West
New York City

Dear Virgil, When The Tribune got YOU[7] they GOT something Terrific and I am congratulating THEM when I write YOU. Thanks to this fresh breeze blowing through and over and AFTER the Musical World I am in stitches, enjoying goose pimples and real shudders, most of the time. I am reminded of Ibsen's play When We Dead Awaken, and, believe me, I am on tiptoe for the Opera to begin and your comments to follow. I did something like it myself once, but that was 25 years ago and since then there hasn't been a ripple to waft a feather out to sea until you began to pull the old beards!     l and k, Carlo

(and laurel)

## TO ARTHUR DAVISON FICKE
18 December [1940]

101 Central Park West
New York City

Dear Arthur, The spectacle of YOU attempting to be philosophical at Fantasia,[8] which is incredibly bad however you look at it, gives me the GIGGLES. And you are misunderstanding my motives concerning the dirty cats.[9] My preparations include a great deal of giving and so anything I buy now would be just one more thing to have to cope with. I intend to keep my erotica by me to the last. They may make my life more easy in a concentration camp. Somehow I must have sensed you were losing your teeth. [. . .] I have lost so many teeth (and hairs) I feel towards you as one of the Roosevelt mothers would feel towards a woman bearing her first child . . . I have sworn off Italian restaurants (tho I dote on them) for the duration. But won't you lunch with *me* Monday* the 23 at the Caviare, 18 East 49 Street. We shall be alone. [. . .]     fourleafed clovers, creampuffs, and 57 swigs of pernod to you! [unsigned]

*I'll tell you all about the preparations for Death THEN.

## TO ARTHUR DAVISON FICKE
23 December 1940

101 Central Park West
New York City

An attempt at a definition, Arthur: When one awakens to the fact that one knows nothing, that all knowledge is relative, that all events are liable to extremely opposed interpretations, that morality is as governed by chic and

[7]Virgil Thomson had become music critic for the *New York Herald Tribune.*

[8]*Fantasia,* 1940, the Walt Disney animated feature based on serious music.

[9]Ficke, who had assisted CVV in assembling illustrations for *The Tiger in the House* in 1920, had some quasi-pornographic, Japanese prints of cats.

fashion as a woman's dress, that people are undependable, unreliable, and unreasonable, that Life itself is incomplete and insecure, he may be said to be comparatively mature.      bloody thoughts to you! Carlo!

It was very pleasant today. [. . .]

TO HAROLD JACKMAN                              101 Central Park West
8 February [1941]                              New York City

Caro Harold, As you remind me this is the sixteenth anniversary of the day Eric Walrond took Donald [Angus] and me to Dorothy P[eterson]'s and we met you and Dorothy and Nella [Larsen]. All I can say is every year I like you better and you have never been sweeter or more efficient than in getting me the P[ittsburgh] Courier so promptly. I wouldn't have missed it. Seldom have I had a greater compliment paid me and from somebody whose opinion I respect very much. Schuyler[1] and I also agree about Native Son,[2] an over-rated book if there ever was one, and one which has done the Negro an inconscionable amount of harm in the minds of many an ofay who has read it.

Rubies, orchids, and everything nice to you! Carlo

TO BLANCHE KNOPF                               101 Central Park West
15 February 1941                               New York City

Grand Duchess, Sweet Puss, Such a lovely time last night and this morning comes the Blue Pamphlet[3] which is the last word in publication chic. I am so happy, especially to have that speech of Thomas Mann's. Is it conceivable that I MIGHT have just ONE more copy, please?

What you seem to have forgotten was that when you spoil people you make life fifty times more difficult for them when conditions make it impossible to spoil them any longer. I told Philip Langner the other evening that if he wanted to be wise he would spend as much time as possible doing things he didn't want to do, as this would be insurance for his future happiness. But we are all different and who knows? [. . .]      l and k, Carlo

---

[1]George S. Schuyler, black editor of the *Pittsburgh Courier*.
[2]*Native Son*, 1940, by Richard Wright.
[3]Entitled *Read at a Luncheon Given by Fannie Hurst, Anne O'Hare McCormack, & H. L. Mencken to Blanche Knopf on December 18, 1940*, 500 copies of the pamphlet were printed for the occasion of the 25th anniversary of Alfred A. Knopf, Inc. The reprinted speech, by German novelist Thomas Mann, is the primary subject of CVV's letter to Blanche Knopf, 18 February 1941.

## TO BLANCHE KNOPF
18 February 1941

101 Central Park West
New York City

Dearest Blanchette, Thanks a thousand times for the extra copy of the luncheon pamphlet. About paragraph two, it contains the whole meaning of life. Life in *any* period or epoch is difficult and baffling* and is only possible to face if one has completely solved the problem of SELF Discipline. On the whole, therefore, if you expect to get any fun or interest or excitement or pleasure out of life, it is BETTER and EASIER and CHEAPER to have this problem solved before one is 20. With plenty of people, for one reason or another, this problem is NOT solved before 20, but alas what torture and pain and unpleasantness etc they have to go through later.[†] If you don't understand this, I'm afraid you don't yet understand the whole meaning of life. [. . .]

   You are a sainted woojums and a scented woojums too!      Love, Carlo
*almost unbearable!
[†]viz P[eter] W[hiffle]


## TO BERNHARD KNOLLENBERG
29 May 1941

101 Central Park West
New York City

Dear Mr Knollenberg, Some time ago we discussed briefly the possibility of my giving the Yale University Library my Negro books and papers. If you still want them I've decided to go ahead with this idea. It isn't a vast collection, like the Schomburg or the Spingarn, nor does it contain many old books (tho I have the rarest of them all, Phillis Wheatley's Poems) but it makes up for that, perhaps, in personality and association items. The material includes: books, many firsts, by Negroes and by whites *about* Negroes, inscribed to me, manuscripts, clippings, files of magazines, a vast quantity of pamphlets and minor items, music, including most of the best collections of Spirituals, phonographs records, including almost complete sets of the famous Blues singers, Bessie and Clara Smith, scrapbooks, photographs of famous Negroes by me (a vast collection) and by others, and a very valuable, important, and personal collection of letters from many of the more important Negroes of the day.

   There would be minor conditions to be met if you accept this collection for the Yale Library, but the more important conditions are these: First, I want the collection preserved as an entity. There may be difficulties in regard to this condition. Your Music Department, for instance, may think they have first claim to the music and phonograph records. I am convinced, however, that the collection will have a greater value if it is kept together as a group of books and papers gathered by the author of Nigger Heaven. Second, I would ask you to put restrictions upon the availability of the material, at least as many restrictions as those with which you would protect the Gertrude Stein manuscripts or your rarer books.

I would suggest that we name the collection The James Weldon Johnson Memorial Collection of Negro Arts and Letters, founded by Carl Van Vechten. I think this name would be of material assistance to you in assembling future material from others.

If you like the idea in toto, let me know. Perhaps you will have some suggestions of your own. In case we ultimately agree on conditions, I propose to ship you the material a little at a time, beginning around July 1, and I think it is extremely likely that I shall still be sending it to you until I die, for even after the present collection is all on its way to New Haven, further material will rapidly accumulate.     sincerely, [unsigned carbon copy]

## TO WALTER WHITE
[24 September 1941]

101 Central Park West
New York City

Dear Walter, One of the points about a nude which I didn't bring out very clearly is that it is noble, classical, and modern, whereas this same statue in pants would be "picturesque darky folklore," unobjectionable, and unnoticed . . . Here are the leaflets I promised you.[4]

The Maine Monument in Columbus Circle includes two nudes. They are sitting but you can get the whole idea from any bus or taxi passing. Take a look next time you go by. They have never created a revolution. Civic Virtue which stood in front of the City Hall for years was to all intents and purposes nude and quite sexy. A discus thrower stood back of the Metropolitan Museum for years. Mr. [Robert] Moses has moved this to Randall Island, I think . . . At the World's Fair practically everything was nude and practically everything was 30 feet high. No fig leaves. Other cities have more nudes. Are we more provincial than St. Louis? Carl Milles' new fountain in front of the Railway Station has twenty or thirty nudes, male and female. The Garden of the Museum of Modern Art (which can be seen by the public from 54th Street) has dozens of nudes of both sexes. Lachaise's Man of heroic size with a terrific penis brazened it out there for months. He has returned to Walter Chrysler's country garden!

[4]Richmond Barthé had executed preliminary drawings for the James Weldon Johnson Memorial Statue featuring a nude figure and he proposed to add at least two others, also nude. Tentatively the monument was to be installed at Seventh Avenue and 110th Street, at the northern entrance to Central Park. See CVV to Walter White, 14 December 1939.

I have been told confidentially that NO statue, work of art or dub, ever got by without a fight! [. . .]     oak leaves and dahlias to you! Carlo

If you want me to meet you or talk to anybody or help in any way, command me. I think psychologically it would be helpful to get this thing done before the election!

## TO CLAUDE MCKAY
22 October 1941

101 Central Park West
New York City

Dear Claude McKay, I am extremely sorry any misunderstanding has arisen in regard to placing your manuscripts in the Yale Library. Your original letter, I discovered, is slightly ambiguous. You wrote: "If you would like to have any of these and want to ask any of the publishers (using my name) it will be all right so far as I am concerned." Both Mr Knollenberg and myself took this offer to be plural, as you didn't write "any ONE of these." Also, of course, in writing, Mr Knollenberg asked the publishers to consult you. I hope, in the circumstances, you will permit the manuscripts to stay where they are, as (1) it is an excellent place to insure your future immortality; (2) Yale is overjoyed to have them and they are a valuable part of the collection. Furthermore, your generosity has already received some publicity. I am also sorry you cannot come in today to see your pictures. It is really shameful that your black and white pictures are not yet printed, but I have been so occupied getting material off to Yale that I have hardly been in the darkroom at all. I do not think it will be long, however, before I'll have these ready. And of course you will have a set as soon as I do. Also I'll ask you again to see your handsome color pictures. Further I've found an old Pearson's and several Liberators or New Masses I'd like you to sign (for Yale) in addition to Arna Bontemps's anthology in which you play an important role.[5]     sincerely, [unsigned carbon copy]
In your second letter about the manuscripts written Sept 20 I find you say "I hope you will get *one or two* of those M.S.S. At least that at Dutton's ought to be obtainable."

## TO ARTHUR SPINGARN
24 October 1941

101 Central Park West
New York City

Dear Arthur, You are being very generous to Yale University, but I felt sure you wouldn't want to be left out of any Memorial to Jim [Weldon Johnson]. It will be a few days before I get your books off to Yale, as I have to list

[5]*Golden Slippers: An Anthology of Negro Poetry for Young Readers,* 1941.

them, but when Mr. Knollenberg receives them he will send you a receipt. I await the other books you promised me with eagerness and *please don't forget I want something personal relating to your brother.** It wouldn't be a Negro collection unless he were represented in some personal way.[6] Herewith the Yale bookplate, the NY Public Library Bookplate of my personal collection (to be shown in Room 112 for two weeks beginning November 17) and, as it includes a Negro (Allen Meadows posed for this!), my own bookplate.

Odilon Redon was the son of a New Orleans Creole mother and a French father who went to America to make his fortune during the Napoleonic wars. Redon was born in 1840 just after his parents landed in Bordeaux. I think there is every chance that he had Negro blood, tho, so far as I know, it has never been suggested. He had dark eyes, large lips, and a swarthy complexion . . . Suppose we look into this.

I enjoyed our lunch very much. Indeed, I always enjoy seeing you.

sincerely, Carlo Van Vechten

*connecting him with the Negro, if possible

## TO LANGSTON HUGHES
17 November 1941

101 Central Park West
New York City

Dear Langston, I LOVED your letter [. . .] And I sent you a postcard last week re At George's Joint.[7] To me the book is entirely devoid of feeling. Nobody in the book has any feeling at all: SO, it becomes monotonous and uninteresting and untrue. After awhile you stop believing it. I have no objections to people drinking and screwing in books. In fact I've written books like that myself, but to make them entirely bereft of mother love, romantic passion, of any regard for propriety, or any inhibitions whatever, is to make them so inhuman that they don't stand up as characters. So I applaud everything you say. [. . .] I can't recall about the hair in the Kauffer drawings [for *Nigger Heaven*] as I didn't look at them from that angle.[8] But THEY ARE ART. Maybe Blanche [Knopf] got 'em fixed according to your desires, but in any case your criticism is not art criticism but an economic or social one. It is highly probable indeed that in a few years EVERYBODY will be having nappy hair again and loving it. Some few sensible persons go in for it now . . . BUT I GET YOUR POINT and the next time you want

---

[6]Joel Elias Spingarn, educator and critic, president of the NAACP.
[7]*Mr. George's Joint*, 1941, by E. A. Wheaton.
[8]E. McKnight Kauffer had made illustrations for Hughes's *Shakespeare in Harlem*, 1942.

to put over something like this, write me about it *too* as I will raise any kind of stink you want me to and I will understand what you are talking about, which sometimes they won't in the office . . . For instance it would be quite legitimate, if he wanted to, for Kauffer to illustrate a modern white novel in hair done in the style of Louis XV. Beardsley did this sort of thing all the time . . . Velasquez and Veronese on the other hand painted biblical scenes in renaissance costumes . . . With these things in mind, it is hard for editors and painters to understand the ways in which Negroes are touchy, but I UNDERSTAND. Well, I hope the hairs will be okay. The pictures, in any case, are beautiful. [. . .] We shall miss you and your distinguished presence very much at the Library today. I got a preview on Saturday and felt as if I were dead.[9] It was very impressive. You'll know when you get laid out at Yale![1]

affection to you and hope to see you in NYC soon, Carlo!

TO R. W. COWDEN                     101 Central Park West
23 November 1941                    New York City

Dear Mr Cowden, In the past when you have invited me to be a judge of the Avery Hopwood awards, I have never been able to accept, but I'm glad you invited me again because this year I accept with pleasure. So send on your manuscripts and instructions when you get ready.

The portrait you speak of BELONGS in the Hopwood Room at Ann Arbor and YOU SHOULD HAVE IT. In the first place it is, I think, the only time Avery was ever painted. In the second place, it is both an interesting work of art and a good portrait of Avery. The painter, Miss Florine Stettheimer, still has her studio at 80 West Fortieth. Like all painters she is temperamental. In any case, she first assured me that she would give the picture to Michigan. Later she changed her mind and said she didn't see why she should. Maybe she would sell it. Definitely, I think you should have it, and if you wrote her asking her to set a price, again she might give it to you or set a low price. In any case, explain to her something about the awards and the room. I'll do what I can which is precisely nothing unless she asks my advice, as already I have begged her to send you the painting and she refused. Let me know what happens.

sincerely, Carl Van Vechten

---

[9]The New York Public Library had arranged an exhibition of the books and manuscripts that CVV had donated to the Manuscript and Archive Division as The Carl Van Vechten Collection.
[1]Langston Hughes had begun donating his papers to the James Weldon Johnson Memorial Collection of Negro Arts and Letters at Yale.

TO GERTRUDE STEIN                    101 Central Park West
31 December 1941                     New York City

Dearest Baby Woojums, I consign this to the air with the hope it will reach you to wish you a merry Christmas (with St Ignatius to help!) but I can no longer be sure of anything as naturally from now on the movements of clippers and ships will be mysterious. I do wish you and Mama Woojums were over here, but wishes are not horses and you and Mama W are certainly not beggars. . . . Fania is learning First AID which means lessons all day and is further a captain of the American Theatre Wing on War Relief. I am trying to get my Negro books off to Yale before the bombs fall . . . You wrote a very sweet letter about Smith [College] and the Ada (named after Ada Byron!) Amanda Fitch Van Vechten Memorial Collection of Books by Women. Nothing whatever is decided about this yet, except that the Librarian at Harvard who is a trustee at Smith is much interested. But they have no treasure room as yet and I am fully occupied with the Yale Library at present. By the way, I've found more items (in storage) for your collection at Yale and have sent them on. I do wish you and Mama W had been here for my show (of MY books) at the [New York] Public Library. You received the invitation, I hope. It is a little like being dead, being all laid out in rows like that, but it is like being an illustrious dead man. I first had the feeling when I saw YOUR show,[2] and I had it again with mine. The first day was very brilliant and everybody was there from Doris Keane to W. C. Handy (the Negro who wrote the St Louis Blues). Virgil [Thomson] is adding to his laurels as a critic and ALL the orchestras are playing his symphonies etc., as I knew they would. He is on the top of the wave. [. . .] I am happy to think of you with a turkey for Thanksgiving. I've just heard from Mary Garden who is in Aberdeen and Mabel [Dodge Luhan] sends her usual sprig of sage. [. . .] Believe it or not, I have been too busy to print pictures of Fania with her white hair, but she has changed her appearance so much since these were taken, rather resembling a Countess of the merveilleuse period now, that I think I shall have to photograph her again. Anyway I'll send something SOON. You are NOW DATING YOUR LETTERS and this is helpful, as Often I can make out nothing from the postmarks and they often arrive way out of order and I like to keep them in order. [. . .] So Love and Kisses to you Both and Fania and I wish you a very happy New Year! BUT WE WISH YOU WERE HERE.      [unsigned]

---

[2]An exhibition of Gertrude Stein's books and manuscripts had been mounted in the Yale University Library in 1941.

## TO HUTCHINS HAPGOOD
[circa 1941]

101 Central Park West
New York City

Dear Hutch, [. . .] Your idea of ghosting an autobiography for some one had me in stitches. Your style and your personality are so definite that the person ghosted wouldn't get much attention, even if you wrote about nothing else. However, I think this is a gorgeous idea and I think you should persuade Harcourt to let you attempt it. Preferably, you should ghost somebody with a terrific personality of his own, such as, par exemple, Elsa Maxwell![3]

I am preparing for death, bombs, destruction, and disasters, ie, getting my manuscripts and books and letters into collections in libraries, museums, etc, where they stand more chance of being preserved and protected. Of course I could dump these into these collections, but I prefer to edit and arrange them. This I have just done for 392 letters of Gertrude Stein (1913–1941) which I have just given to Yale, sealed until GS and I die. Next I am giving my own manuscripts and first editions to the NY Public Library. I am also arranging a series of photographs for the Museum of Modern Art, etc, etc. I have enough to do to occupy me at least till the *next* war or revolution. And in the meantime if I am bombed I die busy!     Much love to you both, Carlo

I ran into Dr. [A. A.] Brill the other day and he said Mabel was coming east for some dentistry, but of course I don't see Mabel any more.[4]

## TO R. W. COWDEN
1 May 1942

101 Central Park West
New York City

Dear Mr Cowden, I regret to say that I have read the plays in the Avery Hopwood Contest with bitter disappointment and increasing lack of interest. It seems to me that none of them deserves a prize, being for the most part, full of holes technically, half-baked intellectually, and casually synthetic in feeling and structure. [. . .] I might say that the order I have placed them in is purely arbitrary. The reverse order would be just as logical and if the other judges prefer the reverse order it is perfectly agreeable to me. I couldn't discover a trace of originality in any of them. I'm sorry to make such an unpleasant report, but I see no point in being less than truthful in the matter if it is worth while for me to judge the contest at all.

I am enclosing the reports of my preferences and I am returning the

---

[3]Elsa Maxwell, garrulous social climbing party giver.
[4]A. A. Brill, Austrian-born Freudian psychoanalyst, for twenty years Mabel Dodge Luhan's mentor.

manuscripts, as you suggest, collect, by American Railway Express.

sincerely, Carl Van Vechten

## TO BERNHARD KNOLLENBERG

101 Central Park West

6 May 1942

New York City

Dear Mr Knollenberg, The last person previously to question me about Max Ewing was Tom Dewey[5] who was a classmate of his at the University of Michigan.[6] Max was one of the best-known "characters" of New York in the twenties which at that time abounded in eccentric characters.[. . .]

Some time ago his cousin Doris Ewing asked me if I would consider writing his biography and sent me two suitcases of his letters to his mother and others, which I still have in my possession. These are wonderful letters as he used to write his mother complete accounts of his more than fantastic activities. I have many letters from Max myself; also I photographed him. His suicide seems to have been caused by his [. . .] notion, which no amount of explanation seems successful in eradicating, that when his mother died he was left penniless. The fact was that she left him over $100,000. I did not see him during the final year and a half of his life, but his letters to me during that period are pathetic and verge on the tragic.

A most amazing book could be made of his life, of which I have given you only the most superficial account above, but I don't think I'll ever write this myself, though anything is possible. [. . .]      Carl Van Vechten

## TO ROY WILKINS

101 Central Park West

10 May 1942

New York City

Dear Mr. Wilkins, Here is the piece about the James Weldon Johnson Memorial Collection at Yale you asked me to do for the Crisis. Altho' I have tried to keep it within the bounds you set, it has gone on a little longer, and it would be easy to make it longer still. If you possibly can, I hope you will print it as it stands, as I have already been obliged to omit mention of some important material. If, however, you find it too long to use in its present form I hope you will do me the favor of letting me cut it myself, as there are certain things I should hate to leave out.

---

[5]Thomas Dewey, governor of New York and Republican presidential candidate. See CVV to Fania Marinoff, 3 July 1944.
[6]Yale University Library had recently purchased some letters written to Ewing and, finding CVV's name in several of them wrote for information. As a result, CVV wrote to Doris Ewing, 14 May 1942, proposing to give the Ewing material she had sent him to Yale as "the nucleus of a Big Max Collection," since Knollenberg "expressed the most violent enthusiasm."

Alexander Woollcott, 1939

Carlotta Monterey O'Neill, 1936

Dorothy Peterson, 1943

Have you any idea how soon you can use this?[7]

sincerely, Carl Van Vechten

I am enclosing the bookplate of the collection which you may wish to reproduce.

## TO OWEN DODSON
24 June 1942

101 Central Park West
New York City

Dear Owen (if I MAY), You certainly shake a jaunty typewriter and write a juicy letter. Your pictures are not even developed yet and Gawd knows when they will be as I am very BUSY, but you will get them soon after they are developed. Before your letter came with the enclosure for Yale (for which, please, many thanks) I had been looking for Rose McClendon as Medea and found *three* which I will send you. These pictures were made the month before she died and it was the last time I ever saw her. She left a ring and as I hadn't heard from her a week later (and didn't know she was sick) I sent one of the maids up with it. When Rose saw her and the ring, she cried, "Carl never would have sent the ring back so soon if he hadn't KNOWN I was dying." The Medea pictures were an idea of my own. She intended to perform the rôle[8] the coming fall and I suggested a tryout in the atmosphere. The costume is a dressing-robe of mine and I ran up the wreath. I am also sending you a picture of Ethel [Waters] as you request. You are aware, of course, that these pictures cannot be re-produced without permission. [. . .] I wish you might have seen Avon Long as Orestes in La Belle Hélène. That was something! Sporting Life [in *Porgy and Bess*] is a bit faint in comparison. He is, as you may have observed, primarily a dancer and he had plenty of dancing in that. Puck in [*Swingin'*] The Dream would be on his Street and The Dreamy Kid of [Eugene] O'Neill and maybe The Playboy of the Western World [by John Millington Synge] Thanks for writing Sterling Brown[9] [. . .] So four golden slippers, jade ap-ples, and a bowl of sapphire dogs to you!     Carlo

## TO CARLOTTA MONTEREY O'NEILL
[11 August 1942]

101 Central Park West
New York City

Dearest Carlotta, I've been working very intensively on the O'Neills this week, cutting off breasts like mad, as you asked me to.[1] I hope to have

---

[7]"The James Weldon Johnson Collection at Yale" appeared in *Crisis,* July 1942.
[8]*The Medea,* a translation from Euripides by Countee Cullen.
[9]Sterling A. Brown, black American educator and poet, late-comer to the Harlem Renaissance, whom CVV hoped to photograph.
[1]Ordinarily, CVV refused to retouch or crop his photographs in any way that would glamourize them, nor is there any evidence that he did so to please this subject.

these ready by early fall! Your letter has something of the old you in it—very sweet & calm and sage—and I'm always happy to find you in that mood! Or myself either. I am photographing This is the Army[2] and it's most amusing having majors order young men to put on drag before my camera.     Love! Carlo

## TO LANGSTON HUGHES
17 August [1942]

101 Central Park West
New York City

Dear Langston, I've been away for a few days and when I come back, I find your letter. [. . .] I've also been reading many Negro letters for Yale, including the correspondence re Mulebone which includes letters from YOU and Zora [Neale Hurston] and Barrett H. Clark and Lawrence Langner and Theresa Helburn.[3] It's a pretty complete tale and your letter regarding Zora's tantrum in your mother's room in Cleveland is wonderful. She had a tantrum in my library at 150 West 55th Street too and threw herself on the floor and screamed and yelled! Bit the dust in fact. You woulda loved it, had it not concerned you. In the Pennsylvania Station last night there wasn't a single porter. I lugged a 90 pound bag (full of letters and books) about a mile in pitch blackness (the roof is glass and they keep the lights out). Your slow eating habits will be a distinct disadvantage to you in a boarding house where you are expected to talk. Better take vitamins. The Everleigh Club in Chicago[4] also had a fountain in the living room. Some of the best families used to fall in.

Affection to you and FM even sends a kiss, after your "Tell Fania I love her!"     Carlo
Monday (I'm off to the [Stage Door] Canteen SOON)[5]

[2]*This is the Army,* 1942, a musical play by Irving Berlin entirely staffed and cast with military personnel.
[3]*Mulebone:* a play on which Hughes and Hurston collaborated but never completed, offered through CVV to the Theatre Guild for production.
[4]A celebrated brothel where, during his college days, CVV used to spell the piano player.
[5]The Stage Door Canteen opened 2 March 1942, under the auspices of the American Theatre Wing, to entertain members of the armed forces. Fania Marinoff was among its first volunteers, and CVV followed shortly. He worked there on a regular weekly basis until it closed in August 1945.

TO MAY [DAVENPORT] SEYMOUR          101 Central Park West
[19 October 1942]                  New York City

Dear Miss Seymour, You said you need a few biographical facts.[6] [. . .] I have always been interested in photographs and photography, other people's as well as my own. Some of my photographs were made in the early nineties, others around 1908–9. . . . I really settled down to photographs intensively in 1932 and I think it was my original intention to photograph everybody and everything in the world! My first interest in photography is documentary, but I see no harm in being honest and as artistic as possible at the same time. My backgrounds, which are a feature in my work, I borrowed from Matisse, but only one person I know has been clever enough to mention this. [. . .]

I am Very, Very eager to look at the pictures as soon as they are arranged (this is curiosity, not a desire to alter anything you have done expertly, I am sure) and if they can be seen early tomorrow (Monday) afternoon will you telephone me before noon and let me know, please?

If there is anything else, command me.

17 Birds of Paradise to you bearing pink ribbon phylacteries in their beaks with the motto: "What a nice girl!"      [unsigned]

TO JOHN MARTIN                     101 Central Park West
23 October 1942                    New York City

Dear Mr Martin, [. . .] I think we had better omit the Gertrude Hoffman[7] notice.[8] I am almost certain I didn't write this. I have been over it a number of times and it seems incredible to me me I could have written that final paragraph. Nor is there the slightest mention of the Ballet Russe or any indication that these ballets had been done abroad, with all of which facts I was familiar. But I hope you will use the passage on the Lindy Hop which I dug out of Parties. [. . .] The idea of using the bookplate[9] as a cover illustration is a marvelous one and I enclose a bookplate so you can go ahead with it. Indeed these matters are ex libris CVV!

I feel a little as if I were dead as a result of these revivals, but I trust to

---

[6]The Museum of the City of New York was mounting an extensive exhibition titled "The Theatre Through the Camera of Carl Van Vechten," November 1942–January 1943.
[7]Gertrude Hoffman, American dancer who in 1912 imported Russian dancers for a short ballet season in New York.
[8]*Dance Index,* October–November 1942, a triple issue entirely devoted to CVV's writings about dance.
[9]CVV's bookplate designed by Prentiss Taylor.

your judgment that people will be interested. And I am very grateful to you for your enthusiasm and the work you have devoted to this number! If I can help in any further way, please let me know!     sincerely, [unsigned carbon copy]

TO DOROTHY PETERSON                    101 Central Park West
[23 October 1942]                               New York City

Dearest Dorothea, [. . .] My draft board sent for me today but they seemed to want a social chat more than anything. [. . .]

Fania was in the W[ashington] DC Canteen when it opened and she was taking meal tickets as she often does here and when the first serviceman entered she got up and shook hands with him and when the first Negro entered she did likewise and explained why. He was followed by six or seven more at intervals.* You will recall I wrote you two or three Tuesdays ago there were forty or fifty sepia hostesses but nothing but ofay servicemen. Well, this Tuesday the reverse was true. But a very black sailor, over six feet tall and most conspicuous, didn't allow this to bother him. He cut in on white dancers and took white girls for partners, not only with impunity but with success. He kept this up for over an hour and must have danced with nearly every girl on the floor. Besides he got acquainted with all the men. I watched this carefully for any signs of an "incident," but saw none. He was polite and danced discreetly, but he talked a good deal and frequently said something which made his partner laugh. I have always said that fear was the only thing that kept Negroes out of restaurants etc and that if they would have nerve enough to go through with it a couple of times all these prejudices (I am speaking of the North) could be broken down in a week. This is pretty good proof.

So love and a basket of magnolias to you!     Carlo
*She left at seven, so I can't give you a report on what has happened since.

TO DOROTHY PETERSON                    101 Central Park West
[circa 26 October 1942]                        New York City

Dorothy, my angel! [. . .] I guess you don't understand about history. It can never be unprejudiced. Whole generations and races and masses of people believed that people were witches; others believed, in even greater number, that if a young girl delivered her maidenhead without wedding bans, she became automatically a social outcast. Historians reflect these mass beliefs. There are those who have believed in the honor and beauty of slavery (including some African chiefs). If a Hindu wrote the history of the West he would be appalled at our casual dispatch of animals. SO, any historian willy-nilly has a point of view and cannot be entirely unprejudiced. There are two ways of getting by this. One is to try to find out what a historian's point of view is. The other is to try to read a historian with the opposite point of view. Pardon this didacticism. As a matter of fact it is much more important for present day or past historians to understand and sympathize with slave owners than not, so that their point of view can be fully explained before it is entirely lost. I thank you for the use of the hall. [. . .] Love and Kisses to you and don't forget that I am spending *all my time* working for the RACE: Night and Day.     Carlo

TO MAY [DAVENPORT] SEYMOUR     101 Central Park West
17 November 1942     New York City

Dear May (if you will pardon the liberty, as I feel we have been hand and glove for years) You certainly know how to give a show and Mr. [Henry] McBride really missed something. What impressed me the most was drawing two photographers and Marian Anderson and Canada Lee![1] I had three hours at the Canteen, then a bite, and home. But I shall make a comeback before Friday. Where was Mr. Scholle? Anyway, thank you, thank you, and will you thank Mr. Smith for his sympathetic cooperation. Please.

I am enclosing an invitation to the dinner on Friday night to tell you when and where you and Ann Seymour are to appear.[2] Your tickets are paid for and your names down as honored guests. You will note that YOUR show is referred to. Mr. Knollenberg is the Librarian at Yale University.

156 camels hair shawls to you and the fragance of myrrh, to say nothing of fifteen bowls of terrapin Maryland and a glass of champagne
    Carl Van Vechten

TO JAMES T. BABB     101 Central Park West
13 December 1942     New York City

Dear Mr Babb, The enclosed lists more material for the James Weldon Johnson Collection which I am sending you tomorrow by insured mail in three packages. It is a fine lot. I can think of nothing I would rather see in the Collection than James Weldon Johnson's letters negotiating with

---

[1] Canada Lee, black American actor.
[2] The James Weldon Johnson Literary Guild sponsored a dinner in CVV's honor on 20 November 1942 at a Chinatown restaurant. He invited May Seymour and her actress-daughter Ann as his guests.

Walter White to become Assistant secretary of the NAACP. The orginial article of agreement (1812)* is an interesting item. At least two of the boxes containing Countee Cullen manuscripts are gems in the Crown of the Collection. The Booker T. Washington booklet is a Bibliographical curiosity of great value. This last, by the way, is so small that it could be easily stolen or lost and special care should be taken to preserve it. There are two autographed items from Paul Laurence Dunbar. I could go on and on about this material. [. . .] Last week I spoke on the Radio on the Bessie Beatty hour and had an opportunity to say a few words about the Collection. As a result, Miss Beatty received a letter from a lady in New Bedford who wrote that she had had a Japanese butler who collected Negro material, that he had in fact over 400 volumes, many of them with inscriptions. As the butler has been sent to a concentration camp she wanted to turn this over to Yale. I foresaw that this case might have legal aspects and I suggested to Miss Beatty that she ask the lady to write to the Yale Library. If anything comes of this, I'd be glad to know about it. [. . .]

sincerely, Carl Van Vechten

*of a slave transaction

## TO LOUIS BROMFIELD
8 January 1943

101 Central Park West
New York City

Dear Louis, I am enchanted by Mrs Parkington. In fact I love Susie. I knew her before you wrote about her, in fact, and part of my love is nostalgic, but it is you who created the nostalgia. I KNEW if I ever opened the book I would never lay it down until I had read the last page and that is exactly what happened. Louis, the whole thing has so much vitality, and charm, and wit (and most curiously, sex!) and the characters are so vividly and accurately presented that it almost seems inspired (like the Bible!). I dare say you consciously had very little to do with it. It is particularly an achievement to have written such a book in the midst of war times and it is indeed a pleasure to congratulate you on ALL Counts . . .

Fania and I send our love to you and Mary!     Carlo

## TO DOROTHY PETERSON
[26 January 1943]

101 Central Park West
New York City

Dearest DeePee, [. . .] There were two Negro junior hostesses in the [Stage Door] Canteen at 5.15 last night which surprised me so much I nearly fainted. I've never seen one at any hour there before on Monday. When Osceola [Archer] appeared, I asked her how it happened and she smiled that mysterious smile of hers and whispered, "I've been working." Then she slipped into the arms of Harvey (ignoring fifteen or twenty cullud service men) and went into a routine on the dance floor. We've had dozens of French sailors every minute the past week and every French person in the place and every person who speaks French hovers over them. I wish the cullud would behave this way. Zora [Neale Hurston] came to see me last night before I went to work and she says when she gets back she wants to work there. I think she would be good, you know. She is going to try to get the Sat[urday] Eve[ning] Post to which she has sold two papers to take a piece from her about the J[ames] W[eldon] J[ohnson] Collection and she is going to work hard for us. [. . .] Duke Ellington refuses to give us any manuscript and I think the secret is that his manuscripts are written down by an arranger. [. . .] Edmund Lowe[3] came into the Canteen and had to be introduced and the O[fficer of the] D[ay] asked me to do it but when I got back to see Ed, an old friend of mine, I discovered he wanted a Stooge with a lotta lines and cues. Well we had a rehearsal or two and I got through with it without a slip up. So they were practically carrying me out of the Canteen on their shoulders when Tom [Mabry] appeared, just too late to witness my triumphs! He says I oughter join Equity. Jimmie Daniels* is coming to be photographed today.[4] I am trying through Lin Yutang and some other Chinese friends to get some Chinese busboys into the Canteen. Tom agrees with me it would be a good idea. [. . .] Incidently, I think the cullud boy who handles the dumbwaiter chez Neptune's Sons smokes reefers hand over fist. His dreamy eyes are always half closed and his demeanour is positively Tropic Night!

So L and K and come back to us SOON!     Carlo
*in uniform

TO CHANNING POLLOCK                    101 Central Park West
[early February 1943]                          New York City

Channing, my lad! I finished your engaging autobiography[5] in two sittings. Few (and they would perforce be authors themselves) know how much actual labor is involved in organizing and executing a book of this kind, but most everybody, I should think, will like it for one reason or another. My reason for liking it is that it is YOU, with your charm and enormous vitality, and even a few of your less lovable traits. I recognized you on every page and felt as though I were listening to you over a table: perhaps

---

[3]Edmund Lowe, film actor.
[4]Jimmie Daniels, black cabaret singer.
[5]*Harvest of My Years*, 1943.

this is the best kind of writing, writing which seems to be like speaking. [. . .]

I think you have been unfair to Avery [Hopwood]'s memory. When he wasn't drunk he was the kindest and gentlest of beings and more loved, I think, than any one else I have ever known. The mere mention of his name today is enough to cause the tears to start in the eyes of dozens of people. He was constantly helping people and some he helped consistently through a period of years. Aside from legacies to friends (he left Fania and me in the neighborhood of $50,000 apiece) he left *in trust* the residue to his mother, but she had only the use of it for a few months and then it went to found the Julie and Avery Hopwood Awards at the University of Michigan, which have been an inspiration to young poets, novelists, and playwrights for many years and will be for many more. What money his mother left to care for her monkey was her own and if she loved the monkey it was a creditable thing to do. I thank you for the use of the hall and I send you my love and continued admiration and a kiss behind the ear for Anna, MP![6]    Carlo

TO CHANNING POLLOCK                101 Central Park West
17 February 1943                   New York City

Dear Channing, I think you will find it was George Tyler who "introduced" [Eleanora] Duse to America. At any rate she was here during the season of 1899–1900 or thereabouts, playing ONLY D'Annunzio's Francesca da Rimini while I was in college and Morris Gest was in Russia. I'm surprised you don't remember this. Morris Gest MAY have directed her final tour in the USA. Of course no one (not even Who's Who) could believe any information Morris gave out about himself. I didn't object to your writing about Avery [Hopwood]'s weaknesses. What I meant when I wrote that you had been unfair was that you had neglected to parade his many good qualities. Perhaps you have forgotten, or never knew, a fact I learned very early in my writing career, that every bad thing you say about a person outweighs a HUNDRED TIMES any good thing. To strike a good balance you have to overdo the other side. Now that you mention it, I think you have been even more unfair to Ren[nold] Wolf[7] than you have to Avery.

[6]Anna Marble Pollock. "MP" stood not only for her maiden and surname but, in CVV's zeal to assign nicknames to nearly everybody, for "Member of Parliament" because of her conservative views. See List of recipients.
[7]Rennold Wolf, a popular newspaper journalist before the First War, and at one time one of Pollock's collaborators on plays.

Most of those who read the book, and didn't know him, will come away thinking Ren was a syphilitic lecher and little more. I KNOW you didn't intend to do this and that is why I mention it. Perhaps in some future edition you can do something about it, if you care to.

Anyway hands across the West Side to you!     Carlo!

## TO BERNHARD KNOLLENBERG
27 February 1943

101 Central Park West
New York City

Dear Mr Knollenberg, Dorothy Peterson's wonderful father died last week at the ripe age of 83 suddenly and unexpectedly. At the funeral at the house [. . .] I sat next to Walter White who told me that he believed that Arthur Spingarn was no longer sure he wanted to leave his fabulous Negro library to Howard and thought he could easily be persuaded to turn it into the James Weldon Johnson Collection. I think it would be an extremely good idea if you wrote to him (without mentioning Walter or me) suggesting that if he had not already made up his mind how he would dispose of his Negro books that you hope he would consider us seriously! But perhaps you have done this already!

Mr Peterson left the Collection any of his books and letters we wanted and yesterday I went over his books with Dorothy.[8] His Negro library was not large, but it is an extremely good one and contains several rare and valuable items such as a Life of Frederick Douglass inscribed to Dorothy's maternal grandmother by the author, several original photographs of Douglass, and a first edition of [W. E. B.] DuBois's The Souls of Black Folk, as rare a book as comes. [. . .] You will recall that Mr Peterson gave us a great number of valuable pamphlets and papers before he died.

Fania and I send you and Mrs Knollenberg our best wishes and HOPE you won't have to spend the summer in Washington!     sincerely,
Carl Van Vechten

## TO BLANCHE KNOPF
[26 April 1943]

101 Central Park West
New York City

Blanche, Grand Duchess Cunegunda Schwartz! Reading Two Serious Ladies[9] I felt at first a good deal as if I were eating dog biscuits with whipped cream while driving around the Rocky Mountains in a hansom cab, but

---

[8]Jerome Bowers Peterson, black American journalist and founder of the New York *Age*. Dorothy Peterson was his daughter.
[9]By Jane Bowles, 1943.

then, suddenly, came that moment in the book (for every reader this will happen on a different page and for some it will never happen at all) when I realized that everything that occurs in it is like life everywhere, at any time and always, like what happened to you and me last Thursday! It is only as mad as life itself!     Love to you, and thanks, Carlo!

TO LANGSTON HUGHES                          101 Central Park West
12 August 1943                                        New York City

Langston! [. . .] I know *why* the riots and so I can understand and they MAY have done some good locally, but the effect on the general public is extremely bad and has given the other side unexpected comfort and ammunition.[1] If such riots are organized the people who organize them should do so publicly and then others would know what they are doing and WHY they are doing it. Ferinstance, the suffragettes broke windows, then waited till they were arrested, then went on a food strike till they were released, then broke more windows and went through the whole program again. Eventually they got the vote. The trouble is in the present case too many people are saying, "Negroes are hoodlums and DANGEROUS. Keep them DOWN." If they had a good reason to break these windows they should have announced it. Propaganda,* as you know, is often more effective than action. Thank you for the use of the hall! Anyway, if the riots were organized† and intended as a lesson to extortionists and exploiters, WHY did they attack pawnshops which hit hard at Harlem? Pearl [Showers] and Mildred [Perkins] tell me many of their friends lost their dearest possessions. Arna [Bontemps] has written the most beautiful paper about me for the Yale Gazette.[2] And Mr K[nollenberg] is writing a piece thanking the principal donors (to date), all this in the October number. The boxes for your manuscripts (seven or eight of them) are still here and will probably be here till you get back as I still hadn't enough [Chicago] Defender pieces for a box yet.[3] The Sun Do Move is not yet boxed because you said I hadn't the final draft yet.[4] But gradually you are piling up in grand style in this

---

[1]In Harlem on 2 August 1943, riots, followed by looting, broke out over discriminatory practices and police harassment in New York, although six weeks earlier civic leaders had urged precautions and negotiations.
[2]"The James Weldon Johnson Memorial Collection of Negro Arts and Letters," *Yale University Library Gazette,* October 1943.
[3]CVV presented material to the James Weldon Johnson Memorial Collection of Negro Arts and Letters in matching cases with hinged covers, sturdily bound in blue buckram with red leather identification labels stamped in gold.
[4]*The Sun Do Move,* 1942, a play by Langston Hughes.

collection and may be studied at leisure by some future historian of American writers in general and the Race in particular. Excuse me for being long winded and allow me to remain affectionately your      Carlo!

*and of course the effect would have been doubled without the looting.

†I have been told by people who should know.


## TO LANGSTON HUGHES

16 August 1943

101 Central Park West
New York City

Dear Langston, What letters *you* write! Maybe I do too. Sometimes I wonder if OUR letters won't be the pride of the Collection. I haven't got around to sending yours to me yet, but will this winter! My remarks on the riot were based on the sworn statements of certain Harlemites that they had been organized for weeks (everybody had his orders). Yours are based on the belief that it was a casual turnout. I have an idea that both of these theories were true. A FEW had planned something, probably, and the mob trailed after. You are right that Harlem is much more indignant about (and much more aware of) these riots than downtown and I don't know anyone more indignant than Pearl Showers and Mildred [Perkins] Thornton. So it isn't all Sugar Hill[5] indignation. Roi Ottley came to be photographed Saturday and definitely we are getting the manuscript.[6] When he saw your new beautiful boxes, he almost swooned and exclaimed, "The Schomburg Collection doesn't keep things like this." Of course, nobody else does and even Yale wouldn't, if I didn't do it myself. The material turned into this Collection is in a condition thanks to my energy and foresight which not many other Collections can boast. It is hard work and endless, but I think it is worth it. I have a DEFINITE FEELING that in LESS than five years Yale will have a chair of Negro life and culture and whoever sits in that chair will have the best source material in the country to guide him. Anyway Ottley promises all letters, manuscripts, what not, in the future. Of course I have the IWO Educational Alliance edition of The Sun Do Move, but I had noted something on the other mss. about waiting for the "final draft" and got confused. I'll have a box made for The Sun Do Move soon. Florence B. Price of Chicago sends me her Symphony in C Minor (manuscript of the full score). This is Harold [Jackman]'s work. [. . .] I expect to be deluged with manuscripts and letters when you return. The boxes will still be here,

[5]Sugar Hill, the west border of Harlem where black aristocracy lived in smart apartments and townhouses.

[6]Roi Ottley, black American historian, donated the manuscript for *New World A-Coming: Inside Black America*, to the Johnson Collection at Yale.

as certain things have to be signed. Besides, I have to catalogue the contents of these boxes before they go and am up to my ears in other matters for the moment. [. . .] Even if you don't reply to other letters, answer MINE. Our correspondence will be historical. [. . .] Bricktop[7] had a birthday last Saturday. Was she up your way?

Dorothy P[eterson] is moving again. So is Dr. Sidney [Peterson]. Have you read a book called Race, by Ruth Benedict? When are you coming back?      fondly, Carlo

TO BLANCHE KNOPF                           101 Central Park West
[circa 16 August 1943]                       New York City

Dear Blanche, you've got something decidedly. There is not only a need for a general book on the Negro question, but there is a demand for it. If it were sufficiently sympathetic and really right, I believe it would even sell to Negroes and many white people are asking themselves questions which are not easily answered save by such a book. Roi Ottley's book[8] is very good indeed and going to sell, but it is almost exclusively devoted to Harlem and is picturesque and descriptive rather than argumentative and controversial. However, it goes a longer way towards being what you want than anything else. Richard Wright could write a humdinger but he is tied up with Harper's probably. Langston could write it if he would. Many of his articles concerning conditions are absolutely tops and he knows the Negro in every state in the Union and in every condition; also he knows the Negro in Africa and Europe. Read Walter White's article in the current New Republic[9] and you will see that he could write it. Walter is very much improved as a writer and stands, of course, as a Negro celebrity. HIS friend Wendell Wilkie could write it and might be persuaded to by Walter. He is very much interested in the subject. Pearl Buck could write it. She has written dozens of articles about the Negro for Negro periodicals. But of course this would be something for the John Day Company. MAYBE Fannie [Hurst] could write it. Dr. Du Bois is too old to tackle this job, but Roy Wilkins, editor of The Crisis (he writes a fine column weekly for the NY Amsterdam News) might be another choice. So might George S. Schuyler, business manager of the Pittsburgh Courier. (He is called the colored Mencken and, indeed, several of his articles were printed by Mencken when he was editor of the [American] Mercury.) MOST books on the subject

[7]Bricktop: Ada Smith, celebrated black nightclub owner in Paris.
[8]*New World a-Coming: Inside Black America,* 1943.
[9]"Behind the Harlem Race Riots," 16 August 1943.

are too dry, too full of statistics, too FAIR to whites, or too sketchy, to do the trick. What you want is an exciting book, not too long, with the facts brilliantly and sympathetically presented, full of examples, but without footnotes or statistics. Why don't you write Langston to ask him what HE thinks about possible writers, contents etc . . . His address at present is Yaddo, Saratoga Springs, NY. It has occurred to me that Clare Boothe might be interested. She gave a ripsnorting speech on the Negro at one of the Herald-Tribune forums and in her preface to Kiss the Boys Goodbye she says that the South invented fascism in its treatment of the Negro.*

Thanks for the use of the hall, and LOVE, [unsigned]

Mr. Van Vechten will NOT write this book or any other just now, thank you!

*Clare Boothe & Langston together could do something terrific!!!

TO GEORGE GEORGE                            101 Central Park West
[summer 1943]                                New York City

Dear George, Whether you are Narcissus or a good artist I can't make out, but your drawings of yourself are excellent: I liked particularly the one of you on the envelope, but the others are good too. In one of your letters shortly before you came here from Salina you spoke of Paris and books and talks about Paris. Have you ever read my Peter Whiffle? This has a lot about Paris which seems to please people and if you haven't read it I'll try to find a copy to send you. [. . .] George, the secret of life is to know what you want always and to go after it while it is there . . . The tragedies of life are caused by those who either know what they want too late or too early . . . I am *sure* you are photogenique and if you ever come back to New York, I'd like to photograph you. . . .

In the meantime five hibiscus flowers to you and a lamb chop!       Carlo

TO ELLEN GLASGOW                            101 Central Park West
22 September 1943                            New York City

Dear Ellen, I was immensely happy to receive so early a copy of A Certain Measure. It is in all respects a fascinating book and a treasure of wit and wisdom, but I think I will ask you to wait to read my considered opinion when it is published in BOOKS where Irita [Van Doren] has invited me to review it.[1] She tells me you are much better and we hope to see you when you pass through New York, but the sad news is we have no cook. . . .

[1]"Most Revealing Prefaces," *New York Herald Tribune Books*, 17 October 1943.

I think "for the duration" (we probably won't have another cook till the war is over) should supplant "it might have been" as the "saddest words," don't you?    Fania and I send love to you, Ellen!    Carlo

TO FANIA MARINOFF                    101 Central Park West
[5 November 1943]                     New York City

Florence Foster Jenkins outdid herself last [night].[2] She was a riot from the start. The moment she appeared on the platform she was a hit. Dressed in pink satin with rhinestone buttons and a big floppy pink garden hat, the kind Billie Burke and Marilyn Miller[3] used to wear, she carried a tiny black lace parasol which she made as if to open while she was singing. This outfit completely brought the house down. She changed to a salmon pink dress, completely covered with black lace, with an enormous orange ostrich fan as an accessory, and again to a pink skirt with a blue velvet embroidered top and a GREEN ostrich fan. Her singing was of a par and got better and better until at the end she sang her own "I sing like a bird" [when] everybody was screaming on the floor. The house was packed and about a hundred were standing and NOBODY left until she had sung five encores at the close.* [. . .] She totters on and off but is good for another ten years, I would say. Rita [Romilly] called up this morning to ask us to dinner before Nora [Holt]'s party and to tell us *she* had been coaching Paul [Draper]. I'll tell you all about this when you come home. I explained to Rita we were tied up. [. . .] Edward III[4] called. He is out of the army and back in New York. And Rosamond Gilder called to ask me to write a piece about Paul for Theatre Arts. I told her I had too much to do at the moment. Your mail is inconsequential and I will keep it for your return. Unless otherwise informed, I am meeting the 9.45 tomorrow night and will be very glad to see you back. [. . .]    All my love, Carlo
I went to call on Alicia [Markova] yesterday and she gets better and better. I called on Anna [Marble Pollock] and Channing says he is very sick and why don't YOU come to see *him*? Anna has improved tremendously and looks her old self. She was sitting in the drawing room.
*There were so many flowers, it looked like General Grant's funeral.

[2]Florence Foster Jenkins, a wealthy matron who gave annual recitals at her own expense, usually in hotel ballrooms and once at Town Hall. Her uncertain soprano voice—remarkable only for its ineptitude—made her into a cult figure.
[3]Billie Burke and Marilyn Miller: frothy musical comedy actresses.
[4]Edward Atkinson, black American actor. CVV numbered his friends named Edward, of whom there were eventually fifteen.

## TO CARESSE CROSBY

101 Central Park West
27 November 1943

New York City

Dear Caresse Crosby, I was happy to hear from you after these long months, and sorry to be obliged to say No. Except under most exceptional circumstances I do not like to let my pictures go out of town and this particular picture holds the dining-room up to such an extent that to take it out would practically create a vacuum! But I am most flattered that you invited my Chirico[5] Who is indeed a beauty!     Sincerely, Carlo Van Vechten

## TO ARNA BONTEMPS

101 Central Park West
31 December 1943

New York City

Dear Arna, A VERY HAPPY NEW YEAR TO YOU! What beautiful and extremely seductive letters you write. ONLY, you really don't have to seduce me. All I want is to be convinced and once conviction is mine I go forward charging into the Future. . . . My difficulties are these: Is my Collection important enough? It doesn't contain any incunabula or extremely rare books on music tho there are some eighteenth and nineteenth century semi-rarities; nor does it contain privately published scores or many first edition scores or manuscripts. If the J[ames] W[eldon] J[ohnson] Collection at Yale was preparation for Nigger Heaven, this collection may be said to be a good working library (in splendid condition) for an acting music critic. [. . .] Also there are phonograph records. My second problem involves the financial stability of Fisk. Could the institution easily be blown away? Has it state support? How many more wars and depressions could it take? My third problem is the worst of all! I think it would be a mistake to name this Collection after myself and would interfere materially with gifts coming in hereafter from others.[6] But I can think of no suitable Negro name to apply to a Collection which includes Wagner and Debussy . . . No suitable name that is with a musical connotation. [. . .]

But I am mad over the idea of breaking down segregation by getting whites to do research work in Negro libraries: that is why you and I have got to find some solution to the above problems or at least to try to find some . . . I send you New Year's Greetings and hope *our* side wins the pennant!     With forty cornucopias of pleasant thoughts! [unsigned carbon copy]

---

[5]Self-portrait of Giorgio di Chirico, willed to the Metropolitan Museum of Art in memory of Fania Marinoff and CVV, 1971. Crosby had requested it for public exhibition.
[6]CVV eventually named this archive The George Gershwin Memorial Collection of Music and Musical Literature and donated it to Fisk University.

TO ANNA MARBLE POLLOCK                    101 Central Park West
22 January [1944]                         New York City

Dearest Nadejda,[7] You seem almost to be defending Channing against attack.
Certainly "attack" was not my intention. My admiration for Channing's
many fine qualities has no rivals. [. . .] I do think that frequently he over-
looks evidence that disagrees with his conclusions and I do not believe
that any one can learn whether natives are contented or not by living several
weeks or months anywhere and talking with Dutch or English speaking
officials. Channing, I feel, is an incurable optimist who believes the world
would be improved if conditions were more to his liking. Personally I am
more sceptical: to me the world moves majestically on fatalistically to its
doom and the mere fact that this one or that one superficially controls
destiny makes very little difference. I cannot quite see the logic or merit
in *any* scheme or branch of politics, and so I am inclined to argue on the
"Red" side with isolationist and tories and on the "capitalist" side with
Communists and Reds. It is impossible, I am sure, to take one side fervently
without overlooking all the truth on the other side and there is truth and
beauty on any side, no matter how you look at it. As for my writing, I
don't like to write and I do not think I have anything very important to
contribute to human knowledge. Photography is as hard work as writing,
but more agreeable to me and here I can contribute a great deal, by doc-
umenting the present age in several fields for important collections. I have
no doubt whatever I am doing something useful here, but the creation of
nostalgia is at best a luxury that is quite unnecessary to indulge. I could
go much further than this. If I liked to write, I would write doubtless, even
if I had nothing whatever to say. But I don't, and I think the most important
thing about life is to live it fully and completely as one feels it and not
according to other people's laws, provided one does a minimum amount
of harm to others. Usually people who live their own lives fully give more
pleasure to others than those who don't; well, even more than pleasure
occasionally. I am not arguing for altruism, either. But you don't have to
defend Channing. His word is self-explanatory and does a great deal of
good, I am convinced, in fields I don't even attempt to explore. [. . .]

   Canteen duty as usual on Monday[8] and love to YOU, as always, on every
day,    [unsigned]

---

[7]Nadejda: another of CVV's several nicknames for Anna Marble Pollock.
[8]By this time, CVV had begun working at the Stage Door Canteen on a regular basis, Monday
and Tuesday nights.

TO HUGH LAING

23 January [1944]

101 Central Park West
New York City

Hello Hugh, I thought you would like to see the accompanying bulletin of the Museum of Modern Art.* I am WORRIED about you. The Perpers[9] speak of your throwing three vertebrae out of place and dancing in a plaster cast. YOU do not mention this altho you speak of the FLU. Will you please begin to take care of yourself a little for the sake of those who LOVE you. Is Antony [Tudor] putting on the Polynesian dances in the musical version of RAIN[1] as all the papers have announced? Alicia [Markova] dined here last night and [. . .] has never looked healthier and in fact looks more like a child than ever. Day before yesterday she worked 20 minutes in the studio and she says everything is okay. The Cellis,[2] who amuse me no end, were here last night and a couple of my boy friends. We showed Alicia's pictures again. [. . .] I saw the Perpers in Sardi's and they went on and on about the Ballet in Chicago and I ate it up. She was even less tender to Nana [Gollner] than you were. [Dimitri] Petroff, you don't mention but she went into that in detail. She said Nora [Kaye] did a magnificent Aurora and when she came off the stage she asked Antony, "How was I?" and Antony said, "You'll be all right, in six years, IF YOU WORK." [. . .] Pearl Showers peed her pants with joy at hearing from you at Christmas. [. . .] You have never been a typist in my presence before, but I like it because you write MORE than when you use a pen. Donald[3] wrote to me and sent me a card at Christmas and so I already had his address. I have a cousin and another friend, most amusing, somewhere in the same sector. I am trying to bring them together† [. . .]. Cocks and balls and things like that are still the rage in New York: so come back soon, please! Lots of love to you both and embrace the beautiful Nora for me, please!

*with *you* & Sono [Osato]

†Well, you know what I mean.

Fania sends love too!

9Kathleen and Leo Perper, directors of Roger Kent Clothing, balletomanes.
1*Miss Sadie Thompson*, 1944, by Cole Porter.
2Vincenzo Celli, Markova's ballet master, and his wife Marian Icell, Scots singer.
3Donald Saddler, ballet dancer. CVV numbered his friends named Donald; Saddler was Donald II.

## TO HUGH LAING
1 February 1944

101 Central Park West<br>New York City

Dear Hugh, You are a very efficient Honey Chile because I got a wire from Alicia [Markova] today, thanking me for the flowers. I am very grateful to you for arranging this. [. . .] A long time ago I suggested to Antony [Tudor] that he do an 1890 ballet with Sousa music. I don't think he cared much for the idea, and certainly it doesn't suit him tremendously, but it does suit Agnes [DeMille].[4] So while she is breaking your back, thinking up new lifts, suggest it to her and let's see what she says. It's a good idea for somebody. Tell her she'll find plenty of waltzes and everything else besides marches (for which he is famous) in his operas: The Bride-Elect and El Capitan. Besides, he wrote some concert music for his band. It could center around July 4 or January 1 and be called Holiday!* So please don't forget me and I'd be sending you photographs by every mail only I don't seem to be taking any now.     Love to you both, [unsigned]

*I want to see Agnes ellemême dancing The Washington Post March (the *two*-step!)


## TO ANNA MARBLE POLLOCK
[13 March 1944]

101 Central Park West<br>New York City

Dearest Anna, It has always been a rule of the American Theatre Wing that any Stage Door Canteen which opens under their auspices is obliged to treat Negro Soldiers like any one else. As one girl at our Canteen expressed it early in the game, "Our orders are to dance with uniforms and not with colors." The Stage Door Canteen in New York is completely democratic in this respect and although there are plenty of colored hostesses, interchangeable dancing is frequent and unremarked, especially as the white soldiers usually grab the colored girls first as they are the most beautiful of the Junior Hostesses. The Negro boys sit at tables with the white soldiers and are frequently joined by them if the cullud boys sit down first. I've never noticed any difficulties with Jews and as you know I practically live at the Canteen. BUT there is occasionally trouble about English sailors. American sailors sometimes* won't sit with them. Waves at my Service Women's Tea Dance have been known to rise when presented with British tars and walk away with the remark "We don't sit with Limeys." In Phil-

---

[4]Neither Tudor nor DeMille acted on this suggestion but George Balanchine choreographed "Stars and Stripes" to John Philip Sousa's music fifteen years later, one of his most enduringly popular works.

adelphia and Washington where there are no colored hostesses there is less mixing and practically no dancing, altho' mixed dancing HAS occurred in Philadelphia. There are no laws against it but the colored boys don't go to these canteens in such great numbers and seldom ask the girls to dance. I am most amused by your Catholic friend. Converts are always the WORST. I know a Jew who has recently been "converted," tho' never having been a religious Jew, I suspect he is not a very good Catholic. However, he talks about it all the time. Recently he was going on at a party and an Italian woman got up and laid him out . . . She said, "Listen. My family has been Catholics since the Crucifixion and we have been kicking the Virgin Mary around for centuries. And upstarts like you come along to act as if you owned her." [. . .]    Love, Carlo

*This sort of behaviour isn't average.

TO FANIA MARINOFF                    101 Central Park West
[3 July 1944]                              New York City

Dearest Babykins, [. . .] As I was leaving the Tea Dance yesterday with Saul[5] we found the sidewalks littered with photographers. I asked what they were waiting for and they explained that Governor [Thomas] Dewey was coming on his way to Pittsburgh. So I sent Saul on to open up the Service Club and went back to see Marion[6] who was in charge yesterday and suggested we ask him to appear at the Dance briefly. She was enthusiastic about the idea and we went up to see the manager of the hotel. He admitted Dewey was coming but was scared to help us. So we applied to the chairman of the Democratic Committee in a room upstairs. He was as helpless as a meadowlark and said he had better see Dewey's press man. We had already learned the press man was with him. SO, I admitted I knew Dewey slightly and said I would brave him. I did when he came in with his wife and party. He remembered me perfectly and was charming but refused to stick his nose into the tea dance (which was right in front of him) because he said [he] was an hour late to an engagement with the Republican Committee. So I introduced him to Marion and he passed on. About half way to the elevator he turned around and came back.* "I heard Max Ewing is dead," he said. "Yes," I replied. "How did he die?" "He committed suicide." "That's awful." "It is. Some day when you have time I'll tell you about it." We had already had this conversation once at Blanche

[5]Saul Mauriber, a decorator and designer CVV met at the Stage Door Canteen who had become his lighting assistant during photography sessions. He continued in that capacity until CVV's death.
[6]Marion Moore, theatrical publicist.

Knopf's and I think he associated my name with Max and wanted to show he remembered me clearly but was not much interested in my replies.

Nora [Holt] appeared at the Seamen's Club with the Walter Florel hat (a present to her from the maker) which is on the current cover of Vogue, red with pink roses. She is terrifically stunning in it.† [. . .] There is a cheque here for you from the US Government (Defense Bonds) which I will deposit for you. And a bill for 60 dollars (six visits) from Dr Garbat. I do not begrudge him this because I am so much better. Saul dined with me last night at the Canton Village and I ate part of his lobster with no ill effects. He is terribly affected by the heat and the Seamen's Club, which is the hottest place I know, almost knocked him out. He sends love to you and Mark [Lutz] wanted to be remembered to you TOO! [. . .]      [unsigned]
*and as casually as that
†I think it would be fun to give a debutante party for Nora some time.


TO HUGH LAING                                      101 Central Park West
8 August [1944]                                    New York City

Dear Ballerino, I am glad I put the fear of god into you, because I got a delightful letter out of you as a result. So here goes about Mia [Slavenska] and the [Lewisohn] Stadium. [. . .] In the first place this aggregation of talent drew about half of what Markova did* and NOBODY was turned away. In the second place [Igor] Youskevitch, in spite of what Mr Martin says, was downright divine. His "beats" were out of this world. I've never seen cleaner entre-chats. Some of the other male dancers had better go into the navy maybe (but I don't mean you, sweet bastard). He is the only dancer I've seen since Nijinsky who can perform Spectre [*de la Rose*] and, generously, after the first one, Mia gave him all the calls alone. [. . .] We are now down to Mia and when I say down I mean down. As a choreographer she would be ideal for [Irina] Baronova as she conceives of dancing mostly in terms of pirouettes and fouettés (she did two or three hundred of the latter in the Pas de Deux from Swan Lake, and probably seven or eight thousand in the César Franck. The latter might have been choreographed by Petipa, so far as any novelty was concerned. [. . .] I have a weakness for Mia making like Salome and she was at her best. Only Theda Bara in A Fool There Was, surpasses this piece of nonsense. I am of an age where I can boast I saw all the Salome dancers of the early part of the century and there is nothing much of their intention that Mia missed, tho the technique of her belly dancing is pretty corny. She doesn't know the first thing about shaking the navel (which however was exposed and em-

bellished with a faint touch of lip rouge). Her dancing as a whole is not clean cut or arresting. Many dancers with a lesser technique and far less beauty make more effect. I have spent many hours during the past week (Fania is still in Massachusetts) going over your color pictures, rearranging them and removing a great great many, to get them into shape for showing. I think I now have them down to pretty much shipshape where they can be exposed to the public and the public will derive much pleasure from seeing them. There are so many beautiful ones, but before there were too many to savour properly. I saw the Perpers at the Ballet and we dished considerably. They want to be at an early showing and they shall be. [. . .] I hate to NAG you, but are you going to arrange for me to do Dim Lustre[†] this fall or NOT? [. . .] Killer Joe[7] is now well enough to take in the sights. Why don't you invite him to see the Ballet one night. He IS Fancy Free and even more. Mildred [Perkins] is away again but Mrs Showers thrives on your love and kisses, as I thrive on your bites. [. . .] I am four inches smaller round the waist and am having all my clothes taken in. Maybe you'd like a report on Mae West.[8] I do not trust the newspapers on this and I think I'll take it in myself. If you want this report, send me further addresses, and stop biting my ankle, you big PRICK.     LOVE, Carlo
*her audience, the biggest of the season, was around 25,000.
[†]and Tally-Ho, please[9]

If you see Archie Savage, send me all the dirt. Is he free again? What did he do with the $10,000, etc.?

I wish I could type like you without making mistakes.

## TO GEORGE GEORGE

11 August [1944]

101 Central Park West
New York City

Dear George, The Theatre Annual has gone to you and I hope this has more success in reaching you than my Poor Blind Bow-Boy! Of course these packages go by ordinary mail and will probably take months in any case, but airmail from you to me is sensational and I have had a letter within six days after it leaves you. Mae West is here as Catherine the Great. She and the play got very bad notices but having seen it twice I am convinced she is much more like the Empress than Katharine Cornell would be, for instance. A good deal of it is bedroomy and would be downright

[7]Killer Joe, U.S. Navy Seaman Frank Piro, celebrated for his jitterbug routines at the Stage Door Canteen and, subsequently, a leading dance instructor in civilian life.
[8]Mae West had just opened on Broadway in her play *Catherine Was Great.*
[9]"Dim Lustre" and "Tally Ho": new ballets in Ballet Theatre's repertory.

lewd if it wasn't so fantastic! In the circumstances it is a good deal like watching Sinbad take a trip on the magic carpet in the movies. It is fun watching all the handsome men in the cast pile in and out of bed with the lady; the meanwhile you can wonder HOW and WITH WHOM in the company they actually enjoy themselves sexually. Some of this speculation is by no means idle! [. . .] Do you think you will be a novelist or an essayist or some such quelque-chose after the Wars, or before the next ones? Your touch gets surer and surer and your descriptions of people and places are very full of arresting bits. [. . .] I am sure it is hotter here than in India, but perhaps less interesting. I enclose a few souvenirs* of our "civilization" and wave my greetings overseas!     Carlo

If you want anything, let me know, but it will take years for you to get it where you are now.

*Pinup Boys and Girls!!

TO COUNTEE CULLEN                    101 Central Park West
9 September 1944                          New York City

Dear Countée, The Piney Woods School, a Negro institution in Mississippi in which I have been interested for a very long time, has plenty of books but needs a library building. With student labor, this can be erected for about $10,000 and the head of the school, Laurence Jones, has asked me and 99 other friends each to raise $100 in one dollar subscriptions. Will you give me a dollar for this worthy purpose? Make the cheque out to the Piney Woods School and send it to me, please.     hearts and flowers to you, Carlo

TO ETHEL WATERS                       101 Central Park West
6 November 1944                          New York City

Dear Ethel, This letter will introduce you to the charming, handsome, and extremely talented Owen Dodson, a good friend of mine who has turned himself into a Committee on Race Relations in Mass Education. He wants to talk with you about a film project and I hope you will listen to him. And if I don't hear from you within a few days I shall be obliged to advertise for you in the PAPERS!     Anyway, Hearts and Flowers and Gold and Pearls to you! Carlo

Ethel Waters, 1936

Anna Marble Pollock, 1939

Hugh Laing, 1940

## TO HUGH LAING
[30 November 1944]

101 Central Park West
New York City

Dear Hugh, It is a bleak day and so I am thinking of you and here are a few of the Dim Lustre Photographs. You'll have some big ones when you come HOME and the Tally-Ho will follow later. I saw the Ballet again Saturday afternoon and now I think I have brought myself up to date on this company,[1] lacking only their Swan Lake which doesn't seem important. Brahms Variations find [Vera] Nijinska making like [Leonid] Massine, [Marcel] Vertès making paper dolls for a pansy drag, [André] Eglevsky making like Gipsy Rose Lee, and the orchestra making like getting paid overtime. Did you see this lengthy opera? It is out of this world. In Constantia [William] Dollar makes like Balanchine and gets so tired with his terrific succession of difficult lifts that he pants like a Newfoundland dog on a July Day. Eglevsky Sweats and Dollar Pants! [. . .] We went to a wonderful dinner last night for William Christopher Handy (St Louis Blues) and Lillian Brown in a tight princess dress with no sleeves but a long train, of crystal beads, with black gloves and a picture hat as big as a cartwheel, black with cerise plumes, sang the Beale Street Blues, as she had circa 1910, i.e., con amore and magnificently. I cried like a baby, I loved it so. [. . .]

   Love to you and Antony [Tudor] and nibble Miss Kaye's pretty ears for me (you may show her the pictures: Miss [Janet] Reed's will follow shortly) . . . Will John Kriza permit me to photograph him when you return? I asked Jerry Robbins to arrange Fancy Free with the three sailors, but you know . . .     Carlo

## TO ANNA MARBLE POLLOCK
2 December [1944]

101 Central Park West
New York City

Dearest Nadejda, [. . .] You don't seem to understand that I don't NOT want to read [George] Santayana: the fact is that I have EIGHT books on hand I HAVE to read before material can be sent away.[2] One of them I read a few pages in each day, that is all I have time for. My desk is piled high with obligations and I am utterly unable to fight my way to the darkroom through all this. And I have nearly 100 pictures developed but unprinted and nearly a hundred more not developed! . . . I am afraid if you go on seeing people who tire you out you will never be able to see ME.

---

[1]Ballet International, a company that survived only one season, 1944.
[2]CVV screened all materials that he donated to his various collections in libraries.

You DON'T HAVE to see people who bring you presents. I was lunching once with Mary Garden at her apartment when the maid announced the Prince Mavracordato. "Tell him to go away," said Mary petulantly, "I can't see him." "But," expostulated the maid, "He has brought you a chinchilla cloak." "Tell him to leave the coat and go away!" Mary said. He did. We all had great fun trying it on. I showed my color pictures of Sebastian[3] last night to the dancers who posed for them and the [Vincenzo] Cellis came. She is a Scotch woman, Marian Icell, who has sung Carmen more often than any other singer and he is the reigning head of the dance world from a professional point of view: as Markova works with him everybody does. He is most amusing and as he knows everything that goes on in the dance world and speaks freely about everybody, he has the world in stitches. Marian is amusing too. Menotti was here, the composer of the ballet, and he brought Sam[uel] Barber, a young American composer who is the nephew of Louise Homer.[4] It was a most exciting evening for Fania and me and I don't think we got to bed at all. Today I am returning to my responsibilities.     So, love and devotion, Carlo

TO GERTRUDE STEIN                          101 Central Park West
27 December 1944                           New York City

Dearest Baby Woojums, I had no sooner received your cable from Culoz[5] than I replied instanter and sent you a fat letter off to Culoz, enclosing all the letters which I had earlier sent to Paris and which had been returned. Now Virgil [Thomson] tells me that he has seen some one who says you are back at the rue Christine. Dear, Dear: I hope all those letters are not lost, but maybe somebody will send them to you from Culoz. Anyway I sent you both another cablegram to Paris, but the cableman didn't like the Mama Woojums and Papa Woojums, so he said he would change this to Father and Mother, which had me in stitches; I explained the relationship as well as I could, so I hope you get the telegram and I'll be glad when airmail will get through to you again. I get airmail letters from soldiers in India in FOUR days sometimes! The war news is frightful for the moment and according to the papers Paris was bombed yesterday; so you will be right in the midst of the battle again. But somehow I am sure you will be

---

[3]*Sebastian*, 1944, ballet by Gian Carlo Menotti, choreography by Edward Caton, with Francisco Moncion and Viola Essen.
[4]Louise Homer, operatic contralto.
[5]During the war, Gertrude Stein and Alice Toklas had been forced to move from the manor house at Bilignin, where they had lived for fourteen years during the summers, to a house at Culoz. The owner had reclaimed the Bilignin house when the lease expired.

all right. Lots of Love and let us hear from you. Fania and I embrace you and Mama Woojums!     Papa Woojums (Carl Van Vechten)

## TO ANNA MARBLE POLLOCK
2 January [1945]

101 Central Park West
New York City

Dearest Nadejda, [. . .] Whether you believe it or not (you *must know* that every cat is different from the others) the cat I wrote you about LOVED being swung by her tail and used to come back and beg for more, rubbing against the swinger's leg and purring till she got another lift. I've written you, I think, about the cat I know who spends most of his time swimming in the tub. Speaking of Laurette Taylor she has just made another terrific hit in Chicago in a piece called The Glass Menagerie. Ashton Stevens compares her to [Eleanora] Duse and the other critics, being younger (the NY critics at the moment haven't even seen Doris Keane) content themselves with raving.[6] [. . .]

My mother used to have the same superstition about a cook that Ann Coleman's cook has. But she didn't call it a superstition. To her it was a law of nature that people shouldn't walk in the kitchen* while she was baking anything like Angel Food. The place called A la Pomme Souflée does not produce perfect ones: they are very hard indeed to make. We have never even tried them here. The only French dishes we attempt are things like bouillabaisse or cassoulet, peasant dishes in which Negro cooks far surpass whites because they "down on them." Most cooks are too tony for the vulgar amounts of garlic, onions, etc., in such dishes. [. . .] I don't follow you when you write "How can any woman care about finery today?" That's like saying that the rich shouldn't dress because of the misery of the poor. There is always *lots* of mud, filth, and disease in the world and girls living today have only today to live. Further if theatres are not only tolerated but demanded in war times, it is the job of the musical comedy actress to be as chic and beautiful as possible and that is the way the returning soldiers like them. They like them that way at the front too as the astonishing success of Marlene Dietrich, who carried some wonderful evening gowns along in her 50 pound bag, proves. Nobody suffers less because other people suffer with him. Quite the contrary is true . . . But I disagree with you quite good humoredly and love you very much and thank you for your letters and for the Saturday Review and for being YOU,     Carlo
*or even upstairs *over* the kitchen.

[6]Laurette Taylor, a celebrated actress since her appearance in 1914 in *Peg o' My Heart,* and an old friend, made her comeback in Tennessee Williams's play.

My enthusiasm over Artist in Iowa is very great indeed. I have never heard of the author [Darrell Garland] before but I sat right down and wrote him. I would be very proud to sign this book myself. Miss Prescott is later Cedar Rapids than I know but if I ever go back there she is the first person I want to meet. What a honey!⁷

TO ANNA MARBLE POLLOCK                    101 Central Park West
[circa January–March 1945]                 New York City

Dearest Nadejda, Your animadversions at what are humorously called the "lower classes" used to shock me a good deal and I even tried to reason with you. Now that I know they are completely unreasonable they no longer shock me, but I worry when you indulge in them thinking to myself that they are causing rises in your blood pressure and postponing our visit to Giselle together, AND the subsequent scandal. ME, I guess I would rather bathe with servants (this is purely hypothetical since I detest sea-bathing and prefer tub-bathing, even to showers) than with most of the rich people I know. As a matter of fact I was brought up to bathe with servants as my father always saw to it that any servants we had had all the pleasures and minor luxuries we had; some day I'll tell you about some of these. And he taught me to respect colored people.⁸ My father indeed was mostly responsible for founding a school for colored people.* [. . .] My experience with all classes of people has been considerably fortified and magnified during the past three years with my work at the Stage Door Canteen, where some volunteer workers *work* and some *don't,* but it has nothing to do with what class they come from except there is always an edge in favor of the "poor but honest class." It IS aggravating to be building a sea wall and to have a union demand that you employ ten men most of whom don't work, but I remember sadly there would be no unions if employers had lived up to their obligations to their men. In other words human nature is frequently hoggish, and whichever side is on top usually behaves badly. [. . .] I am worried about your new virus, but there are so many new drugs nowadays they will pull you out. We are going into a brave new world in so many respects, you know . . . and an insectless one will probably give us fewer ills. However, I've no doubt that without insects something else will arise to annoy us . . . Leonard Bernstein played the Rhapsody in Blue

---

⁷Miss Prescott: a character in Garland's book, 1945.
⁸CVV to Anna Marble Pollock, 30 October 1945: "Race Prejudice is an acquired taste, like olives. Children do not have it and whole races are bereft of it. It is something you have to learn to have."

at the Roosevelt yesterday and was out of this world, but he came in on a breeze and departed on one, as he was holding auditions at the City Center Theatre for his new orchestra and had only half an hour between for us.    Love to you, Carlo

[. . .]

*Piney Woods School in Mississippi

TO GEORGE GEORGE                    101 Central Park West
12 February 1945                    New York City

Dear George, [. . .] At the Theatre Wing Tea Dances for Service Women at the Hotel Roosevelt, we have had groups of blind men recently. They bring their own partners and they stay all the afternoon and DANCE. Men without legs and arms are at the Stage Door Canteen constantly and the clientele of the place has changed a good deal, almost everybody has been abroad somewhere and many have been wounded and wear the Purple Heart. Killer Joe [Piro] is being honorably discharged, stomach ulcers, but he still jitterbugs like an amorous goldfish. The Canteen will be three years old in a minute and I've never missed a performance Monday or Tuesday. You are lucky not to be in the cold foxholes of Belgium or Germany: I get letters from freezing friends in these districts. However, maybe you have other things to put up with, including malignant insects.[9] Did you ever find Ram Gopal? He should be dancing somewhere sometime, but I dare say India is bigger than Rhode Island. Write me again soon. [. . .]

Hearts and flowers to you!    Carlo

TO HUGH LAING                    101 Central Park West
13 February [1945]               New York City

Dear Hugh, Thanks for your wonderful letter, well worth waiting for. I grieve over your illnesses and I am happy you are sufficiently okay at present. I am SURE your Albrecht [in *Giselle*] will be superb and soon or late the best that there has EVER been, because you have deep sincerity in planning your roles and the imagination of an artist. These are the most important qualities for an artist although he can do with some technique too and you have this in abundance, even if not quite to the degree of a Nijinsky, for example. [. . .] We went to the first performance of The Tempest, which isn't very good but is a huge success and doing enormous

[9]George George was stationed with the army in India.

211

business. Zorina[1] moves like a dream and looks very beautiful but when she speaks there is no fire or variety (any vitality is in her movement) and when she sings it is as though she were dead. Still, it is the best thing I have ever seen her do. I wish you might have seen Fania's Ariel, like quicksilver, fire, dragonflies'-flight, and waterfalls: it had *everything* and was one of the great memories of my life in the theatre. [. . .] I could not help feeling all the time we were looking at this performance what a wonderful ballet The Tempest would make, and I wish Antony [Tudor] would think of it occasionally as a possible idea, altho he said once, No more Shakespeare. Perhaps he has changed his mind since Romeo *[and Juliet]* is so firmly established in the repertory. As usual I enclose a few postcards for you. I'm sure you will like especially the one of me making frantic demands on my crew[2] with the air of a demented ballet-master. Agnes [DeMille] is doing Carousel[3] which everybody thinks is Carousal and I think Annabelle[4] is set for it. My friend and busboy Miles White is doing the costumes. Pearl [Showers] has been sick for a week but Fania is an awfully good cook and I am an awfully good cleaning woman. We are running up a party for Lin Yutang and serious thinkers this week, but we prefer you and Antony and the ballet parties to all others and hope we can have some more, if taxes don't take all our money and if we can manage to keep Pearl alive and well at least for emergencies. [. . .] We embrace you both and kiss Nora [Kaye] on the left tit (for tat). Carlo!

TO GEORGE GEORGE                          101 Central Park West
3 March 1945                              New York City

Dear George, I was thrilled by your report that The Blind Bow-Boy had at last reached India. Anything whatever can happen after that. I was not so lucky; in spite of your message to the base censor on the envelope, only ONE photograph arrived. I could of course recognize you from this, but from now on I will number and designate enclosures so that nothing more will get lost without warning. [. . .] License Commissioner Moss has recently distinguished himself by refusing to continue the license of the Belasco

---

[1]Vera Zorina, former ballerina who had turned to acting.
[2]As a captain at the Stage Door Canteen, CVV was responsible for staffing his regular shifts on Monday and Tuesday nights, cajoling young volunteers among his acquaintances to serve as busboys.
[3]*Carousel,* 1945, by Richard Rodgers and Oscar Hammerstein II, a musical play based on Ferenc Molnar's *Liliom.*
[4]Annabelle Lyon, dancer with Ballet Theatre.

Theatre unless the play Trio[5] which deals with gals who love each other were withdrawn. He has been jumped on, as might be expected, from all sides for this. Practically every organization connected with the theatre objects to censorship when it is exercised by one Czar. Anyway the Ballet Russe [de Monte Carlo] is playing the City Center Theatre of which Moss is a member of the board. SO, when the Ballet Russe presented their Frankie and Johnny[6] the newspapers leaped to the opportunity and the headlines read something like this: Commissioner Moss presents Obscene Ballet. Unfortunately this boomerang reacted unfavorably and I saw a much expurgated edition of F and J. It is still most amusing and delightful and I liked it a lot. [. . .] I am reading Black Boy now by Richard Wright AND Murder the Murderer by Henry Miller. The Canteen celebrated its THIRD anniversary last night with the hostesses deep in orchids and the service men mining in a cake ten feet tall. Our Tea Dance for Service Women will be two years old in MAY. [. . .]

Four pounds of caviare, a bird of Paradise, a magnum of champagne, and a woman with frizzy hair, perhaps seven or eight feet tall, to bring books to you!     Carlo


TO ANNA MARBLE POLLOCK                101 Central Park West
[6 March 1945]                        New York City

Dearest Nadejda, I don't take critics as seriously as you do, or as playwrights do. (If they would stop quoting the good notices they get, I would be more inclined to believe what they say about critics.) Nobody was ever more attacked than Ibsen, Beethoven, or Wagner, and of course what Gertrude Stein says, "If there is communication, there is no creation," is true. What she means of course is IMMEDIATE communication. [. . .] But I am an easy mark at the theatre and usually enjoy myself and cry a lot, tho I laugh less easily. [. . .] Looking back at some of Channing's criticisms of plays and actors, I find them none too gentle. He said what he believed, which is all you can ask anybody to do . . . All this business about training, etc. is balderdash. [. . .]     My love to you, [. . .] Carlo

[5]*Trio,* 1945, by Dorothy Howard Baker.
[6]*Frankie and Johnny,* 1938, music by Jerome Moross, choreographed by Ruth Page and Bentley Stone.

TO WALTER VAN VECHTEN          101 Central Park West
[March 1945]          New York City

Dear Walter, [. . .] "After the war" is a curious phrase and means so little. Gertrude Stein says that this war's purpose is to KILL the Nineteenth Century and "progress" and "Security," etc., etc., and that the Twentieth Century will be different.[7] I believe her but exactly what it will be like nobody knows. [. . .] View, a modern magazine, gave a party for Marcel Duchamp, the painter, to which it has devoted an issue. I had a nice time talking to Zorina and others but the high point was when a middle aged writer, quite stinko, began to yell, "I can't stand another minute of this, it's exactly like 1912." This practically killed the bobbysocks who run the magazine but there was some truth in it. Cocktail parties haven't changed much, except for the fact that in 1912 they were new and had some claim to originality. I am glad you were outraged by the bus episode and the Negroes. Negroes who have tried to force an entrance on such occasions have been shot by the driver, afterwards acquitted. But occasionally service men have insisted on taking Negroes aboard and got away with it. However, in the south, better watch your step. They lynch white people too. Stop apologizing for your letters. They are never dull. They are always warm and not self-conscious and they move along in the intended direction and I love your letters. [. . .] I send you four silver earrings and a box of popcorn tied with a purple and silver ribbon; also four painted Spanish beds!      Carlo

TO WALTER VAN VECHTEN          101 Central Park West
[circa 17 April 1945]          New York City

Delightful cousin, I was reminded of you last night when I had a mixture of champagne (which flowed and TASTED like water) and whisky (nobody ever says Scotch or rye or Bourbon any more, just whisky!) at a party given by the Theatre Guild in their new quarters. I got very blotto but feel okay today, very okay indeed (which is my unpleasant habit). In the old days I used to drink myself under the table or bed and retire around 5 to bounce out around 9 feeling like a reborn infant. It usually made people who got drunk with me awfully mad. The Guild has taken over a magnificent private house with French panelling and furniture (Style Louis XVI), chandeliers with crystal pendents, handsome carved marble fireplaces, adjacent to the Museum of Modern Art on West Fifty-third Street. The rooms are enormous, the drawing room being at least 75 feet long and furnished in extreme

---

[7]Paraphrased from *Wars I Have Seen*, 1945.

elegance. I do not see how in such an atmosphere they find it possible to say to an actor, "We cannot afford to pay you $60." Maybe they won't be able to! The supper was buffet but we sat at small tables and I sat with Edna Ferber for a while and listened to her grumble about the World, its wars, works, and women. Then I moved on to Lillian Gish who has lost some of her erstwhile fragility but who looks younger than ever and lovelier than of yore. Agnes De Mille came by too and Tallulah Bankhead, Dick Rodgers, Oscar Hammerstein, Philip Barry, J C Wilson, Paul Osborn, etc., etc. Some of the waiters passed champagne and some passed whisky and soda: I took whichever came my way and lots of it and presently I began to look a little faded. Drink always makes me look older, but YOUNGER the next day! I am not, mind you, describing a GAY party or a GOOD party, or a party I particularly liked. I hope tomorrow when I lunch with Grace Zaring Stone and tomorrow night when I entertain my Merchant Seamen's Club Crew that I can be more enthusiastic about the results. [. . .]   Plum jelly, Hazelnuts, and a quart of cream!   Carlo
I think you put too much postage on letters. The rate for & from service men (and women!) is 6 cents the half ounce airmail (anywhere in the world)

## TO ANNA MARBLE POLLOCK
17 May 1945

101 Central Park West
New York City

Dearest Nadejda, [. . .] Last night Lucia Chase, who backs and dances with the Ballet Theatre, had us to dinner with Markova and we all went to see Martha Graham which is a taste I have never been able to acquire. She is an extremely ugly woman and always holds her mouth open as if she had adenoids. She invariably dances in long skirts that sweep her ankles. [. . .] Miss Graham gets rave criticisms and has a sell-out following. I think she must appeal to frustrated people.[8] Fania is going to the country today (rain or shine, as the saying MUST go these days) with Armina [Marshall] Langner to stay till Monday. I am working on letters *to me* anent Nigger Heaven for the NY Public Library,[9] and this afternoon we are giving a party for the workers at the Roosevelt [Hotel] Tea Dances. The weather seems to be getting warmer.   My love to you, Carlo

[8]Several years later, CVV altered these opinions when he saw her dance again and photographed her, in 1961.
[9]CVV gave his manuscripts, family papers, copies of the books he wrote and their attendant correspondence to the New York Public Library in 1941.

TO WITTER BYNNER                    101 Central Park West
22 June 1945                        New York City

Dear Hal, [. . .] Heaven would be a very friendly place these days: I know
so many who are in Valhalla. I just celebrated my 65th birthday and I
celebrated it far and wide. Arthur [Davison Ficke] is on his feet again; he
was in splendid form when I called on him last, just before he left for the
country. It is very exciting talking to Arthur and Gladys again and I always
enjoy it feverishly. If he enjoys it the same way it must make his temperature
rise, which is bad . . . Incidently, have you noticed how wives of sick men
are always happy, because there is no roaming. Hubby STAYS HOME and
sees no one the wife doesn't see. . . . YOUR Pearl celebrated her 25th Silver
Wedding Anniversary last week with a terrific party at the Witoka Club in
Harlem. [. . .] There was a band of four pieces for dancing and believe me
*your* Pearl is a lively stepper. There were PHOTOGRAPHERS. There was a
complete supper, beginning with Canapés and stuffed celery and cocktails,
going through ham and salad (whiskey and beer) to ice cream and cake
and coffee. And there was a ceremony I have never seen or heard of before:
a REwedding. To the strains of the Lohengrin march Mrs Showers marched
in on the arm of her son and Mr Showers with his daughter on his arm
and were met by the preacher who asked "Do you after 25 years of wedded
bliss take this man as your faithful companion etc for more years until
death do you part, etc" They did. Then the Mendelssohn March. Then
everybody kissed the bride and Mr and Mrs Showers, remarried at long
last, circled the floor in a lone waltz. Fania cried and told Mr Showers she
was touched and that it was beautiful. Whereupon Pearl's consort replied,
"I am devastated."        My respects and blessings to you both and Fania
wafts two kisses your way, Carlo

TO GEORGE GEORGE                   [101 Central Park West
9 July [1945]                      New York City]

Dear George [. . .], Your latest is quite exciting. You have been more places
than any other sojer I write to or know, but it looks as if you were getting
down to business now. I pray for you and wish you luck. [. . .] The picture
I sent you of Scott Fitzgerald was made in 1937 when he was 41, about
three years before he died. His face by that time reflected some of the things
he thought about himself (vide The Crackup) and also drink had taken its
toll on his handsome features. For the twenties he was downright beautiful,
but certainly not fragile. He was a husky sophisticated beauty if not downright rough, except when he was drunk when he thought nothing of spoiling

the face of a waiter or any passerby in any nightclub where he spent most of his later youth. He sometimes got his own face mussed up too.* Tom Wolfe drank to excess too and was constantly fighting but his fights were more of the verbal variety and he used them afterward in some version or other, the way he remembered perhaps, in one or another of his books. Life was a constant source of copy to Tom who wrote like a "creative" genius and might have become one under some circumstance. [. . .] Here is [. . .] an article by Gertrude Stein:[1] All the boys I know in Europe are worshipping at her shrine. They take tours of Paris from Belgium, Berlin, and Marseilles, and then spend their forty-eight hours leave on the rue Christine with GS. Recently she visited Germany in an airplane with three Generals, etc., a five day trip which will probably have literary results.[2] To revert to the SD Canteen, did you know that the NY Times is tearing us down? RUTHLESSLY. We still entertain from 2 to 4000 men a night but that means nothing to the Times. They are extending their plant through from 43rd Street and the Forty Fourth Street Theatre, Sardi's, etc. are doomed. Sardi is being cared for in the new building but that will be too late for US. Believe it or not there seems to be no other place in central New York and unless a place is discovered prochainement or the Times gives us a reprieve we will be dispossessed as of July 31. If you or some of your friends sitting on coral reefs would feel inclined to write bitter letters to the Times or the SDC (224 West 44) on this subject they would be welcome and perhaps HELPFUL. NO pictures in your latest letter: I miss them very much. Do include a couple next time . . .

Hearts and Flowers to you, etc. [. . .]    Carlo

*One of my last views of him was on the floor of the café in the Carlton Hotel in Paris

## TO GEORGE GEORGE
18 July [1945]

101 Central Park West
New York City

Dear George, [. . .] If you boys are getting nothing but pork and beans I don't know where the food is going. Certainly we haven't got it here. Some times no chicken turns up in the market for months at a time. Eggs are nearly as scarce and so is butter. Steaks and roasts practically do not exist, but there is usually plenty of fish and restaurant menus are made up of fish dishes. [. . .] Last Sunday Spivey[3] sang at the Tea Dance, [. . .] and

[1]"The New Hope in Our 'Sad Young Men,' " *The New York Times Magazine,* 3 June 1945.
[2]"Off We All Went to See Germany," *Life,* 6 August 1945.
[3]Victoria Spivey, black blues singer and composer.

she culminated in the Madame's Lament: Everybody goes up stairs but me. Next Sunday BILL ROBINSON! You would like these Tea Dances, I assure you . . . Later I took some of my crew from the Seamen's Club to an adjoining bar to celebrate the birthday of one of them and discovered to my complete embarrassment (I had never visited the place before) that it was as gay as a Garçon's brothel. Suddenly into the midst of this witch's brew* walked an old acquaintance of speakeasy days (I hadn't seen him for twenty years) who was the Boss of the place. If you ever run across my book Parties (which is a pretty accurate account of Post-Great War and Pre-Greatest War days in New York) you will find him set down as the proprietor of a Speakeasy. . . . Incidently books are becoming increasingly hard to come by on account of the shortage of paper: they are all going out of print (no paper except for NEW books) so the arriving generations will have only a limited idea of the books of even the immediate past. I went to two weddings this month and enjoyed them so much (unlimited amounts of the best French champagne flowed from fountains) that I intend to crash all BIG weddings hereafter. [. . .]    C.

No Canteen yet and the NY Times has given us no postponement of the date of closing: July 31. [. . .]

*or should I write Bitches' Rue.

TO GEORGE GEORGE                              101 Central Park West
20 August 1945                               New York City

Dear Edward XII! For the first time you sign off with Edward[4] and so join the hierarchy: I have so many Edwards that I designate 'em by numbers (Edward III [Atkinson] and Edward VIII [Geisler] work on Tuesdays at the Canteen) and you are No XII. Some, like Nine and Seven, simply sign the numerals now and are even called by them generally. Edward III is never called anything else. . . . Some time back I sent you a book, The Folded Leaf [by William Maxwell]. I think it will interest you but it is what I call strip-tease literature. All the boys are just about to take their pants down on every page but somehow they never quite do, altho they make a brave start once or twice. I dare say all this is true to College Life. [. . .] Your description of how Peace [came] to Tinian was most dramatic: you know by now how peace came to everybody. I heard the news in the Canteen (yes we have a new Canteen) and everybody walked solemnly out and got very drunk indeed. Later I was sitting in a bar across the street *trying* to get drunk and a big marine, about six foot six, lumbered up, said "Hello

[4]George George's middle name is Edward.

218

Pop," leaned over and kissed me, then went on out. The celebration, however, was more hysterical than historical. Having been through with a couple of them before, I'd say they mostly ARE. The new Canteen is located in the ex-ballroom of the Hotel Diplomat (it used to be the Elks Club) on West 43rd Street, across from Town Hall. It is garish and big and noisy and a little like a German Beer Garden (without any beer) on a rainy night. [. . .]     And so Hearts and Flowers to you, C.

TO ANNA MARBLE POLLOCK      101 Central Park West
6 November 1945                    New York City

Dearest Nadejda, [. . .] I don't want to move, of course, but it is ridiculous living in an apartment this size with no servants. We haven't gone into what we will do in exchange, because we will be here a year longer at any rate and we may have other ideas then. NO, I never have trouble with sepia friends ANYWHERE and I am sure I wouldn't in hotels where discrimination of any kind is against the law. I never apologize for them or explain them in any way and they are always announced in the proper manner and sent up. The same thing happened at 150 West 55th Street. Very occasionally (it has happened twice)* a new boy on the elevator doesn't understand and makes a slight mistake (no one has been actually rude). But the rest of the help seem to educate them before they make a second mistake. I NEVER say a word. When I speak of greed and the human vices I am speaking of Congress and most of the rich people I know. I don't mean to say poor people are never objectionable, but the rich almost invariably seem to be possessed of the most idiotic ideas. From the way people are behaving in this country at the moment, you wouldn't know that their lives hang by a thread, which will be severed quite neatly if they don't change their tune and get together (whatever the cost) with the rest of the world. Speaking of "stinks" I think the rich are more uncleanly and smellier on the whole than the poor, who make every effort to be respectable in appearance, no matter how difficult it may be. I know one lady who has a bank account which would buy us all out several times who always smells of stale perspiration: I know her at a distance, I might add. Unlike you I am more than reconciled to what lies ahead and aside from my own pleasures which have been considerable, regard the past of the world with considerable loathing. AND NOTHING WOULD INDUCE ME TO REPEAT EVEN MY OWN PLEASANT PAST. So, if nothing better happens, I won't be disappointed, but I HOPE something better *can* happen. [. . .]

  My Love to you, my dear, Carlo
*in twenty years!!

## TO ANNA MARBLE POLLOCK
[circa November 1945]

101 Central Park West
New York City

Dearest Nadejda, So they are going to blow up the world, Good! Two people have said that here this week, Richard Wright and Eugene O'Neill. If people can do no better than they are doing, I must say I agree. The greed and filth and desperate underhandedness of human nature are appalling. [. . .] You must be aware by now that your hero Winston Churchill was about as much in touch with contemporary England as the Dodo Bird. Pigeons, I note, manage to survive, because they behave the same way generation after generation, but the American Indian does too and is NOT surviving . . . So there is no answer to anything, my dear, EVER. Even a life spent in prayer can be ended by an atomic bomb. [. . .]      I love you. Carlo

## TO ANNA MARBLE POLLOCK
6 December 1945

101 Central Park West
New York City

Dearest Nadejda, I do not believe you have read any of my books if you think I have only lately been disillusioned. Or perhaps you have forgotten them. It's quite simple when you understand me. [. . .] On the surface I seem to be an enthusiastic fellow because I hardly ever talk about anything I don't like, and certainly I know how to live and could be happy, I believe, under almost any regime. As for [. . .] elderly couple[s] getting married, my father remarried a woman as old as he when he was 70 and was extremely happy until he died at the age of 86. I see no reason for cutting sex off from the old, if they happen to care for it. Norman Douglas said to me once that the only people who really enjoyed sex were the very young and the very old and it was mostly denied to both of them! Even trying to look young is okay with me, if it gives the tryer any pleasure. Of course he or she knows somewhere that he or she is fooling nobody, but it is a harmless vanity. I believe your mother had some of this. [. . .]      And I send you my usual love and kisses, Carlo

I heard Portia White, the Negro contralto, last evening and was disappointed to observe she was not as good as last year. The trouble with life, and also one of its major excitements, is that you never stay on a level, your books, your paintings, singing, etc. like your health, are always better or worse!

## TO ANNA MARBLE POLLOCK
28 December 1945

101 Central Park West
New York City

Dearest Nadejda, [. . .] Hugh Fullerton's death is noted in the Times this morning. He was on the Chicago American when I started there as a cub reporter and was very helpful to me. (Another good man!) When he left to become Sunday editor of the Chicago Tribune, he offered me double salary to go with him. The American editor, Moses Koenigsberg, met this by trebling my salary (which I think was $20 before they began to work on it). Of course, I am glad I didn't go to the Tribune. Had I done so, I'd probably be in Chicago YET. It takes fleas* to get young men to move. I only saw Hugh once after that, with Percy Hammond.[5] Speaking of getting young men to move, Bill Raney[6] called yesterday to tell me he has been offered a job in Berlin by the government. I don't think he is going to take it and I think he is crazy, but I never give young men too much advice in such a situation: I limit myself to stating my opinion flatly. I am back hard at work on the James Weldon Johnson Collection now that the holidays have begun to float away. My stummick is in a DREADFUL condition as a result of buckets of champagne, etc., I have forced into it, and I am leading the life of a recluse. [. . .]     A very happy New Year to you, my dear!

   And Love, Carlo

*I was fired from the American for "lowering the tone of the Hearst newspapers."

## TO MURIEL DRAPER
8 June 1946

101 Central Park West
New York City

Dearest Madraper, Max [Ewing]'s letters are completely arranged now (there are about 200), but I am holding them until I hear from you that you have nothing else to give me in this line (vide last night's postcard). They are many of them of great interest and do not duplicate others in the Collection. When he wrote to you he wrote to YOU. In a strange way he was obviously in LOVE with you. All he wanted from you, however, was ALL your time, and ALL your attention. I guess he would have given you as much in return, but never his inside, nor even the extremes of his outside. There is not a single letter in the lot that there is any reason for sealing. I will send these to Yale as soon as I hear from you. [. . .] I spend so much time with the dead nowadays that Frank Case's passing was not surprising. Have you seen *Oedipus*?!![7]     My love always, Carlo

[5]Percy Hammond, dramatic critic.
[6]Bill Raney, an acquaintance through the Stage Door Canteen, later a writer and editor.
[7]The Old Vic Company's production of the Sophocles play with Laurence Olivier.

## TO GERTRUDE STEIN

28 June 1946

101 Central Park West
New York City

Dearest Baby Woojums, Well the "testimonial"[8] arrived and it is beautiful and everybody is crazy about it and Papa Woojums is very much touched and feels very nostalgic and wishes he had a white pleated shirt to put on so that he could look and feel the way he did in 1914 [. . .]. You will be interested to know that Selected Works is already completely in galley proofs and that I have corrected all my parts. This is way ahead of schedule but I dare say a printer's or binder's strike can hold us up yet. BUT I HOPE NOT. THIS LETTER IS TO THANK YOU FOR EVERYTHING and to say I HOPE WE'LL be associated always in charming projects of this character, and that I hope I can take some color photographs of you SOON. [. . .] So lots of love to you and Mama Woojums and I'm very excited about the future of Selected Works and Brewsie and Willie and the FIRST READER[9] [. . .]    Papa Woojums!

## TO FANIA MARINOFF

[28 July 1946]

[101 Central Park West
New York City]

Dearest Baby, I hope this habit of Sunday death telegrams is not going to continue . . . This morning, EARLY, there was a ring at the bell and a girl handed me a telegram which, when opened, read, Dearest Papa Woojums, Baby Woojums passed suddenly today your loving Mama Woojums. When I read the date I noted it was yesterday, so I was not surprised to read the news in the morning paper. Montie[1] told me somebody had returned from Paris with news that she was ill, but that is the only thing I heard. Certainly none of her letters had indicated that she had cancer or knew it and it must have been a very quick kind. Why, a month or so ago she was lunching with Eddie [Wassermann], etc. It has upset me a good deal, but she could not have died at a better time for her reputation, nor at a more dramatic time, just after the appearance of Brewsie and Willie and just before Selected Writings comes out. I hope Bennett [Cerf] won't want the preface entirely rewritten. My idea, if he agrees, is to add a note saying that Gertrude saw

---

[8]CVV had edited an anthology, *Selected Writings of Gertrude Stein,* for which Gertrude Stein prepared an introductory note.
[9]*Selected Writings of Gertrude Stein,* 1946; *Brewsie and Willie,* 1946; *The First Reader,* 1946, published in Ireland and dedicated to CVV.
[1]Montie: Lamont Johnson, American actor / director who had met Gertrude Stein while he was in the army in Paris and who was staging the first production of her play *Yes Is For A Very Young Man* in California.

the preface and approved of it before she died. I think she must also have had Montie's cable about the projected production of YES [. . .].

I'll be happy to see you TUESDAY[2] and send you all my love,        Carlo

## TO ALICE B. TOKLAS
28 July 1946

101 Central Park West
New York City

Dearest Mama Woojums, Your telegram was heartbreaking. It came to me early this morning, brought in by a young girl. I hadn't had the slightest preparation for this. Only Montie Johnson told me a few days ago that some one just back from Paris reported Gertrude hadn't been well. But Baby Woojums' letters to me were full of health and cheer and I am so happy she received the preface to Selected Writings and approved. [. . .] It is wonderful to remember I have known you both since 1913 without a break . . . but it is horrible to realize that *her* part of the communication can no longer exist. Those who knew her only through the greatness of her work will never know how great she could also be in friendship! It seems as if Selected Works had been arranged for by Divinity to appear at the exact moment when they are most needed . . . but much more will eventually be revived. However, I always had it in mind to preserve as much as possible of the most important pieces in this one volume so that any reader might form his own conclusions of her work from a study of this book alone. I hope you will write us as soon as you can to tell us as much as you can. You have our very deepest sympathy and love and if you need assistance on any details of all the thousand and one things that will come up now and in the future you can always turn to Fania and
    Papa Woojums!

## TO JAMES BRANCH CABELL
3 August 1946

101 Central Park West
New York City

Dear James, It was quite wonderful hearing from you out of what is known as the BLUE, and more wonderful still receiving another book from you.[3] I read about José Gasparilla, all the pages, last night after dinner and was not surprised to find that none of your old charm or adroit manner of expressing yourself had deserted you. There is even something new added, a deceptive simplicity which is most beguiling. I enjoyed the yarn enormously and what is more believed every word of it.

---

[2]Fania Marinoff was on holiday at Marblehead, Massachusetts.
[3]*There Were Two Pirates*, 1946.

I was considerably shaken, as you were, over Ellen [Glasgow]'s death, which after all was expected and now comes Gertrude Stein's for which I was totally unprepared. Aside from these greater blows, I have been a pall-bearer on five occasions since January 1.

Fania and I seem to be healthy enough at any rate and doubtless are happier than most. She goes into a new play (or expects to) later this month. I am completely and fully occupied [. . .] by photography (and making up Collections of my photographs of celebrated people for various public institutions). [. . .] I hope Priscilla and Ballard are well and I wish you every conceivable felicity.    sincerely, Carlo

TO NOEL SULLIVAN                              101 Central Park West
3 August 1946                                 New York City

Dear Noel, Thank you so much for writing so promptly.[4] Your letter and another from Adelaide Bartelme told me what I want to know. My telegram of notification arrived too late to make it possible for me to attend the funeral which must have been very beautiful and I shall never forget what a wonderful gesture you made in producing Roland Hayes for the occasion. If he is still with you, please thank him for me. I have seen the will and agree with you that it was most impressive. I was especially delighted to learn she remembered your musical society and the Negro organizations. The Piney Woods School, to which she was so generous, was practically founded by my father. But most of all I am pleased that she died peacefully and happily surrounded by loving friends and I hope all that she believed in so staunchly actually happens to her. I learned of Mary's death one Sunday; the next Sunday came a cablegram from Paris announcing Gertrude Stein's death. As I had had no warning of her illness and as she was but a few years older than I am, this was a very great shock to me . . . I have been a pall-bearer five times since January 1, beginning with Countée Cullen's funeral.    our affection to you, Noel, Carlo

TO EDGAR ALLAN POE                            101 Central Park West
15 November 1946                              New York City

Dear Mr Poe, Thanks for your letter which, however, I do not find very helpful. It is my earnest desire to carry out what I believe to be the dying wishes of my dear old friend Gertrude Stein,[5] but it is your job to instruct

---

[4]CVV's cousin Mary Van Vechten Blanchard had died in California.
[5]Gertrude Stein charged CVV with the responsibility of editing her unpublished manuscripts, funded by her estate, of which Edgar Allan Poe was administrator, in Baltimore, Maryland. CVV afterward referred to himself, in print, as her "literary executor."

me how this can be done without friction. Until I receive instructions from you, my hands are tied.      sincerely, [unsigned carbon copy]

TO EDGAR ALLAN POE                                      101 Central Park West
23 November 1946                                        New York City

Dear Mr Poe, Thanks for your letter. I am glad that the sky seems to be brightening somewhat, so far as the wishes of my dear friend Gertrude Stein are concerned.

The will couldn't be plainer: "I desire my Executor hereinafter named to pay to Carl Van Vechten of 101 Central Park West, New York City, such a sum of money as the said Carl Van Vechten shall, IN HIS OWN AB-SOLUTE DISCRETION, deem necessary for the publication of my unpublished letters."[6]

The sums you mention in your letter as available in Baltimore should be more than sufficient to cover the cost of publishing the manuscripts. I am perfectly willing to go to the very considerable labor of editing these volumes, of selecting the material they will contain, of arguing with printers and publishers, etc., and I shall make no charge for these services, but I shall make no move in any direction until I am assured that a certain sum of money is set aside for my disposal if needed; moreover until a substantial part of this sum for immediate needs be deposited to my account in New York.

It is impossible to give any idea in advance of how much will be needed to publish this unpublished work and I will not know about this until I have spent considerable time with the manuscripts. In the meantime prices for printing are advancing rapidly. Naturally I will endeavor to make as advantageous terms with publishers as possible. It is most improbable that all the unpublished work can or will be published at one time; if there is much of it, as now seems likely, its publication MAY extend over a number of years and it will be impossible to tell in advance how much this will cost. However, if there is not too much material to be published, on the contrary, it may all be published at one time. I can make no advance commitments. I await your signal to go ahead.      sincerely, [unsigned carbon copy]

---

[6]CVV is quoting from Gertrude Stein's will, but he capitalized words himself, for emphasis, and he misquoted "manuscripts" as "letters."

TO ALICE B. TOKLAS                    101 Central Park West
29 December 1946                      New York City

Dearest Mama Woojums, Our love to you at New Year's! It is, as you say, horrible about Bernard F[äy][7] and I am curious to know if Francis Rose's[8] remedy comes to anything. You may not have the enclosed [photograph]. Sometimes it is hard to get you to reply to queries and Baby's pictures are a case in point. There were two kinds, one stern, one smiling, and I have been unable to get out of you which one you prefer! [. . .] I was very happy that you liked my Epilogue[9] about Baby. Every time I write about her I get a little nearer to what I want to say, to what I am trying to say, and eventually it may be very good indeed, but a book NO. I can't attempt anything so elaborate with all the other work I have to do. But YOU should write it. Rogers says it is Rinehart and not Houghton Mifflin that want HIS book. He would write something SWEET, if not mystic or profound, and whatever he wrote would be loving. I urged him to go ahead.[1] There is no script of the radio talk, it was impromptu: Bessie Beatty, who interviews celebrities every day, and the Baroness von Trapp[2] and I. [. . .] Well anyway we all talked back and forth, but it started by Miss B asking me what a controversial writer was and I replied "a successful writer." Then I went on to ask why painters and musicians were permitted experiments while prose writers were denied the privilege, at least the privilege is contested . . . and then I said that most of us feel that we don't see pictures on our walls any more because we are so used to them and that Baby felt that way about words and wanted to change them a bit. Etc. Etc. I said something about repetition . . . In reply to other questions I told of her sensitivity regarding pictures, her influence on other writers, and of her importance to GIs . . . Does this give you an idea. [. . .] I mentioned Lady Godiva[3] and YOU several times but never managed to get Basket[4] in. What you write about [Donald] Gallup and the Yale Press is most interesting and of course we'd be delighted to have them publish any unpublished work, IF THEY

---

[7]Bernard Fäy, the French writer, had been imprisoned for collaboration.
[8]Sir Francis Rose, English painter whose career Gertrude Stein had fostered.
[9]CVV's obituary for Gertrude Stein, published in truncated form in several newspapers and completely in *Books at Iowa*, April 1977.
[1]W. G. Rogers, American journalist and friend of Gertrude Stein since the First World War when he was a soldier in France, wrote *When This You See Remember Me: Gertrude Stein in Person*, 1947.
[2]The Baroness Maria von Trapp and her family, the Trapp Family Singers, later the source for the Rodgers and Hammerstein musical play, *The Sound of Music*, 1961.
[3]Lady Godiva, Gertrude Stein's automobile, so named because it was stripped of decoration.
[4]Basket II, Gertrude Stein's white poodle, successor to Basket.

226

WILL CONSULT ME ABOUT IT. I have not heard again from the Baron Poe and I am relaxing until he gives me the green light. BUT if the Yale Press is not publishing Four in America, I must get this script, of course. However, I note on rereading your letter, they intend to do that later when "T Wilder finishes his part of the work."[5] I await a letter from Gallup and I hope he will come to NY to see me occasionally. [. . .]

Donald Sutherland[6] called up. I couldn't see him: it was during the Christmas holidays; the worst of it was I couldn't even remember him. Could you help me about this? [. . .] Christmas Eve in the morning we decided to call up some of our friends to find if they were alone (I wish we might have been able to call you and take you out) and if they were, to invite them to dinner. We called nine straight and they were *all* alone; so we stopped there and took the 9 out, Ettie Stettheimer, Helen [Channing] Pollock who lost both her mother and father this past summer, Rhonda Keane, Doris's daughter (Doris died during the past year), etc. and three young men, a painter, a dress designer, and an actor, who were very much alone and poor. We had quite a cheerful evening and after dinner Ettie invited us up and we had champagne. You may be sure I drank to you and the memory of Baby as I intend to do on New Year's.    OUR very dearest love to you, [unsigned carbon copy]


## TO ALICE B. TOKLAS

101 Central Park West

31 January 194[7]

New York City

Dearest Mama Woojums, I seem to be writing you every day! But things come up. This day it is THIS: Norman Pearson[7] came to see me yesterday and he repeated what Donald Gallup wrote you, that Baby was always asking Thornton Wilder to write the preface to Four in America and so it was necessary to have him do it and also he was the one who had arranged for the publication with the Yale University Press. However, it seems that after Baby died everybody was asking him who was her literary executor and he said pretty generally, I am, having read it in Everybody's Autobiography. So when he read the will he felt pretty cheap and his pride

---

[5]*Four in America,* 1947.
[6]Donald Sutherland, a college teacher who had met Gertrude Stein during her American lecture tour and, subsequently, wrote *Gertrude Stein: A Biography of Her Work,* 1951. He became one of CVV's advisory committee members in editing Stein's unpublished manuscripts, as well as "Donald IV" among CVV's numbered friends until he fell out of favor a dozen years later.
[7]Norman Holmes Pearson, Yale faculty member. See List of recipients.

suffered and I guess he sulked a bit. Anyway he positively refused to have anything to do with ME in the way of business relations and Norman asked me if I objected to signing the contract with the Yale Press rather than Thornton and I replied, Of Course not. Certainly it is the Yale Press that is publishing the book, NOT Thornton. And it seems the Yale Press wants to send the manuscript to the printer immediately, but cannot or will not do so until the contract is signed, and also Norman says this is the way to hurry Thornton with the preface to tell him the book is being put in print immediately. But WHAT SHALL I DO about signing the contract? (The royalties, of course, will go to YOU.) I mean I have no power of attorney to sign contracts. Have YOU? Shall I send it to YOU? Please reply to this *by return mail* as it is a very important point and I don't know what to tell them. Maybe Mr POE could sign the contract, bless his Heart!

I heard the WHOLE of The Mother of Us All[8] the other night. The last part for the first time. There was quite an audience, about 25 people, and Virgil [Thomson] played and sang the score with that expertness which is his in this line. It is magnificent and everybody prophesies great success for it.

So I learn that the reason Knoedler's called me was that there was a squib in the New Yorker that you were selling the pictures!

So we send lots of love and answer, answer, answer!     [unsigned carbon copy]

TO MARY GARDEN                                    101 Central Park West
2 March 1947                                      New York City

Divine Mary, It took WEEKS for your book[9] to get here, but when finally it came I read it through at once, and then waited, and read it through again . . . My dear, you didn't exaggerate when you said you were not a writer! It is as if I were trying to sing Prinzivale![1] It isn't that the style is bad; such matters are easily adjusted and some of the best-known writers have had their books rewritten in the publishers'. It is, that not being a writer, you have left out so many many things of interest. Apparently I know much more about you and your career than you know about yourself. TO give you a concrete example, you were the first woman to run an opera

---

[8]*The Mother Of Us All,* 1947, an opera by Gertrude Stein with music by Virgil Thomson, about Susan B. Anthony, was given its first professional performance in 1949.
[9]This manuscript was eventually published as *Mary Garden's Story* in 1951, extensively rewritten by Louis Biancolli who was credited as coauthor.
[1]Prinzivale was the tenor part in Henry Février's 1909 opera, *Monna Vanna,* one of Mary Garden's triumphs.

company and you have said absolutely nothing about your experiences [. . .].

So this is the worst at once. However, the book is readable and interesting. I read through with no difficulty. It isn't a bore. I realized at once that this is the case and felt at once that you MUST have some one help you rewrite it. Not even that necessarily, but some one to ask you questions and remind you of things and make it richer and MORE HUMAN. It seems, from reading, that your life existed in a vacuum without reference to other people. Of course I could do this, but I actually haven't got the time to rewrite it, although I am willing to HELP. [. . .]

Please don't be impatient and irritated or what not. Remember if you don't see this thing through, somebody else will write a life of you and it won't be yours or what you want to say. It should be done with you, but PROPERLY. Remember that any one who is a writer rewrites a book at least three times, sometimes oftener and that the right way is the long hard way. Remember also, that we cannot adjust this thing by mail, it has to be viva voce. [. . .]

LOVE to you, lots of it, and write me you will be docile* about this, *please!* [unsigned carbon copy]
*This word fits you so little that I am in stitches looking back at it! But maybe you can *assume* docility on this occasion.

TO MARY GARDEN                    101 Central Park West
23 May 1947                       New York City

Dear Mary, Your latest telegram is most discouraging. Your earlier telegram was vague, but I hoped for the best when you wrote, but you haven't written. We'll never get ANYWHERE in telegrams. Write airmail and it gets here almost as quickly and you can and do say so much more. You are, I might say, a very obstinate young lady and apparently ready to argue endlessly to get your own way! I suggested an arrangement to you which is practically ideal and which would send you down to posterity in the best shape possible and you want a foolish compromise.[2] [. . .] I was at my wit's end to find somebody to do your autobiography over [. . .], and if we had found somebody it obviously would have been some inferior person who would have turned out a hackwork that would have been forgotten in a week, because nobody of any importance is going to do ghost writing.

[2]At CVV's instigation, musicologist Herbert Weinstock had agreed to prepare a biography, incorporating material from Mary Garden's manuscript.

But it is all for you to decide. Do you want a good thick book really giving some account of your magnificent career, telling about it in the way it deserves to be told about, or do you want your own cold account of yourself (completely false to the opinions of your disciples, of which Herbert and I happen to be two), made anemic by the stuffy writing of some incompetent hack writer? [. . .] I am devoted to the memory of your past glories, I love you for yourself, but for the life of me I can't understand how you can hold firm to so many opinions about a subject you know less about than the man in the street.

Nevertheless I embrace you and hope for the best!    [unsigned carbon copy]

## TO MARY GARDEN
### 4 June 1947

101 Central Park
New York City

Dearest Mary, Your latest arrived this morning and really deflated me. [. . .] But it is beyond me why, when you have somebody as sympathetic as I am towards you and your career, around to supervise the job, you can let this chance slip by. You say you are more conventional since you have lived in Scotland, but nobody has planned to write an "unconventional" book about you. What [Herbert] Weinstock had planned to do was to write a book which would give people the feeling of you as you appeared on the stage: your book completely fails to do that. You ask: "What has his seeing me in 21 roles to do with his fitness, etc.?" It has this much, Mary, that he has the proper background. He also has the taste and the skill and enthusiasm to write a beautiful book about you and your career, which yours is not. [. . .] A book about you, a GOOD book about you, would make me, for one, very happy and that is my interest. I would do a good deal about that, and have done. Apparently too much! [. . .] But I am not arguing with you; I am stating the case. And I will presently return the manuscript to you, as you ask me to . . . Our love to you. [. . .]

[unsigned carbon copy]

## TO ALFRED A. KNOPF
### 18 June 1947

101 Central Park West
New York City

Dear Alfred, Thanks a lot for the rum. One of the pleasures of suffering from hardening of the arteries is that you are encouraged to drink! I'm sorry I didn't see more of you at the party and I hope you had a good time!    Love,  Carlo

## TO FANIA MARINOFF
[17 July 1947]

101 Central Park West
New York City

Dearest Babykins, Marian Anderson appeared promptly at 11 with several dresses and a bag and we persevered in the heat till 2. She was an endless time changing her clothes, Saul [Mauriber] said on account of her WIG which has to be redressed. I don't wonder she doesn't go out, if she has to put her wig on every time. Even late as it was she wouldn't eat lunch here and there is everything in the house from an alligator pear to two roast chickens and a mango. Mark [Lutz] and I will finish some of this up tonight. He went to lunch with Ettie [Stettheimer] while all this was going on. Saul had to go back home and the house is a shambles which it will take the rest of the day to clean up. The high spot in the photographs of Miss Anderson were done with the Spanish madonna[3] to illustrate the Ave Maria and if some of these aren't incredibly beautiful, I don't know what would be. [. . .]     All my love, Carlo

## TO JOSEPH HERGESHEIMER
2 September 1947

101 Central Park West
New York City

Dear Joe, I am sending all your inscribed books, a nearly complete set, your letters (some 78), and other matters pertaining to you to the Collection of American Literature in the Yale University Library. This is a pretty nearly ideal repository for such matters (not a mark of any kind will disfigure the volumes and they will be guarded by bulldogs) and as near permanence as anything that I can discover. I hope you and Dorothy will be pleased with this decision. I regret that you do not call us when you come to New York and I particularly regret that you have never given me an opportunity of making photographs of you. In any case Fania and I send you both our affection,     Carlo

## TO ARNA BONTEMPS
14 September 1947

101 Central Park West
New York City

Dear Arna, Your recent letter on first reading gave me quite a shock of horror and made every separate hair stand on end; I've had two bad days since. It seems to indicate such a complete lack of comprehension of why I founded the [George] Gershwin [Memorial] Collection [of Music and Musical Literature] and my intentions regarding its continuance that there

---

[3]Spanish madonna: a carved, painted wood statuette in CVV's collection.

were moments during these days when I considered tossing the project aside for ever. [. . .]

The Gershwin Collection is a small valuable (it will be increasingly valuable and much of the material will be unique) Collection intended for the use of serious students. It should not be used as a reading or recreation room by others. These materials are to work with and eventually I hoped professors and students from white colleges in the south who were writing books would come there to work. [. . .] It is obvious that no one could do serious work in a room that has others in it. [. . .]

I also am amazed that we have lost the money that was set aside for the purpose of furnishing such a room. You spoke of this no longer ago than July. It seems incredible that this money would be returned without giving you or me an opportunity to persuade this woman to leave it. In fact it seems incredible that I wasn't notified of the loss of this money at once. [. . .] But I am beginning to wonder if my opinions, let alone my express wishes, are regarded as of any importance.     [unsigned carbon copy]

TO DONALD GALLUP                      101 Central Park West
24 October 1947                       New York City

Dear Donaldo, When you have finished comparing TWO I wish you would next take up Stanzas in Meditation, so that I can shake a book together for CERF, and then (when you get them!) the rest of the plays, so that I can get the play-book to Rinehart.[4] [. . .] I have a letter from Houghton Mifflin this AM and they are interested in Brinnin's biography[5]: they want my opinion on this. I have written them my enthusiasm. Virgil Thomson was here last night. He has talked to [Alfred] Barr of the Museum of M A and Barr says if Alice raises enough stink the picture will NOT be shifted. His explanation is that [Francis Henry] Taylor of the Metropolitan does not care for modern art, that the Metropolitan hasn't any and that he is at his wit's end where to hang this picture when it gets out of the main lobby.[6] My suggestion would be to leave it in the main lobby! Barr added that the Met was fully aware of its value, publicity and otherwise. [. . .]

---

[4]*Two* was scheduled as the first of eight projected volumes of Gertrude Stein's unpublished work; *Stanzas in Meditation* eventually appeared as the sixth, in 1956; Bennett Cerf issued no further Stein titles from Random House; Rinehart published Stein's *Last Operas and Plays,* edited by CVV, in 1958.

[5]*The Third Rose: Gertrude Stein and Her World,* 1959 by John Malcolm Brinnin, based on this early draft.

[6]Gertrude Stein willed her portrait by Picasso to the Metropolitan Museum of Art which in turn attempted to transfer it to the Museum of Modern Art.

Medea[7] is terrific. I've never seen anything so terrific before except Olivier's Oedipus. It mows you down. Lawrence Langner took us to a private showing of the film, Mourning Becomes Electra night before last. It has so much murder and lust and incest that it is sure to be thoroughly censored before it is publicly shown. Gene [O'Neill] likes it, quite unaccountably and most unusually. He even likes Rosalind Russell.     Four white Persian cats to you with blue eyes, Carlo

TO DONALD GALLUP                    101 Central Park West
9 December [1947]                    New York City

Dear Donaldo, Don't send *me* any aspirin or nose-drops, altho I always enjoy a hot toddy! I haven't had a cold, said he knocking hard on wood, since I went on a diet to get thinner. Consequently, I attribute colds to overeating, especially of too much starch. However, I used to suffer with hellish colds and tonsilitis and I certainly am sympathetic with you. [. . .]

The Banyan Tots now think they can sell the movie rights to BOTDRF[8] (God help us all) and want 10%. Of course I'll give it to them. Wouldn't GS love this! They are printing Stephen Spender's Christmas card! They offered to do this and he sent in a poem of 21 pages. However, he is signing some of them to sell which will give BOTDRF a better binding, they assure me. In all my experience I have never met up with anything like the Banyan Tots, and I mean the best by this.

Have you seen the December Harper's Monthly? Katherine Anne Porter scalps Baby in a LONG piece called Gertrude Stein: A Self-Portrait. You might further be edified by a paper called Sex Habits of American Men in the same issue. [. . .]

Here is the Woojums cocktail (apparently invented by me: it is written in my hand in the back of a cocktail book so many years back that I cannot recall any of the circumstances): 5 parts gin, 1 part bacardi, dash of bitters, dash of absinthe, teaspoonful of lemon juice, and a little grenadine. There may be something about this in the letters.

Gladys Ficke has ALL the items missing in our set [of Arthur Davison Ficke's first editions] and you will get them eventually, even if she has to break up her own set, but as I told you her house is too cold to work in at the moment. She also has piles of manuscript. I am asking her for as much as she wants to give us, and hundreds of letters. She has already promised mine as you know. It looks as if Ficke would be sewed up as

---

[7]Robinson Jeffers's adaptation of Euripides' play, with Judith Anderson.
[8]The Banyan Tots, Milton Saul and Claude Fredericks, of the Banyan Press—see List of recipients—published Gertrude Stein's murder mystery, *Blood on the Dining-room Floor* in 1948.

tightly as Hergesheimer before summer comes. [. . .] The Tawny Pipit[9] is now thinking of giving you her father's works inscribed to her mother. I HOPE to get a few cartons off to you myself before January 1!

Hollytoe and mistle to you and some good hot grog! Get well, Donaldo!     Carlo

Neith is VERY slow (she has Indian blood), as slow moving as a glacier. If I were you I would continue to show interest on occasion in my letters and Baby's [Gertrude Stein]. She would have some wonderful letters, really terrific, from Mabel Dodge Luhan, perhaps the BEST. Try for these too.[1]

## TO THE BANYAN PRESS                101 Central Park West
## 9 December 1947                          New York City

Beloved Tots[2] You send me completely! I am floating on soap bubbles. Blood on the Dining-Room Floor in the movies indeed! Of course you may have 10% if you arrange this. [. . .] I want to Photograph Stephen Spender. Can't you arrange this?[3] In copying Stein manuscript I came across the following:

> Kisses can kiss us
> A dusk a hen and fishes, followed by wishes.
> Happy little pair.

This seems so exactly what Mup and Zawy should have on their Christmas card that I present it to you for that purpose provided you credit Miss Stein. Just think, then and there it will become a Stein first edition! Did Donald Gallup write you? Further you are sure to hear from Alice B. Toklas. The only reason you don't see me constantly is that I am living in a whirlpool, a maelstrom if you will, of this and that. Occasionally something gets finished, how I don't know.     My love to you both

[unsigned carbon copy]

## TO CHARLES S. JOHNSON              101 Central Park West
## 10 January 1948                         New York City

Dear Charles, Through me, the widow [Georgia O'Keeffe] of a very famous artist-collector [Alfred Stieglitz] has become interested in Fisk and wants to give a sizeable collection of valuable modern pictures to your institution

---

[9]Tawny Pipit: CVV's nickname for Helen Channing-Pollock.
[1]Neith Boyce eventually bequeathed her papers and those of her husband, Hutchins Hapgood, to Yale.
[2]Milton Saul and Claude Fredericks, nicknamed by CVV the Banyan Tots because of their youth, also nicknamed by him Mup and Zawy.
[3]See CVV to Donald Gallup, 9 December 1947.

which would form the nucleus for a possible future art gallery, as undoubtedly it would attract further important gifts from painters and collectors. I can perhaps best indicate the significance of her proposed gift to
Fisk by informing you that two other parts of the collection are going to
the Art Institute in Chicago and the Metropolitan Museum in New York.
The gift should receive wide publicity and when placed on exhibition should
attract visitors not only from the South but from every part of the United
States. The question is have you the kind of room in which the collection
could be permanently displayed? The size of the gift depends somewhat
on the space you have to offer and could possibly extend to two rooms or
more.

I am invited to a reception in your honor on January 19 so I am aware
you will be in New York on that day. Could you come a day earlier and
dine with us and the donor to discuss this matter from several angles? [. . .]
I hope you can manage this, but please let me know what you can do as
soon as possible so that I will know what night to hold, and I hope very
sincerely that Marie can be with you. [. . .]

As you must be aware I am very disappointed in the present plan for a
listening room in the library. [. . .] However, If no other space is available,
[. . .] I dare say I will be obliged to consent too.      sincerely with our best
wishes to you both, [unsigned carbon copy]


TO KARL PRIEBE                        [101 Central Park West
29 March 1948                          New York City]

Well, Billie* is a real gone girl. She weighs considerably more. Prison fare
must be good. Like June she is busting out all over and is as big as Lil
Green or Ella Fitzgerald now. Unless she bants she will soon have six chins.
A sign on the outside of Carnegie [Hall] assured prospective cats that the
house was sold out. The stage was littered. They not only sat, they stood,
hundreds of 'em. The concert was announced at 11.30[†] and there was
practically no wait. They began at 11.45. Nobody was CPT:[4] all seats were
full. First the band came out: Bobby Tucker, piano, Denzil Best, drummer,
John Levy, bassist, and Remo Palmieri (ofay) guitarist. They got applause.
Then Fred Robbins introduced HER, ALL in black, a little black lace here
and there, the skirt slit at the front showed her legs when she moved.
White gloves, long with no fingers, just caught around the thumbs. Her
hair in a twisted unbraided coronet on top her head; white gardenias on
one side, another pair at her waist, same side. Brilliant earrings. . . . Terrific

---

[4]CPT: late, from the black slang expression, "colored people's time."

applause to which she bowed. She was nervous and perspiring freely, but her first tones were reassuring and were rewarded with a whoop. There was no set program. She turned to the pianist and announced her numbers sotto voce. . . . Some Other Spring, All of Me, Billie's Blues, No Greater Love, Travellin' Light, No More, You're Driving Me Crazy, She's Funny That Way: you know; you're hep. All with that seesaw motion of the arms, fingers always turned in, that swanlake twitching of the thighs, that tortured posture of the head, those inquiring wondering eyes, a little frightened at first, and then as the applause increased they became grateful. The voice the same, in and out between tones, unbearably poignant that blue voice. That BLUE, BLUE VOICE . . . She sang fifteen songs in a row, of course with a microphone, and went off for a half hour intermission. Returned in light blue, embroidery, pearls in her ears, three strands around her throat, black gloves. The gardenias in her hair continued. Sang maybe ten more songs. Then encores, endless encores. For one recall, she sang five songs without stopping . . . Just before the end such a rendering of Strange Fruit, on a darkened stage, with only the piano and very little of that, as I have never heard. One more song and it was the end. 1.45 was the hour. Billie sings again in Carnegie at midnight on April 17. O Lordie, where were you [. . .] on the eve of Easter Sunday, 1948???[5]    [unsigned carbon copy]
*Holiday
†PM.


TO FANIA MARINOFF                               101 Central Park West
[11 June 1948]                                      New York City

Dearest Baby, The weather continues to be icey and it rains all the time. Armina [Marshall] called yesterday and was much astonished that you were in Florida. I told her I was sure you had told her you were going, or at least told Lawrence [Langner]. She wanted you to come to the country

---

[5]Van Vechten appended the following note to his carbon: "The above is a letter by Carl Van Vechten to Karl Priebe and Frank Harriott about Billie Holiday's first appearance after a few months in jail for using narcotics. She has been out about a week.

"This was quite an exciting evening, of course, but my own reservations concerning it are as follows. There is exceedingly little variation in her manner of singing songs and they all sound perilously alike, especially as she seldom sings the actual notes and seldom sings them on the beat. Further practically everything is sung in the same key. Her arm movements are unvaried, and so is her stance. A little of this goes a long way and a whole evening is too much. The only people I knew in the audience were Donald Saddler and John Kriza. The audience was composed of not very bright looking young people of two colors and rather nondescript appearance. She appeals to the cats who rock themselves black and blue at band performances at the Paramount Theatre."

this weekend, but admitted that the weather is hellish out there. Anyway she wants you to come when you get back. [. . .] I was very disappointed in Hamlet.[6] It is NOT in color and the play does not lend itself to treatment of this kind. Whereas Henry V is actually apparently written with the moving picture screen in mind, Hamlet is written for the theatre and you have to cut more than half of it to get it on the screen and the effect is choppy. The actors are good. I'm sure you'll like [Eileen] Herlie, Jean Simmons, and Basil Sydney. Laertes [Terrence Morgan] is incredibly beautiful. Olivier does not look well and The Hamlet we saw of [John] Gielgud is better than this. The [Theatre] Guild is going to "offer" this and Lawrence said a few words at the beginning and said he was going to say more at the end but the applause was so meagre he didn't. [. . .] The housecleaning is nearly done and the men are rolling up the rugs. Your marketing lasted till yesterday and I bought a few things for salad, but no fruit yet. The cheese has not arrived. I'm going to two Harlem parties* this afternoon, and Chester Himes[7] is coming to see me. I had lunch with Tom M[abry] yesterday and he has invited me to see The Heiress[8] next week. Not that I give a damn. [. . .] I've looked high and low for your couch cover among my things and can't find it. I am SURE I have it somewhere, unless you took it back? I'll send you interesting clippings of course, when they come along. There's been nothing else I thought you would enjoy.

All love, Carlo

*One for Claude McKay's exhibition at the Library, the other for a new book. I have been asked to speak at the exhibition.


TO NORMAN HOLMES PEARSON      101 Central Park West
28 September 1948                     New York City

Dear Norman, I am extremely sorry to be obliged to refuse your very first request,[9] but signing pledges of any kind is one of my allergies. Another is "joining." I belong to no political party, to no church, to no club. On the other hand I have opposed Jim Crow (sometimes almost single-handed) for at least fifty years and my opposition has had considerable effect, even on Negroes who have tried to Jim Crow other Negroes. I meet on an average of four or five gens de couleur every day. EBONY once stated, to my everlasting pride, that I had more Negro friends than any other white person

---

[6]*Hamlet,* 1948, Laurence Olivier's film version of Shakespeare's play.
[7]Chester Himes, black American novelist. See List of recipients.
[8]*The Heiress,* 1948, a film based on Henry James's *Washington Square.*
[9]To support the Civil Rights Congress.

in America. [. . .]    A goldfinch and three loaves of bread to you and your wife, [unsigned carbon copy]

## TO ALEC WAUGH                    101 Central Park West
## 25 January 1949                  New York City

Dear Alec, I was enormously touched that you should send me The Sugar Islands with such a nice inscription and I sat right down and read it through. Your style is so ingratiating that I found little difficulty in this. The book is indeed charming. [. . .] My only complaint is that you never permit the Negroes to state their point of view or at any rate you don't back up their point of view.

It would be a pleasure to see you again when you come to New York. I enjoyed seeing Evelyn[1] recently and even photographed him, but I find him definitely changed.    our best to you always, Carlo

## TO GLADYS BROWN FICKE             101 Central Park West
## 5 March 1949                      New York City

Dearest Gladys, Your letter about the poets and painters is most exciting.[2] I hadn't been aware that this was so imminent. But if you charge can you pick and choose? Above all, can you have rules for artists who pay, no matter how little? These are questions that occur to me. Another is Can you, will you, take Negroes? If so I might find you a nice one. The other artists I know are comparatively well heeled and travel with their wives in trailers. We will be happy to see you in April, or, bless you, any time at all! Princeton University Graphic Arts Collection asked for some of my photographs and I sent them 72 including that "great man" one of Arthur . . . Did you or Arthur know Belle Livingstone? She came with Grace Johnson to Tawny Pippit [Helen Channing-Pollock]'s the other night and right away the furniture turned to oak morris chairs, the drinking goblets to cut glass, and the ladies' hair was all done in rats. It is perfectly impossible for me to keep my desk clean. Have you got a recipe for THAT.

Love, anyway, Carlo

[1]Evelyn Waugh, Alec Waugh's brother, the English novelist whose early books were sometimes compared with CVV's.
[2]Arthur Davison Ficke had died in December 1945; his widow planned to establish an artists' colony in his memory at their home in Hardhack, Hillsdale, New York.

Dear John, [. . .] You do not know what kind of cigarette Alice [Toklas] wants, at least you didn't tell me, and she hasn't told me. I am bringing Camels. I hope that is all right. She forgot to mention the penpoints,* so I tried another place. I can get her more of the kind she prefers. You don't mention Rome again or your school. You will be doing me a great favor to go to Rome as my guest as I hate being alone in foreign climes, but I wish I knew whether you really will do it and WHEN as it makes such a difference in my plans. But there will be no time to tell me now before Sunday. We would have such a wonderful time there and you would love it. I expect to fly back from London on November 1, and you also are invited to accompany me there for a few days if you can go. [. . .]

I wish you had been here last night. Brion Gysin[3] gave a wonderful party for me at John La Touche's[4] that lasted all night. Meg Mundy[5] was there and Beatrice Pearson[6] and Nora Kaye (of the Ballet Theatre) and Rosella Hightower who is dancing next week in Paris with the Cuevas ballet, and Gore Vidal,[7] and the Perpers, and Donald Angus (whom Alice will remember) and dozens of others white and Negro and Juanita Hall (South Pacific) sang at 2.30 and two of the Negro boys took off their clothes and danced marvellously, but I missed YOU. Well you will be seeing things they won't and so will I. George George said it was the most wonderful party he had ever been to.

To the Ballet Russe tonight. Two more dinners and I'll be at the airport. Probably you'd better bring a stretcher to take me (after all the limousine they provide will do) to the Hotel Park Elysée on the Rond Point. Perhaps I'll be well enough to dine that night or take you to the Folies Bergere, or whatever.

Will you go?[†]     Love, Carlo

*a letter today says they are not too good. They are very unfashionable here. Everybody writes with a fountain pen.

†Will you go with me?

[3]Brion Gysin, American writer. See List of recipients.
[4]John La Touche, American librettist.
[5]Meg Mundy, American actress.
[6]Beatrice Pearson, American actress.
[7]Gore Vidal, American novelist.

TO DONALD ANGUS                         Hotel Astor
15 October 1949                         11 rue d'Astorg, Paris

Dearest Donald, Thanks for your sweet letter. [. . .] I like Paris BETTER,
altho I am in a constant rage about the telephones, the taxis, the bureau-
cratic office, and once about the douane. I really don't like the place much
and would HATE to live here, it's so uncomfortable and inconvenient, but
the SUN is out and I spent yesterday afternoon with Jean Cocteau and
Jean Marais at a cinema studio in Montmartre, and had a grand time,
photographing at my leisure. Marais was making a scene at a Mirror, and
Cocteau was photographed against the rooftops, also with Chinese boys,
quite a scoop.[8] I have a lot in black and white and color. They were both
sweet. Cleo de Merode[9] will give me a picture, but she will NOT be photographed at this late date. No Arletty yet, and Pierre [Balmain] has gone
to America. She opens tonight in Un Tramway nommé Désire* as Blanche
of course, but I am going to hear Isaac Stern[1] (for the first time) with Eddie
[Wassermann] (NOT EDY). Another thing that has cheered me up is eating
at Larue's which is as divine as ever and more like the old Paris than anything else except the Cirque Medrano, the Luxembourg Gardens or the
Parc Monceau. Of course the Folies Bergere is like the Paris of 1856 and
I agree with you that Jo[sephine] Baker singing the Bach-Gounod Ave
Maria, as Mary Queen of Scots in a wedding dress, is a riot of the first
order. [. . .]     Love to you, [unsigned]
I dined last night Blvd St Germain with a divine Negro boy writer (Mar-
tiniquais).[2] I see a lot of him! He has very amusing ideas about New York
where he has never been. Now I am going to Andre Maurois[3]—Passy—at
noon.
*I have had plenty of this en anglais

TO CHARLES R. BYRNE                     101 Central Park West
[circa late June 1950]                  New York City

Dear Mr Byrne, I was happy to hear from you. It is likely I misunderstood
certain portions of your letter. At any rate we are in agreement now. However, concerning the title there was certainly some objection when the book

[8]Jean Cocteau, the French writer, was making a film, *Orphée*, 1949, with Jean Marais as its
star.
[9]Cleo de Merode, French illustrator.
[1]Isaac Stern, American violinist.
[2]Clément Richer, whose Ti-Coyo books CVV arranged for Alfred A. Knopf to issue in English
translations in America.
[3]André Maurois, French writer.

first appeared, particularly from people who had not read the novel, and it is likely there may be now. That is not the important fact which is that the book is called Nigger Heaven (a tragic and ironic title as any fool who reads the book may see) and no other title would do. That is what you have for sale. If you offered them Black Beauty, for instance they wouldn't know anything about the contents and wouldn't buy the book.

I have consulted George Schuyler and James Ivy, book editor of The Crisis (official organ of the NAACP) about the title this morning and both agree, THE TITLE CAN'T BE CHANGED.

Let me know when you want my introduction and how long you want it. I don't think you'll be displeased with it. If George Schuyler is to write a preface too, I'll get a copy of mine into his hands so that we won't duplicate material.

I am writing Alfred Knopf that he will hear from you presently.

sincerely, [unsigned carbon copy]

The Modern Library edition of Nigger Heaven is the most complete edition as it has the latest corrections and you had better print from that.[4]


## TO DONALD ANGUS
1 July 1950

101 Central Park West
New York City

Dearest Don, You would hear from me oftener (in fact often) if you ever gave me addresses to write to.[5] [. . .] At any rate you have never written better letters and the Anno Santo stamps from Italy make my mouth water. Is the anno santo a bother? This is one of the things I crave to know. I also crave to know if you met Sottsass.[6] She seems quite mad to me and I am sure she will pick you up in Venice or the South Seas or somewhere. [. . .] Did you ever see Richard Buka? I met him at a party recently and he is right smart pretty. He was leaving the next day to play The Corn is Green with Ethel B in Woodstock, but I have him booked for the galleries in the fall.[7] But by far the greatest beauty of all time is the boy who works

---

[4]There was no Modern Library edition of *Nigger Heaven*; CVV must have been thinking of *Peter Whiffle*, revised in 1930. The sixth and seventh printings of *Nigger Heaven* had been revised to substitute song lyrics by Langston Hughes for "Shake that Thing" which CVV had quoted without permission. When ASCAP threatened to sue, he settled out of court and Hughes wrote lyrics for several quoted songs in the novel. The Avon paperback appeared in February 1951, only to be withdrawn from circulation because of complaints over the title.

[5]Angus took long holidays abroad every year; in 1950 he was in Italy.

[6]Fernanda Pivano-Sottsass, Gertrude Stein's Italian translator.

[7]The American actress Ethel Barrymore was appearing in a revival of her 1940 success, *The Corn is Green*, by Emlyn Williams. Booking Buka "for the galleries" was a phrase CVV used frequently in conversation to indicate he had arranged for someone to be photographed.

for the Ritz Delicatessen on Columbus Avenue, around the corner. He belongs to the Nat'l Guard and says he has been called up, so maybe the war is getting worse. What do you hear abroad? You mention the Utrillo scenery in Louise,[8] but don't say whether you liked it or not. Charpentier didn't and refused to go the first night of the revival on that account. Mary [Garden] was sick and couldn't go, but she went to lunch chez Edward [Wassermann] I the next day. The last time I saw Louise at the [Opéra] Comique you could throw quite a big child through the holes in the back drop. [. . .] Desperate letters arrive by every boat from Marguerite D'Alvarez: Write her. I wouldn't be a bit surprised if that number would Do herself in. I sent her a big package of meat.* [. . .] Write her. She just might come to Paris and screw you. Who knows?     Lots of love, [unsigned]
*She has been living off fish.

TO DONALD ANGUS                         101 Central Park West
20 July 1950                            New York City

Dear One (Donald I), Thanks for your letters and cards. Thanks for the peonies. We had a terrific party[9] and I wish you might have been here: garlic ice cream, Valencian rice, and two cakes in the shape of 70. [. . .] Then there was a dinner for Todd Duncan[1] and Ethel Waters, the best public dinner I ever attended, really wonderful, and Ethel was marvellous and ended up by singing. And a testimonial concert for Nora.* Think of it! Nora and Ethel are now highly respected women on the top of the heap while Paul Robeson and Walter White, great men in the twenties, are in the dog house. [. . .] I don't wonder you are getting bored with Paris. It bores the pants off me. Fania says it is only good to buy things in and when you no longer do that, why there is nothing. [. . .]     So lots of love and I hope your hay fever is over. Carlo
*Holt, given by the Negro musicians including the wonderful Wm Warfield who is better than anybody[2]

TO FANIA MARINOFF                       Franciscan Hotel
[15 August 1950]                        Albuquerque, New Mexico

Dearest baby, I had been in Santa Fé about a minute when I ran into Mabel [Dodge Luhan]. Just outside La Fonda. We embraced warmly and she said, "You old fool, I've missed you a lot." Then she asked me to speak to Tony

[8]*Louise,* the opera by Gustave Charpentier.
[9]CVV's seventieth birthday party, 17 June 1950.
[1]Todd Duncan, black American baritone best known for *Porgy and Bess.*
[2]William Warfield, black American bass.

[Luhan] in the car, which I did & she repeated "You old fool." Edward Donahoe[3] was with them, so I saw him too. Anyway she asked me to Taos (they were returning the next minute) & I told her I was going to see Duane [Van Vechten] & would see her too. Edward, who has a house in Taos, ditto. She looks very old. Hal Bynner called & we are driving there tonight with Martha Graham. Tomorrow Georgia [O'Keeffe] is coming for us. Thursday I go to Taos. Edward too. Isherwood is coming for us. Friday is the Tesuque horse fair & Indian dance. Further than that I can't tell you yet but I want to go to Juarez and Santo Domingo. [. . .] The weather continues fine, my bowels move twice a day without pills, my cough is gone, & I feel fine. I hope you are the same. I have written you every day, sometimes twice or 3 times. If you don't get them it is not my fault.

All my love, Carlo

TO MABEL DODGE LUHAN                      101 Central Park West
1 October 1950                                          New York City

Dearest Mabel, It was fine seeing you too (I loved being called An Old Fool) and Fania is very happy that [we] are again en rapport. So I sent you all those things so you could in a way catch up with me and my activities which are quite different now from in the past. Somehow, I wanted you to KNOW, because you have played a very important part in my life (I told a dinner party this recently) making me acquainted with beauty when I didn't even know how to spell the word. More than that, indeed. . . . But you *know* how callow I was, and what you did. Perhaps better than I do. [. . .]

I am glad you sent the [CVV] material to the U[niversity] of [New] M[exico]. A young man[4] there recently wrote to me; he is writing a thesis about me. This material should help him.      Fania and I send love to you and Tony, Carlo

I am more impressed with the Southwest than I have ever been before. You are responsible for interesting me there too!

TO PRENTISS TAYLOR                        101 Central Park West
23 October [1950]                                    New York City

Dear PT, [. . .] Your letter was gossipy and newsy and I have so little to offer. Ettie Stettheimer is most ill and has been taken to a hospital, but her friends must ignore this and write or telephone the Dorset [Hotel] as usual.

---

[3]Edward Donahoe, numbered Edward IV among CVV's friends named Edward, had worked as an editor for Alfred A. Knopf during the 1920s.
[4]Edward Lueders: See List of recipients.

The part of Miss Waters's Memoirs in the October issue of the Ladies Home Journal is sensational in all respects. How that cumbersome conservative magazine happened to publish all this rape and bastardy and adultery is beyond anybody, but they did. The book which contains much more material will be out in October or November, some time. I can't wait. Meanwhile I am speaking at a dinner for Ethel on Sunday at the Park Sheraton and so is Miss Holt. I never see Langston except at public gatherings. No reason, except he is busy and so am I. I haven't seen Angus for ages, but he is okay or somebody would telephone. They always do. [. . .] As you know Mencken is dying. It makes me feel old to see them falling away all around me. But I may survive a moment. My latest adventure is ear devices. I haven't got them yet, but I go every day and repeat words I hear in a machine. I hope I can hear them through my new appliance which I haven't tried yet.      Love, Carlo

Don't miss the baritone Wm Warfield if he comes to Washington. He is sensational.


TO BRION GYSIN                                101 Central Park West
16 December 1950                              New York City

Dear Brion, I don't know if this will reach you, as you wrote me a month ago and perhaps by now you are in Helsingfors or Oslo or Lucca or Mallorca or wherever. [. . .] Your remarks about Arabs amuse me very much and probably are very true. As you say, there are those who like kindred performances (like High School Boys in the lavatory at a dance or Princeton freshmen), but such minor pranks are not for me. I want the works, long and continuous, with subtle and brazen variations in minor and major keys, ending with a shower of roses and a display of Roman candles, and possibly a High Mass in C major with all the Priests in embroidered vestments and the choir boys nude. We had a hurricane which blew the roof off the adjoining synagogue. We were giving a Party for Edith Sampson, the Negro Member of the UN (52 people were asked for cocktails: 17 arrived, stayed for dinner and practically all night). It was a grand romp and like one of the major rites of the Rosicrucians. At the end I was exhausted and felt the weight of my 70 years, but for the most part I hobble about spryly on my wooden legs, see intensely with my glass eye, and hear a good deal that is bad for me with my hearing-aid. I miss you a lot. In the first place you are picturesque, downright beautiful, indeed. Added to that you speak your pieces with wit and fantasy and imagination. I am happy to have a picture of you, but it would be nicer to see you in person. Alice

[Toklas] is okay and writes me often. I have at last persuaded the Yale Press to publish the remaining unpublished works of Gertrude Stein, about eight thick volumes. I did this by promising them a preface to the first volume by Alice B Toklas, after securing her promise she would write it.[5] I expect the first volume will be out this spring. The NY City Ballet is giving performances the like of which I have never seen in the ballet world, far superior to that overpraised Sadler's Wells. Hugh Laing and his wife [Diana Adams] have joined the company and Melissa Hayden has turned into the greatest ballerina [. . .] in a long time.[6] [. . .] Write me again soon. In the meantime I embrace you and wish you a merry Christmas and a fine New Year. We are having a party on New Year's eve with champagne if you want to fly over.    Love, Carlo!

TO MABEL DODGE LUHAN               101 Central Park West
21 December 1950                   New York City

Dearest Mabel, [. . .] You [. . .] say in this letter that you have left all your papers to ME. As I have made a great study of libraries, college and public, in the past ten years, I'll know exactly what to do with them and put them all where they will be cherished and loved for generations, that is, if you die first. We are exactly the same age but I think you will outlive me by several centuries. The wars and rumors of wars remind me of our experiences in Florence just before the FIRST ONE and DURING. It will be much worse in Europe now. What those poor people who live in Europe have gone through since the days of the Romans! Cause and Effect, Cause and Effect! The Greeks warned them in their plays. Do you recall Orestes who killed his mother because she had killed his father, and in turn he was pursued by the furies for the rest of his life. Wagner knew about it too. When Brunnhilde saved Siegmund, she knew her father wanted to, but as he had commanded her *not* to, he had to dole out punishment. That is why I am sure every last one of us is punished for any bad deeds we do whether they seem to be for the best or not. I feel sorry for the poor Rus-

---

[5]Alice Toklas wrote none of the prefaces to the eight Yale volumes. Janet Flanner, American correspondent for *The New Yorker* (Genêt) and journalist, wrote the first one; subsequent volumes were introduced by American writer Lloyd Frankenberg, Virgil Thomson, American-born French writer Natalie Clifford Barney, French art dealer Daniel-Henry Kahnweiler, Donald Sutherland, Donald Gallup, and CVV.

[6]CVV to Richard Rutledge, 8 February 1959: "I would say that at the moment Melissa is the world's greatest dancer and probably the most versatile dancer who has appeared in our time."

sians.* But of course *they* feel sorry for *us,* unarmed and unprepared as we are, as they don't understand the laws of Cause and effect. [. . .]

Did I tell you about our Christmas decorations? A Spanish shawl over the piano, Chinese New Year's cards under the glass top on the round Biedermeyer table, Mexican tin Christmas trees, Hopi dolls and Tesuque bowls, a Mexican hat on the ceiling in the drawing room, Chinese butterfly kites at the windows, a Japanese FISH kite over the main doorway, Victorian angels and a Portuguese Victorian decoration in the Victorian Room. [. . .]    Fania and I send Love and Merry Christmas to you and Tony, [unsigned]
*whose first crime was to murder the Czar & his family.

## TO BRION GYSIN                    101 Central Park West
2 September 1951                    New York City

Lovely Brion, You DO write the most heavenly letters, even when nothing happens to you and I think a book from you in the form of letters would be something. [. . .] I looked up phimosis and have never seen one but it used to have a slang name which may come to me.* And I have never seen it but somebody told me once the cure for it was slamming a window down on your prick. I am not so sure that would be fun. Anyway I haven't got phimosis. Anna May Wong is in town and I guess I told you I have a new restaurant and the cold weather is upon us and I read a good deal and pray. I am by way of being elderly, but I have no beard save that surrounding my sacral dimples. I miss you constantly and I discover that you add enormously to the savour of NY life with your beauty and your foreign (shall we say?) TOUCH. But don't bring back any phimosis, please.    Much love and do not forget ton    Carlo

Can you send me Paul Bowles' address.
*it hasn't. Maybe next letter.

## TO DONALD GALLUP                  101 Central Park West
5 September 1951                    New York City

Dear Three, [. . .] Four[7] IS naive, I am convinced of it. Like most over-educated men he is extremely unacquainted with the mores and ideals of decent human behaviour. I also discovered he was somewhat naive about Gertrude and Alice as people and certainly most naive about what had to be done to get people to write prefaces for nothing, etc., etc. But he is a

---

[7]Donald Sutherland, who had been numbered Donald IV.

Donald Gallup, 1947

Edward Lueders, 1951

James Purdy,

good boy (he drinks as much as I do, maybe more) and certainly his book is brilliant, if difficult.[8] No one can review it. No one is good enough. [. . .]

I am sorry about Pavlik's letters, but I think you undertook to write or edit a book about 5 times as hard to do as Notre Dame de Paris, for example. Editing, indeed, is more difficult than composition, because errors are not smiled on with editing. Poor boy, but you MUST finish this book.[9] I have never heard you swear before. [. . .]     Avocadoes and grilled Panama Shrimps to you, Carlo

A terrific letter from Alice. She is distinctly pleased, tho with RESERVA-TIONS.[1] I saw Rogers last night at the ballet, and he seems to have reservations too. My great niece almost named her 3rd son Jehosophat but compromised on Carl[2]


## TO EDWARD LUEDERS

1 October 1951

101 Central Park West
New York City

Dear Fifteen, By ALL means, let me be Carlo II. It sounds kingly! I've sent the mss to Mabel Dodge Luhan as you asked me to and shall bite my nails until it returns. [. . .][3] Definitely there would be NO advantage in submitting a longer mss. I think I told you before that this draft reads like a finished mss. Aside from making typographical corrections and changing a few errors of fact, I see no need for further work. When it is ready I'd like to have you send it first to Knopf, and if you will tell me when you want to send it, I'll be glad to prepare him. I am by no means sure he will publish it, but as my publisher I think he should have the first crack at it. The title is most important and the working one won't do.[4]

Better come to New York before I am laid away. I haven't more than 35 or 40 more years to live. 35 more would make me 106. I go to New Mexico regularly every 17 years, so that won't do. [. . .]

Please let me know truthfully what the faculty makes of OUR book. And you haven't yet asked any favors of me.     Caviare and champagne to you, Carlo II

[8]*Gertrude Stein: A Biography of Her Work,* 1951.
[9]Donald Gallup was editing a selection of letters written to Gertrude Stein, published as *The Flowers of Friendship,* 1953. He was having grievous difficulties in deciphering Pavel Tchelitchew's handwriting.
[1]About the jacket and design of Sutherland's book.
[2]Carl Van Vechten Shawber.
[3]Edward Lueders had written his dissertation for a doctor of philosophy degree about CVV and had sent it to request permission to submit it for publication. It was published by the University of New Mexico Press as *Carl Van Vechten and the Twenties,* (1955).
[4]"More on Wine Than Oil," a quotation from Rabelais.

O yes, I don't think there is any reference to it in your (our) book but in The Autobiography of Alice B. Toklas, Gertrude Stein refers to a Mrs Van Vechten coming to see her. That was *NOT* the present incumbent. It was my first wife, divorced, & deceased.

## TO MARK LUTZ
[April 1952]

101 Central Park West
New York City

Dearest Bino, TWO Specials arrived from you today. One at dawn, the next at daybreak. [. . .]

Essbees[5] see too much of each other and a party of them alone turns into a gossip fest. A few girls makes them more reasonable. The best Essbees know this and act accordingly, saving their exclusive parties for the bedroom. Occasionally I give an all-male affair, but it seldom works out well. I mean I get bored. [. . .]

I can't think of anything I want for my birthday so you can send me a carnation as usual.

I shop at Manganaro's later today. Hal [Bynner] dines here Monday. I lunched with Miss Ettie [Stettheimer] today. [. . .] Miss Ettie is regaining her health and strength and bad temper rapidly and even talks of giving me a birthday party. [. . .]

so love to you, sir and mister,

## TO JOHN BREON
28 April 1952

101 Central Park West
New York City

Dear John, Your letters are wonderful and I can see that you ARE in love, and it makes me very happy, because I've known for a long time you never have been in Love. It will do a lot for you and will make you quite different and the NEXT TIME you may be even more in love. For it is seldom that any one is in love only once (it DOES happen) and the *first* time is seldom permanent, and if you do get over this, don't get cynical about it. Realize that it was something that had to happen and how and why are unimportant, the sooner the better, and keep an open mind and heart, and it will happen again. I am not PRAYING that you will get over this time, but warning you that you MAY. But whatever and however, you will become a better boy through this. [. . .] Your letters, you know, are contradictory,

---

[5]Essbees: In the CVV-Lutz private vocabulary, this was an abbreviation for "sexy boys," derived from their euphemism for homosexuals, "strange brothers," prompted by Blair Niles's 1932 novel, *Strange Brother*.

full of passion and confusion, but I am sure you will be all right NOW. You've never been so frank WITH YOURSELF before. You have INDICATED A GOOD DEAL without saying it. But you'll breeze through it all in the end and it's going to be OKAY. [. . .]     Love to you, John, whatever and however, Carlo

Somehow I like you more now!

## TO MABEL DODGE LUHAN

16 June 1952

101 Central Park West
New York City

Dearest Mabel, I hope you are better.

Frieda[6] has come and gone. We saw her twice. She was more elegant than at Taos, and indeed at times, imposing and distinguished. I can't help being fond of her: I was immediately when I met her in Taos. And there is no doubt she is a personality, "a character." She said, "Mabel is growing sweeter and sweeter, I believe, as she grows older." As most people tend to progress the other way, this tendency must be applauded, and appreciated! [. . .] Fania is going to Europe and I am considering a Caribbean tour, by airplane, this time, but nothing is definite in life. It is HOT here, as you can well believe.     Love to you and Tony, Carlo

Tomorrow I'll be 72! I can still walk.

## TO FANIA MARINOFF

12 July 1952

101 Central Park West
New York City

Dearest babykins, I was awake all night Thursday July 10, worrying about what had become of you. On Friday your BAD letter came and gave me a miserable day. We have such powers of wounding each other (often unconsciously) that we must love each other very much. Certainly, I never felt more tender towards you, more sorry to see you go.[7] [. . .] Far from being the first off the boat, I believed I was the last. The dock was crowded with people down to see their friends off, and the ship's officer said as I stepped down the plank, "lively now, sir." [. . .] Yesterday Mark [Lutz] came over and we had rather a horrible day. I was thinking of your letter* most of the time and hating to have you unhappy, especially unjustifiably. [. . .] I forgive you for being bad, and me too, if I was. I love you very much, and please try to be happy and have a good time.     All my love, Carlo

---

[6]Frieda Lawrence, D. H. Lawrence's widow.
[7]Fania Marinoff was on a North Cape Cruise, to be followed by a holiday in Paris.

This is the second letter to Oslo. The first one has enclosures. Don't write on both sides of Cunard airline paper. It shows through & is hard to read. But *write* please.

No phones. No letters.
*Your second letter helped a little

TO DONALD ANGUS                                    101 Central Park West
12 July 1952                                       New York City

Dearest Mr Angus, Sir and Mister, I got a letter from you today (July 12) asking me to write you in Rome till July 13 which is pretty difficult, and it is the first time you have indicated where I could write you. This goes to Paris, as you suggest . . . It is hot here, as usual and, aside from the election has been a pretty calm summer. To be sure Ruth Ford got married to Zachary Scott[8] in Chicago. I came near going to this: Alvin Colt[9] and I were the sole invités. Ruth had beds for us in addition to one for Z and herself and she urged prettily but it was too hot. Flying on the Fourth would have been uncomfortable and even dangerous and the Republican Convention made Chicago seem uninviting . . . Then Alice de la Mar gave a red white and blue barn dance for Pavlik [Tchelitchew] and Charles Henri [Ford] in Westport on the 4th and for similar reasons (having no desire to be strewn along the highway on the dawn of the Fifth) I decided not to go. The party was grim, tho pretty, I am informed, and cost $3,000. Pavlik, who appeared briefly TWICE, allowed he would rather have had the money. Leontyne Price has made a sensation in Porgy and Bess. With [William] Warfield and Cab Calloway in the company she has stolen the notices. The Sat Review of Literature gave her a PAGE, and they played two weeks in Dallas to $85,000. They are now getting similar raves in Chicago, and just now her engagement to Warfield has been announced. [. . .] FM is in Norway. I am mostly seeing Aileen Pringle who loves New York and heat and we do odd and exotic things like eating planked soft shell crabs (baby ones) marinara. Don't let any one tell you that Wish You Were Here[1] is thrilling. Everybody is mostly nude, but the baskets are hand-made if any, the legs and faces insupportable. [. . .] I am thinking seriously of dashing rapidly through the Caribbean by AIR, but I have thought of

[8]Ruth Ford and Zachary Scott, American actors. Ford was an early and frequent photographic subject for CVV.
[9]Alvin Colt, scenery and costume designer.
[1]*Wish You Were Here,* by Harold Rome, based on the 1937 play *Having Wonderful Time* by Arthur Kober.

this before without result. The NY City Ballet is having a sensation abroad and Jerry Robbins's The Cage and The Pied Piper are the hits. [. . .]

I kiss your hand, Herr et Monsieur, and call me on your return.     Love, Carlo

## TO MABEL DODGE LUHAN
3 September 1952

101 Central Park West
New York City

Dearest Mabel, [. . .] Did I tell you that at Muriel's funeral, Paul said, "Three things are indestructible: Music, Love, and Muriel Draper. We have them all here today." As we know, Music and Love are destructible, and Muriel proved to be too.

Did you get Mickey Spillane?[2] It's nonsense but amusing nonsense. I won't send you Gertrude [Stein]'s new book because I don't think you want it.[3]

Fania is back, the weather is cooler, and the NY season is beginning with a bang, with indeed, the Balinese dancers.

I am reading Djuna Barnes: Nightwood.[4]

I have aches and pains in my right arm and am reminded forcefully that I am no longer an infant.     Love to you, Carlo     Both

## TO DONALD GALLUP
26 November 1952

101 Central Park West
New York City

Dear Three, I spent the better part of this afternoon at Arthur Spingarn's office, extracting letters (LS, ALS, and letters signed by Richetta Randolph, his secretary, from James Weldon Johnson to AS on matters relating to the NAACP) from VERY dusty files. It was dirty work but we found quite a horde of letters and others still exist in earlier files not immediately available.

Also today Virgil [Thomson] sent me a rough draft of his preface to Bee Time Vine.[5] He says you already have a copy. Parts of this do more to explain the genius of Gertrude than anything hitherto in print, and I like

---

[2]CVV to Bruce Kellner, 8 August 1952, about one of the then popular Mickey Spillane murder mysteries: "But it's good fun, not too dirty, and I wouldn't say sexy at all, except perhaps to novices. In fact I am sure Mickey has a success in nunneries."
[3]Mrs Reynolds, the second Yale volume of her unpublished work, 1952.
[4]A reissue with an introduction by T.S. Eliot.
[5]Bee Time Vine, 1953, volume 3 of the Yale Edition of the Unpublished Writings of Gertrude Stein.

the way he has gone over every piece, now with a feather duster, now with a hammer, but he has brushed out or POUNDED out as much as he can of meaning, sound, or provocation. I am pleased, and still more pleased by the fact that this piece is ready so soon. I am already worrying about Volume IV and long to get to YOU and Sutherland.[6]

I should add that we saw [Georges Feydeau's] Occupe Toi d'Amélie the other night, a farce of which I caught the original production in 1908, and were completely enchanted. This is a reconstruction, complete, terrifyingly complete, of a form as dead as the dodo. So much harder to reconstruct than Molière, for this earlier playwright can be studied any day at the Comédie. I was in hysterics most of the time and so was the rest of the audience. On Sunday we met [Jean-Louis] Barrault and [Madeleine] Renaud chez Bobsie [Mrs Gilbert] Chapman.

Last night a new Hindemith-Balanchine ballet, [*Opus 54*] stillborn, I'm afraid, but it has some terrific moments and the music is gorgeous. By the way what has happened about Hindemith? Does he refuse to greet me with a lens in my hand?[7] [. . .]      Sweetbreads to you, rain from Heaven, and six pug dogs (housebroken)    Carlo

## TO HONORABLE DOROTHY BRETT          101 Central Park West
3 July 1953                                            New York City

Dear Brett, I think Fania has told you we have to MOVE[8] and we are in the throes of packing and assorting. We have no place yet and I don't actually know when moving will be imminent, but it will probably take place some time in the next twelve months. So don't be surprised if we don't write you too often. [. . .] Mabel [Dodge Luhan] telegraphs that she has had a bad accident. Isn't it terrible for one so active, but as one gets older bones get more brittle and one has to be more careful. So often elderly women break their hips. Mabel *would* be different and make it the collarbone, but the latter is harder to set or to mend too. The weather is frightful here: BAKING us all in a casserole: why go to Hell? But we are managing to get our chores done.      Love to you, Carlo

[6]See CVV to Brion Gysin, 16 December 1950, note 5.
[7]CVV had asked Donald Gallup to arrange for him to photograph Paul Hindemith, the German composer then teaching at Yale.
[8]The apartment house at 101 Central Park West was going cooperative.

## TO DONALD GALLUP
11 February 1954

146 Central Park West
New York City

Dear THREE, I was very much interested in your report on [the Albert C.] Barnes [Foundation] and I think if you can manage another entree (when your opinions will either change or solidify) you might do another article, but don't write it *before* you go again. [. . .] Barnes never cared for Picasso (Alice Toklas once wrote me that a mutual love for Picasso and Matisse in a collector was either extremely rare or actually impossible.) However, the good (or bad) doctor has at least two excellent examples from every one of Picasso's various periods, including that very early Spanish picture. The "old masters," gadgets, Pennsylvania Dutch hinges, etc etc. can be accounted for by Barnes's theory of art which was not based on chronology, but on "influences," "resemblances," and the like, and most of the arrangements are based on this theory. Matisse once said to me that it was impossible to see French pictures of the periods represented without visiting this Collection. "Nowhere in France," he went on, "can anything like it be seen." I have visited the collection at least 8 times (perhaps more). At one time, indeed, I was the Doctor's "white-headed boy," due to our mutual interest in Negroes. [. . .]     Minuets to you, white wigs, and embroidered waistcoats, Carlo

## TO DONALD GALLUP
27 February 1954

146 Central Park West
New York City

Dear Three, Stop ribbing me about the innocent Yale students and the still more innocent Librarians. If they are upset by the naive Mr Kellner's scabrous contes, I am sorry for them. What will they do, if Yale is offered a large slice of Hemingway correspondence. What will they do, indeed, with Miss Stein's notebooks?

I was not exactly bored by [T.S. Eliot's] The Confidential Clerk, nor was I much interested either. The first act is pretty hard to take. I slept through most of this. The second and third acts are "sources of innocent merriment." And I sat up with a bang when Aline MacMahon announced that everybody had his wish when it was obvious that no one had. I liked the ladies generally, and didn't like the men much.[9] I like Mr Eliot better than Noël Coward, but NOT MUCH BETTER. [. . .] This week we see the Kabuki and The World of Sholem Aleichem. Last night we saw a VERY STRANGE film

---

[9]Aline MacMahon, Ina Claire, Joan Greenwood; Claude Rains. Douglas Watson, Newton Black, Richard Newton.

at the Museum of Modern Art: The Diary of a Parish Priest: Preview. Eliot is milk porridge compared to this! [. . .]     Rock candy to you, licorice, bears' paws, and stag horns, Carlo

## TO ALICE B. TOKLAS                    146 Central Park West
## 27 March 1954                         New York City

Dearest Mama Woojums, [. . .] I am excited about [Sir] Francis Rose's drawings for the [Alice B. Toklas] Cook Book. They are probably too good for Harper's. Don't be surprised if they are refused. [. . .] We have no dishwasher or clothes washer, or garbage disposer, or PIG, [. . .] Really there is nothing modern about our kitchen, except we've never had a really good stove before and the refrigerators work so rapidly (there are two) that it scares you. [. . .] My bathroom is the most amusing room in the house. It is papered with covers (vintage of 1914) of Le Rire, Le Sourire, Fantasio, and La Vie Parisienne.[1] [. . .] We had about 60 at a party and could easily have had sixty more. People were invited from 5–7. Many stayed until midnight. [. . .] Drinks were served by a barkeeper and our Pearl [Showers] and Mildred [Perkins] attended to other matters. I wish you had been here. So does Fania. She had a happy birthday. [. . .] I shall give my birthday party in the morning as the apartment is best when the Eastern sun shines in. I expect to serve cold borscht, crabmeat salad, and champagne. (O yes, Creme de marrons!) Thanks for the use of the hall and pardon this garrulous letter.     Fania and I send eternal love, [unsigned carbon copy]

## TO MABEL DODGE LUHAN                  146 Central Park West
## 29 March 1954                         New York City

Dearest Mabel, [. . .] I am helplessly upset about your cataracts. So far, I have avoided the usual gifts of old age, such as cataracts and prostate trouble, but doubtless, like Job, I'll be afflicted by these later. I'll be 74 in June, so I am getting on. I understand fully why you don't feel like writing. You probably don't feel like reading either. I decided the other day that death comes when you tire of EVERYTHING. I am already tired of parsnips (which I adored), of Pineapples, of Bach, of the Opera (O how tired I am of that!) and the theatre (but I still enjoy moving pictures and the ballet), of travel, of avocados, of THINGS. God, how tired I am of THINGS. Write me only when it is easy for you, and much love to you and Tony.     from Fania & Carlo

[1]French magazines.

TO CHESTER HIMES                    146 Central Park West
23 April 1954                       New York City

Dear Chester, [. . .] For an old gentleman on the way out I do seem to be quite lively. As for the race, it seems to be doing even better than usual. Someday we will all wake up to the fact that EVERYTHING has been changed. This agreeable ending will come with a rush, like the spring flowers and leaves after a fallow winter. The most extraordinary things will happen with nobody paying any attention (paying any mind would be a more harmless way of saying this). [. . .] I am grateful to you for keeping the [James Weldon Johnson] Collection in mind.[2] When there is no distinction between the races, it will be pleasant to have a repository like this where one can examine what the race did single-handedly. [. . .]     Easter Eggs, Shish Kebab, broiled kid, and Raumschnittle, Carlo

TO EDWARD LUEDERS                   146 Central Park West
13 October 1954                     New York City

Dear XV, I haven't heard from you since July. Probably I haven't written. Anything arranged [. . .] about my Negro photographs?[3]

I spent a night at a [Dave] Brubeck jam session and the next day he spent with me HERE being photographed, also Paul Desmond, his sax player. I took a great shine to them both and I am pretty sure they didn't dislike ME.[4] But so many times I meet people and see them for several hours under great intensity and grow to like them better than SOME old friends, and then I see them no more. But that can't happen with Dave, because I can track him down to some nightclub. He is a doll and so is Paul. By the way, Dave's FIFTH child is on the way: He's a prolific bastard, n'est-ce pas? I'll send you some photographs when they are ready. They are not even developed YET.

I have been writing an Yvette Guilbert cover for Angel records, and two books reviews (The Rainbow Bridge by Mary Watkins Cushing, a biography of the great Olive Fremstad and Forgotten Altars, by Marguerite D'Alvarez) for the Sat Review. Also plan to do a piece on the ballet for Lincoln Kirstein's

[2]Chester Himes had begun depositing his manuscripts and books with CVV for the Yale Collection.
[3]During the 1940s, CVV had established the Jerome Bowers Peterson Memorial Collection of Photographs of Celebrated Negroes at Wadleigh High School for Girls in Harlem; when the school closed, he offered the collection to the University of New Mexico where Lueders was teaching.
[4]CVV to Bruce Kellner, 23 October 1954, re Brubeck: "I prefer [. . .] those long Rossini-like monotonous crescendos that stretch out endlessly like the moon of my delight in the orient."

Center Magazine and of course I am busy with photographs, collections, etc.     My very warmest greetings to you and yours, Carlo

TO ROY WILKINS                                     146 Central Park West
28 June 1955                                       New York City

Dear Mr Wilkins, I have had a wonderful 75th birthday, but your letter, representing the NAACP, was the climax.[5] Thank you!     sincerely, Carl Van Vechten

TO WALLACE STEVENS                                 146 Central Park West
30 June 1955                                       New York City

Dear Wallace, Thank you for your very kind letter. I had a ball, but you know what it's like because you had one last year. As you perhaps know, I devote myself pretty completely to photography nowadays and would like very much to photograph you, if you would be so good as to let me know IN ADVANCE some time when you will be in New York and what hours you might have free.[6]     sincerely, Carlo

TO KAREN BLIXEN                                    146 Central Park West
17 September 1955                                  New York City

Chère Madame, It is with not a little emotion that I write to you, and you will please believe it is an unusual experience to write to a stranger. But you are no longer a stranger. You have, indeed, become a part of me. Why I have waited so long to read you, I'll never know, but from the very first words in Out of Africa, I understood that I had found an important friend & ally.[7] Never before have I been made to feel so deeply the personal power of the written word. Until the book was finished I was like one possessed. So it was an ultimate pleasure to meet Bent Mohn & ply him with questions.[8] I want to Know everything about you. Curiously, that is unnecessary,

---

[5]CVV to Bruce Kellner, 5 April 1955: "Fisk is giving me a doctorate! [. . .] I dare say all this extra activity will bring on some fatal disease, if it is only exhaustion." 18 May 1955: "I do hope people will not begin to hail me as Doc, but I expect the worst." 29 May 1955: "Tomorrow I become by magic an LLD—without writing a thesis." CVV to Edward Lueders, 30 May 1955: "Dear Doctor Lueders, *Dr*. Van Vechten speaking!"
[6]CVV never photographed Wallace Stevens.
[7]CVV to George George, 9 September 1955: "I have never enjoyed anything more than Out of Africa & immediately plunged into Seven Gothic Tales. I have you to thank for these. I'll never get over it & I am already very different!" CVV to Bruce Kellner, 20 September 1955: "I am MAD about them and have written a love letter to the Baroness Blixen."
[8]Bent Mohn, a literary critic for the Danish publication *Politikan*, then visiting in America.

Karen Blixen (Isak Dinesen), 1959

Ned Rorem, 1956

Sandy Campbell and Donald Windham, 19

too, after reading your books. They speak for the author & leave very little unsaid. Is it clear to you that you have created by your will and your art a tremendous admirer on this Western Shore? May I hope to hear from you? May I lay twelve dozen yellow roses at your feet? with much love, Carlo Van Vechten

pour Madame la Baronne Blixen!

TO ALICE B. TOKLAS                    146 Central Park West
16 November 1955                      New York City

Dearest Mama Woojums, Please do not be unhappy. I wouldn't do anything to make you unhappy for the world. Forget all about Knoedler's and coming to New York.[9] When Henry McBride first broached the matter to me we were both excited and enchanted that you would come over (could is a better word) and that the pictures could be shown to New Yorkers. Everybody among Gertrude's and your friends that I have approached has felt the same way. You, quite obviously, are not enthusiastic about the idea, and, as you are not, let us forget about it. No one will urge you to do anything you don't want to do.

I enclose a request from London which is YOUR province.[1] So will you please answer this? It was forwarded me by the American publishers of Last Operas and Plays.

Lots of love to our blessed Mama Woojums from Fania and

but we are very disappointed we won't see you here. [unsigned carbon copy]

[9]CVV to Bruce Kellner, 31 October 1955: "Knoedler's, the leading art gallery (commercial) in NYC telephoned me today that they want to give a show for Gertrude's pictures (mainly Picassos). They will borrow even the ones she sold. All expenses of packing, shipping and insurance both ways will be paid and Alice's plane fare will be paid both ways so that she may visit the show. I have written Alice and await her reply with baited breath." 10 November 1955: "Alice is probably coming to New York and the show will probably be given, but nothing is settled YET, altho she has nodded approval. [. . .] Alice of course will have several galas of her OWN and as I wrote you there will be parades and fireworks and general rejoicing." 17 November 1955: "Dear Bruce, Miss Toklas no longer tentatively on her way. Something is the matter—perhaps she is too old to undertake so tiring a visit. Perhaps she has no further inclination to shake hands with the public. Anyway her responses have become the reverse of enthusiastic and I have written her to concern herself no longer with the project. Perhaps this will make her determined to come. I HOPE SO."

[1]Alice Toklas handled requests from Europe concerning Gertrude Stein's writings.

## TO LILLIAN GISH
### 30 January 1956

146 Central Park West
New York City

Dear Lillian, Fania read your interesting contribution to The Spiritual Woman[2] some time ago and doubtless wrote you of her enthusiasm, but I delayed as I have been too swamped in work these last weeks for a man of my venerable years. Last night, however, I read what you had to say with pleasure, and profit. Every word glitters with wisdom and if you can strike subsidies out of hard-hearted senators by your efforts, you will have done something of historical significance. Yet it is obvious that Art should be subsidized, a fact that is readily recognized when our government sends cultural ambassadors abroad.

I am writing this on the day that Mencken died and of course all of us must think of this. However, what a BLESSING the manner of his death![3]

We send our best love to you, Carlo

## TO CHESTER HIMES
### 4 February 1956

146 Central Park West
New York City

Dear Chester, I've read The Primitive with great excitement and have sent copies around with great success where I though they would do the most good. [. . .] In some ways it is an improvement, this abridged edition, because it moves so fast that you can't lay the book down (in other words the lays prevent you from laying) but I missed some scenes and characters from the original, missed them very much indeed. [. . .] Your new book about Harlem socialites sounds most promising and I burn to see it finished and published. You should have known A'Lelia Walker. Nothing in this age is quite as good as THAT. Her satellites were shocked and offended by her appearance in Nigger Heaven, but she was nicer to me after that, even than before. I miss her. She always treated me to champagne when we had locked ourselves in her boudoir and locked the toadies and sycophants out with a bottle of beer apiece. What a woman! What you write about people who understand that Negroes are human is very marvellously put and thanks for the compliment to me. You see, like everybody else who goes into this new world, at first I had a Messiannic complex (My God, how DO you spell it). But one day I came home shouting, "I HATE a Negro! I HATE a Negro!" It was my salvation and since then I've had no trouble at all. From that point on I understood that they were like everybody

---

[2]*The Spiritual Woman*, 1955, by Marion Turner Sheehan.
[3]Felled by a debilitating stroke in 1948, H. L. Mencken was unable to read or write during the last eight years he lived, but he died quietly in his sleep.

258

else, that is they were thieves and cut-throats, generous and pious, witty and wise, dumb and foolish, etc., etc. But you put all this very nicely. How understanding you are! Most Negroes wouldn't understand this about their own people, let alone US. Write me when you have time. [. . .] Chitlings to you, pig's knuckles and sauerkraut, and hominy grits, I am in favor of seceding from the SOUTH.     Hands across the seas, Carlo

## TO WITTER BYNNER
1 March 1956

146 Central Park West
New York City

Dear Hal, [. . .] I must say I always love your verse, and so does Fania. You have the happy faculty of transforming light verse into something rich and strange, thoughtful and even tragic on occasion. You wear cap and bells with a purple tinge: the cap is made of ermine and the bells are indeed CHIMES. You are the king of the madcap troubadours and the Archbishop of topical verse. I award you an Oscar, an orchid, and a diploma. Seriously, you have seldom done anything better.[4] [. . .]

Fania, after a very difficult fall, is at last coming out of her two serious operations in July–August. I don't believe she has ever been better. I am pretty much the same, entangled somewhat in my collections to institutions but I propose presently to emerge from these entanglements before I expire and make my assumption or descent into the Inferno. [. . .]     Love to you both:[5] I send you a cracker and a parrot to bite on it!   Carlo

## TO PETER DAVID MARCHANT
25 April 1956

146 Central Park West
New York City

Dear Peter, Your letters are full of honey, milk, and meat and deserve swift replies. [. . .] You ask me if I have ever approached the Great Garbo to be photographed. The answer is NO. I know her and have even dined at Aileen Pringle's in Santa Monica with Garbo and Jack Gilbert,[6] whom I knew better. But perhaps she has been photographed enough. I find I can add nothing to the others. I'd like to photograph her when she is considerably older to find if anything remained of the celebrated features. She was never one of my enthusiasms, my taste running more to wilder music and stronger wine. Certainly I do want to photograph you and ALWAYS love to be photographed myself in almost any medium at almost any time. Also I

---

[4]Bynner had sent CVV his most recent collection, *Book of Lyrics,* 1955.
[5]Robert Hunt, Bynner's companion.
[6]John Gilbert, silent film actor, frequently costarred with Greta Garbo.

consistently like the results, if they faintly resemble me, no matter how many puffs under the eyes. When I say "resemble me" I hasten to add "or my character." Probably I originally embarked on photography so that I might photograph myself. Incidently you should try Kodak Tri-X (black and white film), a new film which astonishingly requires a minimum of light. The results are amazing and really unexpected. You seem to be mistaken about my photographs of Nesbitt.[7] They were taken quite recently when she played in Gigi. You also seem mistaken about the photograph of F. Scott Fitzgerald, NOT taken "in the cruel movie sunshine" but in front of the Hotel Algonquin and in no sunshine at all! [. . .]

And I offer you 17 dachshunds (housebroken), 4 bowls of Indian rubies, and a plate of garlic icecream,     Carlo

TO CHESTER HIMES                          146 Central Park West
[April 1956]                              New York City

Dear Chester, [. . .] In your latest letter you write, true, without much enthusiasm, that you have started a new book. I do not believe I ever started a book with enthusiasm. The enthusiasm comes when the characters assume shape or begin to assume shape and you actually KNOW what you are writing about. Earle Hyman, cullud, has made a sensation in a piece called Mr Johnson.[8] He has been hailed as the actor of the century (white or Negro). But in the audiences who go to see him one seldom sees a Negro face and I am forced to the conclusion that there is seldom one of our people with enough enthusiasm for the race to show it openly. Most of the time I consider this unimportant and nobody's business, but at the moment with the South howling the Negro down and the Supreme Court raising the Negro high, it is politically of VAST importance to seize on every high spot. It is typical perhaps. I do not think it is the Negro who has appreciated YOU (Of course, I am the exception) or danced in the street in your honor. Perhaps the Negro cannot bear to see himself treated seriously in fiction or on the stage. [. . .] Let me know how you are getting on with your book and in general. I have no doubt but that you are intended for fame and fortune!*     with fond regards, Carlo
*Even if you weren't I'll insist until my dying day that Lonely Crusade is a great book.

---

[7]Cathleen Nesbitt, English actress.
[8]Mr. Johnson, 1955, by Norma Rosten, based on Joyce Cary's novel.

146 Central Park West
New York City

Dear Peter, I can't tell you how much I enjoy your letters. I don't seem to find time to write many letters recently but I cannot resist writing *you!* Your letters are endlessly attractive, full of questions and answers, and allusions and CRACKS* and really devilishly fine letters. Another one please. [. . .] Don't worry about a typewriter. Your letters are clear as crystal (at least in their APPEARANCE: the square ROOTS are frequently intriguingly ambiguous). The Whirlpool of Life is occasionally better than Greed and [Erich von] Stroheim said if he had seen it before he had done Greed he would have engaged FM for Trina.[9] Holbrook Blinn played McTeague. I am aghast by the way these pictures are rusting in studio vaults somewhere. I hope Burt Lancaster or Gregory Peck won't be engaged for the next one, but I'm certain Lana Turner[1] will be engaged for Trina. There is no argument re Gershwin's songs. They are his masterpieces. Still I am fond of An American in Paris and the Concerto in F. I have seen Porgy and Bess, man and boy, many more than seven times, but not through enjoying it, altho I delighted in some of the performers. I don't like the recent version at all, too much restoring.† (The original cuts were made by George and Alec Smallens.) [. . .] You are correct about Virgil [Thomson]. He has ALWAYS had everything pigeonholed whether it be his opinion of marrons déguisés or of Toscanini. He never leaves you for an instant in doubt.‡ Personally, I LOVE The Mother of Us All (both words and music). [. . . Aaron] Copland is most loveable. He is an old friend and the moment he sees me he begins to giggle and never recovers. One time or another I must have told him something funny. Anyway I haven't needed to repeat this. [. . .] I want to tell you that your most mystical theory is that I stem from [William] Congreve. This is absolutely correct. I had an English teacher at the University of Chicago who dwelt in and out of season§ and I was steeped in the plays while still a baby. My copies are dated around that era. But Incognita which you mention so frequently in the thesis,[2] I was not familiar with and it was a sweet gesture to present it to me. [. . .]

[9]Frank Norris's novel, *McTeague,* 1899 was filmed in 1915 with Fania Marinoff and remade ten years later with Zasu Pitts in her role.
[1]Lancaster, Peck, and Turner, were popular film stars of the period.
[2]"Carl Van Vechten: Novelist and Critic," Peter David Marchant's M.A. thesis at Columbia University, tracing CVV's development from Restoration comedy.

Buttered radishes, Indian saris, and 15 (presumably housebroken) Siamese pussies from your scatological and devoted friend     Carlo

*and *personal* opinions to FM.

†I don't care for the scenery either.

‡about his opinion of anything!

§on Congreve


TO PETER DAVID MARCHANT          146 Central Park West
25 June 1956                     New York City

Dear Master (what is your title, anyhow) Marchant, [. . .] I always enjoy your letters, probably more than any others I receive. Presently they will be in my collection in the NY Public Library. Your letters are not as spontaneous as you in person, but they are MORE prepared and certainly not lacking completely in spontaneity. They are, in their field, works of art.

I am glad the medics have uncursed you. It was NOT Sembrich as Sieglinde, but Fremstad. At the moment I do not recall her appearance (I speak of Sembrich) in Wagner, tho she must have sung the Bird in Siegfried, at least in the bathtub. Tell your mother I can easily recall the day when Gladys Cooper's[3] photograph was in Every window on Bond Street, but certainly elsewhere as well. Had I known you wished to see Carmen ([Emma] Calvé) I could have shown it to you. That one is framed and Signed and on the wall. But I was really quite shocked to hear you scorn Il Barbiere [*of Seville*]. That is why you got dubbed a snob. This opera is quite honi soi qui mal y pense with me, almost my eldest son. I have never heard it referred to as much under Mozart and never read a word in its dispraise. So you sounded to my softened ears like a naughty school boy who wrote bad words on a fence. Otherwise our attitude towards music is entirely different. I know what I don't like: Elgar, for instance, but I never would object to others liking it or even playing it in my presence. I adore much music that is considered cheap by others besides you, but I have my pigeon-holes and do not compare such music with that of a higher genre. It is hard to explain all this, but if I don't succeed, ply me with questions. You are so enthusiastic about music you DO like that it shocks me to have you dislike so firmly music to which I am addicted for one reason or another. That is why I called you snobbish. Probably intolerant would be more what I meant. Next time we play the gramophone (I can be as English as your papa) I'll let you select the scores. [. . .]     Hands across the East River, Carlo


[3]Gladys Cooper, English actress appearing on Broadway in Enid Bagnold's *The Chalk Garden.*

146 Central Park West
New York City

Dearest Miss Peterson, Beautiful. Fania is in the country and I am taking a much needed rest after a miscarriage or a sunburst, or a bad housemaid's knee or something. Anyway while the heat was playing havoc (90% and as humid as a bowl of soup) I keeled over and developed a splitting head ache. The doctor said nothing organic. Prescribed COMPLETE REST, put me to bed (I slept 14 hours without waking) and told FM that I was working too hard in the heat at my age. The next day I slept 9 hours and since then I have been taking it EASY. However, there's still so much work to do that I shudder. Perhaps I'd better burn everything up and forget it. My birthday party was earlier than this and was sensational. First a small dinner at the Capri (Mildred was working in the country and couldn't come in). Beverly Sills (a new ofay singer and a fine one, very handsome with the most beautiful natural RED hair), Bruce Kellner, Saul [Mauriber], Marinoff and Nora [Holt] (of course you would have been present had you been in town). Then we came back to the house where we were greeted by Reg[ina] Wallace, Josephine Premice,[4] Bill Warfield, my new biographer Peter Marchant, Carmen de Lavallade,[5] Alvin Ailey,[6] CARL WHITE,[7] Alvin Colt. Only champagne was served, with supper at midnight. The guests began to straggle home at 2.30. It was MARVELLOUS. Carl has a scholarship to go to Stuttgart. What a boy! Also the show opened in Albuquerque. The head of the gallery there is a painter and probably always careless about sending material, but I have photographs of the show and gallery and both are ducks. Further the head of the gallery Raymond Johnson is beginning to get excited and enthusiastic and I am pretty sure it's going to be all right. There isn't very much more to tell you at the moment, but doubtless there will be later.[8] I suppose you travellers know all about Althea Gibson,[9] daughter of a Harlem mechanic. It occurs to me that one of the reasons Southerners devote themselves to keeping Negroes out of their social and educational midst is for fear they will EXCEL. Not an unjustifiable fear. That is why they talk so much about the race "keeping its place." An

---

[4]Josephine Premice, black American singer.
[5]Carmen deLavallade, black American dancer.
[6]Alvin Ailey, black American dancer and subsequently choreographer.
[7]Carl White, black American tenor, named for CVV, Walter White's son.
[8]An exhibition of the Jerome Bowers Peterson Memorial Collection of Photographs by Carl Van Vechten of Celebrated Negroes, at the University of New Mexico.
[9]Althea Gibson, black American tennis champion.

unreconstructed Northerner was here last week. He won't even shake hands with a cracker or hold converse with him. So I hope you are having a ripping time.     Love, Carlo

## TO ALFRED A. KNOPF
30 October 1956

146 Central Park West<br>New York City

Dear Alfred, I think it would be impossible for any one, save in some secret way, to set down his share of the story, to write a frank O'Neill story. Undoubtedly Carlotta [Monterey O'Neill] will have her version prepared and she has already rewritten her diary. Probably anything unfavorable to Gene in her possession has been destroyed. Princeton, Yale, and the Museum of the City of New York share his manuscripts. They have already been informed that if they give out anything she doesn't desire given out she will withdraw the mss. She will INSIST on reading any biography. [. . .] Moreover, I think she will be able to protect his reputation even after she is dead, for a generation or two. Then, everybody who knew him will be dead. The only way to preserve the unadulterated story is to get affadavits from numberless people, including wives and children of Gene (Lawrence Langner has already written his), organize and publish these in some far distant future, without risk of getting sued.* Please do NOT let any one see this letter and do not quote from it. It is for your private eyes, but better keep it in some safe place because this subject will come up many times. Every publisher in America will be after the story.     With love, Carlo
*Of course, this would be an expensive procedure, because most of the witnesses would require a ghost writer.
P.S. Is he worth all this trouble?

## TO JAMES PURDY
18 November 1956

146 Central Park West<br>New York City

Dear Jaime: Voltaire remarks so truly: Le Superflus est une chose necessaire, and my motto is A little too much is just enough for me!

63:Dream Palace is NOW My Dream Palace.[1] The pranks of Fenton Riddleway, the exasperating behaviour of the greatwoman, the huddled belligerency of Claire, the unholy purposes of Parkhurst, all fascinate and bewilder and repel me. Somehow I felt as tho I were watching sexuality

---

[1]63: Dream Palace, 1956, privately printed. CVV was largely responsible for publicizing James Purdy's work through this book and Don't Call Me By My Right Name, 1956, also privately printed, by sending out several copies to friends.

264

on TV or watching orchestral instruments enjoying orgasms with each other. I pray that your books will never end and then they do, quite unexpectedly with the word "motherfucker." [. . .] I want to send some of your wet-dream palaces around and I find your publisher ridiculously slow in shipping. We must think of a better plan. You should be very happy and perhaps a very little mad. Wave your arms, Jaime, wave your arms.

> Said a morbid and dissolute youth
> I think Beauty is greater than Truth,
> But by Beauty I mean
> The obscure, the obscene,
> The diseased, the decayed, the uncouth.

yours in threnody and wild roses, Carlo

## TO JAMES PURDY
25 November 1956

146 Central Park West
New York City

Dear Jaime, [. . .] Think of your receiving letters telling you to stop! You must be as famous as Maria Callas,[2] who receives decaying vegetables and Japanese babies with leprosy and even arthritis! . . .

Last night I saw the very tall, very naked Geoffrey Holder, as black as licorice, white plumes gathered on his already high head to make him look taller and blacker gaily disport himself on the Metropolitan Opera Stage [in *Aida*], a nude white girl at his doubtful mercy. The stockholders and abonées were ravished, raped, and left to perish in their boiling emotions, like baby squid devoid of their poisonous shoe polish. What a military spectacle! Tonight I watch Geoffrey again at the YMHA in a program of bountiful and beautiful obscenities. Would you were with me! What progress and manly lust we cultivate in North America. [. . .]

I wring your hand and lift my slight and graceful ankle as tribute to you and your works!

Shall we tell you that is a cold Sunday afternoon with high wind? I rather think we shall.

November 25 (for three days this year: on the third we eat Goo-Goo![3])

[unsigned]

---

[2]Maria Callas, controversial operatic soprano. See CVV to Peter David Marchant, December 1956.
[3]Goo-Goo, a Chinese dish CVV had recently discovered in a restaurant.

TO PETER DAVID MARCHANT        146 Central Park West
[December 1956]                  New York City

Dearest David, I was much touched to receive a letter from YOU at Christmas time, and I thank you heartily and hope you feel better at New Year's.

Your mention of cigarette pictures reminded me I had thousands in the 1890s and nothing disturbs me more than that they have all disappeared. Some of them were pasted in my theatre scrapbooks, now in the drama department of the NY Public Library, most of them I must have given away. One of them I remember with pleasure, must have been left in a country house we once owned in Northern Michigan. When we sold it, we left everything intact in the house as it was too far from home to bother clearing out.

As I remember it, I seem to have been giving away things and changing my collecting habits constantly. What became of my birds' eggs or my stamps, I couldn't tell you. There remains not a vestige of these.

I do not believe the Sandor Szabo on television was the same one I photographed. Both Sandor and Szabo are as common in Hungary as Kate Smith would be here. The Szabo I photographed was a wrestler, but the picture was taken 25 years ago and he is probably teaching in some gymnasium now, or maybe he has become a cop.

Miss [Beverly] Sills is not only "engaged" but married and living in Cleveland. She has not, however, deserted the stage. Just now she would have been superb in Candide. Mattiwilda [Dobbs] was glorious. A warm and brilliant coloratura and the best Gilda in my experience and I have heard [Nellie] Melba, [Emma] Eames, and Bessie Abott, to say nothing about the current [Hilde] Gueden who always leaves me as cold as a sardine in the icebox. There is a rumor Mattiwilda returns to do the Queen of the Night. Anyway we hear her Jan 7 as Zerbinetta. Eileen Farrell sings Ariadne. The mass hypnotism that created the [Maria] Callas furore is disturbing. I do not think, speaking honestly, that Maria la Divina is as good as Elvis Presley.[4] In any case she is no better. She is dull as dish water with no temperament. Her Norma was exactly like her Lucia. Both were nothing. Her voice is actually unpleasant. She sings without excitement or even emphasis. Her acting is worse than her singing. I shall not attend further performances. I heard Norma twice to be sure, and would not have heard

[4]CVV to Bruce Kellner, 22 September 1956: "I heard him with amazement and I am convinced that his appeal is purely (or impurely) sexual. And as he does not appeal to me on that basis, I have discarded him forever, unless he comes around with his hand-organ to sing at my door."

Lucia if we had not been taken. She is a complete bust.[5] If you want to know anything else, Carlo can give you a true picture.

Love to you in which Fania joins me and don't try to write.[6] [. . .]
Carlo

TO DOROTHY PETERSON  146 Central Park West
23 February [1957]  New York City

By misrepresentation Mrs. [Martin] Benson [Rita Romilly] did get us to go to the Dances at the Museum of Modern Art. She had told me they were Asian dances of different countries. She did not mention Gurdjieff, that old fake. I had seen something of that kind in NYC with Muriel [Draper] and when the first one began I knew what I was in for. So I sat patiently and wide awake until they were over, but when Rita demanded how I liked them, I said, "not at all: I was frankly bored. When I see Western dancing," I went on, "I prefer to see something arranged by Balanchine. These dances were not for an audience. They were intended to improve co-ordination in the dancers themselves." I had previously asked Rita where these dances were made and when she told me Paris, I was convinced that this was a semi-professional show troupe to show the public what the old man could do. Then I asked Rita if she could do these dances. She replied enigmatically, "Some of them a long time ago." Coordination is NOT Miss Romilly's strongest talent. It was a very dull evening and she will not easily rope me in again. [. . .] Incidently the Danses Sacrées were presented as Sacred Dances. There was no applause and the audience sat as quietly as at a Christian Science Church.

I hope you are feeling better. I send you our love, Carlo

---

[5]CVV to an acquaintance, educator Richard Rutledge, 8 February 1959: "Even when she sings well I do not like the quality of her tones. Her top is too edgy to give me any pleasure. [. . .] Callas seems to include among her admirers people with her own bad taste. Fancy a young man shouting Bravo Callas, before [Leonie] Ryzanek had sung a note. At first it would appear that Callas would be Verdi's ideal for Lady Macbeth as he said he wanted a lady with 'a harsh voice who produced edgy tones.' But Ryzanek sang the music so beautifully that one forgot what Verdi pretended he craved." CVV to Bruce Kellner, 11 January 1959: "Maria Callas is a disagreeable bad-singing slut, and I have no intention of ever taking the trouble to hear her again."

[6]Peter David Marchant was growing steadily weaker from an incurable illness of which he died two months later. CVV to Philip Marchant, 2 February 1957: "I learned of your brother's death this morning with very mixed feelings, indeed. It was certainly a great loss to me personally and to the world. His mind was brilliant and, had he lived in full strength, his future writings would have been a very great gift, indeed. His thesis about me showed very great promise and indubitably he was destined to be a most important writer."

## TO SANDY CAMPBELL
4 April 1957

146 Central Park West
New York City

Dear Sandy, I LOVED Orpheus [*Descending*] more than a little. I don't believe any one else has seen what I see in it, but I'm sure I'M right even if Tennessee W[illiams] does not agree with me. In the first place, it is a play about what happens to a man and this fact should be emphasized by STARRING only a man. In the second place it is a play about the SOUTH and what happens to a good man in the really horrible south. (For instance, it is a man who is practically seduced by silly women, and the women are so real that they stink with actuality: I know them all.) They are the kind who paw ignorant Negroes who afterwards are lynched for seductions the women commit. In fact a good deal of the play is intended to show you what happens to good humored, innocent Negroes who happen to be beautiful. The sheriff is certainly not in love with his wife but his sacred manhood resents another man, particularly a handsome one, having anything to do with her. Of course Val hasn't, but she tries unsuccessfully to have something to do with him. So Orpheus descends into this Southern Hell, whereas the original tamed the denizens of that place and even the savage beasts by playing his lyre. I think the meaning of the play is somewhat distorted by Miss [Maureen] Stapleton's performance. She does not seem to be physically attractive enough to play the part and certainly she plays it with little inner conviction. In the end the author leaves us with the object of his play: the unfortunate Negro and with one of his seducers. You may take it or leave it. The play moved me very much and I think it did the audience too, judging by the applause in the end. Lois Smith and Cliff Robertson killed me with their performances.     My love to you both, Carlo

## TO JAMES PURDY
13 April 1957

146 Central Park West
New York City

Dearest Jaime, [. . .] We give millions to Arabs so they can eat cockroaches again, but nothing to our teachers and our postmen, so that they can LEARN to eat cockroaches. My opinion of Mr [Dwight D.] Eisenhower is very low indeed. In fact only a handful of presidents have held my respect. [. . .] Fortunately we don't HAVE to understand the Virginians, who should be spayed and shot at birth to prevent future contretemps. How any people can consider the color of the skin a matter of superiority is certainly cracked as you submit. [. . .] Now the papers are arguing about whether moslems will accept communism! I really shudder at the mentality of the governing and publicity classes. [. . .]    My love (it is still warm here), Carlo

Your bulletin about Testicles not making the man is a classic,[7] but I think they probably do make such men as inhabit this planet, at least for the most part. [. . .]

TO PRENTISS TAYLOR                     146 Central Park West
29 May 1957                            New York City

Dear Mr Prentiss, Certainly, you NEVER spoke of your household arrangements until recently, but your household arrangements are certainly your own business and I do not begrudge you your confidences in this respect. Quite the contrary. Enlist a harem and you do not lose MY friendship or even love. YOUR time is YOUR time as Rudy Vallee does NOT sing.[8]

My only objection to your review of Miss Sprigge's quite awful book[9] is that you mention Noël Coward as her photographer instead of ME. I regard this simply in the light of bad taste! Miss Toklas would find more to object to. She loathes La Sprigge and will not even talk of the book. [. . .] I will not tell her (Alice) that you write: "it contains some material that has not been available before."

Fania, of whom you write, is on a cruise in European and African ports and I, enfin, have taken the occasion to visit the deep South. Aside from the excessive heat, this was a wise move. I found Nashville as of yore, hated Atlanta, and am mad for New Orleans, Charleston, and particularly Natchez, all new to me. [. . .] I loathed the hotels (in fact motels everywhere are far superior to hotels and in Natchez I discovered such a charmer of a motel that I could easily decide to live there.) Naturally I wasn't there very much, but I did see every one of the important houses from top to bottom and met EVERY châtelaine. Incidently, if you are still ignorant, as I was, Natchez rhymes with matches or snatches. New Orleans owned me for a week, I ate everywhere, drank everywhere, and loved everything. [. . .][1]

[7]James Purdy's letters frequently took the form of advertising spoofs.
[8]Rudy Vallee, the popular singer from the 1920s, endlessly sang a song entitled "My Time Is Your Time."
[9]*Gertrude Stein: Her Life and Work,* 1957, by Elizabeth Sprigge.
[1]CVV to Chester Himes, 13 July 1957: "In New Orleans I ran into an old friend from Harlem, Lizzie Miles, an old time blues singer whom I hadn't seen since 1925 or thereabouts. We embraced on one of the principal streets and she took me to a wonderful band session. Otherwise I ate well there, enjoyed the picturesque streets and drank Ramos gin fizzes. [. . .] Atlanta I loathed, but I visited Atlanta University and saw the Countee Cullen Collection. Charleston was a delight. Catfish Row is now a fashionable apartment house and it is flanked by Porgy and Bess Shops."

Langston [Hughes]'s play [*Simply Heavenly*] got wonderful reviews, but I am only seeing it next week. Langston invited me to the opening but I left New York the day before and I have just returned.

I have managed to involve myself in enough work to take up my time till I visit my heavenly home (that is why you see me so seldom). [. . .] In a minute I will be 77 but you can see that I still have a sharp tongue and a warm heart. Everything else is all right too and in frequent use!

My love to you, and have a good time!     Carlo

Have I introduced you to James Purdy, the author of the minute? [. . .]

TO JAMES PURDY                          146 Central Park West
6 July 1957                             New York City

Dearest Jaime, Naturally I cried a good deal after reading Dame Edith[2] on 63 Dream Palace! What a woman! What a review! It is only one in a thousand years that any writer is blessed with such a Godmother, and please do not forget that you have a saintly Godfather too! How lucky you are, kid. Pee your pants, no longer! Spread your wings and fly into all the desolate corners of the world and tell the millions how happy (or unhappy) you are. In other words, create and write and convince the world of your greatness! [. . .]

I never eat tripe anywhere. I loathe it. I also loathe chitlings and possum and venison and pineapples and napoleons and eclairs, but I LOVE mouse cheese and eat beads of garlic cheerfully and even lovingly.

You are right about NY. Over this Fourth weekend there isn't a soul in town and taxis wander the streets without customers. NY is so free of people that some actually get LONELY. You bet I don't. I plan to spend today entirely alone, doing odd jobs. Nothing pleases me MORE.

You MUST see The Pride and the Passion.[3]

Dear Woojums, my compliments and my love,     Carlo

---

[2] Dame Edith Sitwell, the English poet, had become James Purdy's leading defender, after CVV. CVV to James Purdy, 14 February 1957, when he was about to meet her: "Do not be afraid of Dame Edith except in appearance. She is nine ft tall and quite broad and looks like the leaning tower of Pisa if it were straight, but she is usually affable and ALWAYS will be with you."

[3] *The Pride and the Passion*, 1957, an action movie that CVV admired because of Sophia Loren's appearance in it.

TO JAMES PURDY                          [146 Central Park West
11 July [1957]                          New York City]

Dearest Jaime, [. . .] Obscenity is variable according to the personality. Perhaps the most obscene piece of music I know is also the most beautiful: The Prelude to Tristan und Isolde which accurately describes a FUCK. To me I cannot see how an audience can sit through it without a sexual thrill or at least a cockstand, but from the bland expressions on people's faces I think many of them take it as calmly as the Overture to William Tell. But to judge that 63 Dream Palace is obscene is to believe Water Cress is obscene because it has the same initials as Water Closet. [. . .]

As you so sensibly submit [Dwight] Eisenhower is a grinner. I do not recall a picture of Lincoln grinning altho he found himself in much the same situation that Eisenhower does. He did something about it, but Eisenhower grins through it. [. . .]     Love, indeed, Carlo


TO LANGSTON HUGHES                      146 Central Park West
19 November 1957                        New York City

Dear Langston, [. . .] I am up to my neck working on my collections, photographs, and two prefaces, but expect to emerge in time to go to heaven.

with the warmest possible greetings (I wish to GOD you would stop signing yourself "sincerely." One is sincere with the butcher. It is taken for granted one is sincere with one's friends. Certainly I get letters from no one else in the world with such a conventional signing off.)     Carlo


TO DORIS JULIAN                         146 Central Park West
24 February 1958                        New York City

Dear Princess Doris, I wore the stigmata of Saint Dorisita to the opera last night and offered Leontyne Price quite a competition! [. . .] Leontyne was too divine last night. Dressed in pale green with a pink rose on her breast she looked like a brown angel. Do not forget me please.     love, Carlo


TO FANIA MARINOFF                       146 Central Park West
29 January 1959                         New York City

Dearest Baby, It is raining this AM, I feel miserable, I am hovering on a cold and I must go to the dentist at 10.30, but I am happy that I heard from you at last and that so far you are happy.[4] [. . .]

---

[4]Fania Marinoff was off on another cruise to Mediterranean ports, Greece, Turkey, and Israel.

But now I may have to have my broken tooth pulled. It will be a bad job digging out the roots. I certainly won't have it done today as Armina [Marshall] called on Wednesday to say that two seats had just been returned on the center aisle first row.[5] Naturally she is selling them. I have heard nothing from the Scotts. BUT the Baroness [Karen Blixen] who was here last night to be photographed reported that Ruth whom she knew in Denmark and London had telegraphed her yesterday she had two seats for her. For tonight. The dinner was good: Oysters, Capon, French peas, new potatoes and strawberry bavarian cream was excellent. Nobody here but the Baroness's secretary [Clara Svendsen] and Saul [Mauriber]. The Baroness was in a fine form and delightful altho she had posed for Cecil Beaton[6] in the afternoon. She permitted endless pictures and left only at 10.30. She was excited to be photographed in color, an experience she never had before. She is having a wonderful time and is mad for New York. I think she will be here when you get back. She inquired all about you and saw your room this time. She loved especially the Boule dressing table and the rose porcelain mirror. She goes to Boston in a week or two but returns to New York and expects to be here most of March. [. . .]

I have a terrific number of pictures to print, and more to do on collections than I can manage even with the time at my disposal, but I always feel more comfortable when you are here. By the way Mildred [Perkins] changed her day [. . .] so she could cook dinner and serve it last night.

with all my love,

Continue to enjoy yourself. The world seems to be cracking up and travel will be increasingly difficult.     Carlo

## TO FANIA MARINOFF
31 January [1959]

146 Central Park West
New York City

Dearest Baby, I'm afraid Requiem [*for a Nun*] is a flop save for the performance of Bertice[7] which took all the applause. It is a bad play and a dull one. There is no interest in any character except the Negro girl and so you have no feeling about what happens to Ruth [Ford]. She talks interminably in ONE KEY, that in which she berated you for giving your Boule cabinet to Eleanor Perényi.[8] Zachary [Scott] is good and so is Scott

---

[5]*Requiem for a Nun,* 1959, William Faulkner's novel-in-play-form.
[6]Cecil Beaton, English photographer and designer.
[7]Bertice Reading, black American singer playing her first professional dramatic role.
[8]Eleanor Perényi, American writer and editor, daughter of CVV's friend, novelist Grace Zaring Stone.

McKay but Bertice steals the show. I enclose the morning paper notices. PLEASE PRESERVE these carefully because they go to Yale. The Baroness [Karen Blixen] was there with Leo Lerman who actually let her sit alone for the intermissions while he strolled in the lobby. Naturally I took his place by her side. Saul [Mauriber] was with me, but he strolled the lobby too. It was a very brilliant audience. [. . .] I DID go back stage tho and Ruth said NOTHING about the buckle or the telegram. Zach thanked me for the telegram. I do not see this play running. [. . .]

I am in for a siege with my tooth and will have to go practically every day for a while.

Cole just telephoned that Eileen Herlie has read the play, heard the music and will DO the the Countess.[9]

All my love to you and continue to have a fine time. Tonight Mattiwilda [Dobbs] in Lucia [di Lammermoor] at the Opera. I am taking Don Gallup and we are dining at the Canton Village.     Carlo

## TO VIRGIL THOMSON
27 March 1959

146 Central Park West
New York City

Dear Virgil, I am a little disappointed in your biography:[1] I should have preferred a more informal approach, with occasional ribaldry. Probably Mrs Hoover was not acquainted with this side of your nature. However, your personality has its serious, even its noble, side too, and this is fully exploited in this volume full of awards and virtues, and enthusiasms. I missed your quarrel with Gertrude [Stein] and believe this inclusion would have added zest to these rather dull pages. However there is much in the Paris chapters that is excellent. Occasionally I was sure that a man would have done better by you than a woman, but John Cage[2] does even less with your extraordinarily brilliant personality. I reiterate I am disappointed and feel that this is NOT the definitive biography.     Much love from Carlo

---

[9]Coleman Dowell (later a novelist) had taken an option to transform *The Tattooed Countess* into a musical play. CVV had often been approached for permission to dramatize it, but memories of a film version in 1925, updated and nearly unrecognizable as *A Woman of the World* with Pola Negri, had made him chary. The preliminary score, however, included "seven enchanting songs, precisely in the right mood, and with lyrics that Cole Porter or W. S. Gilbert might have envied," he wrote to playwright and theater reviewer Robert Downing, 2 May 1957. English actress Eileen Herlie was only one of several prominent actresses who considered the role.
[1]*Virgil Thomson: His Life and Music,* 1959, by Kathleen O'Donnell Hoover.
[2]John Cage, American avant-garde composer.

## TO SANDY CAMPBELL
12 April 1959

146 Central Park West
New York City

Dear Sandy, It has indeed been too long since I have seen you and Don[ald Windham], but I have been caught up in the meshes of fate. That fascinating witch, the Baroness [Karen Blixen], has been partly responsible because I turn up everywhere there has been a chance to see her. She comes here for MORE photographs tomorrow. There are certain aspects I have missed. I prefer her with her hair showing and in BROWN. Also I think gloves improve her scandalously thin arms. This time I hope that Saul [Mauriber] can catch us together in a fond embrace. I did not manage that in black and white last time, but the color pictures of this sexy scene are magnificent. You must see these some time.

Is it true you are moving to Brooklyn? Everybody I know will soon live there and then I will see nobody ever because I am allergic to Brooklyn, not to Brooklyn itself which I find fascinating, but allergic to going there. And at night I am always fearful I will be raped and eaten up by children on the street like a hero out of Tennessee [Williams]. [. . .]     I love you both and send my love freely to you both, Carlo

You and Don MIGHT be interested in Lonnie Coleman's Sam, just out. It is quite a frank book. In fact it is an OPEN book.

## TO DONALD WINDHAM
2 August 1959

146 Central Park West
New York City

Dear Don, Even if you have no brother I assume that The Bathtub[3] is autobiographical to some degree, if only emotionally. There is always an au delà to your writing and I often sit and wonder about the before and after of your stories and about the emotions of your characters. It is extraordinary how youth takes offence easily and burns his bridges fast. I was intensely emotional about people until I grew up, say at about 60, and used to cut them off "without a shilling" so to speak for imagined insults and hurts. With me there was no turning back and usually when I cut somebody off it stuck. People have cut me off too. Sometimes I have not known why. Latterly I am more philosophic and don't care why. And I myself am kindlier.

I am trying, perhaps unsuccessfully, to show how your books burn into me to make me think and feel. I think you will understand what I am TRYING to say!     love, Carl the Patriarch

---

[3]"The Bath Tub," a chapter from Donald Windham's memoir *Emblems of Conduct*, 1963.

## TO FANNIE HURST
5 February 1960

146 Central Park West
New York City

Dearest Fannie, Zora [Neale Hurston]'s death has affected me profoundly. I had not heard from her in perhaps fifteen years and had no idea where she was. But I discover, as sometimes happens too late, that I loved the girl. I have learned before through other deaths that I am inclined to miss Negroes more than white people: they are so much warmer (as a rule so much more intimate without being offensively so). My heart has been broken many times as a result of these endearing qualities. [. . .] It seems a dreadful trick of fate that we shall never see her again. She was a remarkable personality and a remarkable writer. Had I known where she was or that she was poor I would of course have sent her some money, almost a blank cheque for her to fill in. Fortunately, Scribner was her last publisher, and the Times obit couldn't be more distinguished about anybody. I have asked the Yale Library to give a show of her work, etc. I am writing you, because somehow we always shared Zora, a common annoyance and a common love, something we will both remember with a great deal of pleasure.[4]

I embrace you, Carlo Patriarch

## TO ALICE B. TOKLAS
31 May 1960

146 Central Park West
New York City

Dearest Mama Woojums, [. . .] Now comes my 80th birthday and the [New York] Public Library has prepared a great surprise for me. My name is to be carved in stone letters, six inches high, on one of the four columns in the lobby of the Fifth Avenue entrance under the caption: Generous Donors to the Library. Most of the other donors are names like Rockefeller, Vanderbilt, Ford, Tilden, Lenox, and Astor, so Papa Woojums feels like a millionaire. No doubt this will enhance my credit. There will be a party after the unveiling. A record magazine is devoting the June number to me.[5] And there will be some parties, including a big Negro party. As a man of eighty I feel exactly the same as I did at 18.

I am well, and so, thank God, is Fania and we hope you are. You write you are going away but you give me no address and do not say if your

---

[4]CVV wrote to Donald Gallup the same day: "Anyone who knew her would never forget her. [. . .] She was like a breeze or a sunflower, a child of nature. I loved her."
[5]*American Record Guide,* June 1960, with articles about CVV, a reprint of one of his essays, and a large selection of his photographs of musicians.

mail will be forwarded. Anyway you will be back here one day at 5 rue Christine and will get this.

You do not tell me how you are progressing with your book[6] or what happened about E A Poe.

always love from Fania and Papa Woojums to Mama Woojums,
Carlo, Papa Woojums, Magus Patriarch, et Beau Mage, etc, etc, etc.


TO FANNIE HURST                           146 Central Park West
5 July 1960                               New York City

Dearest Fannie, I am certainly glad that I begged you to do the piece on Zora [Neale Hurston]. It is a chef d'oeuvre, a masterpiece and while I read it I cried. You make all the girl's faults seem to be her virtues. As a matter of fact, they were NOT faults, they were characteristics. There's quite a difference. What it comes down to is the fact that Zora was put together entirely differently from the rest of mankind. Her reactions were always original because they were her OWN. When she breezed into a room (she never merely entered), tossed a huge straw hat (as big as a cart wheel) on the floor and yelled "I am the queen of the Niggerati"* you knew you were in the presence of an individual of the greatest magnitude. You have certainly written the greatest obit I have ever read and perhaps cheered Zora in whatever department of oblivion she has CHOSEN to reside.

With love to you always, Carlo, the happy octogenarian

Fania says that Zora's remark about me, quoted by you, is more extraordinary than anything else that has been said of me by any other member of the race.[7]

*a term she herself invented


TO DONALD GALLUP                          146 Central Park West
29 August 1960                            New York City

Dear Three, Advance copies of Purdy's book, The Nephew, have arrived and I have read it with interest and pleasure. It is completely different from his past work in subject matter and is quite an extraordinary performance. Written, as usual, with enormous skill, it might be described as a brilliant combination of Henry James and Mrs Wiggs of the Cabbage Patch.

[6]*What Is Remembered*, 1963, Alice Toklas's memoirs.
[7]"If Carl was a people instead of a person, I could then say, these are my people." Quoted in "Zora Neale Hurston: A Personality Sketch," *Yale University Library Gazette*, July 1960.

I had a bad fall on the street yesterday, but aside from sundry bumps I seem to be all right.[8]

I am done with my Columbia Interviews, that is I have done all I can do without completely rewriting them.[9] Alfred Knopf wants me to turn this into a book, but this would be much harder work than writing a book from scratch and I do not write books any more. The material was not chosen for a book and it would have to be completely redone. [. . .]

yrs with love   Carlo

TO NED ROREM                                    146 Central Park West
7 October 1960                                  New York City

Dear old Ned, Thanks for sending me The Prostitute or The Pastry Shop.[1] I have never thought of you writing prose, but you have turned out a brilliant bit of bravura. I congratulate you. Of course it should be played by a male whore in drag* (a young Barbette)[2] but Ruth [Ford] is the next best thing and when I talked with her she seemed very enthusiastic. I said it needed music and she assured me that you had already written a score for it. I am returning the script to you with this.

Love to you, dear Ned   Carlo
Betty Allen[3] gave a great recital this week in Town Hall.
*T. C. Jones would be fabulous.[4]

TO DONALD WINDHAM                               146 Central Park West
10 December 1960                                New York City

Dear Don, [. . .] I'd love to see Forster's Maurice, but I suppose I'll have to wait a little for that, even if it is possible that I will not outlive him.[5] The Ballet season seems to be better than usual. I have seen a great many

---

[8]CVV to Bruce Kellner, 30 August 1960: "I [. . .] have a few bumps as souvenirs, but nothing interior seems to be damaged. The adjacent peasantry were surprisingly wonderful when the accident occurred and picked me up tenderly and carried me to the nearest chemist where I was bathed and annointed. I felt like Christ after the Cross!"
[9]CVV taped his memoirs for the Columbia University Oral History project; then, dismayed by his own repetitions and errors, he made extensive hand-written revisions to "A Rudimentary Narration."
[1]These plays were written by Ned Rorem in 1960 when several of his friends were writing plays. This one—a monologue—remained unproduced until 1970.
[2]Barbette, celebrated 1940s transvestite entertainer.
[3]Betty Allen, black American soprano.
[4]T. C. Jones, celebrated 1950s transvestite entertainer.
[5]E. M. Forster wrote Maurice in 1911 but it was not published until after his death, in 1971, because of its homosexual subject matter. Forster allowed some friends of his to read it in manuscript, however.

performances and they all seem to be perfection, and I am no lenient critic of the ballet. Incidently, Agnes de Mille writes me that after working for four years on it she has at last finished her History of the Ballet and after she has collected the photographs (another year's work) it will be published.* Balanchine's Liebeslieder Waltzes are pure heaven, and angels' saliva. He has a new group of young men with long legs, and they are very good, altho I've seen handsomer. I loved your Cambridge photograph: you look so mystic and wicked. AND incredibly beautiful. [. . .]

I hope you both have a happy Christmas and I have a copy of Markova's book [*Giselle and I*] for you when you return.     Love and kisses pour dearest Sandy and Don,    Carlo

The new RCA recording of Verdi's Requiem with Leontyne Price etc., is out of this world.

*Agnes has a remarkable article, "Advice to a Young Dancer," in the December Atlantic.

TO SANDY CAMPBELL                    146 Central Park West
27 December 1960                     New York City

Dear Sandy, Instead of your usual post card I received a longish letter this time, and loved it. Thanks for the encomiums. What you say of the patriarchs is just, but sometimes we have our bad moments and burst into violent rages. I dare say it all depends on our companions, tho I can be patient with fools. You and Don[ald Windham] have all the qualities you describe TOO, and probably Forster and I reflect them!

Purdy DID receive The Warm Country[6] and loved it. Purdy by nature is not generous and it is quite different for him to want letters about his own books and to be able to think that others may want letters about theirs. I am enthusiastic about Purdy, as you know, but it is very difficult for me to write him about them and I never do until the time arrives when I HAVE to say something. Probably this is because his understood demand brings about a tension. By the way it has been a long time since Don's story about a piece of furniture and I have not heard from him when another story will be published.[7] I HOPE soon. [. . .]

Love to you both, come back soon, and whenever you come back, you had better start somebody looking up an apartment or else you will be

[6]*The Warm Country,* 1960, stories by Donald Windham published in England.
[7]Chapters from Windham's memoir, *Emblems of Conduct,* 1963, had been been published irregularly in *The New Yorker.*

cheek by jowl with Christ and have to put up with a manger.      You are both loved and I stroke your handsome backs, Carlo

## TO CHESTER HIMES

146 Central Park West
30 January 1961                                          New York City

Dear Chester, [. . .] It is a great relief to know some one who can write about other things occasionally besides the Negro "problem." [. . .] Long ago (perhaps nearly 40 years) I said to James Weldon Johnson, The Negro "problem" will be settled by the artists. It is coming nearer to be every year; the writers, the painters, the actors and singers have done the most. The writers the least, because most of them "harp" on the problem. [. . .] This sort of thing MUST eventually bring about changes with those dumb creatures who constantly reiterate the Negro is inferior. [. . .]      [unsigned]

## TO SANDY CAMPBELL

146 Central Park West
26 February 1961                                          New York City

Dear Sandy, Your telling Alice [Toklas] about my honors did no harm as the Yale one occurred almost immediately after you told her and it was something! I have a medal and a citation to show for it.[8] The [National] Institute [of Arts and Letters] was announced in the papers almost the day after, which is what I had to wait for; so your indiscretion did no harm, but it might have because Alice is as indiscreet as they come and would have told everybody.

I should have made the Institute in the twenties when I was writing my novels, but the Institute was very stuffy then and altho I was proposed I was black balled many times as some of the stuffier members were shocked by my wicked books. However, everything comes to him who waits or grows old enough and if I live to be 140 I shall probably be made Mayor of New York (God forbid) or a Cardinal or a rabbi. [. . .]

The excitement of the moment is mostly Leontyne Price who has since I wrote you about her [*Il*] Trovatore made an even greater success in Aida. This week she sings [*Madame*] Butterfly. I go to all of her performances with rapture. She is sui generis and there is nobody like her. At the close of the season she leaves immediately for La Scala in Milano and maybe you will hear her there. I plan a lunch party for her and 20 guests.

Of course you may send Peter for an autograph on his forehead or his

---

[8]CVV was awarded the Yale Medal, given by the alumni association, because of his generosity to the library.

ass, as you prefer. I am amazed that you have never seen this edition or noticed it in the Bibliography which I am sure I gave you. The photographs and lithographs are so good that at least one of them was stolen at the engravers.[9] [. . .]

If you are in a film with [Simone] Signoret, tell her that I am mad for her in every department and that the French poster of Casque d'Or[1] is now the principal decor of the foyer. Don't tell Yul Brynner[2] anything, nor Jimmie Merrill[3] either for that matter: I have a distinct allergy for both of them.

You and Don[ald Windham] are so nice about my books that I would write more for you if I could, but this elderly gentleman has written about all that he wants to. [. . .]     Love to you indeed, Carlo

## TO EDWARD LUEDERS
[circa May 1961]

146 Central Park West
New York City

Dear XV, Here is the first night [*Tattooed*] Countess program. It played exactly four performances, each of which was ghastly.[4]     my compliments, Carlo

## TO CHESTER HIMES
24 June 1961

146 Central Park West
New York City

Dear Chester, Your last (latest) letter was brief and does not mention your lady companion. In fact you write: *I* am now living in a studio apartment. Has anything happened to your companion of yore. Nothing has happened to mine but a great deal has happened to me otherwise. I am now 81. Just the same I feel as I did when I was 18, except that I have more sense. Also my health is better. I never felt better and I never seem to have serious illnesses. I stopped smoking thirty years ago, but I believe I drink more than ever, mostly vodka and Jamaica rum. NO whiskey, except a very

[9]Sandy Campbell has an extensive collection of CVV's books. "Peter" refers to the 1927 boxed and illustrated edition of *Peter Whiffle;* the "Bibliography" refers to Klaus W. Jonas's *Carl Van Vechten: A Bibliography,* published by Alfred A. Knopf, 1955.
[1]*Casque d'Or,* 1947, French film. See CVV to John Breon, 23 November 1961.
[2]Yul Brynner, stage and film actor.
[3]James Merrill, American poet.
[4]CVV to Bruce Kellner, 4 May 1961: "The musical Countess may not last till Saturday. [. . .] I had no hopes for the piece in the end and my worst fears were justified. You will certainly hate this travesty, if you see it. [. . .] The house last night was entirely (save for the critics) composed of acquaintances and friends." CVV to Mark Lutz, 5 May 1961: "Well, it ended like a giant firecracker all at once with a big BANG. The audience was brilliant; the applause was staggering. The notices were the worst I ever read. Fortunately not a single word of mine was used. Also fortunately Cole[man Dowell] repeated this fact endlessly to every one. [. . .] I am not unhappy about the failure except for Cole who is deeply injured."

occasional bourbon on the rocks, and NO GIN. I love Strega, but I detest campari.

At this advanced age I have been voted into the [National] Institute of Arts and Letters. I was too daring for the sober set that governed the Institute when I was writing books, but now that Henry Miller is a member there is little reason to keep me out. [. . .] Langston Hughes was initiated with me. Dr DuBois already belongs and I can probably get you in when you write another serious book. [. . .]

Yesterday FOUR BOOKS came from you which will go presently to the James Weldon Johnson Memorial Collection of Negro Arts and Letters in the Yale University Library. You have always been fine to me and the Collection and I shall never forget it. [. . .]      Carlo

TO ALICE B. TOKLAS                          146 Central Park West
24 June 1961                                 New York City

Dearest Mama Woojums, [. . .] I loved the photograph of you, Don Windham, and Jose Quintero[5] at Tre Scaline. Was this taken on the terrasse? I never ate anywhere else there. Sandy [Campbell] is back, full of you, and full of Rome. He is looking hard for an apartment.

Fania is over her virus, has learned to use a hearing aid, sees better, and is altogether improved in health.

I do not understand what Mrs. Stein[6] can do to you re Picasso. Gertrude's will plainly says these pictures are yours until you die and that you can sell anything when you need money. I hope this is settled by now.

I have asked you several times about the Knapiks.[7] You used to write about them, but I have forgotten what you wrote and your letters are at Yale. They have opened a gallery and I went to the vernissage. I found them both charming. They have nice pictures too, small and not too important, but charming.

The [National] Institute [of Arts and Letters] is fun: I meet old friends whom I haven't seen for years and old friends like Virgil [Thomson]. The food is wonderful (they have gigot saignante which I can get nowhere in New York outside of 146 CPW) and there are no expenses: everything is paid for by the foundation. [. . .]      Lots of love to you, dearest Mama Woojums, Papa Woojums!

[5]Jose Quintero, theater director.
[6]The relatives of Allan Stein, a nephew to whom Gertrude Stein had willed her estate after Alice Toklas's death, had begun their (eventually successful) attempts to gain control of paintings in the Stein Collection.
[7]Harold and Virginia Knapik, friends of Alice Toklas.

## TO CHESTER HIMES
8 August 1961

146 Central Park West
New York City

Dear Chester, If my letters touch you, it is nothing to what your letters do to me. This last one is a masterpiece and it makes sense. You are at last, I believe, growing and beginning to understand what one has to face sooner or later, the mysteries, the agonies, and wonders of life. There is seemingly no solution for any of this. We actually have to learn how to grin and bear it. Some people prefer to be angry and scowl and to grind their teeth, but the other method is the better one and when you say you have decided to pursue pleasure you seem to have perceived this. I have always wanted you to write a book to top Lonely Crusade and I think you can, a book about loneliness and sorrow and every kind of torture that flesh is heir to. You can write about Negroes or white people, but no race problems this time, please. When you have written this book you will be able to return to America, but I think it would be a mistake to come back before. You actually have many admirers here, some people actually love you, but no one more than     Carlo

## TO WILLARD MAAS
24 October 1961

146 Central Park West
New York City

Dear Mr Maas, I'd be delighted to see you and your friend Mr [John] Schneider, but I seriously object to being dubbed a "neglected" novelist. I gave up novel writing in 1932 for various excellent reasons, one of which was that I had become more interested in photography, a field in which I have achieved notable success. Moreover my books are read in English courses in many colleges, I have recently become a member of the Institute of Arts and Letters, a young professor is writing a book about me and two well-known painters are painting my portraits. If you still believe I am neglected read [Mark] Schorer's book on Sinclair Lewis, at least the references to my name. I cannot even be called forgotten. But if you want to write about me under another heading call me (En 2,8748) and I will arrange to see you both.     sincerely, Carl Van Vechten

## TO JOHN BREON
23 November 1961

146 Central Park West
New York City

Dear John, I've had letters from you and a very sweet letter from Charlie,[8] but for the past two weeks I have been feeling rotten and while I have kept some engagements it has been at a sacrifice of sense and I finally

---

[8]Charles Cerbone, a friend of John Breon.

devoted myself to the doctor and his beneficial injections. I have one to-morrow and it is perhaps the last. Just as I was getting well SIMONE SIG-NORET came to see me, and that naturally gave me a great uplift. She is all that I had hoped for and considerably MORE. She promises to come for photographs. I am hoping this will actually happen.[9] [. . .]

It is curious that you should write about Gamiani. I have a copy of the illustrated edition. The illustrations are in color and most scabrous. The book is fascinating. Musset wrote it on a wager that he could write a dirty book without using one single dirty word. He won the wager.[1]

Bruce Kellner who is writing a book about me is about to finish it and get married (I am the best man).[2] The book is marvellous[3] and we are giving him a wedding dinner. This all occurs three days after Christmas.     Love to you both, Carlo

TO ALICE B. TOKLAS                    146 Central Park West
29 January 1962                        New York City

Poor dear Mama Woojums, A letter arrived, inscribed for you by Joe Barry, in which you said you had had another fall, but Joe, or you didn't describe the accident, and it was not until I saw Maurice Grosser and Virgil [Thomson] that I learned it was the hip. Poor dear Alice, really you do have a bad time and you expect the next time will be the head! Let's not have another fall please. While all this was going on, unbeknownst to you, Fania sent you a letter and a Japanese jacket lined with sheep's wool. We have not heard from you about this and she has worried a lot for fear you have not received it because it was taken over by two young men in Paris briefly. They report they left it with your concierge. Of course your silence is quite understandable now and she will not worry any longer. [. . .]

I was done in by the holidays: too much food, too much champagne and vodka, too many parties, theatres, ballets, what not. [. . .] As a finale I collapsed and saw a series of medicos, ending in injections and other medications. I am well now, as a result, without salt. I have missed very little in the way of good food or intoxicating liquors. So I am happy as a hermit now.

---

[9]CVV to Bruce Kellner, [November 1961]: "Simone Signoret spent the afternoon here and it was something! She is even more beautiful & thinner than her pictures. What else can the good lord give me?"

[1]*Deux Nuits d'Excès* by Alfred de Musset, published under the pseudonym Gamiani.

[2]CVV to Margaret Wilcox, 3 November 1961: "Bruce has told me the joyful news [. . .] and I am delighted. Probably you are too good for the old boy, but maybe he can make a lie out of this opinion."

[3]*Carl Van Vechten and the Irreverent Decades*, 1968; CVV is referring to a manuscript draft.

Fania, more prudent than I, is very well indeed.    much love to you, dearest Mama Woojums, from Fania and Papa Woojums

I hope you are getting on well with your book.[4] I long to read it. Donald Gallup speaks of a new cook book[5] which I don't know about. Who published this and where?

## TO WITTER BYNNER
[circa January 1962]

146 Central Park West
New York City

Dear, dear Hal, Thanks for your note. The first thing I did when I was elected to the Institute was to propose your name. The secretary called me at once to advise me that the name had already been proposed by Paul Horgan.[6] She suggested that I might shift my proposal to second Horgan's nomination. This I did with pleasure. Glenway Wescott[7] was the other seconder. You should have been in long ago. So should I but my books were too scandalous to pass muster with the old maids who ran the club then. I daresay some of your poems shocked them too. Anyway I'm happy you are in. At present I am making a series of mounted photographs for the Institute of members of the Institute. I was so certain that you would be elected that yours was one of the first I made. [. . .]

I had so much to drink over the holidays and ate so much that I was in pretty bad condition by the 10th of January. So I took a course of shots with my physician and was so bored with the stuff that I laid off drinking. This may not be forever and again it may.    Love to you and Bob, from Fania and Carlo

## TO JAMES B. MERIWETHER
24 May 1962

146 Central Park West
New York City

Dear Mr. Meriwether, I had met Mr. Faulkner several times before, once in Charlottesville, Virginia, and several times at Bennett Cerf's, his publisher. We had even talked about photographs but they never had got beyond that stage until that night in 1954. We were giving a small party and a young lady named [Jean] Stein [. . .] called up. She had sent us a letter of introduction and we had written her to call us. We asked her immediately to join us and our friends. "Would you mind," she asked, "if I brought a

---

[4]*What is Remembered*, 1963.
[5]*Aromas and Flavours*, 1958. CVV apparently forgot he had written an advertising blurb for the book when it was published.
[6]Paul Horgan, American novelist.
[7]Glenway Wescott, American novelist.

friend." "Certainly not," I replied. When the bell rang I answered it myself and was surprised to see Miss [. . .] Stein clinging to the arm of William Faulkner. During the course of the evening I asked him if he would mind being photographed. He seemed to be pleased with the idea. It was easy to do so because my assistant was there: we had everything set up (camera and lights). So we excused ourselves and went into the studio and remained there until I had taken ten or twelve pictures. I have never seen Mr. Faulkner since, but, curiously enough, I may see him this afternoon when he is scheduled to receive an award at the Installation Ceremonies of the Academy of Arts and Letters. However, it is distinctly possible he may not come. He did not attend the President's dinner for Nobel Prize Winners.

sincerely, Carl Van Vechten

## TO EDWARD LUEDERS
19 August 1962

146 Central Park West
New York City

Dear Fifteen, Mabel Luhan's death upset me a great deal, although she was in a bad way, mentally unsound, nearly blind, and unable to walk with her leg recently broken in two places. So death came as a relief to HER. I recalled the brilliant past and how much she had meant to me. Mabel was a great woman and she completed my education. She had some bad qualities and the worst one was what made her great. She adored to change people. I loved what she did for me and accepted her guidance with pleasure. The people who disliked her FOUGHT against her influence.[8] Incidently I forgot to quote Mabel on the subject of having offspring. I don't think the couplet was hers, but it often sprang from her lips.

> Sons of great men oft remind us
> We should leave no sons behind us.

As I recall, the lines were inspired by Browning's son [Pen]. [. . .]
Love to you, toujours et Immer.     Carlo

---

[8]CVV to the Honorable Dorothy Brett, 19 August 1962: "Mabel was a remarkable woman. She had some bad qualities, but, on the whole, these are what made her great. She manipulated people as if they were putty. She had an enormous influence on me, and she taught me more, probably, than anybody else had been able to. When she influenced some one, if he loved it (I did) you loved her; if you struggled against her influence and many did, you hated her. This accounts for the diversity of opinions about her."

## TO EDITH JABLONSKI
### 3 September 1962

146 Central Park West
New York City

Dear Ditta, What a lovely letter you wrote me from Bay City. When I talk of death, it doesn't mean I expect to die immediately. It is only that I want to leave my affairs in better than first class order. I have known so many people who didn't and how much trouble they caused as a consequence. That is why I have given so many things to Museums and Universities. I do not want to bother my heirs to carry out my intentions. Besides they could not decide all the things I wanted done.[9] [. . .]

I have been very busy with photography and this is to tell you and ED that Esquire is publishing a long article by me on this subject in the December issue, together with four pages of photographs.[1]

Love to you, XIV, and die Kinder, The enclosed cheque is for Carla's birthday.[2]    Carlo

## TO ALICE B. TOKLAS
### 21 September 1962

146 Central Park West
New York City

Dearest Mama Woojums, I am copying you! I have a broken wrist! I fell down, shamefully, on Madison Avenue which is unpaved at present and is as uncertain in its rocks as a pass in the mountains. However, it only hurt me for two days, AND NIGHTS. The new way is to leave it unbandaged, let the blood flow through and let NATURE do the mending. Also, I take a particular kind of heat, but NO plaster cast! And no setting! [. . .] Bruce [Kellner] came back [from Paris] with messages. He was overwhelmed by you and we were happy with the messages. Virgil [Thomson] telephoned that he sees you in November. He has changed his mind about Dr Faustus [*Lights the Lights*] and NOW wants to set it to Music, as nothing really came of Kupferman's attempt at this. The servant problem is worse. We have nobody again. But we are happy in our loneliness and disorder.

Mabel [Dodge Luhan]'s son, John Evans, went to Taos for the funeral (he would be about fifty now) and will spend the winter there with Tony,

---

[9]Three months earlier, CVV had written to Edward Lueders, 1 June 1962: "Altho I have no present intention of dying, I want my affairs to be neat when I DO die and I spend a great deal of time figuring how to make this possible. You not only can't take it with you, but it is also true that occasionally you can't think of a way to do anything with certain papers and objects, but I am doing my best."

[1]"Portraits of the Artists," *Esquire*, December 1962. CVV to Bruce Kellner, 18 July 1962: "I got my list from Esquire this morning, a rather peculiar list, but not unreasonable. They might have been happy business men's choices."

[2]XIV: Edith Jablonski's husband Edward, CVV's fourteenth numbered Edward; the Jablonski's daughter, Carla, was named after CVV.

Who, he reports, is extremely frail. I sent you the Villager, with the BEST obituary of Mabel that appeared. I hope you received it.

The weather is good, we are good, with the exception of my fractured wrist, and we both send love to dearest Mama Woojums.

Carlo, Papa Woojums

Isak Dinesen's death affected us more deeply than Mabel's.

## TO PAUL WILLIAM MACDONALD[3]      146 Central Park West
13 October 1962                       New York City

My very good new friend Paul (if you will permit me!) [. . .] It is a great pleasure to me to have you collect me together with Gertrude [Stein] and I will try to help you over the corners. Besides, I like you plenty enough for yourself. [. . .] Somewhere you have written me that you do not possess Music After the Great War. I have a copy of the first edition of this book and can think of no one I would rather give it to than you. [. . .] My music books are all rare, but I will try to dig some out for you. [. . .]

The new Philharmonic Hall, of which you have probably heard even in San Francisco, is a disappointment. The acoustics are awful and the band sounds as if it were playing under water, or under a wet blanket. Also there is practically no place to pee and you have to walk about a mile before you can accomplish this act. The spaces are fabulous and the staircases numberless. The place is all Glamour and makes no SENSE.

I will send the book under separate cover.

yours with very warm greetings, Carlo

[. . .] You must pardon me if I tell you I think Paul MacDonald is a very fine name. The Wm or William in the center weakens it and is not so euphonious.

## TO HENRY VAN DYKE            146 Central Park West
24 October 1962                  New York City

Dear, dear Henry, This time I really LOVED your letter. It shows you can write. The impersonal literary epistle DIDn't. If you would make your commercial stuff more personal, more like your talk, you would have no difficulty selling it. [. . .] Become freer and more daring, breathe deeply and easily, let your hair down and take off your pants. You are much too congested, inhibited, and tied to a TREE. [. . .] The priest story is interesting,

---

[3]In honor of CVV's 83rd birthday, Paul MacDonald reverted (because CVV had admired it) to his actual name—Paul Padgette—from his foster name.

but not entirely novel. I have heard of monks behind the high altar in the choir in a church in Florence who permitted pleasant indignities during a service, but it seems it is only in foreign churches where there are often strangers there to view the Murals that one is allowed to visit such intimate places during a service.

My life is quite proper but I continue to receive vast numbers of joyously indecent letters. [. . .]

Anyway, I send you my love, and suggest you write me some more.
Carlo

TO ALFRED A. KNOPF            146 Central Park West
19 December 1962              New York City

Dear Alfred, You started something when you published a book by Walter White. Then you introduced me to Walter & HE introduced me to James Weldon Johnson, Langston Hughes and ever so many more and I eventually wrote Nigger Heaven. Well what we started has eventually progressed to James Baldwin, John A. Williams, *and* JOHN OLIVER KILLENS.[4] I have read Then We Heard the Thunder with amazement and a very real emotion. It is a great book, a very real book, and a very true book. The Negro has at last learned to say what is really on his mind. It is shameful that what is described in these pages had to occur, but the things did occur and only a Negro could really describe [. . .] them accurately. Well, one has at last— and I am proud that you and I started a movement that has become so lusty.

Love to you and Madame Blanche & happy Christmas
When will this book be published?      [unsigned]

TO PAUL MACDONALD            146 Central Park West
[26 January 1963]            New York City

Dear Paul, [. . .] I think I wrote you that I didn't like Who's Afraid of Virginia Woolf.[5] I am reading the play now and I like it better. My reaction to the produced play was that the audience screamed with laughter all the way through. I did not find the play funny and so this attitude of the audience annoyed me. "Annoyed" is hardly a strong enough word.

I enclose more photographs. If you like these I will continue to send

---

[4]These three young black authors were writing (more directly and militantly than Johnson and Hughes had written) about the black experience in America, although White's *The Fire in the Flint,* 1924, and *Rope and Faggot,* 1929, anticipated their work.
[5]*Who's Afraid of Virginia Woolf,* 1963, by Edward Albee.

them. I have literally thousands. Under separate cover I am sending you a Russian calendar which I hope you will amuse you.

my affection to you, Carlo

Some day when you feel like it, you might tell me more about your business or professional life and something about your intimate friends.

TO EDWARD LUEDERS       146 Central Park West
28 February 1963         New York City

Dear Sir and Mister, What a loverly letter! [. . .] I am glad you understand about growing older. Browning's poem Grow Old Along With Me is a masterpiece of understanding. The only persons who do not understand are the physically vain. I have never belonged to this class and every minute I grow older I feel freer and happier than I ever felt before. I must exclude another class: those who suffer from serious illnesses and perhaps the un- happily married or those burdened with the care of some one. Also, of course, those who are not provided financially for a long life. I have always managed to do exactly what I wanted to do, but somehow I find with age, it is easier to have one's own way without interruption. Very often it pleases me to please others. [. . .]

Yesterday I sent you an addition to my Bibliography. The annual number of Dance Perspectives, with my piece on Alvin Ailey. The editor changed the title. My title was lighter: Roses for Alvin.[6]

Persevere and Love to you and Judy, Carlo

I am posing for a group picture: authors of the 20s & 30s for Esquire. I wouldn't think many of these would be alive, but they think they have found enough.[7]

TO PAUL PADGETTE       146 Central Park West
18 June [1963]         New York City

Dear Paulet, I was disappointed that I didn't hear from you on my birthday. [. . .] Of course your new name card was birthday enough for anybody but that came several days ago.[8]

---

[6]"Eloquent Alvin Ailey," Dance 62, a bonus offering to subscribers to Dance Perspectives, not offered for sale.
[7]CVV to Bruce Kellner, 17 March 1963: "Friday I was photographed for Esquire. It was intended to be a group from the twenties and thirties, but all of these are dead; so they decided on a group of any old timers. So we sat, like the Last Supper, Virgil Thomson, Man Ray, Marcel Duchamp, Caresse Crosby, Dawn Powell, Glenway Wescott, Kay Boyle, William Slater Brown, Matthew Josephson, Malcolm Cowley."
[8]See CVV to Paul MacDonald (Padgette), 13 October 1962, note 3.

FM got sick on Saturday and her illness still persists. Consequently she shared none of the festivities yesterday. Presents and cards and telegrams and telephone messages arrived all day and I shall be days in thanking people. In spite of all the unfortunate illness, it was the nicest birthday I ever had. I was 83, but I felt about 16. [. . .] Dick Banks's[9] party for me started at 6.30. His apartment is very attractive and his pictures hang in every room, including Gertrude Stein and Markova. The guests at the party included Nora Holt and a friend, Pamela Drexel, Marian Seldes,[1] Bruce Kellner and his wife, Donald Angus, Aileen Pringle, Jimmie Daniels, Mabel Mercer,[2] Tallulah Bankhead, and assorted youths. Champagne flowed freely and several times during the evening the guests stood up in front of me and saluted me. Toasted me, that is. Mabel sang several songs, including *my* Sunday in Savannah,[3] Tallulah sang and both sang together. What a party! I never had it so good! [. . .]     Much love to you, dearest Paulet. I wish you had been here.   Carlo

TO LANGSTON HUGHES                 146 Central Park West
2 June 1964                        New York City

Dear Langston, you and I have been through so many new Negroes that we are a little tired of it all. BUT I am really excited about the group you have brought together. LeRoi Jones, who appears to be somebody, I photographed long since.[4] I wonder when he & [James] Baldwin will have a fight! It will be a big one. I am very happy to receive your book[5] with its beautiful inscription.     Much affection to you   Carlo

It was certainly old home week at Rita [Romilly]'s. I had a really wonderful time.

TO EDWARD LUEDERS                  146 Central Park West
31 August 1964                     New York City

Dear Edward XV, [. . .] Quite suddenly, with no warning at all (I became aware of it one evening, saw my doctor the next day and was fitted with what I am pleased to call a chastity belt the same day) I have developed

---

[9]Richard Banks, American composer and portrait painter.
[1]Marian Seldes, American actress, a friend since her childhood.
[2]Mabel Mercer, black English-born cabaret singer.
[3]It was Mabel Mercer's invariable practice to include *Sunday in Savannah* in her program whenever CVV attended her performances in New York.
[4]LeRoi Jones (now Amiri Baraka), black novelist succeeding Hughes's generation.
[5]*Something in Common and Other Stories*, 1963, or *New Negro Poets: USA* (Langston Hughes, editor), 1964.

a hernia which with my bad knee makes me in the future a fairly immoveable object. However I am invariably adjustable to circumstances and none of it bothers me excessively. The only alternative seems to be an operation which at the moment I do not desire. [. . .]

I read a great deal, always seemingly, very long books. At present I am spellbound over Sartre's St Genet, a fabulous book, 600 pages concerned solely with ass.[6] It is too hot to work in photography. The acids refuse to react in hot weather. But fall approaches and soon I will be making pictures again.

Fania is in the pink and sends her love as does your Patriarch side-kick,     Carlo

## TO EDWARD LUEDERS
3 October 1964

146 Central Park West
New York City

Dear Edward, [. . .] I envy you your opportunity to take your son and his girl friend to a concert. I never had the luck in my childhood because my parents were more over middle age by the time I went to concerts and were formed in their tastes while I invented mine.

Our domestic affairs are improving: We are getting back a cook who was formerly with us for 35 years. She is a superb cook and we love her. So Fania feels better. Mildred [Perkins] can't come for two weeks (she has to give notice where she is) but she sent a substitute for the two weeks. FM has every kind of nerves there is and she has had a grand time to exploit them.     Love to you and I am waiting for the book[7] impatiently, Carlo

No word about Bruce [Kellner]'s book. I see him tomorrow when he comes down for the ballet with his wife who is expecting in January.

## TO PETER FRANCIS O'BRIEN, SJ
20 October 1964

146 Central Park West
New York City

Dear, dear Peter, It is about time I was reminding you to read Colette who is a complete mistress of the art of writing, and who knew more about the human heart than any author who ever lived. She recreated the novelette

---

[6]*Saint Genet*, 1964, Jean Paul Sartre's critical biography of French writer Jean Genet.
[7]Edward Lueders had written a second book about CVV, for the Twayne series on American authors. CVV had read the book in manuscript and responded with unqualified enthusiasm, but its release had been delayed. *Carl Van Vechten* was published in January 1965, a month after CVV's death.

form and made a work of genius out of it. Try to find The Ripening Seed or Cheri and The Last of Cheri. But anything by Colette will do and I think some of her is in paper.     much love to you, Carlo

Did I send you a picture of Aileen [Pringle]?

**TO HENRY VAN DYKE**                    146 Central Park West
20 October 1964                          New York City

Dear Henry, Purdy roasts [Orville] Prescott and the [*New York*] Times in his book and naturally he gets roasted back. BUT the Herald Tribune devoted a page with high praise to Cabot Wright last Sunday [. . .] and remember that Purdy only gets what he asks for.[8] Don't be too naive about reviews. Everybody gets bad ones.     Love to you, Carlo

**TO DONALD WINDHAM**                    146 Central Park West
16 December [1964]                       New York City

Dear Don, [. . .] I congratulate you on your good fortune in finding a generous publisher so soon. But you must remember that this is not a gift or even a loan. It is a payment against your royalties. I always liked to take royalties when they came rather [than] in advance. Mr. Scribner of course is an ass. I have heard stories before. It is too bad Max Perkins[9] isn't alive, he would spank the old man. The title and your description excite me very much.[1] There are already two books on this limitation of this subject, one by Thomas Mann,[2] the other by Christopher Isherwood.[3] Both are masterpieces. I hope the third will be too.     Love to you both   Carlo

Fania is better, and I am in the pink. I have just realized that I am only 5 years younger than Alice Toklas, Mary Garden & Natalie Barney, whom I have been regarding as old ladies![4]

---

[8]*Cabot Wright Begins,* 1964, a roman à clef by James Purdy.
[9]Maxwell Perkins, the editor at Charles Scribner's Sons responsible for shaping the careers of F. Scott Fitzgerald and Thomas Wolfe.
[1]*Two People,* 1965, by Donald Windham, a novel about a love affair between a middle-aged American man and an Italian boy.
[2]*Death in Venice,* 1911.
[3]*A Single Man,* 1964.
[4]Four days after he wrote this letter, CVV died in his sleep.

# Index

Wylie, Elinor, 62, *83*, 89, 105
Wynn, Ed, 145

Yale University Library, 177–83 passim
Yale University Press, 226, 228

*Yellow Jacket* (Hotchkiss), 136
*Yesterday's Children* (Coates), 135
Youskevitch, Igor, 204

Zorina, Vera, 214